University Textbook Series

May, 1988

Especially Designed for Collateral Reading

HARRY W. JONES
Directing Editor
Professor of Law, Columbia University

ADMINISTRATIVE LAW AND PROCESS (1985)
Richard J. Pierce, Jr., Dean and Professor of Law, University of Pittsburgh.
Sidney A. Shapiro, Professor of Law, University of Kansas.
Paul R. Verkuil, President and Professor of Law, College of William and Mary.

ADMIRALTY, Second Edition (1975)
Grant Gilmore, Professor of Law, Yale University.
Charles L. Black, Jr., Professor of Law, Yale University.

ADMIRALTY AND FEDERALISM (1970)
David W. Robertson, Professor of Law, University of Texas.

AGENCY (1975)
W. Edward Sell, Dean of the School of Law, University of Pittsburgh.

BUSINESS ORGANIZATION AND FINANCE, Third Edition (1988)
William A. Klein, Professor of Law, University of California, Los Angeles.
John C. Coffee, Jr., Professor of Law, Columbia University.

CIVIL PROCEDURE, BASIC, Second Edition (1979)
Milton D. Green, Professor of Law Emeritus, University of California, Hastings College of the Law.

COMMERCIAL TRANSACTIONS, INTRODUCTION TO (1977)
Hon. Robert Braucher, Associate Justice, Supreme Judicial Court of Massachusetts.
Robert A. Riegert, Professor of Law, Cumberland School of Law.

CONFLICT OF LAWS, COMMENTARY ON THE, Third Edition (1986) with 1987 Supplement
Russell J. Weintraub, Professor of Law, University of Texas.

CONSTITUTIONAL LAW, AMERICAN, Second Edition (A TREATISE ON) (1988)
Laurence H. Tribe, Professor of Law, Harvard University.

CONTRACT LAW, THE CAPABILITY PROBLEM IN (1978)
Richard Danzig.

CORPORATE TAXATION (1987)
Howard E. Abrams, Professor of Law, Emory University.
Richard L. Doernberg, Professor of Law, Emory University.

CORPORATIONS, Second Edition (1971)
Norman D. Lattin, Professor of Law, University of California, Hastings College of the Law.

i

CORPORATIONS IN PERSPECTIVE (1976)
Alfred F. Conard, Professor of Law, University of Michigan.

CRIMINAL LAW, Third Edition (1982)
Rollin M. Perkins, Professor of Law, University of California, Hastings College of the Law.
Ronald N. Boyce, Professor of Law, University of Utah College of Law.

CRIMINAL PROCEDURE, Second Edition (1986) with 1988 Supplement
Charles H. Whitebread, II, Professor of Law, University of Southern California.
Christopher Slobogin, Associate Professor of Law, University of Florida.

ESTATES IN LAND & FUTURE INTERESTS, PREFACE TO, Second Edition (1984)
Thomas F. Bergin, Professor of Law, University of Virginia.
Paul G. Haskell, Professor of Law, University of North Carolina.

EVIDENCE: COMMON SENSE AND COMMON LAW (1947)
John M. Maguire, Professor of Law, Harvard University.

JURISPRUDENCE: MEN AND IDEAS OF THE LAW (1953)
The late Edwin W. Patterson, Cardozo Professor of Jurisprudence, Columbia University.

LABOR RELATIONS The Basic Processes, Law and Practice
Julius G. Getman, Professor of Law, University of Texas.
Bertrand E. Pogrebin, Member, New York State Bar.

LEGAL CAPITAL, Second Edition (1981)
Bayless Manning.

LEGAL RESEARCH ILLUSTRATED, 1987 Edition with 1985 Assignments Supplement and 1987 Assignment Update
J. Myron Jacobstein, Professor of Law, Law Librarian, Stanford University.
Roy M. Mersky, Professor of Law, Director of Research, University of Texas.

LEGAL RESEARCH, FUNDAMENTALS OF, 1987 Edition with 1985 Assignments Supplement and 1987 Assignment Update
J. Myron Jacobstein, Professor of Law, Law Librarian, Stanford University.
Roy M. Mersky, Professor of Law, Director of Research, University of Texas.

PROCEDURE, THE STRUCTURE OF (1979)
Robert M. Cover, Professor of Law, Yale University.
Owen M. Fiss, Professor of Law, Yale University.

PROPERTY, Second Edition (1975)
John E. Cribbet, Dean of the Law School, University of Illinois.

TAXATION, FEDERAL INCOME, Fifth Edition (1988)
Marvin A. Chirelstein, Professor of Law, Columbia University.

TORTS, Second Edition (1980)
Clarence Morris, Professor of Law, University of Pennsylvania.
C. Robert Morris, Professor of Law, University of Minnesota.

WILLS AND TRUSTS, THE PLANNING AND DRAFTING OF, Second Edition (1979) with 1982 Supplement
Thomas L. Shaffer, Professor of Law, University of Notre Dame.

WILLS, TRUSTS AND ADMINISTRATION, PREFACE TO (1987)
Paul G. Haskell, Professor of Law, University of North Carolina.

LABOR RELATIONS

THE BASIC PROCESSES, LAW AND PRACTICE

By

JULIUS G. GETMAN
Professor of Law, University of Texas

and

BERTRAND B. POGREBIN
member of the New York Bar
Adjunct Professor of Law,
New York University Law School

Westbury, New York
THE FOUNDATION PRESS, INC.
1988

COPYRIGHT © 1988 By THE FOUNDATION PRESS, INC.

615 Merrick Ave.

Westbury, N.Y. 11590

Library of Congress Cataloging-in-Publication Data

Getman, Julius G.

    Labor relations: the basic processes, law and practice / by Julius
G. Getman and Bertrand B. Pogrebin.

      p.   cm. — (University textbook series)

    Includes index.

    ISBN 0-88277-652-5

    1. Labor laws and legislation—United States. I. Pogrebin,
Bertrand B. II. Title. III. Series.

KF3369.G48 1988

344.73'01—dc19

[347.3041]   88–16438

                                        CIP

G. & P.—Labor Relations UTB

To
Dan, Mike, Poppy, and Jason
JGG

To
Letty
BBP

*

FOREWORD

This book is an attempt to describe legal doctrine in a way that explains its relation to the realities of industrial relations in five major areas: union organizing, collective bargaining, grievance mediation, strikes and picketing, employer-employee cooperation. It also explores the division of power between federal and states in enforcing employer and employee rights.

One of the puroses of our collaboration was to combine the insights of an academic with practical experience and those of a practicing lawyer with a penchant for academic analysis. We hope that the resultant mixture of explanation and criticism reflects that both authors have some familiarity with the way in which reality and law interact in the world of labor relations. The book is not intended to be comprehensive, but to give the reader a sense of the basic structure and rationale of the law and understanding of the way it reflects and shapes labor relations.

The Introduction, Chapters 1, 2, 3, 5, and the beginning of Chapter 4 were written primarily by Getman, and the last half of Chapter 4 and Chapter 6 dealing with preemption were written primarily by Pogrebin. We hope that the book does not overly reflect either the fact that Professor Getman is President of the American Association of University Professors, which serves at times as a union for faculty members, or that Mr. Pogrebin is a management lawyer. Rather it is our hope that it shows the commitment which both of us have to the fair treatment of employees and to the basic policies protecting free choice and fostering free collective bargaining.

For several years, writing of the book was used as a pedagogical adjunct to the Labor Law Seminar at Yale Law School and the final product was much helped by the research done by several generations of Yale law students who took the seminar. We are considerably in their debt. The students who helped (many are now experienced labor lawyers and at least three are law professors) included the following:

Stuart Bauchner	Deborah D. Dupire
Linda Benedetti	Cynthia Estlund
Richard Boldt	Sherry Fingarette
James Bowen	Karen Fitzmaurice
Oscar R. Cantu	John Gill
John Colwell	Jose Gonzalez
Eric Corngold	Cornelius Grealy
Tom Distler	Susan Grebeldinger

David L. Gregory

George C. Harris

Maria O'Brien Hylton

Gary Issac

Samuel Issacaroff

Bruce C. Johnson

Dawn Johnson

Wayne Jones

Wesley Kennedy

Celia Kirsch

Thomas C. Kohler

Sara Korn

Niki Kuckes

Ron Kuerbitz

John Libby

Thomas Lim

Daniel Livingston

Ed Mansfield

Valerie Marcus

Beth Z. Margulies

Stephen J. Massey

Byron Ndaki

Sheldon Pine

Arnold Pinkston

Joseph Ruby

Susan M. Sacks

Adina Schwartz

Liz Shollenberger

John W. Simon

Rafael Ventura–Rosa

Gilda Villaran

Martin Vranken

Wendy A. Wolf

Perry Zirkel

We apologize for my omissions which are the result of two moves and poor recordkeeping. Along the way we have been helped by a variety of other people. Bert Pogrebin acknowledges the help of Craig Benson and Richard Kass, who helped in the preparation of the manuscript. Professor Getman acknowledges the research assistance of Dan Anderson and Adriana Capistran and the editorial help of Christy McCrary at the University of Texas School of Law and the secretarial assistance of Barbara Mianza at Yale Law School, Shirley Walker at Indiana University School of Law, and Barbara Bellamy at the University of Texas School of Law. Ms. Bellamy played a particularly helpful role which included the contribution of several valuable unsolicited ideas. Her personal involvement with the book was one of the factors that made it possible to complete it.

JULIUS G. GETMAN
BERTRAND B. POGREBIN

June, 1988

viii

SUMMARY OF CONTENTS

Chapter I

UNION ORGANIZING

Chapter II

COLLECTIVE BARGAINING

Chapter III

THE ENFORCEMENT OF RIGHTS UNDER
COLLECTIVE AGREEMENTS

Chapter V

REGULATING THE NATURE OF UNION MANAGEMENT RELATIONS

Chapter VI

FEDERAL PREEMPTION OF STATE LABOR LAWS

Appendices

TABLE OF CONTENTS

Chapter III

THE ENFORCEMENT OF RIGHTS UNDER COLLECTIVE AGREEMENTS

Chapter IV

UNION ECONOMIC PRESSURE: STRIKES, PICKETING, AND BOYCOTTS

TABLE OF CONTENTS

*

TABLE OF CASES

References are to Pages.

*

LABOR RELATIONS

THE BASIC PROCESSES, LAW AND PRACTICE

*

INTRODUCTION

The most significant event in the development of U.S. labor law was the enactment of the National Labor Relations Act. Its passage marked completion of a major transformation. For over a hundred years, labor relations had been governed by a confused body of common law precedents derived from non-labor cases and applied by judges lacking knowledge of industrial relations. The law was hostile to unions, whose interests were subordinated to those of employers and employees who opposed unionization. The law's application varied with the political power of labor in different areas of the country, but in almost every jurisdiction concerted activity was vulnerable to adverse legal actions and employers were free to take reprisals against union members. The NLRA was intended to reverse the law's basic direction, to make it uniform, rational, responsive to the legitimate claims of labor, supportive of employee choice with respect to unionization, and favorable to collective bargaining.[1] One of the key aspects of the new law was that it was to be administered by the National Labor Relations Board, a panel of knowledgeable experts who would bring to their decisions understanding of the realities of labor relations.[2] The role of the courts, already limited by the Norris–LaGuardia Anti–Injunction Act, was to be further reduced by giving the Board exclusive jurisdiction over labor law questions, subject to limited judicial review. This book describes the labor law and labor relations systems that have developed since the Act's passage. In all cases, the basic policies have been altered or rendered different from their original concept, sometimes by direct statutory amendment, sometimes by the impact of new policies or unforeseen developments. The early promise of the Act has never been fulfilled. Its achievements have been limited by confusing general statutory language, ill-defined or competing policies, and from human limitations interacting with bureaucratic considerations. Despite its inadequacies, the goals of free choice and free collective bargaining remain important, and the labor relations scheme that has developed under the Act has achieved significant social change.

Part I. The Statutory Scheme: The Interplay of Change and Consistency

A. *The Wagner Act*

Section 7 has been at the heart of the NLRA from its passage until the present. It grants to employees "the rights to self-organization to join or assist labor organizations to bargain collectively through representatives of their own choosing and to engage in concerted activities

1

for the purpose of collective bargaining or other mutual aid or protection." These rights are effectuated through elections that determine whether employees desire union representation. The Act seeks to protect employee choice in this regard through unfair labor practice provisions that prevent employers from using their economic power over the employees to frustrate section 7 rights. The broadest of the original unfair labor practices, now section 8(a)(1), makes it unlawful for an employer "to interfere with, restrain, or coerce employees in the exercise of the rights guaranteed in section 7." Section 8(a)(2), which was aimed at preventing employer involvement in employee organizations generally and the establishment of "company unions" in particular, prohibits employer "domination" of or even "assistance" to a labor organization. Section 8(a)(3) was aimed at preventing employer retaliation, such as blacklisting, discharging union supporters, or making discriminatory pay cuts. It prohibits "discrimination to encourage or discourage membership in a labor organization." Section 8(a)(5) was intended to prevent employers from disregarding the wishes of the employees for union representation. It requires an employer to bargain with the representatives chosen by his employees. The meaning of the duty to bargain was not defined but the Act specified that the "representatives designated *   *   * by a majority of the employees in a unit *   *   * shall be the exclusive representative of all the employees in the unit." Unlike labor laws in other nations, the Wagner Act did not seek to regulate the relationship of the parties once recognition was achieved and good faith bargaining begun. The focus of the statute was on eliminating barriers to organization and requiring collective bargaining once the employees had chosen to be represented. Neither union nor management desired governmental involvement in setting wages and working conditions.

A unique and important feature of the Wagner Act was the resolution of conflicting claims concerning the representation of the employees through elections supervised by the NLRB. The Board was assigned the task of determining when an election was to be held, the basic unit in which it was to be held, the eligible voters, and the result.[3]

Passage of the NLRA also served to nationalize labor relations policy. Previously each state was free to establish its own labor policy, but section 7 was intended to limit the states as well as employers. It was soon held that states could not legislate with regard to matters that came within the Board's sphere of regulation, even if their laws were consistent with the national act.[4]

B. *The Taft–Hartley Amendment*

The Wagner Act became law during a period when labor was politically powerful and its cause was understood to be advanced by the Act's passage. The power that unions obtained under the statute became politically unpopular in the period immediately after World War II, which was marked by significant numbers of strikes in major industries. In 1947, Congress after prolonged emotional debate enacted the Taft–Hartley Act,[5] which sought to limit the power of labor unions and to put the government in a more neutral position with regard to the issue of unionization. Both supporters and opponents of organized labor viewed its passage as fundamentally altering the law's approach to labor management relations, yet the Taft–Hartley Act was as noteworthy for what it did not do as for the changes it made. It did not eliminate the original unfair labor practices. The Act's election process remained intact, and the Board's central role in labor relations was, if anything, expanded. The Board acquired jurisdiction over union unfair labor practices, which increased its case load and expanded application of the preemption doctrine. By not amending the basic provisions of the Wagner Act, the Taft–Hartley amendments established their permanency. Taft–Hartley did, however, make significant changes in the NLRA. It added union unfair labor practices to the law and specifically recognized a right to refrain from concerted activity. Union unfair labor practices included restraining employees in the exercise of section 7 rights, refusing to bargain in good faith, and, most significantly, engaging in secondary activity. Section 8(b)(4), the provision that outlawed most secondary activity, constituted a major rejection of the concept that it was legitimate for employees of different employers to make common cause with each other—a concept previously embedded in the sweeping language of section 7 with regard to concerted activity.

The Taft–Hartley Act resurrected the possibility of injunctions against union activity that violated the secondary boycott provision, and it forbade closed shop agreements which required the employer to hire only union members.

C. *The Landrum–Griffin Amendments*

In 1959, after a series of well-publicized hearings in which various union abuses of power were revealed, the NLRA was amended once again by the "Landrum–Griffin Amendments," with the avowed purpose of preventing organized labor from using its economic power as an organizing device. The secondary boycott provisions of the Act were made stronger, contract clauses by which organized employers agreed not to deal with non-union employers were made unlawful, and picketing for purposes of recognition or organization was severely limited.

D. *The Basic Statutory Legacy*

Certain basic decisions incorporated in the original Wagner Act have remained crucial to the U.S. system of labor relations. These include the establishment of the NLRB and its major role in enforcing the policies of the Act, the law's minimal control over the bargaining process, and the system of exclusivity by which a single union designated by a majority represents everyone in a bargaining unit. It is this latter, almost unique, approach that has most distinguished U.S. labor law. Exclusivity has led to uniform working conditions for similarly situated employees. It has permitted the widespread use of seniority and unit-wide grievance systems, both of which have provided significant limits on managerial decision making. The grievance systems have given unions a visible shop-floor presence and have given employees significant job protection.

It was implicit in the doctrine of exclusivity, together with the policy against discrimination on the basis of union membership, that a union that did not represent a majority could not undertake to bargain even on behalf of its members. Thus, enormous consequences under this statute attached to majority selection. A union either represented everyone in a unit or no one. This consequence made it almost inevitable that informal processes of determining majority sentiment would either be abandoned or discouraged in favor of the statutorily specified election process. Exclusivity therefore mandated that the election process be carefully monitored to be sure that its results were in fact an indication of majority choice. The concept of exclusivity also required that the employer's ability to deal with individual employees or other groups or unions be severely limited and that the protection of economic pressure be limited to its use by the incumbent when one existed. Because exclusivity meant that unions in almost every case would act as the bargaining representative for employees who did not wish to be represented, it inevitably led to significant legal concern with the relationship between the union and such employees. Thus the courts read into the NLRA a duty of fair representation, a concept that has required considerable explication. The courts also have devoted considerable effort to determining the amount that unions might legally charge such employees for their unwanted services as bargaining representative.[6]

Part II.   The Failure to Develop a Consistent Labor Law Policy

A.   *Statutory Vagueness and Contradiction*

The various statutes that combine to form the National Labor Relations Act have markedly different visions of the appropriate role of government in the regulation of labor relations and different approaches to the legitimacy of unions using economic pressure in pursuit of goals other than improving wages and benefits. Moreover, both the Taft–Hartley and Landrum–Griffin amendments reflect in their provisions uneasy compromises between fiercely contending political forces. The language of the Act, as a result, is overly general, often confusing and contradictory. Nowhere is this more obvious than in the provisions dealing with strikes and other forms of concerted activity. Section 7, its original language largely intact, announces a broad right to "engage in concerted activities for the purpose of collective bargaining or other mutual aid or protection." Section 13, another of the Act's original provisions, specifies that "except as specifically provided" "nothing in this Act * * * shall be construed so as either to interfere with or impede or diminish in any way the right to strike * * *." This language is in sharp contrast with the language of section 8(b)(4), which makes it an unfair labor practice "to engage in, or to induce * * * any individual * * * to engage in, a strike or a refusal * * * where * * * an object thereof is * * * forcing or requiring any person to cease using, selling, handling, transporting, or otherwise dealing in the products of any other producer, processor, or manufacturer * * *"—language the literal prohibitions of which are violated in almost every strike in which the strikers seek to prevent pickups or deliveries. The Act thus contains language recognizing the common goals of organized labor and language that, if read literally, would outlaw almost all strikes and most inducements to strike. Similar tension exists between the policy favoring free collective bargaining developed by the Wagner and Taft–Hartley Acts and section 8(e), which prohibits agreements by which unions seek to enlist the support of an employer in favor of their organizing efforts elsewhere. The difficulty of construing a provision whose language reflects compromise rather than a unified vision is best revealed by section 8(b)(7), which prohibits picketing for recognition or organizational purposes in vague language, the reach of which is limited by a complex series of provisos and exceptions. There is almost no way to interpret parts of this section that does not do violence either to its language or its policy.[7]

Aside from its internal inconsistencies, the Act has had to be harmonized with other statutory and societal policies. The bankruptcy, antitrust, and civil rights laws all limit behavior otherwise sanctioned by the NLRA. More fundamentally, the Act has from the beginning been interpreted in such a way as to minimize interference with managerial authority and entrepreneurial decision making. This counter-policy to the Act's declared purpose of giving employee representatives a voice has become increasingly important during the Act's development. As a result of it, the reach of collective bargaining has been limited; management's right to eliminate jobs, close down operations, and limit union access to employees has been expanded. From very early on employees who exercised their right to strike were subject to being permanently replaced. All of these conclusions were reached without regard to, or in spite of, the language of the statute. They reflect what may be thought of as the Act's "capitalist exemption."

B. *The Disappointing Performance of the NLRB*

The vision of labor law policy established through the vehicle of
an expert Board knowledgeable about labor relations and supportive
of collective bargaining has never been realized. There are a variety
of reasons why the Board so little resembles the vision of its earliest
advocates. One is the political nature of the appointments process,
which sometimes has been used to reward labor for its support and
sometimes has been used as a way of punishing labor for opposing the
President's policies. The judicial nature of the task has mandated the
appointment of lawyers, which has typically meant politicians with
little or no labor relations background, former Board employees, or
those with only partisan experience. Those with reputations as neutral experts have rarely been asked, and when asked, have generally
declined.[8] Few Board members have ever been involved in the
organizing process, which takes up so much of the Board's time. Few
have actually been at the bargaining table and fewer still have any real
personal first-hand experience with strikes. Indeed, only a small
percentage have ever been union leaders or even members. While
some come from the ranks of management, only a few have experience that is directly relevant to the tasks of the Board, and, of course,
individual experience in this regard tends to be skewed. All of this
might be less significant if the make-up and procedures of the Board
were such as to permit it to develop true institutional expertise so that
it could ultimately draw upon its own experience and whatever is
known about labor relations by scholars and experienced people in the
field. Unfortunately, this is not the case. The way the Board is
constructed, those who are responsible for announcing its policies and
applying its decisions have very little to do with those who have field
experience, who interview employees, or who hear the cases. Those
who investigate in an unfair labor practice proceeding are part of the
regional office staff that is responsible to the General Counsel, not to
the Board. Cases are not heard by the Board members but by
administrative law judges. For reasons of administrative neutrality,
the Board members have little contact with the regional offices or the
administrative law judges.[9] Although it has been administering the
National Labor Relations Act for over fifty years, the Board has never
engaged in an effort to determine empirically the impact of employer
or union conduct. It has not required or even permitted the introduction of evidence as to what impact particular conduct had on employees. It has stated, "in evaluating the interference resulting from
specific conduct, the Board does not attempt to assess its actual effect
on employees, but rather concerns itself with whether it is reasonable
to conclude that the conduct tended to prevent the free formation and
expression of the employees' choice".[10] Thus the elaborate structure
of Board rules, which will be described in this treatise, is not
grounded in any respect on factual data. It rests rather on guesses or

assumptions. There is nothing in the collective activities or experiences of the Board that ensures the accuracy of the assumptions upon which these rules are based. As has been pointed out by a respected scholar, "the Board's staff consists mostly of lawyers and a few researchers who are primarily concerned with the statistics of the Board's own operations . . . what the Board lacks notably is specific information about labor management practices and employee attitudes and reactions which may be pertinent to its work and to any systematic means of monitoring the impact of the Board in court and NLRB doctrine upon industrial practice." [11] Thus the Board's decision-making processes fail to provide a bridge between Board members and the complex world of labor relations.

Less understandable than its own failure to investigate reality is how little effort the Board makes to incorporate into its decisional process what is known by others about various aspects of labor relations. To read through a volume of Board opinions is to be struck by the perfunctory nature of its opinions and the lack of sophisticated analysis when the Board does undertake to analyze a labor law issue. Its effort is almost always confined to elaborating its own doctrine and treating as established reality its previous assumptions.

The Board has had to apply its myriad of doctrines and sub-doctrines to the complex facts of labor relations. The result would be confusion and uncertainty even if there were significant continuity on the Board. However, given the political nature of the Board and its tendency to change complexion with the political environment, the problem becomes magnified many times. New Boards are always in a position to distinguish away most of the precedent that is harmful to their political values and to refuse to accept much of the rest. The matter is further complicated by the fact that the Board often attempts to adjust its doctrine or to articulate it in such a way as to avoid judicial rejection. This has meant a significant difference between doctrine as announced and as applied.

For those reasons, the Board has supplied neither expertise, nor clear doctrine, nor consistency.

C. *The Increasing Role of the Courts*

The assumption that the Board would have special expertise was intimately related to the Act's policy of minimizing the role of courts. This policy predated the NLRA, having begun with the Norris–LaGuardia Anti–Injunction Act. The scheme of the NLRA envisioned no role for the courts with respect to the representation election process and only a limited one of enforcing Board orders with minimal review with respect to unfair labor practices.

For a variety of reasons, the courts have played a far more significant role than the Act's drafters contemplated. The courts have used the enforcement process to incorporate into the NLRA their own visions of desirable labor relations policies, rejecting with regularity the Board's legal conclusions, its policy determinations and its findings of fact. The idea that courts would simultaneously defer and enforce has never been realistic, and there are special reasons why it was unlikely to come about with reference to the NLRA.

1. The reasons advanced for deferral to the Board—its expertise and neutrality were quickly perceived to be fictional. As it became obvious that the Board was performing the function of an adjudicatory body, applying or interpreting general language, developing doctrine, and finding facts, the reasons to defer seemed less compelling.

2. Because of its concentration on the NLRA, the Board was not in the position to undertake the important task of harmonizing NLRA policy with the policy behind other statutes and laws. This became increasingly important as other labor related statutes and policies were developed. The courts have primary responsibility for harmonizing the NLRA with the policy favoring arbitration with the anti-discrimination and the anti-trust laws, and of developing the law dealing with the relationship between the employee and the union.

3. As labor law became more complex and as unions acquired more power, the labor injunction reemerged as an important technique for preventing strikes in violation of national policy. Because the Board lacked injunctive power this approach increased the role of courts, which then had the primary responsibility for determining the legality of strikes. As an exception to the Norris–LaGuardia Act, an injunction may be issued when a union violates a no-strike clause over a dispute subject to grievance arbitration. Determining whether these standards are met requires the courts to interpret collective agreements.

4. Many judges resisted aspects of NLRA policy either as an infringement upon the free market or as inconsistent with the rights of employees. These values inevitably manifested themselves through more stringent review of Board decisions.

D. *The Growing Importance of Other Agencies*

   1. Other Federal Agencies

When it first began, the National Labor Relations Board was the primary agency through which national labor law policy was established. Gradually, however, other tribunals have come to play an important role in defining labor relations policy. The Labor Department enforces the LMRDA amendments, dealing with internal union affairs, and ERISA, which regulates pension programs. The EEOC enforces federal laws prohibiting discrimination on the basis of race, sex, or age. All these statutes have had an important effect on labor relations and collective bargaining. Once it was decided to allocate significant authority to other agencies, the effort to centralize labor policy-making in the Labor Board was effectively terminated.

2. Arbitration

Primary responsibility for interpreting collective bargaining agreements has for some time belonged to labor arbitrators. This happened first by choice of the parties who discovered that arbitration effectively supplements the bargaining process. After the Supreme Court's Steelworkers Trilogy, the encouragement of arbitration became an objective of the law.[12] The Board's *Collyer*[13] decision extended this objective to areas in which Board and arbitral jurisdiction overlapped. On occasion the policy favoring arbitration has conflicted with the policy favoring free collective bargaining. This has confused decision making by the courts, the Board, and arbitrators. It has interfered with the enforcement of statutory rights.

3. The Reemergence of State Law

The role of the states, which was insignificant during the two decades from 1947-1967, has since become increasingly important. State labor law has been applied to the great expansion of public sector unionism during this latter period. In almost all cases the basic rules have been patterned primarily after the NLRA, but important differences have been maintained. While the concept of free choice has been universally adopted, that of free collective bargaining has been significantly altered in the public sector. The right to strike has generally been either replaced or supplemented by some form of mandatory adjudication in establishing wages and working conditions. The scope of bargaining has been reduced and certain mandatory clauses restricting the union's role are frequently inserted into agreements as a matter of law.

State law has also reemerged because the doctrine of federal preemption has been reduced. State tort, contract, and public interest regulation have been increasingly permitted in situations coming within the NLRA. State courts have been permitted to develop new doctrines protecting job rights even as to employment relations supposedly governed by the NLRA. In many cases, the application of state law undercuts national labor relations policy.[14]

Part III. Basic Policy Changes

A. *The Declining Role of Collective Bargaining* [15]

One of the least predictable aspects of the law's development has been the retreat from collective bargaining. The Act originally seemed to envision collective bargaining as the end product of mature labor relations, the process by which employee participation and industrial peace could be achieved, management rights protected, and rival claims articulated and resolved. There is evidence to suggest that collective bargaining has frequently been successful in achieving these goals. Where it has not been defeated by union indifference or management intransigence, it has helped employees to achieve greater power, wealth, and dignity. The widespread use of seniority as a result of collective bargaining and the almost automatic limitation on the employer's right to discharge have helped to establish the idea that employees through their work develop a legally enforceable claim to their jobs and that most management decisions affecting significant employee interests must be based on legitimate, objective standards. Through bargained-for pensions and supplemental benefits, employees under collective bargaining are provided protection for their old age and a cushion against unemployment. It is noteworthy that in all these areas the benefits achieved through collective bargaining have been gradually made available to employees more generally. Collective bargaining has given American unions a visible, significant presence on the shop floor, it has brought many of them great resources, political power, and economic leverage. For many employers this system, while limiting control and possibly raising labor costs, has provided stability. It has reduced quit rates, encouraged the development of reasonable rules uniformly applied, helped to create a sense of common enterprise, and thereby often promoted productivity and efficiency. Through collective bargaining, labor and management have developed a private system of dispute resolution culminating in arbitration, the success of which has been widely acknowledged and which has given impetus to private and public efforts to develop similar systems in different areas throughout society. Despite this record of achievement, the judicial attitude towards collective bargaining has increasingly become one of suspicion, hostility, and indifference. This is manifest in a variety of ways.

1. Increased Tolerance for Competing Approaches

At one time the courts were suspicious of employer-developed programs for worker involvement, which were held outlawed by the Act as efforts to provide the form of collective bargaining without its substance. Currently such programs almost uniformly receive judicial approval. They are perceived as techniques for making labor relations cooperative rather than adversarial. Related to this development has been the courts' willingness to find that programs developed to institute a significant employee role can have the effect of making employees managers and hence remove them from the Act's jurisdiction. This approach has been applied most significantly to higher education under the *Yeshiva* doctrine,[16] but it has also been applied to other professional employees and has the potential to reduce a significant portion of the Act's jurisdiction.

2. Reducing the Scope of Collective Bargaining

By narrowly defining "wages," "hours," and "conditions of employment," the Board and the courts have reduced the commitment to collective bargaining significantly. They have held that employers are not required to bargain about such things as plant closings that lie at the "core of entrepreneurial control."

3. The Increasing Governmental Role in the Establishment of Terms of Employment

The failure of collective bargaining to effectively deal with questions of race and sex discrimination led the government to insist through the Civil Rights Act that employment relationships incorporate the policies against discrimination in a variety of important ways. Similarly, disclosure about union corruption and mishandling led to the passage of ERISA, which has limited and directed bargaining about pensions. The development of the law dealing with unjust discharge may be seen as an acceleration of this trend. Not only have the courts gradually annexed the concept of "just cause" originally developed by and limited to collective bargaining agreements, but also they have, in some cases, refused to recognize the primacy of collective bargaining in this area.

The movement away from collective bargaining is reflective of the reemergence of market economics as a technique for the evaluation of legal institutions. Under traditional economic theory, collective bargaining is an inefficient way of regulating labor supply and conditions of work. The NLRA was passed at a time when the market was discredited in dealing with labor relations. Currently, however, the reexamination of legal institutions through the medium of free market analysis has gained enormous momentum. In addition, collective bargaining is increasingly perceived as overly adversarial. Other forms of employee relations coming under the general rubric of "worker participation" are thought to be more cooperative. The vision of the U.S. system as adversarial in contrast to Asian and European countries, in which a more cooperative model of employee relations is utilized, is quite common even though the data on which the assumption rests are difficult to ascertain and the rights of employees in these countries to their jobs and extensive collective bargaining has been ignored.

It is not surprising that the courts' vision of collective bargaining is skewed. The problems dealt with in collective bargaining, the techniques and methods of collective bargaining, and its reliance on relative economic strength are all foreign to the experience of most judges. It is the reflection of collective bargaining derived from cases, scholarly writings, and media depictions that furnish the courts' conception of the process, and for a variety of reasons these currently portray an unfavorable image of the process.

B. *Limiting the Right to Strike*

As already noted, the right to strike was significantly reduced by the 1947 and 1959 amendments, which prohibited secondary boycotts and recognitional picketing. A variety of other doctrines have either made strikes unlawful or else reduced the protection available for employees who engage in them. Strikes are rendered unlawful if they occur during the term of a collective agreement; if they are about issues that do not come within the statutory phrase "rates of pay, wages, hours of employment, or other conditions of employment"; if a union is seeking an unlawful clause; or if its proposals violate the antitrust laws. Strikes may be unprotected because the goal is something beyond the employer's control, because the message is disloyal, because the method is indefensible, or because it is not called by the incumbent union. Protected strikes can be responded to by lockouts or permanent replacement. Honoring a picket line may lead to discharge. In all of these ways, the right to strike is constrained and reduced. One of the major trends in labor law is to reduce the right to strike to make it less attractive, and to channel its use into a limited sphere.[17]

Part IV. The Protection of Free Choice

What has remained most constant about the National Labor Relations Act over the years is its emphasis on free choice and its focus on the election process as the means of determining that choice. More than anything else, the major accomplishment of the National Labor Relations Act has been to resolve questions concerning the representation of employees through the election process. The elections have been conducted fairly and have overwhelmingly tended to reflect the employee choice at the time. However, the question of whether the election process actually works properly is one which is being debated with increasing emotion on both sides. From the current perspective of most of organized labor, the Act's inability to protect free choice is demonstrated by the union movement's failure to organize more effectively. Labor leaders argue that the Board has failed to provide an environment in which free choice can be effectuated. The Board permits employers to delay elections, to threaten and discipline employees, and to utilize their greater access to employees to either directly or indirectly promise rewards for voting against representation. From the perspective of management, the Board has often unfairly overturned elections truly reflective of employee choice and it has frequently imposed on management and employees unions rejected by a majority of employees.

One significant element of free choice has been the policy against retaliation on the basis of union membership or activity. This policy continues to be important, but throughout the history of the NLRA it has been subject to important practical and legal limitations. Legal enforcement of this policy has been regularly interfered with by competing considerations.

Both the Board and the courts resist reinstating employees who might have been or could have been discharged for legitimate reasons. Courts have been sympathetic to employers who close down marginal aspects of business in response to unionization. The protection of capital investment permits employers to respond to strikes by replacing the strikers and to respond to unionism by shutting down all or sometimes part of a business.

The Board cannot monitor its cases to insist that reinstated employees in fact return and remain. Studies suggest that most do not.[18] There are many other ways in which employers can make union activity costly for those who engage in it without incurring significant liability.

For all of these reasons, free choice becomes a relative concept that characterizes decisions made after a complex process in which debate and access are both limited; decisions which, for various reasons, may lead to harmful consequences.

Part V. Summary

As the overview suggests, the law governing union organizing, collective bargaining, strikes, picketing, grievance handling, and relations between the federal government and the states are complex and frequently contradictory. One of the things that makes labor law both fascinating and frustrating is its lack of coherence; its mix of pro- and anti-union aspects, its ambivalences with respect to collective bargaining, and its contradictions with respect to strikes and picketing.

FOOTNOTES

1. Magruder, A Half Century of Legal Influence on the Development of Collective Bargaining, 50 Harv.L.Rev. 1071 (1937); I. Bernstein, The New Deal Collective Bargaining Policy (1950).

2. J. Gross, The Making of the National Labor Relations Board (1974).

3. NLRA, § 9.

4. See generally, Meltzer, The Supreme Court Congress and State Jurisdiction Over Labor Relations, 59 Columbia L.Rev. 6 (1959).

5. The development is traced out generally in Getman & Blackburn, Labor Relations: Law Practice & Policy, 1983 (pp. 1–39).

6. These concepts are developed in Chapters 2 and 3.

7. See generally, Meltzer, Organizational Picketing and the NLRB: Five on a See Saw, 30 U.Chi.Law Rev. 78 (1962).

8. We cannot think of a single Board member appointed during the past 30 years who, prior to appointment, had standing as a neutral expert. We are aware that Professor Meltzer of the University of Chicago Law School was offered the chairmanship by President Nixon, but declined. There are probably other such cases of which we are unaware.

9. See Murphy, The National Labor Relations Board—An Appraisal, 52 Minn.L.Rev. 819 (1968).

10. 33 NLRB Ann.Rep. 60 (1969). For a fuller discussion of this issue see Getman and Goldberg, The Myth of Labor Board Expertise, 39 U.Chi.L.Rev. 681 (1972).

11. Bernstein, The NLRB's Adjudication—Rule Making Dilemma Under the Administrative Procedure Act, 79 Yale L.J. 571–577 (1970).

12. The cases which involved enforcing the promise to arbitrate and enforcement of arbitral awards are discussed in Chapter 3.

13. In *Collyer Insulated Wire Co,* 192 N.L.R.B. 837 (1971). The Board announced a policy of refusing to hear cases which dealt with matters either pending or subject to arbitration. The *Collyer* doctrine is discussed in Chapter 3.

14. The relation between federal and state law is discussed in Chapter 6. For a discussion of the nature of state regulation, see Edwards, The Emerging Duty to Bargain in the Public Sector, 71 Mich.L.Rev. 885 (1973).

15. See Getman, The Courts and Collective Bargaining, 59 Chicago Kent L.Rev. 969 (1983).

16. In *NLRB v. Yeshiva University,* 444 U.S. 672 (1980), the court held faculty members generally to be managerial employees. See Chapter 1.

17. See Chapter 4.

18. See Weiler, "Promises to Keep: Securing Workers' Rights to Self–Organization Under the NLRA," 96 Harvard L.Rev. 1769 (1983).

Relevant Books, Articles, and Suggested Reading

BOOKS:

Gorman, Labor Law Basic Text (1976).

(Somers, ed.), Collective Bargaining: Contemporary American Experience (1980).

Wellington, Labor and the Legal Process (1968).

Slichter, Healy & Livernash, The Impact of Collective Bargaining on Management (1965).

Flanagan, Labor Relations and the Litigation Explosion (1987).

ARTICLES:

Bernstein, "The NLRB's Adjudication—Rule Making Dilemma Under the Administrative Procedure Act," 79 Yale L.Journal 571 (1970).

Getman & Goldberg, "The Myth of Labor Board Expertise," 38 Univ.Chicago L.Rev. 681 (1972).

Estreicher, "Policy Oscillation at the Labor Board: A Plea for Rule Making," NYU 37th Annual Conference on Labor Law, Chapter 10 (1984).

Attleson, "Reflection on Labor Power and Society," 44 Maryland L.Rev. 841 (1985).

Craver, "The Vitality of the American Labor Movement in the Twenty–First Century," Univ. of Illinois L.Rev. 633 (1983).

Klare, "Judicial Deradicalization of the Wagner Act and the Origins of Modern Legal Consciousness 1937–41," 62 Minn.L.Rev. 265 (1978).

Finken, "Revisionism in Labor Law," 43 Maryland L.Rev. 23 (1984).

Klare, "Traditional Labor Law Scholarship and the Crises of Collective Bargaining Law: A Reply to Professor Finken," 44 Maryland L.Rev. 731 (1985).

Stone, "The Post War Paradigm in American Labor Law," 90 Yale L.Journal 1509 (1981).

Getman, "The Courts and Collective Bargaining," 59 Chicago Kent L.Rev. 969 (1982).

Chapter I

UNION ORGANIZING

Part I. Introduction

One of the prime goals of the National Labor Relations Act was to effectuate free choice for employees with respect to the issue of union representation. However, because the Act contemplated a system of exclusive representation for all employees in a bargaining unit, freedom of choice was from the beginning a majoritarian rather than an individual concept. The Act provided for its implementation through representation elections regulated by the National Labor Relations Board. This system remains at the heart of the Act. When the Board's processes are complete, either all employees in a unit or none will be represented by a union. The group to be represented must be identified in advance and then polled in some way to ascertain their preference. Much of the Board's work involves determining when elections are appropriate and who may vote in them. Thereafter, the Board seeks to regulate employer and union conduct so that elections will accurately reflect the wishes of the majority of employees in the unit polled.

The concept of free choice is a vague one and the Board has not developed a consistent theory or definition over the years. For example, if an employee initially favors union representation but later changes his mind because he becomes persuaded by the employer that in some vague way the advent of the union might jeopardize his economic future or that unionization would be futile given the employer's likely resistance, is his vote against representation a reflection of free choice or is it coerced? Board opinions reflect a variety of different answers to this question. The confusion is compounded because the Board has learned little over the years about which campaign tactics, if any, are likely to sway employee choice. For very sound reasons, the Board does not collect evidence about the impact of employer or union tactics in particular cases. For reasons less convincing it has never investigated these issues by rule making or empirical investigation. As a result, debate within the Board has reflected both the different political values and the empirical assumptions held by Board members at various times. These differences have led to abrupt changes in Board doctrine as well as to more subtle shifts in the application of its rules that have taken place whenever the political alignment of the Board has changed substantially. It is thus impossible to predict over any substantial time period how the Board is likely to rule on complex issues or subtle fact patterns. To have a meaningful knowledge of NLRA law it is necessary not only to be conversant with current doctrine but to understand the competing viewpoints, the areas of potential change, as well as the areas of common agreement.

Part II. The Election Process

A. The Employment Relationship

1. Statutory vs. Common Law Approaches

Rights under the Act are granted to "employees." [1]   Before an election can be called, it must be concluded that these for whom representation is sought are in fact employees for purposes of the National Labor Relations Act.   The definition section of the Act, section 2(3), merely provides the circular explanation that the term employee "shall include any employee."   Nowhere in the statute is the basic concept defined with particularity, although the term is narrowed by specifically excluding the following categories: (a) agricultural laborers, (b) domestic servants, (c) independent contractors, (d) supervisors, (e) employees subject to the Railway Labor Act, and (f) public employees whether federal, state, or local. [2]   In applying the exclusions, the Board and courts have had the most difficulty with the distinction between employees and independent contractors.   The original Wagner Act did not contain such an exclusion, and the Board originally sought to interpret the term "employee" by reference to the applicability of the Act's policies.   Thus the Board held that newsboys who might not have been servants at common law were employees because they were dependent upon the publisher for their livelihood. In *NLRB v. Hearst Publications,* the Supreme Court affirmed. [3]   The Court stated that "[t]he mischief at which the Act is aimed and the remedies it offers are not confined exclusively to employees 'within the traditional legal distinctions separating them from independent contractors.'"   Congress responded in 1947 when it specifically excluded "independent contractors" from the definition of employees. [4] In *NLRB v. United Insurance Co.,* [5] the Court recognized the policy change intended by the new definition.   It concluded that the failure to define the term "employee," a term with a rich common law history, together with the exclusion of "independent contractors," established a statutory policy of determining employee status by common law principles.   Under such principles, the right of control over the way the job is performed by the claimed employee is supposedly the crucial test.   If the alleged employer retains the right of control, the worker is an employee; if the worker has the right of control over his own working conditions, he is an independent contractor. [6]   What the Board has often done in response to this statutory limitation on its discretion has been to use the language of the common law test, but, nevertheless, in cases of gross disparity to base its characterization on the underlying economic relationship between the parties. The Board generally has tried to apply the right of control test in such a way as to prevent individuals or groups who have effective economic control over others from avoiding the reach of the Act by the tactic of giving discretion about the mechanics of job performance to those who otherwise would be employees.[7]

The Board's insistence on evaluating the economic relationship is reflected in its analysis of certain occupations, such as selling or truck driving, in which an employee necessarily works by himself or herself and out of the immediate presence of the alleged employer. In such cases, the Board generally has based its determination on the extent to which the alleged employee is dependent for her livelihood upon the employer and the decisions of the employer.[8] Application of the right of control test has not varied as much as other Board doctrine in recent years because it has primarily been administered by the regional directors, a group well versed in Board doctrine and less political than the Board members themselves.[9]

If an employer has the ability to change the relationship to include or exclude factors consistent with the right of control test, the very presence of this power has been used by the Board to establish an employment relationship.[10] While the courts consider this factor as evidence, they have been unwilling to accept its controlling significance.[11] Behind this is an important policy question of the extent to which an employer can intentionally manipulate relationships in order to avoid the reach of the Act. At first blush it would seem to be entirely appropriate, much like people arranging their affairs to minimize taxes. On the other hand, to remove people from the protection of the statute to prevent the exercise of rights granted by it seems contrary to the basic policy of section 8(a)(1), which prevents an employer from changing conditions of work in such a way as to interfere with the exercise of rights under section 7.

2. The Distinction Between Management and Labor

a. THE SUPERVISORY EXEMPTIONS [12]

The exclusion of supervisors from the Act's coverage reflects several policies that have been influential in administration of the NLRA: (a) that free choice needs protection against employer manipulation that could follow from permitting representatives of management to participate in the election process;[13] (b) that certain employees do not need protection because they already have an adequate role in their economic destiny by virtue of their employment status;[14] (c) that permitting a union voice with respect to any aspect of supervision would improperly blur the line between management and union and therefore prevent people properly on the management side of the line from performing their tasks adequately.[15] The definition of supervisor in the statute is very broad, including "any individual having authority in the interests of the employer to hire, transfer, suspend, layoff, recall, promote, discharge, assign, reward or discipline other employees or responsibly to direct them or to adjust their grievances or effectively to recommend such action, if, in connection with the foregoing, the exercise of such authority is not of a merely routine or clerical nature but requires the use of independent judgment." [16]   As might be expected with a definition of this breadth, the issue of whether a particular person or group constitutes supervisors arises frequently, and no clear line between supervisors and lead workers can be discerned, particularly with reference to such qualities as "responsibly to direct" or "effectively to recommend." The issue is made even more difficult by the fact that the constant or routine use of such power is not necessary for an employee to be held a supervisor.[17]   Some regional directors and Board members have applied the statutory language in a fairly literal fashion, in which case they have found most challenged employees to be supervisors. Others have sought to determine the issue by reference to the Act's basic policies, addressing themselves to such questions as: Do the challenged employees seem to need the Act's protection in terms of their wages and working conditions? Do they consider themselves a part of management or a part of the work force? Are they in a position to coerce other employees if they are included in the unit? Are they included in management discussions and otherwise treated as management by the employer? No general key to decisions is apparent. This issue more than almost any other is decided on a case-by-case, tribunal-by-tribunal approach. The slow trend of the cases, however, has been towards greater willingness to find employees to be supervisors and away from analysis in terms of the Act's policies.

b. THE MANAGERIAL EXEMPTION

The definition of supervisor, broad as it is, does not theoretically include all people who generally would be considered a part of management. Because it focuses on the relation of the alleged supervisor to rank-and-file employees, it does not include those whose role involves planning, articulating, or carrying out high-level policy, but who have no supervisory role. It is not at all clear that any high officials exist who do not exercise at least some supervisory authority, but the Board and the courts have dealt with the possible gap by creating an exemption in the category of covered employees for "managerial employees." The Board defined this group in *Ford Motor Company* as those executive employees who "formulate, determine and effectuate management policies." [18]   The Board did not treat managerial employees as a group. Instead it sought to exercise jurisdiction over them selectively, depending upon the function of the particular managerial employee.[19]   The Supreme Court in *NLRB v. Bell Aerospace*

Co. adopted the Board's definition, but it held that all such employees are excluded from the Act's protection.[20]

Both supervisory and managerial exemptions are usually used to exclude certain individuals from voting and from the bargaining unit. Occasionally, however, the exclusion of a group of employees on the grounds of supervisory or managerial status will make an entire unit inappropriate.

In *NLRB v. Yeshiva University,* the Supreme Court applied the concept of managerial employees to deny the Yeshiva faculty as a group, and by obvious implication most other university faculty members, the right to unionize under the NLRA. Because of their traditional role in university governance through professional committees and votes in academic bodies, the Court held that all faculty members were managers: "It is clear that Yeshiva and like universities must rely on their faculties to participate in the making and implementation of their policies. The large measure of independence enjoyed by faculty members can only increase the danger that divided loyalty will lead to those harms that the Board traditionally has sought to prevent."[21] That the term "like Universities" was meant to be read broadly is suggested at various points in the opinion where the Court indicates plainly that its conclusions about the critical policy-making role of the faculty were meant to apply not only to Yeshiva but to "mature educational institutions" generally. The Board has followed three different approaches in applying *Yeshiva.* At first it seemed to limit it to cases in which many individual faculty members played key roles in the administration of the institution.[22] Most often it has held faculty members to be managers when there was the appearance of collegial responsibility and a well-established institution.[23] Then it applied it whenever there was even the appearance of collegial governance. The Board has even applied *Yeshiva* where faculty power has been achieved through collective bargaining.[24] On some occasions, however, the Board has rejected managerial status on the grounds that faculty responsibility does not approach the standards of faculty governance described by the Court in *Yeshiva.*[25] Thus the Board varies between limited and expansive application of *Yeshiva.* There are many reasons why literal application of the *Yeshiva* exemption would be unfortunate. First, there is the fact that active roles in university governance do not give faculty control over their own wages and many aspects of working conditions. (Hours of teaching, vacation, etc.) Second, many universities contain elaborate structures of faculty governance but limit final decision making to full-time administrators. In such cases, the Board should decide how fully to consider the realities of academic power. Third, the *Yeshiva* decision, which was decided by a sharply divided Court (5–4), is fundamentally at odds with the basic national policy of free choice with respect to unionization. Most commentators have been critical of the opinion, pointing out that the Court ignored the extent to which faculty members are vulnerable to arbitrary decisions by university administrators.[26] Nor did the Court in its opinion explain why the problem of union-created divided loyalty is more acute for faculty members, whose institutional commitment is normally increased by the professional standards to which the various faculty unions are committed, than for other groups of employees. Moreover, the Court in *Yeshiva* treated faculty as a unit, attributing to faculty members generally the institutional authority exercised by some of their colleagues, an approach never previously employed. The special approach undoubtedly reflects the Court's conclusion that traditional collective bargaining is particularly inappropriate for academic institutions. This does not mean, however, that the *Yeshiva* approach will be so limited. It provides a tempting technique for those employers who seek to avoid unionization in enterprises that differ significantly from the traditional manufacturing and retailing enterprises in which the Act has been applied.

The Board has thus far applied *Yeshiva* only once outside the academic context. In *FHP Inc. and Union of American Physicians,*[27] it found a group of physicians to be managers because the governance system of the hospital in which they worked included committees of physicians that played a role in determining some aspects of health care policy. The extension of *Yeshiva* from faculty to physicians does not seem to be a major step because those being denied coverage in both cases are professionals, groups to whom unionism is a recent phenomenon. The case indicates, however, that now groups other than those with a special history of institutional governance may be made managers because of a committee system in which less than half of the group takes part. The implication is that, at least as to professionals, a committee system may be an alternative to unionism, even if established unilaterally by the employer. The concept of employer-established committees replacing unionization was at one time clearly rejected under the NLRA as a technique for thwarting employee choice, but it is reemerging today in a variety of different contexts with court and Board approval. (This point is discussed more fully in Chapter 5.) The *FHP* case seems to be part of that development. In today's climate, the possibility of utilizing committees to have nonprofessional but skilled workers declared to be managers should not be discounted, especially for those workers without a history of collective bargaining.

The trend of decisions concerning coverage has mirrored the changing approach to enforcement of the Act taken by the Board and courts. The first decisions by the Board were guided by an effort to protect those thought to be economically vulnerable. Congress rejected this approach and instead provided a standard with a long common law tradition that was developed for other purposes. The resulting doctrine as developed by the Board was confusing, technical, and frequently disingenuous. The line between employees and supervisors and that between employees and independent contractors became increasingly difficult to discern. A major area for legal maneuvering as part of the organizing process was provided.

As unionization spread to white-collar professions, the courts began to intervene more frequently, to ensure that the Act as administered did not conflict with the wholehearted commitment of higher level employees to management. The doctrine of "managerial employee" was adopted by the courts and served to limit efforts by unions to expand their base of influence to include professional and higher level employees. This doctrine eventually resulted in major sections of the academic profession being excluded from the Act. The Court rejected the broad applicability of collective bargaining upon which the Act was originally premised in favor of a labor relations system with which it was not really acquainted but which seemed preferable to the Court. The Board has pursued the new policy with conceptual purity, untempered by investigation into reality. The result has been the termination of collective bargaining relationships at many institutions and a dramatic decline in organization among college and university faculty. In the course of this process a major new technique for union avoidance may have been created for some employers. Resolving the limits of this technique is certain to involve considerable litigation, serious efforts at amendment, and continued diversion of union efforts from organizing and collective bargaining to legal and legislative programs. Thus the issue of coverage shows movement from a broad labor policy favorable to unionization to a technical approach recognizing managerial interests and traditional ways of doing things.

B. Unit Determination

1. The Concept of Appropriate Unit

When a union organizes, it almost invariably limits itself to a portion of the employer's work force. It may, for example, attempt to organize employees only at one or two locations or only in a single department, such as drivers or maintenance employees. It may organize production workers generally, but exclude such groups as professionals, clericals, and guards.[28] Most unions will choose the largest unit in which they think they will be successful. Thus, implicit in an organizing drive is the union's concept of an appropriate unit.

When it begins to organize, a union seeks to obtain pledges of support from employees in the unit. These pledges customarily take the form of authorization cards signed by the employees designating the union as their bargaining representative. At the point at which the union feels it will be successful in an election, generally always after it has obtained a card majority in the unit it is organizing, it will formally request recognition from the employer. When that request is rejected, as it is in the great majority of cases, the union will petition for an election.[29] Even if the union has cards designating it as bargaining representative signed by a majority of employees in an appropriate unit, the employer may refuse to grant recognition and require the union to prove its majority status in a Board-conducted election. The employer's right to insist upon an election is probably absolute so long as he does not engage in conduct thought likely to interfere with the validity of the election.[30]

The employer may challenge the union's desired unit on the grounds that either a larger or smaller group is called for. The very fact of challenging the unit will normally cause some delay in holding the election, which most employer representatives believe works in their favor—a belief supported by data. The process is so constructed that by challenging the appropriateness of the unit an employer has the ability to delay the onset of the election for a considerable period and the onset of bargaining for even longer. Because the Board has delegated much of the day-to-day task of unit determination to its regional directors, the initial step in the process is a hearing on the questions of unit and eligibility conducted by a regional office representative.[31] The issues in the hearing are primarily factual, focusing on the employer's labor relations policies and the employees' duties. The hearing officer, who may not be an expert at conducting hearings, will typically seek to avoid error by permitting considerable leeway in the evidence submitted. Thus, where the employer's operation is a complex one, the hearing can be prolonged for many weeks. The parties then submit briefs to the regional director, who decides on the basis of existing precedent whether the union's proposed unit is appropriate and if so which employees should be included. After the regional director's decision is issued, the employer may petition for review by the Board.[32] The very act of seeking review involves a delay of about a month, and, if the Board grants the petition, an additional delay of six to eight months is likely. If the union wins the election, the employer may obtain additional time by refusing to bargain with it, which is also the only way the employer can challenge the Board's determination on the appropriateness of the unit. When this happens an unfair labor practice will be filed. The unfair labor practice proceeding will be quick and perfunctory, establishing that the union won the election, that the union was certified by the Board, and that the employer has refused to bargain. On this basis, the Board will find the employer guilty of violating its obligation to bargain under the Act. The Board's order to the employer to bargain has no binding legal force. The employer may continue to refuse and thereby require the Board to begin an enforcement proceeding in the court of appeals. The issue of the appropriateness of the unit will then be litigated before the court as the primary question in the unfair labor practice charge. If the court of appeals reverses the Board, the entire matter must be begun again. If the court of appeals upholds the Board, it will issue an order enforcing the Board's order. The employer at this point has been instructed by a court to bargain with the union, and failure to comply is punishable as contempt. Until this point, however, there is no legal penalty attached to any of the employer's tactics. The entire process of delay may take years, and the employer's cost will be only his legal fees. By the end of the legal process, the union may well be too weak, and its membership too discouraged by the delay, to bargain effectively. Thus the law does little to prevent employers from using the issue of unit determination as a significant delaying technique. What keeps this from happening regularly is that employers do not want the turmoil, disruption, and diversion of resources that constitute the price they pay for keeping the representation matter open. They would prefer the quickest election in which the union is defeated. This preference will be balanced by concern for the composition of the unit for bargaining should the union win. As a result, employer counsel during a representation proceeding will agree to an election in a unit at a time they consider favorable to their client.

The possibility of delay that the law offers puts employers in a favorable bargaining position to offset the momentum generated by the union's organizing drive. The typical election is held in accordance with an agreement by the parties at a time acceptable to the employer and in a unit, which may put the union's victory in doubt. Board personnel seek to encourage such agreements, and although the Board has the statutory power to set the terms of the election, it will routinely accept whatever the parties agree to.[33]

When, because of the absence of agreement between the union and the employer, the Board or its regional director has to determine the unit, it has broad discretion under the statute to choose from among the possible appropriate units.[34] The Board has traditionally limited itself to determining whether the unit sought by the union is an appropriate unit, not the "only" appropriate unit or the "most" appropriate unit.[35] If the union seeks an election in one of the appropriate units, the Board will grant its request. Therefore, it is in the union's interest for the Board to recognize the greatest possible number of appropriate units.

In determining whether the unit sought is appropriate, the Board seeks to ascertain whether the employees share a "community of interest."[36] This in turn depends upon the answer to two questions:

1. Are the employees in the proposed unit covered by a common labor policy and similar terms and conditions of employment?

2. Are there other employees whose jobs and working conditions are so intertwined with the group sought that to exclude them would mean that both:

    a. the union would bargain for them *de facto* if it won (i.e., the employer could not practically provide them with different wages and working conditions), and

    b. they would not be in a position to obtain effective representation independently? [37]

In deciding whether employees share the requisite community of interests, the Board addresses itself to a wide variety of factors: methods of compensation, hours of work, employment benefits, supervision, training and skills, job functions and situs, contact and interchange with other categories of employees, integration of work functions,[38] and bargaining history (whether—and how effectively—a particular unit was ever previously represented).[39] The Board also considers "extent of organization," i.e., the boundaries of the group the union has organized. The latter poses something of a legal problem because section 9(c)(5) provides that "[i]n determining whether a unit is appropriate . . . the extent to which the employers have organized shall not be controlling." The issue that the Board has wrestled with on numerous occasions is whether it can consider a factor as relevant without, on occasion, giving it controlling weight? In general, the Board has concluded that the language of the statute means that extent of organization may not regularly be used to make an otherwise inappropriate unit appropriate but that it may be looked to as a factor in designating an appropriate unit.[40] This is obviously a very fine line that leaves it open to the Board to either consider or ignore extent of organization in particular cases.

Although the Board has not developed hard and fast rules, it provides the parties with guidelines for agreements through a complex network of presumptions that are routinely employed. The most significant of the Board's presumptions and one that is helpful to unions is that in most industries a single facility is presumptively appropriate.[41] A typical example is the Board's policy that where a retail store has a warehouse operation, a separate warehouse unit is presumptively appropriate if there is geographic separation, separate supervision, and no substantial integration of employees. This presumption is applied in manufacturing industries,[42] retail operations,[43] and the insurance industry.[44] The number of factors considered and their generality means that many different units may be justified in most situations and also that the Board can usually find a basis in precedent for denying a contested unit. The Board's decisions with respect to unit are rarely overturned. Because the issues are complex, factual, and rarely involve significant legal issues, the courts of appeals have been willing to accept almost any conclusion reached by the Board.

When the parties cannot agree and the question of appropriate unit is presented to the Board, it is almost certain to be because of the employer's insistence that the unit sought by the union is too small. Given the sporadic and costly nature of union organizing today and the prevalence of multi-unit employer enterprises, it is often the case that union chances of victory depend upon the Board's willingness to conduct the election in a single location. If the Board insists on a large multi-location unit, the union will lose, or it will not even be able to get the necessary showing for an election. Thus the larger the unit that the Board insists on, the better off employers are. The current Board has been less willing than its predecessors to assume the appropriateness of an election in a single location.

Typical of the Board's new approach is *Ohio Valley Supermarket, Inc.*[45] The union had sought an election in a single retail store. The regional director, on the basis of the Board's presumption that such a unit is appropriate, ordered the election. The full Board reversed on the basis of the company's integrated approach to labor relations at the three stores. This approach has given employers who are not vulnerable to a single pervasive organizing drive the power to insulate themselves against limited union organizing efforts by centralizing the administration of their labor relations program.

In addition to a general willingness to find that the presumption of appropriateness for a single location has been overcome, the current Board has specifically rejected the presumption in the health care industry where it has essentially established a contrary assumption requiring proof that there is some disparity between the unit sought and labor relations policy at other locations before it will hold that a single location is appropriate.[46]

2. The Choice Between Conflicting Appropriate Units

Unit determination becomes especially complex in situations where different unions are competing for interrelated or overlapping employee groups. When two unions are seeking elections in different units, it is possible that both units sought are appropriate. In that case, the Board will make a more careful analysis using many of the factors listed above to choose the better of the appropriate units. It will also frequently take into account the wishes of the employees in the smaller unit, i.e., whether they wish to be included in the larger unit. Employees' wishes are polled through special self-determination election procedures.[47]

The self-determination elections may be used where a craft or department seeks severance from an existing unit. They may also be used where such groups seek a representation election in a small unit where there is no existing larger unit but where at least one union is seeking the larger, more inclusive unit.[48] Self-determination elections may also be used where a union is attempting to add a group of unrepresented employees to an existing unit [49] and must be used for professional employees pursuant to section 9(b)(1) of the Act.

C. Factors Affecting the Appropriateness of an Election Petition

In order for an election to be held, a petition must conform to certain standards established by the Board.

1. Jurisdiction

First, the employer must come within the Board's jurisdiction. Statutorily this is almost impossible to avoid for private sector enterprises.[50] The Board's jurisdiction by statute covers all enterprises which "affect commerce." [51] Except for limitations based upon the definition of employees under the Act, the Board's potential jurisdiction thus extends to almost any kind of business. The Board, however, has voluntarily limited the scope of its jurisdiction by issuing "jurisdictional standards" that are a waiver of jurisdiction over employers whose volume of business falls below the dollar limits set for a particular industry.[52] Before processing a petition, or at least before holding an election, the Board ascertains whether the employer meets the standards. The right of the Board to adopt such standards is specifically recognized in section 14(c) of the Act. However, that section specifically forbids the Board from making its standards more restrictive.

2. Showing of Interest

An election petition may be filed by a union or an employee and in limited circumstances by an employer.[53] If filed by the union, the Board, for reasons of administrative necessity, declines to proceed to an election unless the union can show support by at least 30 percent of the unit—usually by having the employees sign authorization cards designating the union as bargaining representative. Because the 30 percent requirement was developed to protect the Board's resources and not to prevent employers from having to undergo the hardship of an unnecessary election, the Board does not permit the adequacy of a union's showing of interest to be litigated or even contested by an employer.[54] The Board does not permit the employer or a rival union to inspect authorization cards in order to challenge the validity of the 30 percent showing.[55]

3. Timeliness and Blocking Charges

An election is not timely if a valid election has been conducted within the preceding twelve months, nor is an election timely within a year of a union's certification.[56] In addition, the Board generally will not proceed to an election while unfair labor practice charges are pending that relate to any of the employees covered by the petition.[57] Sometimes, if the charging party files a request to proceed, the Board will do so.[58] When such a request is made, the requesting party agrees not to use the alleged unfair labor practice as a basis for challenging the election.

4. The Union's Ability to Prove Majority Status

One of the most significant decisions the Board and the courts have made about freedom of choice is that it is better ascertained through an election after a campaign than through the initial willingness of employees to join the union or sign cards authorizing the union to bargain on their behalf. The language of the statute does not require such a result. The Act in section 9(a) states only that "[r]epresentatives designated or selected for the purposes of collective bargaining by the majority of the employees in a unit appropriate for such purposes shall be the exclusive representative of the employees in such unit for the purposes of collective bargaining. . . ." Section 8(a)(5) requires an employer to bargain with a union so designated, but the act does not specify that the majority can only be established through an election. An employer is free to recognize a majority union without an election.

Congress at various times has rejected a proposal that would require an election before a union is entitled to recognition. At one time the Board took the position that an employer might be required to bargain on the basis of cards unless he or she could demonstrate a good faith doubt as to the card's validity.[59] Gradually the Board's position on this topic changed until it recognized the ability of an employer to insist upon an election where there was an atmosphere free of unfair labor practice even in the face of a union card majority. This approach was upheld by the Supreme Court in *Linden Lumber Div. Summer & Co. v. NLRB.*[60] In *NLRB v. Gissel Packing Co.,*[61] the Supreme Court suggested that an employer who has learned of the union's majority status independently of the cards might be required to bargain without an election, but thus far this has proved to be a virtually empty set. The Board does not require an employer to bargain until he has had the opportunity to make the case against unionization. This position has sometimes been explained on the grounds that formal secret ballot elections are recognized as important events by employees while cards are likely to be signed unthinkingly because of peer pressure or to get the union organizer off the signer's back. While there is much comment to this effect in the cases and law journals, what data there are suggest that signing a card is an important event that is likely to reflect the employee's choice at the time.[62] The election process enables the employer to campaign against representation. Thus the policy favoring elections ultimately rests on the important consequences that attach to a union victory and the desirability of permitting an employer the opportunity to respond to the union's campaign for unionization.

D. Obtaining an Election When a Collective Bargaining Relationship Exists

After a union has been selected, Board rules favor stability over freedom of choice. This preference is revealed in a variety of Board doctrines.

1. The Certification–Year Rule

Once a union has been certified, the employer must treat its majority status as conclusively demonstrated for a period of at least one year. Even if it has reliable indication during this period that the employees have changed their minds and no longer wish to be represented, the employer must continue to bargain with the union and otherwise deal with it as the representative of his employees.[63] The reason for this doctrine is the assumption that stability is best achieved by permitting the union to bargain for a substantial period without concern that failure to come to a quick agreement will jeopardize its claim to speak for the employees.

2. The Contract Bar Doctrine

This doctrine prevents employees, rival unions, or the employer from challenging the status of an incumbent union for a period of up to three years during the existence of a collective bargaining agreement,[64] with the sole exception that a rival union or a group of employees can petition for an election during an "open period" between ninety and sixty days before the termination of the existing collective bargaining agreement.[65]

The contract bar doctrine is designed to promote stability in the collective bargaining relationship.[66] Limiting filing to the open period provides a long period during which the parties can administer the contract, work out problems, and stabilize their dealings without the distraction of a rival union's claims. The open period ends sixty days before contract expiration. The point of denying petitions during this so called "insulated period" is to ensure a normal bargaining environment that isn't distorted by the pressures of rival claims and the related uncertainties that those claims engender.[67]

Sometimes parties to a contract reach an agreement or a new contract before the open period for rival petitions. The "premature" negotiation of a new contract, however, cannot prevent a challenge that is timely according to the open period based on the old contract's expiration date.[68]

3. Craft Severance

Board doctrine makes it difficult for a union that seeks to compete for part of an existing unit to obtain an election in which the employees in the part sought to be broken away vote their preferences between challenging and existing unions and units. Such a process, generally called "craft severance," has historically been attempted by unions that have sought to organize employees in a particular craft or occupational specialty rather than on an industrial basis. The Board's craft severance rules, which were announced in *Mallinkrodt Chemical Works*,[69] specify the factors that the Board will consider in deciding whether to hold such an election.[70]

The rules are so constructed as to put a burden on a union seeking to fragment an existing unit. The union must show much more than that which is normally required to obtain an initial election. In seeking an initial election, a union need only show that a substantial number of people in an appropriate unit favor it. In a craft severance hearing, the union must show its own experience in representing employees, must show that the employees as a group have maintained their separate identity, must show that this group had not participated fully in the existing unit, and must show that they are not integrated into the production process. Even if it succeeds in so doing, the union may be denied an election if the Board concludes that the current system has produced "stability in labor relations" that might be "unduly disrupted by the destruction of the existing patterns or representation." [71] It is not clear precisely what is meant by stability of labor relations, but most Board opinions in which established relations are challenged will deny craft severance on this basis if the parties have been able to successfully negotiate agreements in the past, particularly if they have done so without many strikes having taken place.[72]

4. The Presumption of Continuing Majority

Before bargaining rights are established, an employer has the right to reject even overwhelming card-showing majority and to require a union to prove its right to representative status through an election. After a union has been recognized, however, the employer can rarely force it to prove its right to continued recognition through another election. As the rules discussed above demonstrate, during the certification year and the life of a contract a petition would be untimely. Even at the end of the certification year or the termination of the contract, an employer is not entitled to an election as a matter of course. An employer is required by the presumption of a continuing union majority to maintain recognition. Failure to do so will make him vulnerable to an unfair labor practice charge alleging a failure to bargain in good faith unless he can show (a) that the union in fact had lost its majority status—something that is extremely difficult to demonstrate at a Board hearing long after the fact, or (b) that there was objective evidence to support a good faith doubt as to the union's majority status. In such case, the withdrawal of recognition and insistence upon a new election is legitimate so long as it is not raised in the context of illegal anti-union activity by the employer.[73] At most times the Board has been extremely reluctant to accept as adequate employer evidence suggesting that he or she had reason to doubt the union's continuing majority. At different times the Board has rejected most of the criteria that would support a rational conclusion that the union had lost its majority. For example, in *National Car Rental Systems, Inc.,*[74] the employer withdrew recognition from his shop's union after he had replaced all of his work force in an economic strike. In holding this to be an unfair labor practice, the Board stated "new employees, including strike replacements, are presumed to support the union in the same ratio as those they replace." The employer's knowledge of such matters as resignations from the union, refusal to pay dues, and the setting up of a rival union by a substantial portion of the work force have all been held insufficient to establish good faith doubt, even when these factors have occurred in combination.[75] The Board's policy has been so extreme that the concept of good faith doubt clearly misdescribes it. Instead of an effort to determine motive, the Board has sought to discourage employers from putting at issue the union's continued right to represent employees. The Board has generally taken the position that if the employees no longer want to be represented by a union, they can themselves call for an election through a decertification petition. This position aimed at removing the employer from the issue of the union's continuing status is not an irrational one, but because the Board has not articulated it directly it has lent itself to confusion in terms of judicial review and to subtle changes by subsequent Boards. The courts using the concept of good faith doubt have been more willing than the Board has been in the past to accept the employer's withdrawal of recognition based upon factors that would suggest to a neutral observer that the union had lost its majority status.[76]

The presumption of continuing majority also applies in successorship cases. If an employer that acquires the assets of another is found to be a successor, it has "an obligation to bargain with the union which represented the predecessor's employees." Such an obligation will arise as a result of the presumption of continuing majority if the union makes a bargaining demand at a time where the new employer has hired "a representative" complement of employees, if the former employees of the predecessor constitute a majority of the unit.

The Supreme Court dealt with the circumstances necessary for such an obligation to arise in *Fall River Dyeing & Finishing Corp. v. NLRB.*[77] In that case, the Court, upholding the Board, dealt with the standards to be applied in determining the three requirements for recognition: successorship, demand, and majority status.

The Court held that the question of successorship was properly evaluated under the Board's "substantial continuity" test, which focuses on the acquisition of the predecessor's assets, on whether the new employer produces the same product or provides the same service as its predecessor, and most significantly on whether the basic jobs of the employees continued as before. The Court stressed the importance of this latter measure. "Of particular significance is the fact that from the perspective of the employees their jobs did not change."

The Court also upheld the Board's "continuing demand" rule under which it was held that "when a union has made a premature demand that has been rejected by the employer this demand remains in force until the moment when the employees attain the "substantial and representative complements." If, at that point, a majority of the employees were employed by the predecessor, an obligation to bargain arises, either on the basis of the union's certification if that has been within the past year, or else because of the presumption of continuing majority. Presumably the difference between the two situations is that the union's entitlement to recognition is "conclusive" during the certification year, but is "rebuttable" under the presumption of continuing majority.

The nature and power of the presumption of continuing majority was left unclear by the Court's opinion. Justice Brennan clearly intended for it to be more than a method for making factual conclusions in the face of an ambiguous record. His discussion treats the presumption as a rule of law expressing a preference for continuity over free choice in successorship situations. This conclusion is explicit in the Court's discussion, which noted that both the certification year rule and the presumption of continued majority "are based not so much on an absolute certainty that the union's majority status will not erode . . . as on a particular policy decision." The policy decision that the Court refers to are policies that require that momentary shifts in employee choice, brought about by changed circumstances, be ignored:

> "They [the presumptions] enable a union to concentrate on obtaining and fairly administering a collective-bargaining agreement without worrying that unless it produces majority support and will be decertified . . . the presumptions also remove any temptation on the part of the employer to avoid good faith bargaining in the hope that by delaying it will undermine the union's support among the employees." [78]

Analyzing the situation from the perspective of the affected employees, the Court concluded that in successorship situations continuity was of more importance than free choice:

". . . During a transition between employers, a union is in a peculiarly vulnerable position. It has no formal and established bargaining relationship with the new employer, is uncertain about the new employer's plans, and cannot be sure if or when the new employer must bargain with it. While being concerned with the future of its members with the new employer, the union also must protect whatever rights still exist for its members under the collective-bargaining agreement with the predecessor employer. Accordingly, during this unsettling transition period, the union needs the presumptions of majority status to which it is entitled to safeguard its members' rights and to develop a relationship with the successor."

"The position of the employees also supports the application of the presumptions in the successorship situation. If the employees find themselves in a new enterprise that substantially resembles the old, but without their chosen bargaining representative, they may well feel that their choice of a union is subject to the vagaries of an enterprise's transformation. This feeling is not conducive to industrial peace. In addition, after being hired by a new company following a layoff from the old, employees initially will be concerned primarily with maintaining their new jobs. In fact, they might be inclined to shun support for their former union, especially if they believe that such support will jeopardize their jobs with the successor or if they are inclined to blame the union for their layoff and problems associated with it. Without the presumptions of majority support and with the wide variety of corporate transformations possible, an employer could use a successor enterprise as a way of getting rid of a labor contract and of exploiting the employees' hesitant attitude towards the union to eliminate its continuing presence." [79]

The Court's arguments are almost all directed to the conclusion that employee's choice during this period is likely to be untrustworthy, ephemeral, and, if given effect, harmful both to their own self-interest and industrial stability. Thus the presumption should be applied even if counterfactual. Indeed, quite close to the surface is the conclusion that as a factual matter the presumption is likely to be wrong. In light of the discussion, it is not surprising that the Court majority in *Fall River* does not even address the factual evidence supporting or contradicting the presumption; if the Court so easily accepted the application of the presumption in this situation involving a small majority and a long hiatus, it is difficult to imagine how the presumption could be overcome.

The majority opinion explicitly supports the Board's approach to the presumption rather than the approach generally taken by the courts of appeals that focuses more on whether there is reason to doubt the presumption's factual accuracy. It is far from certain, however, that the appeals courts will apply the doctrine in the manner advocated by the dicta in *Fall River*. The policy preference is not made absolute by the opinion and the Court at one point refers to the presumption as rebuttable. The absence of discussion by the Supreme Court as to the grounds for overcoming the presumption leaves the courts of appeals free to apply their own standards. This is not an issue the Supreme Court is likely to deal with again in an effort to police the court of appeals; and, if it does, in the future it is not clear whether it would reaffirm *Fall River* in this respect. At least three members of the Court do not accept Justice Brennan's reasoning. Given their existing precedent it is likely that some courts of appeals will continue to apply an evidentiary approach to the presumption, particularly in non-successor cases. Such cases can easily be distinguished from *Fall River* because the Court noted in *Fall River* that "the rationale behind the presumption is particularly pertinent to the successorship situation," and it stressed the special vulnerability of employees in successorship situations. However, once post-*Fall River* authority exists for treating the presumption as an evidentiary matter, such precedent is likely to be applied in successorship cases as well. Thus it is unlikely that the current confusion about the force of the presumption of continuing majority will be overcome by the *Fall River* decision.

The Court in *Fall River* argued that its holding did not place an insufferable burden on successor employers. In *Howard Johnson Co., Inc. v. Detroit Local Joint Exec. Board,*[80] the Court held that a purchasing employer normally has the option to hire its own work force. An employer that is in a position to do so can avoid the presumption of continuing majority simply by decreasing the percentage of its predecessor's employees it hires. Although if it can be proved that it refused to hire the former employees to avoid union recognition it will be held in violation of Section 8(a)(3).[81]

E. Judicial Review

1. The General Policy Against Court Intervention

It is difficult for an employer and sometimes impossible for a union to obtain judicial review of a unit determination. Under the statute, only a "final order by the Board" is reviewable.[82] In a very early case, *American Federation of Labor v. NLRB,*[83] the Supreme Court held that Board decisions about the conduct of an election are not final orders that are subject to review in the normal course. The Court's concern was to prevent the use of litigation to delay elections, thereby prolonging the campaign or frustrating freedom of choice.[84]

Generally, if the Board decides not to hold an election, its decision is unreviewable because there is no final order under section

10(f). For the same reason, a union that objects to a unit cannot raise the issue readily no matter whether it wins or loses the election.[85]

2. Exceptions to the Policy Against Judicial Review

In *Leedom v. Kyne*,[86] the Supreme Court held that district courts have jurisdiction to enjoin the conduct of an election where the Board acted in a clear violation of a direct statutory mandate; In *McCulloch v. Sociedad Nacional de Marineros de Honduras*,[87] the Court permitted review where the Board's assertion of jurisdiction was in conflict with U.S. foreign policy (because it sought to conduct elections among the crews of ships registered in other countries). Some of the language in these opinions may be read to create broad exceptions to the general policy of *American Federation of Labor v. NLRB*.[88] The concept of violating a statutory mandate, for example, potentially suggests routine judicial review in all situations, since the party seeking review always claims that the Board exceeded its statutory authority under section 9. In *Boire v. Greyhound Corp.*, the Supreme Court subsequently, however, reasserted the policy of keeping district court review of election determinations very limited. It held that the district court could not enjoin an election in order to test the employer's claim that the people involved were not really employees, but independent contractors. Recognizing and rejecting the broad implications of its earlier opinions, the Court stated: "The *Kyne* exception is a narrow one not to be extended to permit plenary District Court review of Board orders and certification proceedings whenever it can be said that an erroneous assessment of the particular facts before the Board has led it to a conclusion which does not comport with the law." [89]

As the above discussion might illustrate, the issues involved in determining when to hold an election and in designating eligible voters are generally technical and dry, but highly important. It may well be that these rules are more significant to the process of union organizing and the nature of the collective bargaining than the better known and far more often discussed issues of campaign regulations that are dealt with below.

Part III. Regulating the Campaign—Ground Rules

A. The Statutory Scheme

Labor Board elections are almost always preceded by campaigns by the employer and union, seeking to convince the employees to vote either for or against representation. The Board regulates such campaigns through the unfair labor practice provisions of section 8, and through its authority under section 9 to investigate and determine representation questions. Where the Board proceeds under its unfair labor practice jurisdiction, the process may or may not involve judicial review. If either party believes that the other has committed an unfair labor practice that threatens the integrity of the election, it may file an unfair labor practice charge any time within six months of the time the allegedly illegal act took place. The charge is investigated by the regional office.[90] The regional director (sometimes with advice from the Board in Washington) decides whether to issue a complaint. If the regional director decides not to issue a complaint, the charging party may appeal the decision to the Board's Office of Appeal in Washington. Reversal in such cases is quite rare. If the complaint is dismissed, the charging party may not obtain judicial review of this decision.

This is a highly questionable approach that is a relic of the exaggerated deference to the Board's expertise that marked the early days of the Act and the view of the General Counsel as a public prosecutor of labor violations. Because any claim of unfair labor practice must be presented to the Board initially, this approach creates the possibility of Board error uncorrectable by the courts. There seems to be no reason why Board doctrine rejecting charges should be given greater weight than Board doctrine establishing unfair labor practices.

If the regional office decides to issue a complaint, a hearing is held before an administrative law judge. The parties to the hearing are the Board's General Counsel acting through the regional office and the respondent. The charging party may be present with counsel, but typically does not play a major role in presenting the case. After the hearing, the administrative law judge makes findings of facts and conclusions of law. If the judge finds that an unfair labor practice has been committed, he or she will recommend a remedy. In election cases where the unfair labor practices allegedly have been used to object to the election, the typical remedy will set aside the election and require the respondent (usually the employer) to post notices promising that it will no longer interfere with its employees' rights to self organization. In cases of severe unfair labor practices, where the union can demonstrate a card majority, the employer may be ordered to bargain with the union as a remedy.[91] The decision of the administrative law judge may be appealed to the Labor Board itself which will decide the case on the basis of the record before the administrative law judge and written briefs. The decision by the Board either sustaining or dismissing the complaint is subject to review in the courts of appeals. Typically, both the court with jurisdiction over the regional office and the D.C. Circuit have jurisdiction. The court of appeals is required under the Act to affirm the Board's decision if it is supported by substantial evidence.

The Board's unfair labor practice jurisdiction is clearly spelled out in the statute. Section 7 gives to employees the right to "self-organization to form, join or assist labor organizations . . . and

. . . to bargain collectively through representatives of their own choosing." These rights are protected by section 8(a)(1), which makes it an unfair labor practice for an employer "to interfere with, restrain or coerce employees in the exercise of the rights guaranteed in section 7" and by section (8(b)(1)(A)) which makes it "an unfair labor practice for a labor organization to restrain or coerce employees in the exercise of rights guaranteed in section 7." A close reading of the statute makes clear that more severe restrictions are placed on employer conduct than on union conduct since section 8(a)(1) prohibits "interference" with section 7 rights and there is nothing comparable in section 8(b)(1)(A), which prohibits only restraint or coercion. The Supreme Court held this difference to be quite significant in the *Curtis Brothers* case,[92] in which it rejected a Board doctrine that held that organizational picketing by a minority union violated section 8(b)(1) because it restrained employees in the exercise of their right not to engage in concerted activity. The Court's opinion left no doubt that if the Act prohibited "interference" by unions it would have upheld the Board. The statutory difference undoubtedly reflects the conclusion that employers, because of their economic power over the employees, pose a greater threat to free choice than do unions.[93]

The Board's claim to regulatory power beyond that specified in the unfair labor practice provisions is more problematic, but it has a long history. It was first exercised in the *General Shoe* case, decided in 1948,[94] in which the Board described its function to be the maintaining of "laboratory conditions" in Board conducted elections. It has been invoked many times since then. It has regularly been upheld by the courts, even though the statute contains no express grant of such authority nor any language which implicitly suggests it.

The basic policy that underlines the laboratory conditions language and many of the Board's other decisions is that employees should be free to make an informed and carefully reasoned choice. As conceived of by the Board, the concept of informed, reasoned choice has two major policy implications:

1. In order for their choice to be informed, employees must be given a chance to learn about and discuss the pros and cons of unionism.

2. In order for their choice to be reasoned, employees must be protected against efforts to frighten, deceive, or unfairly manipulate them into voting for or against unionization, particularly on the basis of the employer's economic power over them.

There is considerable tension between these two elements of free choice. As will be shown more clearly below, the concept of informed choice suggests the importance of open debate, while the concept of reasoned choice suggests the need for protection against various forms of communication.

B. Employer Rules Prohibiting Union Activity

1. Solicitation During Non–Working Time

a. IN GENERAL

The concept of informed choice conflicts with traditional concepts of employer property rights because it requires some ability for the employees to learn about and discuss unionization on the employer's property during the course of the working day, and employers might otherwise use their power to prevent such discussion. One of the first major decisions about the reach of the National Labor Relations Act was *Republic Aviation Corp. v. NLRB.*[95] The case involved the discipline of employees for distributing union literature on their own time in the company parking lot and the discharge of an employee for passing out authorization cards in violation of company rules that prohibited distribution of literature and solicitation on company property. The company rules were enacted before the unions came on the scene and were not motivated by the desire to prevent unionization. The Board held and the Court agreed that both the rules themselves and their enforcement violated the Act. The very existence of the rules was deemed by the Board to be an "unreasonable impediment to self-organization." The Board viewed the opportunity to solicit at the plant as "uniquely appropriate for the employees' exercise of their right to full associational freedom." The Court agreed, holding that the Board properly balanced the employer's interest in discipline and efficiency against the employees' opportunity to organize. The Board's doctrine specified that it is "within the province of an employer to promulgate and enforce a rule prohibiting union solicitation during working hours. Such a rule must be presumed valid in the absence of evidence that it was adopted for a discriminatory purpose." On the other hand, the Board concluded that "it is therefore not within province of an employer to promulgate and enforce a rule prohibiting union solicitation by an employee outside of working hours, although on company property." The Board has maintained this position from the earliest days of the Wagner Act until the present. There has been disagreement, however, about how clearly the employer must spell out the employees' rights. The Board generally had taken the position that rules which merely announce that employees are prohibited from soliciting during working time were prohibited, because they do not make clear that employees could solicit on their own time.[96] The current Board overturned that interpretation, holding that such rules were valid and that they indicated "with sufficient clarity that employees may solicit on their own time."[97]

b. PRIVILEGED BROAD NO–SOLICITATION RULES

Republican Aviation left open the question of what evidence would suffice to overcome the presumption of invalidity and permit an employer to promulgate a lawful rule prohibiting solicitation in working areas during non-working time. In general, the Board proceeds on a case-by-case basis in determining when the presumption is overcome, but it has special rules for department stores, hospitals, and restaurants. These facilities all have working areas frequented by the public (or used for essential patient care) and may be validly held off-limits for solicitation.[98] Even in such institutions, the reach of the valid no-solicitation rule is limited to those areas in which solicitation would threaten to substantially interfere with efficient operations.[99] Employers have argued that they are within the special class of institutions in which solicitation could pose particular problems, but in most cases these efforts have been rejected both by the Board and the courts.[100] In concluding that the Act has been violated, the Board does not find (and the courts do not require it to do so) that the no-solicitation rule actually interfered with union organization. To sustain a section 8(a)(1) finding, it is enough to conclude that the employer's conduct has a general tendency to interfere with section 7 rights.[101]

c. THE CONCEPT OF A DISCRIMINATORY RULE

A no-solicitation rule as first promulgated may be discriminatory in two ways. It may treat union solicitation differently from other forms of solicitation, in which case it is *per se* invalid, or it may be promulgated in order to stifle union activity. In general, absent discrimination there are two types of prima facie valid rules: those seeking to prevent people other than those scheduled to work (whether or not employees) from coming into work areas, and those seeking to limit solicitation by employees while performing their jobs or during down time during working hours.[102] The meaning of solicitation in this context is not clear because no-solicitation rules were originally directed at commercial activity and not at normal employee discussion. No-solicitation rules are not the same as no-talking rules. Efforts to penalize employees for talking about the union during working time are carefully analyzed and are generally found to be discriminatory on the grounds that other forms of discussion have been permitted in the past.

d. THE DISCRIMINATORY ENFORCEMENT OF AN OTHERWISE VALID RULE

By far the greatest number of cases dealing with the validity of no-solicitation rules have concerned allegations that the rules have been applied in a discriminatory fashion. The enforcement of no-solicitation rules is a special branch of the law dealing generally with employer retaliation for union activity, which is discussed below. Regardless of how reasonable the rule, the employer may not treat union activity less favorably than other activity. In particular, it may not distinguish between pro- and anti-union activity.[103] A general crackdown in enforcement after the onset of union organizing is also not permitted.[104] Reasonable rules against solicitation by outsiders for commercial or political causes, however, may be applied to union activity if employees are not at their normal work station but are seeking to solicit in working areas during normal work time. The enforcement of the rule is generally permitted when the union activity is different in kind or degree from the activity previously permitted.[105]

e. NO–DISTRIBUTION RULES

The Board distinguishes between rules prohibiting oral solicitation and rules limiting the distribution of literature. Solicitation by distribution of literature may be prohibited during non-work time in working areas.[106] The Board reasoned that literature presents more of a legitimate problem in working areas and that it is not necessary for it to be distributed in working areas in order for it to be effective, except in unusual circumstances.

C. Union Rights of Access and Reply

1. The Limited Right to Respond to Captive Audience Speeches

Employers are permitted to make anti-union speeches to their employees on company premises during work time without permitting the union to respond. In *NLRB v. United Steelworkers of America 86 (Nutone)*, the Supreme Court announced this general right of employer and qualified it by stating that the Board could find a violation where it concluded that the employer's refusal to grant equal time "truly diminished the ability of the labor organizations involved to carry their messages to the employees" or created an imbalance in the opportunities for organization communication.[107]

Thus the *Nutone* case apparently delegated to the Board the task of balancing on a case-by-case basis the opportunities for communication by both employer and union. The Court's opinion did not, however, describe how the Board was to measure whether an appropriate balance existed. The Board, lacking the ability to make quantitative judgments, has responded by assuming that no imbalance exists so long as the union has some ability to reach the employees through traditional means of organization such as telephone, mail, and meetings at union headquarters. This approach has been utilized by different Boards regardless of their attitudes towards unionization.

The Board has at all times in its history been loath to find an imbalance and only rarely will it require an employer to grant the union equal time.[108]

2. Access to Company Premises by Union Organizers

The Supreme Court dealt with the right of nonemployee organizers to enter upon the employer's premises in order to make contact with the employees in *NLRB v. Babcock & Wilcox,* in which case the Court stated without much explanation that "[a]n employer may validly post his property against nonemployee distribution of union literature, if reasonable efforts by the union through other available channels of communication will enable it to reach the employees with its message and if the employer's notice or order does not discriminate against the union by allowing other distribution." Although the Court drew a distinction between the rights of employees and the rights of non-union organizers, it did comment that "the right of self-organization depends in some measure on the ability of employees to learn the advantages of self-organization from others. Consequently, if a location of a plant and the living quarters of the employees place the employees beyond the reach of reasonable union efforts to communicate with them, the employer must allow the union to approach his employees on his property." [109]

Despite subtle differences in the language employed, the Court's opinion in *Babcock* was similar in approach and outcome to its approach in *Nutone.* In both cases, the Court apparently delegated to the Board the task of making determinations in individual cases about the adequacy of the union's opportunities for reaching the employees with its message. In both cases, the Board with the approval of the courts of appeals has avoided the task by creating an almost inflexible presumption of adequacy for traditional union methods of reaching the employees. An adequate balance for these purposes has been found whenever the Board determines that the union has "some possibility of communication." [110]

Neither the Board nor the courts will find an imbalance justifying access on the basis of what seem to be glaring differences between the employer's and the union's opportunities to communicate with the employees. As Judge Edwards stated, summarizing existing law, "an employer may deny a union access to company property unless the union meets a heavy burden of showing that no other reasonable means of communicating its organizational message to the employees exist." [111] This approach has been applied, especially by the courts, even to such obvious areas of employer advantage as hotels and lumber camps where employees live on the premises. The only exception is the shopping mall, and this exception seems based on the notion that greater disruption of commercial interests will occur if unions solicit at public areas adjacent to such malls.

Board precedent in the resort hotel situation is mixed. Access was approved in *Grossingers,*[112] a case which combined extreme anti-union animus by the employer and almost no opportunity for the union to get its message heard. The court of appeals affirmed that in such cases the majority of employees "cannot be reached by any means practically available to union organizers." Probably more typical is *NLRB v. Kutsher's,*[113] in which the court denied enforcement of the Board's access order, distinguishing *Grossinger's* on the basis that there was no anti-union animus and that there was potential for adequate access at Kutsher's because the employees could be reached as they walked across a public road. In *NLRB v. Tamiment, Inc.,* the union was denied access to a completely self-contained resort community because it had not demonstrated that it had made reasonable—but unsuccessful—efforts to communicate through other channels.[114]

In *Sabine Towing v. NLRB,* the Court denied a Board order of access to a tug boat. The Court noted that resident seamen went ashore frequently and could be reached on the decks, in bars, etc. It stated: "This is clearly not one of the rare situations where nonemployer access to an employer's property is required by *Babcock & Wilcox."* [115]

As the resort and tugboat cases demonstrate, the circuits impose a severe burden of proof on the union before permitting the Board to grant access. The Board cannot prospectively determine that there will be a lack of access, notwithstanding the admitted difficulty of making organizational contacts. Before an access order becomes a possibility, the union must first make a serious effort to overcome the difficulties.[116]

In 1978, in *Sears, Roebuck & Co. v. San Diego County District Council,*[117] the Supreme Court appeared to adopt the restrictive interpretation of *Babcock* and *Nutone* sketched above when it declared: "While *Babcock* indicates that an employer may not always bar nonemployer organizers from his property, his right to do so remains the general rule. To gain access, the union has the burden of showing that no other reasonable means of communicating its organizational message to the employees exist or that the employer's access rules discriminate against union solicitation." [118] Thus the "balancing" metaphor used by the Supreme Court was largely ignored because the law's concern seems to be almost entirely with the protection of property rights. Indeed, the announcement and enforcement of these rules represent one of the earliest examples of the Court's rejecting Board decisions consistent with the Act's policies, in support of traditional employees' property rights.

The Board has recently changed its approach somewhat. In *Fairmont Hotel* it announced that it would henceforth engage in a case-by-case analysis of the competing interests of employer and employees in order to tell whether access should be granted.[119] The Board stressed the "mandate" of the Court in *Babcock & Wilcox* "to accommodate" each right "with as little destruction of one as is consistent with maintenance of the other"—which language, the Board stated, "recognized that the claim of a party to one or another of these rights will have varying degrees of strength depending on the facts of the particular case."

The Board's stress on balancing rights seems to offer unions hope of greater access because the availability of alternative means of communicating was made subordinate to the balancing process:

> "It is the Board's task first to weigh the relative strength of each party's claim. . . . Only in those cases where the respective claims are relatively equal in strength will effective alternative means of communication become determinative." [120]

It is still too early to tell how *Fairmont Hotel* will be applied. The first applications seem promising from a union perspective. Thus in *Emery Realty, Inc.,*[121] the Board held that a union had a right to distribute organizational material in a hotel arcade. The Board evaluated the union's interest as a very strong one. "The section 7 right of employees to organize which the union here seeks to assert through its organizational solicitations is at the 'very core' of the interests the National Labor Relations Act seeks to protect." Under the facts of the case, the Board found the employer's property interest in preventing solicitation to be "relatively weak." Accordingly it stated "that the availability of reasonable alternative means by which the Union could have communicated its message is not determinative under a *Fairmont* analysis." [122]

Whether this case is likely to be a precursor of future Board decisions remains to be seen. Over the years, the Board has in many situations shifted from careful balancing to decision by rule. If this happens, a rule more favorable to union organizing efforts may develop. It appears as likely, however, that the Board will gradually fold into the balance the availability of alternate means of communication for the union, in which case the resulting rule will be much like the Board's previous approach.

Another interesting question is whether the *Fairmont* approach will be used to give unions greater right to reply to captive audience speeches under the *Nutone* decision. At this moment this appears unlikely because the employer's property interest is almost always a powerful one in such cases. The formal *Fairmont* analysis thus would invariably lead to an evaluation of alternative means in captive audience cases, a standard traditionally unfavorable to unions. Thus, while the indications are that the *Fairmont Hotel* approach will improve access at least temporarily for unions, it is doubtful whether it will significantly alter the balance.

3. *Excelsior* Lists

In 1966, the Board established the *Excelsior* rule—requiring employers to make available lists of names and addresses of eligible voters prior to NLRB-conducted elections.[123] In *NLRB v. Wyman–Gordon Co.,*[124] the Supreme Court upheld the Board's authority to do so. On the same date that it promulgated the *Excelsior* rule, the NLRB also announced its decision in *General Electric Co.,* a case that involved the denial by an employer of a union's request to respond to a captive-audience speech. The Board that had considered modifying its rules regarding union access decided not to make any change in these rules, pending a determination of the impact of *Excelsior:*

> "In light of the increased opportunities for employees' access to communications which should flow from *Excelsior,* but with which we have, as yet, no experience, and because we are not persuaded on the basis of our current experience that other fundamental changes in Board policy are necessary to make possible that free and reasoned choice for or against unionization which the National Labor Relations Act contemplates and which it is our function to insure we prefer to defer any reconsideration of current Board doctrine in the area of plant access until after the effects of *Excelsior* became known." [125]

Since *Excelsior* and *General Electric,* the Board has had two techniques available for going beyond the traditional line of cases and affording additional protections for unions seeking to organize an employer's premises. First, the Board could determine, under *Nutone,* that there has been "an imbalance in the opportunities for organizational communication." Second, the Board could resume the inquiry into equal access rules that it deferred in *General Electric.* During the years that have elapsed since *Excelsior* and *General Electric* were decided, the Board has done neither of these things.

Nutone's suggestion of case-by-case balancing seems to be ignored today, as it was prior to *Excelsior.* Nor has the Board kept its promise to study the effects of *Excelsior.* This is understandable because such a study would require a sophisticated research design beyond the Board's capabilities. The only way for such a determination would be for the Board to underwrite a study by outside researchers, an approach the Board has not heretofore taken. The Board instead has simply assumed that the *Excelsior* lists substantially improve a union's ability to communicate with the employees. The value of *Excelsior* lists, however, is far from clear. Since elections are generally held a short time after the *Excelsior* list is received, the only way for a union to take advantage of *Excelsior* lists is through general mailings. It should not be surprising therefore that empirical data suggest that unions are normally at a significant disadvantage in getting their message across as compared to employers.[126]

The development of the law dealing with access parallels the development of the law more generally. The initial approach of the Board stressed the crucial importance of employee ability to learn about unionization, a statutory interest that was deemed to override significant employer property rights. The courts after a short period of deference to the Board rejected this approach. They determined without empirical information or an understanding of the dynamics of organizing campaigns that union access to employees through outside channels was normally adequate. They delegated to the Board a more limited factual inquiry that the Board is incapable of making on a case-by-case basis. The result has been confusion, technicality, and a basic scheme that permits employer campaigns on the premises, directed by professionals, while limiting union campaigns to informal early gatherings, home visits, and meetings away from the employee's work.

Because the rules distinguish between employees and outside organizers and because they deny unions the opportunity to deliver formal talks on the company's premises, the law requires unions to place reliance upon informal employee discussion as one of the major vehicles for getting its message to the employees. Thus the union's chances of success are inevitably dependent upon the quality of the inside organizing committee, the articulateness of the people selected, and the esteem in which they are held by fellow employees.

Part IV. Regulating Campaign Content

A. The Need to Protect Freedom of Choice

Battles over the Board's role, its understanding of labor relations, and its biases towards or against unions have been most bitterly fought out with respect to its evaluation of employer campaign tactics in general and employer speech in particular. Two basically different approaches have alternated depending upon the political make-up of the Board as well as the philosophy and activism of reviewing courts.

1. The Liberal Activist View

During most of its history, the Board has adopted an activist view of its role based on a vision of campaigns that assumes the potency of campaign tactics and the need for careful regulation on the grounds that freedom of choice is fragile. In particular, the Board has frequently assumed that reasoned choice is vulnerable to suggestions of employer retaliation. Not only direct threats, but also a variety of different types of speech and conduct have been prohibited because they are thought to portend the possibility of economic reprisal for union activity. It also has been generally assumed that suggestions of reprisal, both direct and subtle, are successful in getting employees to vote against unionization.[127]

2. The Conservative View

Republican-era Boards are generally noted for four basic approaches to campaign regulation.

1. Tolerance for employer speech marked by a reluctance to characterize any but the clearest indications of retaliation as threats.

2. A more flexible view of other campaign tactics so that their legality is determined by a case-by-case approach rather than through the application of per se rules.

3. A reluctance to set aside elections on the basis of conduct not amounting to unfair labor practices.

4. A generally more benign view of employer campaign tactics together with a notable reluctance to remedy unfair labor practices through the issuance of bargaining orders.

The conservative view of campaigns has recently been bolstered by a body of academic thinking not easily characterized as pro-employer or anti-union, suggesting that the impact of campaign tactics on employee voting behavior has been exaggerated and that Board regulation of campaign tactics is an inefficient, arbitrary, and misleading way to protect employees' freedom of choice. The position that the potency of employer campaign tactics has been exaggerated is currently quite controversial. It has been rejected by various Board members, by important academic commentators, by the overwhelming majority of unions, and by management consultants and employer representatives. It has been accepted by a limited number of academics, accepted by a few influential union organizers, and accepted with qualifications by some Board members.[128]

B. Protection Against Threats of Reprisal

1. The Constitutional Issue

It is well settled that overt threats of economic retaliation by employers directed towards employees who support the union are not an exercise of free speech but are instead a violation of NLRA section 8(a)(1) as a form of interference with the right of self-organization protected by section 7.[129] Employers these days, for a variety of tactical, legal, and ethical reasons, rarely make direct or overt threats. They do, however, suggest that the consequences of unionization might be harmful, without directly mentioning reprisals. Because such statements may well be a sincere expression of the employer's economic philosophy, under traditional first amendment analysis they should be constitutionally protected unless they contain overt threats. Nevertheless, the Supreme Court in *NLRB v. Gissel Packing* [130] adopted a highly restricted approach to employer free speech rights under the Act. The case itself involved an employer who argued that the union was a "strike happy outfit" and warned that a strike could put the company in economic jeopardy and lead to its closing. He warned the employees to "look around Holyoke and see a lot of them out of business." The Board concluded that the employer's conduct made a fair election impossible because it "reasonably tended to convey to the employees the belief or impression that selection of the union could lead the (company) to close its plant or transfer the weaving operation." The employer argued that its statement amounted to no more than an exercise of its first amendment rights of free speech. The Supreme Court rejected this contention, holding that the employer's speech contained impermissible threats of reprisal:

> "Any assessment of the precise scope of employer expression of course must be made in the context of its labor relations setting. Thus an employer's right cannot outweigh the equal rights of the employees to associate freely . . . and any balancing of those rights must take into account the economic dependence of the employees on their employer and the necessary tendency of the former because of that relationship to pick up intended implications of the latter which might be more readily dismissed by a more disinterested ear."

On the basis of this analysis, the Court restricted an employer's first amendment right to discuss the effect he believes unionization will have on his company to "prediction . . . carefully phrased on the basis of objective facts to convey an employer's belief as to demonstrably probable consequences beyond his control. . . ."

The Court stated that an employer was not constitutionally protected in expressing his belief that the union might lead to plant closing even if his belief was sincere "unless which is most improbable, the eventuality of closing is capable of proof." In responding to the argument that "the line between threat and prediction thus drawn, is too weak to withstand constitutional scrutiny," the Court commented that "[A]n employer . . . can easily make his reasons known without engaging in internal brinksmanship . . . at least he can avoid coercive speech simply by avoiding conscious overstatement. . . ." The Court's assurance that an employer can easily make his views known without coming close to the brink would have been more convincing if the Court had explained how the question of possible harmful effects resulting from collective bargaining could have been addressed legally. Perhaps the Court really meant for the employer to stay away from the issue of possible harmful effects, because it

deemed it to be too frightening to employees. If so the Court chose
to ignore the fact that there is a respectable economic argument to the
effect that unions and collective bargaining might lead to plant closing
or transfers of work.[131] This is not, however, an argument that can be
conveyed solely by objective fact without distortion because it is based
upon assumptions about likely union behavior. It is also difficult to
discuss this issue fully and openly without leaving some room for
employer discretion. As will be discussed more fully below, the law
currently protects employer discretion with regard to plant closing and
transfer of work in circumstances where there is no obligation to
bargain about such decisions. An employer may go out of business
altogether in retaliation for a union vote or make substantial changes
in the way it conducts business without even discussing the decision
with the union. To refer to these rights during an organizational
campaign would probably be an unfair labor practice. Thus the Court
assumes employee ignorance that it is unlawful to correct.

2. The Issue of Statutory Construction

Throughout its history the Board has been continually faced with
deciding whether statements by employers suggesting possible adverse
economic consequences of unionization constitute threats. The *Gissel*
case did not resolve this issue. The Court was concerned primarily
with the constitutional issue. It set forth a standard for judging
whether employer statements touching upon the issue of plant closing
were constitutionally protected expressions. Whether or not the
Court intended in its discussion to deal simultaneously with the issue
of statutorily defining a threat, it provided little guidance to the Board
for judging threats other than those directed to this issue.

A variety of common employer statements of other types may also
be perceived as implied threats. For example, in a typical campaign
speech, the employer will almost always make at least one of the
following types of statements: [132]

1. Stress the importance of the vote in a way calculated to
    create some apprehension, e.g., "Your vote will be one of
    the most important decisions you will ever make."

2. Mention generally that the advent of the union might "make
    things worse."

3. Suggest that unionization would disrupt existing good rela-
    tions and that the company would no longer be in a position
    to respond to individual requests for special favors flexibly.

4. Indicate that collective bargaining will be very difficult since
    the employer "has no intention of meeting unreasonable
    union demands. I intend to bargain hard [and if the union
    rejects my position you will probably be dragged out on
    strike.]"

All of these statements may be taken as threats by a person who is acutely attentive to nuances of possible retaliation, or they might be treated as the employer's predictions of harmful consequences that will flow from unionization regardless of his own wishes they may also impart relevant information given to the employees about the way in which the employer might legitimately respond to the union, or as a response to overblown union claims.   It should be noted that the question turns not upon what the employer intended, but upon how the message is likely to be perceived by the employees.   Thus the issue of separating threats from legitimate expressions of opinion turns on the model of employee voting response that the Board and the courts adopt.   The Board has almost always assumed that employees are attentive to the campaign and that they will note the form of expression chosen.[133]   There is conflict, however, about whether the employee's response will be shaped by the precise language used or by the suggestion of coercion emanating from the speech and from the nature of the employer's campaign.   An example of the conflicting approaches is contained in *NLRB v. Golub Corp.*[134]   In that case, the employer made the following statement in its campaign statements: "The union has been making many promises.   Promises to make demands which could be excessive.   Companies that have been forced to meet excessive union demands have been known to be forced out of business."   And again: "Large chains which have been forced to sign up with the unions have been known to increase the work load of all their individual employees by reducing the number of employees in order to offset the higher costs.   They find that they have to get the same amount of work done by fewer people to remain competitive." The majority of the Board found that these statements were a threat.

The court of appeals reversed the Board's conclusion by carefully analyzing the language used.   Speaking for the majority Judge Friendly stated: "But as the dictionaries tell us, a threat of reprisal means a threat of retaliation and this in turn means not a prediction that adverse consequences will develop but a threat that they will be deliberately inflicted in return for an injury. . . .   Nothing in these communications could reasonably be interpreted as a threat to make the employees' lot harder in retaliation for their voting for the union. The only fair reading is that the employer would take these steps solely for economic necessity and with regret."   In contrast, the dissenting opinion by Judge Hays stated: "An employer can dress up his threats in a language of prediction.   'You will lose your job,' rather than 'I will fire you' (and fool the judges).   He doesn't fool his employees.   They know perfectly well what he means."   It is notable that both Judges assume careful attention by the employees to the statements made.   Their difference is over the likely response of employees.

The decision in *Golub* was pre-*Gissel,* and *Gissel* seemed to require a far more restrictive approach to employer speech, thus suggesting that it endorsed the minority opinion. However, opinions similar to *Golub* were issued by courts of appeals shortly after *Gissel.* The first major departure from the approach used in *Gissel* came in *Boaz Spinning Co. v. NLRB,*[135] in which the Sixth Circuit set aside a NLRB ruling that two pre-election speeches had exceeded permissible limits and had contained impermissible threats. The speeches in large part discussed the results of unionization at other plants whose employees had voted for representation. The employer noted that the other textile plants had been forced to close because of inability to function competitively. The message was quite similar to that contained in material condemned by the Court in *Gissel.* The Sixth Circuit, citing pre-*Gissel* cases, stated that:

> "the right of free speech in a union organizational campaign is not to be narrowly restricted . . . nor is the right of free speech to be unequally applied as between employers and labor unions. There is no basis for adopting a narrow restrictive rule for one party and a liberal one for the other."

This evenhanded equating of union and employer speech is obviously inconsistent with the logic of the *Gissel* opinion, which, because it is based on the employer's economic power over the employee, necessarily infers a double standard for employer speech and union speech. In *Gissel,* the Court specifically stated that it was necessary to "take into account the economic dependence of the employees on their employers" and recognize that a worker might pick up implications "that might be more readily dismissed by a more disinterested ear."

The Ninth Circuit in *NLRB v. Lenkurt Electric Co., Inc.,* reformulated the Supreme Court's language with respect to the difference between prediction and threat, in language that was widely cited: "Thus an employer may not impliedly threaten retaliatory consequences within his control, nor may he, in excess of imagination and under the guise of prediction, fabricate hobgoblin consequences outside his control which have no basis in objective fact."[136]

Most recently the Seventh Circuit under the leadership of Judge Posner has taken the lead in redefining the *Gissel* standard. The opinion that came closest to directly repudiating the *Gissel* approach is *NLRB v. Village IX, Inc.* In that case, the employer guaranteed to the employees that if the union was voted in he would be out of business within a year. "The cancer will eat us up and we will fall by the wayside. . . . I only know from my mind, from my pocketbook how I stand on this."[137] Judge Posner found that the *Gissel* standard was satisfied because the employer's vision of the union's economic impact while hazy and imprecise was consistent with respectable economic theory.[138] The opinion ignores the fact that the employer in the *Gissel* case had more of a factual basis for the statements, found by the Supreme Court to violate section 8(a)(1), than did the employer in *Village IX* whose statement the Seventh Circuit held to be permissible.

The circuits vary one from the other and often within a single circuit with respect to the distinction between threats and predictions, and the latitude that the circuits are willing to give employers to discuss the possible harmful effects of unionization. What seems clear, however, is that no circuit applies the *Gissel* approach strictly and that the general movement is towards greater permissiveness.

The Board itself has never adhered strictly to the standard set forth in *Gissel*. In *Birdsall Construction Co.,*[139] for example, the employer told his employees that financial problems would confront the firm if the union succeeded in gaining representation. The employer had deliberately located his plant inland to obtain lower labor costs even though this location necessitated his trucking goods from Rivera Beach, Florida, to Miami and Fort Lauderdale. If required to work under a union contract, he might as well eliminate his trucking costs and relocate on the coast, he told them. This prediction of plant closing was deemed not to be a threat of retaliation, although it clearly would have been under either the language or approach used in *Gissel*. The employer, for example, did not know that the union demands would match those made on the coast. He had no proof that the shipping costs plus union demands would not still leave him in a favorable competitive position. More recent Board decisions show a similar willingness to permit employers considerable latitude to suggest by reference to hypothetical situations that unionization will harm the employees without either specifying the harm or setting out a factual predicate.[140]

In general, both the Board and the courts of appeals are currently applying a standard at odds with their previous approach by permitting statements that harm will flow from unionization without specifying the nature of the harm or its source. There are still, however, decisions holding that ambiguous references to harm or prediction based on conjecture and surmise are unlawful. If past history is any guide, a treatise that focuses its discussion on the current state of the law is likely to be quickly outdated, and counsel who rely on the most recent precedent are destined to be disappointed. What is most important is to recognize that this is an area in which the law has constantly fluctuated and that this state of affairs is almost certain to continue because the cases vary so much in tone and detail while the adjudicators are almost certain to vary in attitude, bias, and assumption.

3. Interrogation

Unless they are counseled to avoid it, employers or their representatives will often question employees either about their support for the union or else about the grievances that gave rise to the organizing effort. Although there are many reasons other than the desire to coerce that might lead to such behavior, traditionally the Board has held that both types of questioning violate the statute—the former as an implied threat, the latter as an implied promise. The courts of appeals have always been uneasy about the Board's categorical treatment of interrogation, but they have generally gone along with the Board's basic approach, which has been that interrogation is unlawful unless certain safeguards are present.[141] These safeguards were set forth by the Board in two major opinions, the most recent of which was *Struksness Construction Company.*[142]

The circumstances under which a poll would be valid under *Struksness* were as follows:

1. The purpose of the poll was to determine the truth of a union's claim of majority status.

2. This purpose was communicated to the employees.

3. Assurances against reprisals were given.

4. The employees were polled by secret ballot.

5. The employer had not engaged in unfair labor practices or otherwise created a coercive atmosphere.

If all these requirements were not met, the Board would hold the employer's actions an unfair labor practice regardless of the employer's motivation and regardless of whether the circumstances otherwise indicated that the employees questioned felt threatened. An employer that simply assured its employees that it would not take reprisals or that told them the purposes of its polling would not meet these standards and its questioning would therefore constitute a violation. Under *Struksness,* the Board would set aside the election even if the employer interrogated only a few employees in a larger unit. The assumption was that the fact of interrogation would quickly become generally known. The Supreme Court referred approvingly to *Struksness* in *Gissel,* and there have been favorable references to *Struksness* in many court opinions.[143] Nevertheless, the courts often insisted upon greater flexibility than the Board was willing to display. The Second and Eighth Circuits both held specifically that interrogation could be noncoercive even if all the conditions set out in *Struksness* were not met.[144] They inquired into such factors as the employer's general response towards unionization, and the nature and circumstances of the interrogation.

In *Rossmore House,* the current Board explicitly adopted a more permissive approach to the interrogation of open union supporters about their support for the union.[145]   In its opinion, the Board cited court of appeals' decisions that had rejected *Struksness* and stated that, henceforth, greater flexibility would be shown.   The *Rossmore* approach has been upheld on appeals.[146]   As a result, the current status of the *Struksness* standards is questionable.   It is clear that they are no longer dispositive, but the Board has not indicated whether they will be looked to as guidelines, and it is similarly unclear how they will be treated by reviewing courts.

With respect to solicitation of grievances, the Board's approach has traditionally been less clear than with respect to interrogation about union membership.   At times the Board has prohibited any discussion of employee job attitudes, and at times it has permitted employers to ask about discontents where the questioning has not been clearly tied to the union.   The current Board takes the latter approach at least, and probably also takes the position that asking about grievances even in a discussion of the union is not coercive *per se*.[147]   It is thus quite possible that the Board and the courts will have switched positions, with the Board being more lenient of interrogation than the courts.

4.   Grants and Promises of Benefits by Employers

From very early in its history, the Board has treated the grant or promise of benefits during the course of a union organizing campaign as a blatant form of interference, equivalent to a threat of reprisal.   It has not distinguished between unconditional promises and grants and those expressly conditioned upon a union defeat.   The Board has never explained the vice that makes an unconditional grant or promise disruptive of employee rights although it has consistently affirmed its mischievous potency.   The Supreme Court in *NLRB v. Exchange Parts Co.* undertook to provide the missing rationale.   It announced that "the danger inherent in well-timed increases in benefits is the suggestion of a fist inside the velvet glove . . . employees are not likely to miss the inference that the source of benefits now conferred is also the source from which future benefits must flow and which may dry up if it is not obliged." [148]

Thus the authoritatively announced rationale of the law is that employees when given or promised benefits will react as though they were threatened.   This implied threat traditionally has been viewed by the Board as sufficiently powerful that employers were forbidden from even announcing the decision to bestow benefits decided upon for reasons unrelated to the campaign sooner than they would have done otherwise in order to convince employees to vote against representation.[149]   Employers have not, however, been prohibited because of the existence of a representation campaign from granting benefits they would otherwise have granted, nor have they been prohibited from making announcements that they would otherwise have made. Indeed, failure to do so would itself violate the Act.

There has been a great deal of litigation before the Board over the years directed to the question of whether an employer varied his business conduct with respect to the grant or promise of benefits in an effort to influence the campaign. Past Boards have placed the burden upon the employer to establish that its conduct was not an effort to influence the campaign.

The current Board, bound by the Supreme Court's holding in *Exchange Parts,* has continued to treat grants or promises as unlawful interference when it has found them to be made in order to influence the campaign. It has, however, lessened the impact of the doctrine outlawing grants and promises by being less apt to find a promise in an ambiguous statement and less likely to find that a promise or grant was made in order to influence the campaign. It has also reversed the longstanding rule prohibiting an employer from announcing benefits sooner than he would otherwise have done in order to influence the campaign.[150]

5. Unlawful Benefits From Unions

The Supreme Court extended its concern about the coercive impact of benefits to unions in *NLRB v. Savair Manufacturing Co.,* in which the Court held that a union's offer to waive initiation fees for all employees who signed cards before an election interfered with employee free choice.[151] The Court reasoned that employees might be tempted to sign a card in order to avoid the initiation fee and then feel compelled to support the union because the fact of their having signed a card would become known. The Court also viewed the practice as improper because it would permit the union to claim support it did not have. The Court assumed that such a misleading claim of support would be helpful to the union and that any votes it thereby acquired would not be an expression of free choice. Finally, the Court concluded that "the failure to sign a recognition slip may well seem ominous to non-unionists who fear that if they do not sign they will face a wrathful regime should the union win." The conclusion seems to be based on an unconvincing and patronizing view of employees who vote in representation elections. Why, for example, would employees who know of the conditional offer assume that other employees who signed cards were not doing so in order to take advantage of the offer? Why would they be persuaded to vote contrary to their own attitudes towards unionization in any case? The fear of a wrathful union regime if it is at all a reason why employees sign cards and existing data suggest it is not, should be the same whether or not the union offered a conditional waiver. Some of the language of *Savair* suggested that even a nonconditional waiver would be improper. Such a conclusion might have a major impact on union campaigns because most unions currently do not require dues or initiation fees until the union wins the election and a contract is signed. The Board, however, held that such general waivers were not covered by *Savair*. The Board's holding was upheld on appeal and it has not been challenged by the current Board.

6. The Laboratory Conditions Doctrine

As mentioned above the Board has long claimed the authority under the "laboratory conditions" doctrine to set aside elections for conduct that does not constitute unfair labor practices. In supporting the propriety of such an approach, the majority of the Board stated in *General Shoe*: "It is the Board's function to provide a laboratory in which an experiment may be conducted, under conditions as nearly ideal as possible, to determine the uninhibited desires of the employees . . . when in the rare extreme case the standards drop too low, laboratory conditions are not present and the experiment must be conducted over again." [152] It is difficult to imagine a more inexact or confusing metaphor. It describes neither how the Board functions nor what the appropriate standard is or should be.

First, the metaphor suggests that the election environment is actively established and controlled by the Board when in fact it is the parties who shape it by their campaigns.

Second, the metaphor suggests a need for pristine purity and shutting out improper influences when the Act contains no warrant for such a standard, but seems rather to have contemplated a rough-and-tumble atmosphere common to labor relations. This counter image is supported by section 8(c), which states that "the expressing of any views, arguments or opinions or the dissemination thereof, whether in written, printed, graphic, or visual form shall not constitute or be evidence of an unfair labor practice under any of the provisions of this Act if such expression contains no threat of reprisal or force or promise of benefit."

Third, the laboratory conditions metaphor is inconsistent with the Board's statement that it will interfere only in "rare cases." By juxtaposing the purity of the laboratory with the assertion that it will interfere only rarely, the Board is simultaneously announcing conflicting approaches: one a commitment to purity—which is inconsistent with much traditional behavior, thus justifying regular intervention—and the other a willingness to accept any but the most egregious conduct. This statement contains the elements of a confusion that has plagued the Board over the years.

Finally, the laboratory image, particularly when reinforced by the use of the term "experiment," suggests an environment in which events can be observed easily and causality definitively determined by the Board, neither of which is so. It also suggests that little is lost and much is gained simply by rerunning the experiment, setting aside an election inconsistent with a pristine idea of free choice.

The Board's authority to invoke the laboratory conditions doctrine which has been claimed by all Boards of whatever political persuasion, has been recognized without exception by the courts of appeals. The courts have accepted rulings under the doctrine as part of the law and have even on occasion denied enforcement to Board decisions on the grounds that the Board had not properly applied one of the rules established under the laboratory conditions doctrine. Despite its bipartisan acceptance to date, the doctrine flourishes under activist Boards and wanes under conservative management-oriented Boards such as the current one. While the current Board has not disclaimed the authority, it has rarely exercised it, and it specifically has announced that it would no longer set aside elections for campaign misrepresentations that had previously been one of the major aspects of the doctrine (see discussion below). It is to be expected that the current Board will be loathe to apply the doctrine because the doctrine rests in significant part upon an assumption, that the current Board rejects, that employee free choice may be easily interfered with by reminders of employer economic power unrelated to direct or implied threats. This is an assumption that apparently is favorable to unions because it limits the boundaries of acceptable employer campaign tactics. It has been regularly challenged by Boards such as the current one, many of whose members believe that the Act previou·ly has been administered with a pro-union bias. The review of the doctrine that follows should be read with its current questionable status in mind. Nevertheless, the doctrine and the decisions that have composed it provide a baseline of non-overruled cases of which counsel must be aware in advising clients; and they express an approach constantly being put forward for acceptance. It is of course quite possible that the Board may return to the laboratory conditions doctrine or decide to acknowledge it more positively as the Board's composition changes.[153]

a. INDIVIDUAL AND SMALL GROUP MEETINGS

In *General Shoe Corp.,*[154] the case that gave rise to the laboratory conditions doctrine, the company's general and personnel manager met with small groups of employees in the managers' offices to urge them to vote against the union. Their statements were moderate in tone but the Board set aside the election because of the coercive impact that it found to inhere in meetings held in the "locus of final authority." In subsequent cases the Board broadly defined the locus of final authority for these purposes, eventually taking the position that any discussion of the union by high company officials away from the employees' work station would interfere with free choice. In *Peoples Drug Stores Inc.,* the Board announced that "[T]he very fact that employees were summoned by management representatives to a place, removed from their work stations . . . imparts to the place selected its character as the "locus of final authority in the plant." [155] The Board has also assumed that home visits by high company officials would be coercive, and in *Peoria Plastics Company* it stated that it would set aside any election in which such visits were made regardless of the actual comments made by the employer.[156] There is a curious contradiction implicit in the combination of *General Shoe* and *Peoria Plastics* in that one assumes that employees are particularly vulnerable away from familiar surroundings, and the other announces that they are especially vulnerable in their own homes.

The entire set of opinions dealing with this question represents the Board at its worst, attempting to generalize about employee state of mind without either empirical information or the use of labor relations studies, on the basis of its supposed expertise. Behind all of these assumptions, the Board may be indulging a more general assumption, namely that any discussion by high company officials with rank-and-file employees is likely to be coercive regardless of where it takes place. The Board may well have felt inhibited from articulating this presumption because of its obvious conflict with the employer's first amendment rights. The Board has not always taken a categorical approach to this question. Employer-oriented Boards such as the current one have traditionally dealt with the issue of meetings off the shop floor between high company officials and employees on a case-by-case basis, and when the content of the employer's speech has not been threatening, they have generally found some reason for saying that the circumstances of the meeting were not coercive.

b.   The Need for an Atmosphere Conducive to Sober Thought

(1) The 24–Hour Doctrine

The Board held in *Peerless Plywood Co.* that any speech to a large group of employees on company premises within 24 hours of a scheduled election would be grounds for setting aside the election. Such speeches were described as "unwholesome and unsettling," and inconsistent with "that sober and thoughtful choice which a free election is designed to reflect." [157] The *Peerless Plywood* doctrine has not been applied to meetings at which attendance is voluntary although this is often a fact that is difficult to determine after the meeting. The Board generally assumes that a meeting was not voluntary unless the employer stated specifically that employees were not obliged to attend.

(2) Appeals to Prejudice

In *Sewell Mfg. Co.*, the Board stated that it would set aside elections in which one or the other party utilized "appeals or arguments . . . to inflame the racial feelings of voters in the election." The Board justified its decision on the grounds that the Board "has the responsibility . . . to ensure that the voters . . . cast their ballots . . . in an atmosphere conducive to the sober and informed exercise of the franchise." The Board drew a distinction for these purposes between statements "temperate in tone" and those "not intended or calculated to encourage the reasoning faculty." [158] The initial effect of the decision was to set aside elections in which employers used appeals to bigotry to defeat unionization. However, with the passage of the 1964 Civil Rights Act shortly after the *Sewell* decision, such appeals became less frequent, in part because work forces became more integrated and in part because such statements supplied evidence of discrimination. Much of the litigation following *Sewell* has concerned union efforts to appeal to employees on the basis of racial or ethnic solidarity, a technique particularly likely to be employed when the work force is largely black or made up of members of an ethnic minority. The Board has generally permitted unions to raise racial issues in this fashion, drawing a distinction between appeals to bigotry and appeals to racial pride.[159] The courts of appeals have been less accepting than the Board of such union tactics, reasoning that if racial appeals are improper when employed by an employer, they also should be improper when used by a union.[160] The entire line of cases demonstrates the inevitable difficulty of the Board's assuming the role of censor. Why should employees be denied a union because racial feelings were expressed during the course of the campaign? Moreover, it is unlikely that a campaign based on prejudice would help many employers because it leaves open to the union the response that it is the employer's goal to keep the employees separated and the union joins them together. Yet the Board is understandably reluctant to certify the result of a vote achieved by racist appeals.

The Board has never used its reasoning in *Sewell* as a general warrant for setting elections aside when irrational or emotional appeals have been made. It has on occasion, however, set aside an election where the employer has linked the trade union movement to communism.[161] However, the precedent with respect to this is old, sporadic, and unreliable.

(3) Third Party Behavior

Because only employers and labor organizations can commit unfair labor practices, the Board has frequently been faced with determining whether to attribute to the employer the conduct of a third party that urges the employees to vote against unionization. Boards favorable to unions have been prone to find an agency relationship based on either economic ties or knowledge by the employer of the third party's anti-union campaign. Such Boards have also required a clear disavowal by the employer in order to negate the assumption of responsibility under such circumstances.[162] Even where the Board does not hold the third party to be the agent of the employer or the union, it might set the election aside if it concludes that the conduct of the third party made the exercise of free choice impossible. Where the third party is found to be acting independently, all Boards have required far more serious statements or actions than when the conduct is attributable to the employer or the union.[163] For example, direct threats of job loss by a third party are not likely to be sufficient for setting aside an election unless they are made repeatedly or under circumstances in which the employees are likely to think they come from the employer.[164]

c. MISREPRESENTATION

The Board's treatment of campaign misrepresentation is the area of the laboratory conditions doctrine in which the rival approaches have been most clearly articulated and in which the Board has switched back and forth most obviously, as first one approach and then the other has commanded a majority. From very early in its history the Board has debated whether it should attempt to ensure the accuracy of campaign statements made by the parties. At first the Board took the position that its role was not to police the campaign in this fashion. However, the Board began to insist that an effort to be accurate be made and as it did so it came to adopt a strict requirement that campaign propaganda be accurate. This approach led to conflict with reviewing courts, which either took a more lenient view than the Board or else insisted that the Board apply its standards with scrupulous impartiality. On occasion the courts overturned elections that the Board had sustained.[165] Faced with judicial resistance and internal dispute, in 1962 the Board attempted to modify and codify its rules with regard to misrepresentations. In *Hollywood Ceramics Co.,*[166] the Board articulated the circumstances under which it would set aside an election on the basis of campaign misrepresentations:

> "We believe that an election should be set aside only where there has been a misrepresentation or similar campaign trickery, which involves a substantial departure from the truth at a time which prevents the other party or parties from making an effective reply, so that the misrepresentation whether deliberate or not

may reasonably be expected to have a significant impact on the election."

The Board went on to state that even where a misrepresentation was substantial, the Board still might refuse to set the election aside if the Board concluded that it was not likely that the misrepresentation affected the outcome of the campaign because of a factor such as independent knowledge by the employees. Despite the appearance of precision involved in having articulated rules that set the standards by which misrepresentations would be measured, the *Hollywood Ceramics* doctrine did not end the confusion over the applicable standards. The most glaring weakness was that the Board was almost never in a position to know whether the misrepresentation affected the outcome. Forced to speculate, the Board inevitably would have its pro- or anti-union biases reflected in its decisions. The courts that accepted the articulation of the doctrine continued to set aside elections based on their conclusion that the Board had applied the doctrine in a biased or inaccurate fashion. In particular, the doctrine was likely to be interpreted to require that union statements concerning gains achieved elsewhere be precisely accurate. The Fifth Circuit's statement that "assertion[s] concerning wages . . . are . . . the selfsame subjects concerning which men organize and elect their representatives to bargain" [167] was widely cited with approval by other courts of appeals even though it stated a view of campaign effectiveness neither obvious nor supported by any empirical information. The study of representation campaigns that was conducted by Professors Getman, Goldberg, and Herman concluded that such campaign misrepresentations were unlikely to have been noted by the employees and that even those who had some idea of what the union had claimed were not influenced by it.[168] In 1976 the Board in *Shopping Kart, Inc.* stated that except in very unusual circumstances it would no longer set aside elections based on misrepresentations.[169] The majority in *Shopping Kart* relied heavily on the Getman, Goldberg, and Herman study, and the dissent attacked it vigorously, suggesting that it was inadequate, procedurally flawed, and misleading. The decision in *Shopping Kart* was widely criticized. Some saw it as granting a license to the parties to lie and others saw it as leading to a new approach as suggested in the study, whereby the Board would be less protective of free choice. *Shopping Kart's* life was brief. In slightly more than a year, after a member of the majority resigned, *Shopping Kart* was overruled in *General Knit of California, Inc.,*[170] in which the Board returned to *Hollywood Ceramics.* The prevailing opinion in *General Knit* was very critical of the *Shopping Kart* majority for relying upon the study:

> "While we welcome research from the behavioral sciences, 1 study of only 31 elections in 1 area of the country—although it may provide food for thought—is simply not sufficient to disprove the assumptions upon which the Board has regulated

election conduct, especially since, in our experience, statements made by either side can significantly affect voter preference."

The majority did not specify how it had learned about the impact of campaign statements. *General Knit* was itself short-lived. Soon after the Reagan Board was established, *General Knit* was overturned in *Midland National Insurance,*[171] in which the Board returned to *Shopping Kart* without further discussion of its empirical basis. The Board simply announced that in its view the *Hollywood Ceramics* doctrine rested upon a misleading and patronizing view of employees as incapable of properly discounting campaign propaganda. And it concluded: "We will no longer probe into the truth or falsity of the parties' campaign statements and . . . we will not set elections aside on the basis of misleading campaign statements."

The courts of appeals have been willing to go along with either approach although they have been critical of the Board's inability to maintain a single policy for any length of time. Nonetheless, efforts by the parties to have one or another of the Board's opinions rejected as arbitrary have failed. The Board has continued to apply *Midland National Insurance* and the courts have accepted it. Indeed, as the minority had feared the Board has extended the view of employee competence contained in *Midland National Insurance* to other cases, and it has cited *Midland National Insurance* to support limiting its campaign oversight in other areas.

C. The Board's Basic Approach to Campaign Regulation

Almost every policy decision that the Board or the courts have had to make in regulating campaign content has involved a choice between efforts to protect its vision of reasoned choice and permitting the transmission of information that might make informed choice more likely. In protecting against threats, for example, the Board has on occasion limited the employer's ability to transmit legitimate information about the possibility of harm resulting from the economic consequences of unionization. By limiting the employer's promise of benefits and ability to solicit grievances, the Board prevents employees from finding out how far the employer would be willing to go to satisfy their concerns without unionization. Similarly, by rigidly preventing interrogation, the Board foreclosed the possibility of a dialogue based on the interests and needs of particular employees. In the *Peerless Plywood* 24–hour rule preventing employers from holding mass meetings within 24 hours of the election, the Board obviously prevents undecided employees from hearing the position of the parties just prior to the election on the theory that such statements would create too much pressure upon them.

Board rules concerning inflammatory appeals, home visiting, and discussions in the locus of authority all prevent employees from hearing aspects of the employer's position. The rules concerning union access place a similarly low priority upon the ability of employees to learn the union's position, although in such cases the competing interest is the employer's property interest rather than protection against coercion. Generally, in enforcing the Act, the Board and the courts have assumed a rough equality between employers and unions as the result of which the Board and the courts have limited the ability of the unions to be heard.

During the past decade there has been a significant academic debate about the extent to which unlawful employer campaign tactics affect voting behavior. The Getman, Goldberg, and Herman study, concluded that, in general, unfair labor practices by employers do not change votes and that the costs of campaign regulation outweigh its benefits. The conclusions and methodology of the study have been challenged on a variety of bases. The most significant criticisms have involved a reexamination of its findings applying highly sophisticated mathematical analysis to the study's data. Using a technique called "probit," Professor Dickens concluded that direct threats of reprisal made by the employer directly to the employee are effective in influencing votes.[172] Dickens' conclusions have been accepted and relied upon by other commentators, particularly Professor Weiler.[173] These conclusions have themselves been questioned and the Getman and Herman study's findings supported by additional data collected and analyzed by Professor Cooper.[174]

One who carefully examines the available data and commentary cannot easily determine the extent to which it is possible to coerce employees into voting against unionization by threats. Not only are the data subject to varying interpretations but the issue tends to activate the preexisting attitudes of many labor relations experts. Some are swayed by their distaste and condemnation of employer efforts to win elections by frightening employees who are exercising their statutory rights. Others are swayed by a general condemnation of regulation, their contempt for the Board's efforts, or both. The sharpness of the academic debate obscures the fact that there is considerable agreement among sophisticated commentators. Almost all agree that much behavior traditionally found by the Board to unduly influence employees does not do so. There is no scholarly support for the laboratory conditions approach and none for the conclusion that employees are threatened either by ambiguous statements or by grants or promises of benefits. Almost all commentators agree that there is and has been too much law in this area.

While it is generally true that union supporters favor greater limits on employer campaign tactics and management supporters favor opening up the campaign, it is not at all clear that unions benefit from campaign regulation. Except for bargaining orders for serious unfair labor practices, the remedies employed by the Board are generally inadequate, if one assumes that employees were dissuaded from supporting the union by the original unfair labor practices. More significantly, in other areas, the law has been shaped in ways unfavorable to unions by the assumption that unions are often beneficiary of legal help in achieving incumbency. This is most noticeable in the law regulating and limiting use of economic pressure by unions and their supporters (discussed in Chapter 4). Thus, from the unions' point of view, the tradeoff may not be worth it.

Part V. Insulating Protected Activity From Economic Consequences

A. Retaliation Against Union Members

1. The Importance of Motive

One of the abuses that the Act was meant to stop was the discharging and blacklisting of union supporters. Not only does such conduct automatically reduce the number of union backers, but also it serves as a warning to the remainder of the work force. Section 8(a) (3) of the Act was directed against such employer conduct. It makes it an unfair labor practice for an employer "by discrimination in regard to hire or tenure of employment or any term or condition of employment to encourage or discourage membership in any labor organization." [175] The policy behind this section was said to be to insulate the employees' decision as to union membership and activity from their job rights.[176] Employers rarely take reprisals openly today. Various forms of anti-union discrimination remain, however, and many employers and their advisors still believe that discharging union supporters is a good way to squelch organizational efforts or to ensure that the representation election will not end up in a union victory. While there is disagreement as to how widespread this practice is, no one doubts that it goes on.[177] A great deal of Board litigation still concerns the question of whether employer action that purports to apply discipline for some offense was in fact retaliation. In such cases, the issue before the Board turns on the employer's motivation. Was the employee discharged because of some perceived infraction or was the action taken in response to the employee's union activity? [178] The Board's ability to answer this question properly is important to its effectiveness in enforcing the Act. All sides agree that union supporters should not be protected against normal discipline and that employers should not be able to retaliate and intimidate through discriminatory exercise of their right to hire and fire. This agreement in principle rarely solves particular cases. It is common for there to be some evidence of infraction and some evidence that the employer was punishing the employee for his union activity. In seeking to evaluate the employer's motive, the Board looks to such things as the importance of the rule violated, whether other employees were punished similarly in the past for the same violation of company rules, whether the employer was aware of such infraction and did it seem willing to tolerate such behavior before it found out about the employee's union activity. How determined did the employer seem to be to defeat the union and did it manifest a willingness to violate the law for this purpose? In close cases, and most section 8(a)(3) cases today are of this type, the outcome is likely to turn on the Board's judgment as to the strength of the competing interests. Is it more important to uphold rights under the Act or to uphold the right of an employer to discharge workers found to be unsatisfactory? Traditionally the Board has been more concerned with protecting statutory rights than with the employer's prerogative, although the strength of this commitment has varied depending upon the makeup of the Board. In general the courts of appeals have been concerned that the Board might go too far and force employers to employ clearly unsatisfactory workers whom they would have discharged anyway, in order to vindicate statutory rights. As a result, Board findings of violation are frequently overturned. The issue of the standard of review to be employed in such cases has been before the Supreme Court on a number of occasions. In each case the Court has sided with the Board and reminded the courts of appeals not to review findings of discriminatory discharge with special concern, but to uphold the decision of the Board whenever substantial evidence is present in the record to support it.[179] Despite the Supreme Court's reaffirmation of the Board's primacy, the courts of appeals have continued to review Board decisions in this area with particular closeness. This is not an issue as to which the Supreme Court is capable of overseeing the courts of appeals. The factual content of the cases varies too much and the meaning of substantial evidence is too ambiguous for the courts of appeals to feel bound to affirm Board decisions that conclude that a discharge was not warranted. They need only to acknowledge the deference due to the Board and then they are essentially free to oversee as carefully or as loosely as their own attitudes dictate.[180]

2. Mixed Motive Cases

Employers frequently discharge marginal or unsatisfactory employees whom they know or consider to be union supporters. The Board has consistently held that the action is not made lawful by the presence of legitimate grounds nor by the fact that the discipline may have been partly motivated by misconduct. As long as the employee's union activity or membership played a role in the decision, discipline violates the Act. The Board's approach has not fared well in the courts of appeals, several of which not only overturned Board decisions regularly in mixed motive cases, but also rejected the Board's standard. Historically, the circuits have been in conflict with each other over the proper treatment of mixed motive cases. The Eighth Circuit tended to uphold the Board in mixed motive cases. But the First and Fourth Circuits employed what they called the "dominant motive" standard, requiring that the Board's General Counsel establish not only that an improper motive for discharge existed, but also that any lawful motive that also existed was rejected and the discharge predicated on the improper grounds.[181] The D.C. and Ninth Circuits on various occasions employed both the "in part" and the "dominant motive" standards, and the Fifth Circuit used a "50–50" type test, requiring the Board to establish that the force of the unlawful motive for discharge was "reasonably equal" to that of the lawful one.[182]

The Board, in order to improve its record on appeal, adopted a new standard for judging mixed motive cases, in *A Division of Wright Line.*[183] The new approach was derived from the Supreme Court's decision in *Mt. Healthy City School District v. Doyle,*[184] in which the Court established a standard for discharges motivated in part by Constitutionally protected activity. Essentially the *Wright Line* test is the Board's old mixed motive standard dressed up in the language of burden of proof. It works as follows. The General Counsel has the burden of proof to establish that protected activity under the Act was a "motivating factor" in the employer's decision. Once this has been achieved, the burden shifts to the employer to demonstrate that the employee would have been discharged in any case. It should be noted that if the employer meets his burden of proof he establishes that this is not really a mixed motive case but a case of discharge for some other reason. The *Wright Line* test was approved by the Supreme Court in *NLRB v. Transportation Management Corp.,*[185] but it is still too early to tell how much affect this will have on the courts of appeals. Regardless of the legal formula, the courts will still be able to deny enforcement in cases in which they believe that an employee merited discharge. In such cases, they may conclude that the General Counsel had not met his burden of proof or that the employee would have been discharged in any case. This question is complicated by the fact that the current Board is less likely to find 8(a)(3) violations than its predecessors and thus would have done better on appeal even without the Supreme Court's affirmation of the *Wright Line* test.

3. The Use of Lawful Employer Speech in Determining Motive

A significant issue that sometimes arises is whether the Board may consider a lawful anti-union speech in determining the motive for a discharge. Although section 8(c) provides that expressions of opinion are not to be considered evidence of unfair labor practice, the Board considers such statements as part of the background of the case. In *Wright Line,* one element of the General Counsel's prima facie case was employer anti-union animus. Evidence of animus included employer speech. Whether or not the employer's statements were violative of 8(a)(1) was not ruled on.

Prior to the *Wright Line* decision, the Board regularly looked to lawful employer speech in evaluating the employer's motive in discharging a union supporter. This approach is inconsistent with the language of section 8(c), which provides: "The expressing of any views . . . shall not . . . be evidence of an unfair labor practice under any of the provisions of this Act." From time to time Board section 8(a)(3) findings have been set aside by the courts of appeals because of inconsistency with section 8(c).[186] In general, the Board has prevailed by arguing that the employer speech was not used as evidence of an unfair labor practice but was merely looked to as background. Although this argument merely masks the inconsistency with section 8(c) through characterizing the use of the speech as background rather than evidence, the Board's approach is easily understandable. Employer speeches and statements are a measure of its opposition to unionism and therefore an indication of its willingness to take action. The point becomes clearer if one imagines two employers, one that conducted no campaign, and the other that has conducted a vigorous one. It is natural to assume that the employer that has not conducted a campaign is less likely to have violated section 8(a)(3) than the one that has. Suppose an employer characterizes union supporters as "incompetents and free riders." Such a statement would be an expression of his right of free speech, but it also would cast some possible light on his motive if a group of union supporters were discharged shortly thereafter. The problem is that 8(c) announces a standard at odds with common sense.

4. Retaliation vs. Economic Motivation

In several cases the Board and the courts have disagreed about the application of section 8(a)(3) where the employer has terminated a portion of his business immediately after the employees voted for union representation, claiming that he did so for economic reasons and not because of anti-union animus. The Board has held that such terminations constitute reprisals against the employees because they voted for the union and hence are violations of the Act. The courts have generally been more accepting of the employer's claim that his action was a legitimate business decision. Typical is *NLRB v. Lassing*,[187] in which the Court of Appeals for the Sixth Circuit stated: "The advent of the Union was a new economic factor which necessarily had to be evaluated by the respondent as part of the overall picture pertaining to costs of operation. . . . Fundamentally the change was made because of reasonably anticipated increased costs, regardless of whether this increased cost was caused by the advent of the Union or by some other factor entering into the picture." The courts' approach is inconsistent with the policy of section 8(a)(3) because it permits employees to be put out of work as a direct consequence of exercising their statutory right to choose union representation. The court's distinction between union animus and business considerations is in fact a distinction that does not describe a difference because most employer resistance to unionization is ultimately based on the assumption that the advent of a union will be economically costly to the employer. The approach of the courts, however, is not merely based on a misinterpretation of the statute but rather is reflective of a general effort by the courts of appeals to interpret the National Labor Relations Act in such a way as not to interfere with economic efficiency and to leave intact the employer's ability to make purely economically motivated decisions.

B. Plant Closings

1. The Darlington Standards

There is one situation in which open retaliation against employees for engaging in protected activity does not violate the Act even where there is no economic justification and that is when the employer closes down his business entirely. The Supreme Court so held in *Textile Workers v. Darlington Manufacturing Company.*[188] That case arose when the employees of Darlington Manufacturing Company voted for union representation. In response, the stockholders voted to dissolve the corporation. Darlington discontinued operations and sold the plant. The Board found that Darlington thereby violated section 8(a)(3). The Board also found that Darlington "occupied a single employer's status with another respondent, Deering Milliken and its affiliated corporations." A separate order was directed to Deering Milliken making it liable for back pay to the same extent as Darlington and ordering Deering Milliken to offer the discharged employees positions at other locations to the extent that they were available. The Fifth Circuit sitting *en banc* denied enforcement. The Supreme Court remanded. It stated that if Darlington should be regarded as a single employer, it was privileged to go out of business even if "the liquidation (was) motivated by vindictiveness towards the union. . . ." On the other hand, the Court held that the closing down of the Darlington plant might constitute an unfair labor practice because of its impact on other parts of the Deering Milliken enterprise. It announced a three-step test to determine whether a plant closing violated section 8(a)(3): if the persons exercising control over a plant that is being closed for anti-union reason, (1) have an interest in another business, whether or not affiliated with or engaged in the same line of commercial activity as the closed plant of sufficient substantiality to give promise of their reaping of benefit from the discouragement of unionization in that business, (2) act to close their plant with the purpose of producing such a result, and (3) occupy a relationship to the other business which makes it realistically foreseeable that its employees will fear that such business will also be closed down if they persist in organizational activities, an unfair labor practice would have been made out. The case was returned to the Board to make findings on the issue of purpose and effect and then to the court of appeals to consider whether Darlington was a single employer under the newly established test and to review the Board's findings.

It is difficult to understand why the Court adopted such a test in cases of partial closing. It apparently requires the Board to examine the employer's motives to determine whether he was acting solely out of a refusal to continue in business with a union representing his employees in which case the closing would be legitimate, or whether he was also motivated by a desire to chill unionism in other plants, in which case it would be improper. The clear implication is that section 8(a)(3) of the Act is concerned with those who observe the employer's conduct, but not with those directly affected, a premise not usually accepted in section 8(a)(3) cases. The test seems at odds with the Act and unworkable. Whatever the employer's motive, there is likely to be some coercive effect on employees in other parts of the business, but the Court requires more than the mere likelihood of coercion, it also requires that coercion be intended.

It was not clear after the *Darlington* case how broadly the Supreme Court's language was to be interpreted. If the Board is willing to conclude that news of anti-union closing would spread rapidly and to assume that employers intend the natural probable consequences of their action, then almost all cases of partial closings constitute violation under *Darlington.* However, the Board did not at first adopt such an approach.

Immediately after *Darlington,* the Board applied the strict-intent focused standard to both intra-plant and inter-plant operations. In *Motor Repair, Inc.,*[189] the Board held an anti-union closing of one out of six of an employer's garages was not a violation because it could not be shown that discouraging unionization elsewhere was the employer's purpose. In *Morrison Cafeterias,*[190] the Board and court allowed one of many cafeterias to be closed for anti-union reasons simply because there was no contemporaneous organization elsewhere, despite a showing that the employer told other employees of the closing so as to discourage unionization. Subsequent case law involved a slow but steady transition to a less rigorous, more traditional "mixed motive" discrimination standard.

In *Plastics Transport, Inc.,*[191] the Board found a violation on the basis of an anti-union closing of the intra-state part of an integrated intra- and inter-state trucking business. The Board paid lip service to the *Darlington* proof requirements, but the Board found 8(a)(3) and (5) violations without extensive inquiry into either the purpose or effect of the action.

In *George Lithograph Co.*,[192] the employer closed down his mailing operations for anti-union reasons. The Board short circuited the *Darlington* analysis in holding that the employer's action would necessarily chill other employees located on the same premises and under the same management in exercising their section 7 rights: "We conclude that Respondent's closure of its mailing division with the openly avowed purpose of blocking the mailers' organization activities in the mailing department could not but operate as a deterrent to the exercise of Section 7 rights by the remaining employees . . . (W)e may reasonably infer that the chilling effect of the conduct at issue on other employees was entirely foreseeable—and hence intended—as a consequence of that conduct."

The Board does not apply the *Darlington* chilling requirement to cases of anti-union subcontracting.[193] If the Board determines that an employer subcontracted to avoid dealing with a union, it will find his conduct to be an unfair labor practice and it will usually order the employer to reopen the portion of his business discontinued.

2. Runaway Shops

The *Darlington* opinion does not apply to cases in which the employer trans͟ ͟rs its business to a new location in order to get away from a union. If such behavior can be established, it constitutes a violation of section 8(a)(3).[194] There have been very few such cases, however, because of the reluctance by the courts in particular to characterize major decisions which have some economic justification as retaliation in violation of section 8(a)(3). It is noteworthy that the past decades have witnessed a major shift of economic activity from the unionized Northeast to the South and Southwest. Despite the likelihood that much of the plant movement has been motivated in part by the desire of management to operate without unions, there has been almost no application of section 8(a)(3) to the process.

C. The Concepts of Discrimination and Protected Activity

1. The Statutory Scheme

Most cases of employer retaliation are analyzed under section 8(a) (3) of the statute, which makes it an unfair labor practice for an employer "by discrimination in regard to hire or tenure of employment or any term or condition of employment to encourage or discourage membership in any labor organization." Although the term "discrimination" suggests that the Act is violated only when union members and nonmembers are treated differently, any form of retaliation is normally held to violate this section even if the employer is operating under a policy that does not distinguish between union and non-union members. For example, in *Republic Aviation Corp.*,[195] the Supreme Court affirmed the Board's conclusion that section 8(3) was violated when the employer disciplined employees for violating a no-solicitation rule even though the employer argued that there was no discrimination because the rule was applied to all cases, not only those involving union solicitation. The Court rejected this argument, which has also been inferentially rejected in cases involving retaliatory lockouts, stating: "It seems clear, however, that if a rule against solicitation is invalid . . . a discharge because of violation of that rule discriminates within the meaning of Section 8(a)(3) in that it discourages membership in a labor organization." The meaning of this passage is not obvious because it seems to elide the different requirements of the section, but the necessary implication is that so long as the employer treats employees who engaged in protected activity under section 7 differently from the way he would treat them had they not engaged in such activity, his action constitutes discrimination for purposes of the Act.

The same result could have been reached by applying section 8(a)(1) because the employer's conduct restrained and coerced the employees in the exercise of their section 7 rights to self-organization and to form, join, or assist labor organizations. Whenever section 8(a)(3) is violated there is also a violation of section 8(a)(1), which has been held to encompass the other subsections of section 8(a).[196] Section 8(a)(1) applies independently to issues such as employer speech and interrogation in which action has not been taken against employees, and to cases in which the employees are engaged in activity protected by section 7 but where there is no labor organization involved. For either section 8(a)(3) or (1) to apply, the activity against which the employer is retaliating must be protected by section 7. This is not obvious from the language of the statute because it is possible for employer discipline of union supporters to discourage membership in a labor organization even if the action to which the employer is responding falls outside the scope of section 7. Indeed, studies suggest that discharges of union adherents are likely to be perceived the same way regardless of the reason for which the employer acts. Nevertheless, the Act has always been interpreted to permit employers to retaliate against unprotected activity regardless of its impact on protected activity.[197] The policy has been less clear with respect to retaliation against supervisors whose actions could not be protected because they are not employees under the Act. The Board from time to time has held that discharging supervisors because of their open pro-union activity interfered with the rights of the other employees under the Act. This approach has not been well received by the courts and current Board.[198]

2. The Reach of Section 7—The Concept of Concertedness

Read literally, section 7 applies to almost any action jointly undertaken by a group of employees. The literal language is misleading, however, because a single employee may engage in concerted activity and group action may fall outside the Act's protection.

The clearest case of concerted action by an individual would be the effort by one employee to organize a union. Even if no one else joins in, the action is concerted because its purpose transcends the individual, and such conduct clearly comes within the statutory purpose of legitimating union activity. In general, action by an individual seeking to make common cause with other employees is held protected. Other activity by individual employees is less clear. What of the individual who protests against his working conditions, making no claim to speak for any one else? Any such protest has the potential to help employees generally. The Board traditionally has sought to differentiate between individual griping and action undertaken on behalf of the group, but the distinction has been hard to draw in practice.[199] A similar issue arises when an individual seeks to enforce some statutory protection outside the NLRA for herself, but in such a way that her actions might benefit others. In *Alleluia Cushion Co.,*[200] the Board held that despite his failure to involve others, an employee had engaged in activity protected by section 7 when he complained about safety conditions and then wrote to the state OSHA when his protests were not responded to by the employer. The Board reasoned that "[s]afe working conditions are of great and continuing concern for all within the workforce." It concluded that any effort to enforce occupational safety laws would be within section 7's protection unless the other employees specifically disavowed the effort. The Board continued to apply this approach despite difficulty with the courts of appeals for some time. The courts generally, but not unanimously, took the position that action by an individual could be concerted only if it was on behalf of other employees or intended to enlist the support of other employees.[201]

In a 1984 decision, *Meyers Industries, Inc.,* the Board overruled *Alleluia* and adopted the definition of concerted activity taken by the majority of the courts of appeals. The facts in *Meyers* made out a strong case for protection. The employee had been discharged for refusing to drive an unsafe truck and trailer concerning which he had filed a report with the Tennessee Public Service Commission, and for making earlier complaints about the safety of the vehicle. Another employee had complained in the dischargee's presence about the same truck. The Board found that there was no concerted activity because the record did not show that the two employees "in any way joined forces."[202]

The Board's order dismissing the complaint was overturned by the Court of Appeals for the D.C. Circuit, which remanded the case to the Board "for reconsideration of the scope of concerted activities" under section 7.[203] The opinion by Judge Edwards, a former labor practitioner and professor, took the position that the Board improperly concluded that the language of the statute and its own prior precedent required the result which it had reached. Judge Edwards pointed out that the Supreme Court had recently approved a decision by the Board holding that an individual was engaged in protected concerted activity when, acting in accordance with his rights under a labor contract, he refused to drive a truck that he had reason to believe was unsafe.[204] Judge Bork dissented on the grounds that if the employee's actions could be deemed concerted, "almost any actions might be so characterized and the qualifying word that Congress wrote in the statute would effectively be removed from it." More recently, the Board has begun to adopt a more expansive view of section 7 than it did in *Meyers Industry*.[205] Thus, the meaning of concertedness remains doubtful when a single employee acts to secure group rights not under a collective agreement without being motivated by the desire to make a common cause with fellow employees.

3. Non–Statutory Limits on the Reach of Section 7

Protected status may be lost for a variety of reasons not spelled out in the statute. Breaches of contract and violent, unlawful, or indefensible conduct are unprotected. One area in which pro- and anti-union Boards have regularly differed concerns their willingness to characterize minor misconduct as protected. The Board has generally held that misconduct that occurred as part of a general course of protected activity did not make the employee liable to discharge. The stated standard by which the Board has judged such cases is whether the misconduct is so severe as to "render the employee unfit for further service." [206] The standard has been applied in a variety of situations. The Board has held protected such activity as taking company cards that the employees objected to signing, or interrupting a company meeting to talk on behalf of the union, and it often has permitted name-calling and violent language. The current Board has been far less willing than most of its predecessors to hold such activity to be protected. It has regularly characterized minor misconduct as "insubordination" or as violence and hence it has held it to be unprotected.[207]

Part VI. The Board's Remedial Power to Protect Freedom of Choice

A. Remedies Under the Act in General

1. Limits on the Board's Remedial Power

The Board's remedial power under the NLRA is broad but not unlimited. The Supreme Court has held that the Board can only impose a remedy to correct the harm done by the offending party's violation. It does not have the authority to punish a union or employer in order to deter future misconduct.[208] Thus, for example, the Board may not fine, decline to exercise its jurisdiction over or seek to blacklist from government contracts, parties that regularly violate the Act. In the area of union organizing, the Board's remedial authority is exercised most frequently to set aside elections and to order the undoing of benefits or reprisals improperly granted or imposed. In cases of discriminatory discharge, the employee is ordered reinstated without loss of benefits or seniority and with back pay (minus interim earnings) plus interest, computed from the time of the discharge until such time as the employee is offered full reinstatement.[209] Any employer or union unfair labor practice occurring after the filing of an election petition is grounds for setting aside the election. The Board also will order the offending party to post notices stating that it will no longer violate employee rights under the NLRA. When either employer or union conduct violates the Board's laboratory condition standards, the Board will order the election set aside but will not order the posting of notices.[210] Thus in practical effect, with the exception of bargaining orders, the consequences of ordinary unfair labor practices and the consequences of conduct interfering with laboratory conditions are virtually the same.

2. The Board's Injunctive Power

Under section 10(j) of the Act, whenever the Board decides to issue a complaint it has the power to petition for an injunction in the Federal District Court in which the unfair labor practice allegedly took place or in which the respondent resides or is doing business. For example, such authority might be exercised to order discharged employees immediately reinstated without going through the elaborate and time consuming procedures normally required. The regular use of this power might have a substantial effect on the election process and outcome by demonstrating to employees the Act's potency and the Board's determination to protect them. However, the Board does not exercise this power. Despite criticism from labor and from academics, the Board over the years has resolutely refused to intervene while the election process is going on. Perhaps the Board is fearful of making an error that will affect the result of an election; perhaps it assumes that its regular unfair labor practice procedures and remedies are adequate. If the latter, the Board probably misconceives the potency of its remedies. Studies suggest, for example, that only a small percentage of discriminatees in fact return to work, and those who do, usually do so long after the election has been held.[211]

B. Bargaining Orders

1. To Remedy Election Violations

a. WHERE THE UNION HAD OBTAINED A CARD MAJORITY

The Board's preference for an election discussed above, is not absolute. Where unfair labor practices by an employer are thought to preclude the holding of an election that will truly reflect employee choice, the Board, under authority conferred by the Supreme Court in *NLRB v. Gissel Packing Co.,*[212] may order the employer to bargain with a union not chosen by a majority of his employees in a representation election. The Court stated that such orders were appropriate where the Board found that the employer had engaged in (a) "outrageous" and "pervasive" unfair labor practices that could not be remedied, or (b) "less pervasive practices which nonetheless still have the tendency to undermine majority strength and impede the election process." [213] In the latter situation, the Board can issue a bargaining order only when it finds that "the possibility of erasing the effects of past practices and of ensuring a fair election (or a fair rerun) by the use of traditional remedies, though present, is slight and that employee sentiment once expressed through cards would, on balance, be better protected by a bargaining order." [214] It should be noted that this formulation requires a finding that majority sentiment had once been expressed through the union's obtaining a card majority, and then an additional finding that the employer's unfair labor practices precluded the holding of a fair election at any point in the immediate future. The Court's language makes clear that the Board is required to decide not only whether the employer conduct in question had a coercive effect on the election campaign just completed, but also the likelihood of its continued impact or recurrence in a subsequent rerun election.

In the cases immediately following *Gissel,* the Board did not address itself seriously to the questions posed by *Gissel.* It simply announced its conclusions, using the language of the Supreme Court as a formula to be invoked when the Board chose to issue a bargaining order. This approach to the mandate of *Gissel,* however, proved unacceptable to the courts of appeals. In several cases they denied enforcement of bargaining orders or remanded to the Board for further findings of fact,[215] and in some cases the courts, expressing displeasure with the Board's performance, made their own determinations of the impact of employer unfair labor practices and their likely effect on the outcome of a subsequent election.[216] The Board's failure to make detailed findings concerning impact is not surprising given that it lacks the ability to do so. It refuses to hear evidence after the fact, rejecting testimony as to a past state of mind as unreliable and subjective, relying instead on its own views as to the reasonable tendencies of such acts to coerce. It is for this reason the Board has not taken subjective evidence concerning the impact of unfair labor practices; despite all the years in which the Board has been regulating unfair labor practices, there is no data base from which it may draw the conclusions that the Supreme Court asked for in *Gissel*. The courts of appeals have not questioned the ability of the Board to make the findings called for by the Supreme Court. To the contrary, the theme running through their opinions is the failure of the Board to make such findings with the degree of care that *Gissel* seemingly commanded.[217] The accusation that the Board when asked to make specific findings has responded instead with "a litany, reciting conclusions by rote without factual explication"[218] has been quoted repeatedly by the courts of appeals.

It is not surprising that when the Board orders an employer to bargain with the union not elected by his employees, the courts have been reluctant to grant enforcement merely on the basis of the Board's assumed expertise.[219] Such cases involve different and more significant interests than does the enforcement of an order directing an employer merely to cease and desist from interfering with his employees' rights or even to bargain with a union chosen by the employees. In neither of the latter situations does the Board's order appear to run counter to the exercise of employee free choice. In the *Gissel* situation, however, it does. Since the Board's powers are supposed to be remedial rather than punitive, the sacrifice of employee free choice arguably inherent in a bargaining order could not be justified solely to punish the employer for engaging in improper conduct.[220] The use of a bargaining order in a *Gissel* situation can be justified only if there is good reason to believe that the employees' failure to choose union representation in a NLRB election was the result of employer coercion and did not, in fact, represent the true desires of the employees.[221]

Another factor that helps to explain the close scrutiny given the Board's post-*Gissel* decisions is the requirement that the Board's order be responsive to the facts of the particular case.[222] As noted above, the criterion in most unfair labor practice proceedings is whether the conduct in question has a general tendency to interfere with the employees' exercise of their statutory rights. The impact in the particular case is not critical. So long as the issue is cast in general terms, for a court to disagree with the Board would require it to challenge the basic assumption of Board expertise in judging impact. When, however, the issue is cast in narrower terms—that is, whether this employer's conduct has tended to prevent employees from expressing their choice on the question of unionization—the courts can disagree with the Board's conclusion without challenging the basic assumption of Board expertise.[223]

While the courts have often referred to the requirement that the Board make specific findings as to both the immediate and continuing impact of the employer's conduct and the likelihood of its recurrence, the courts have not specified how the Board is to make these difficult determinations. Thus, the basic problem confronting the Board is that of devising acceptable rules about the impact and probability of recurrence of unfair labor practices. The task is a formidable one. As former Chairman Miller has stated: "No decisional task has more perplexed the Board, or confounded the courts. . . ." [224]

Even if the Board were capable of making a realistic assessment of the extent to which unfair labor practices affected votes in the original election, how could it determine whether the impact would continue? To make this determination it would be necessary for the Board to consider factors such as the effect of the passage of time both in dissipating the coercive impact upon the affected employees and in changing the composition of the work force between the two elections. Yet the Board has been reluctant to consider these factors, arguing that to do so would be to permit the employer to profit by the delays inherent in the procedure for remedying unfair labor practices.[225] Some courts have accepted this argument; others have not.[226] But in no case have the courts really required an elaborate inquiry into the question of potential changes. They have enforced bargaining orders without such inquiry, and when the courts have themselves made impact determinations, they have largely ignored this factor, focusing instead on the nature of the unfair labor practice and the conditions that existed at the time.

Board opinions make clear that the nature of the unfair labor practices involved is significant in impact determinations. The Board has rarely elaborated, however, on the weight assigned to this factor or on the basis upon which various types of illegal behavior are differentiated. Instead, the Board frequently employs epithets such as "flagrant" or "egregious" in place of explanation.[227] Some principles can, however, be deduced from the Board's opinions. First, an unfair labor practice that is viewed as "deliberate" or "calculated" is more likely to lead to a bargaining order than one that is not.[228] Second, much turns on the significance of the interest being endangered. If the employer's statements or acts can be characterized as threatening either a significant economic interest, such as retention of jobs, or a fundamental legal right, it is more likely to lead to a bargaining order.[229] Third, acts of reprisal, particularly discharges, are considered to be extremely effective in swaying votes and very difficult to remedy.[230] Not only is there a great deal of language to this effect in Board opinions, but also the coincidence of section 8(a)(3) violations and bargaining orders is notable. Fourth, promises to correct the grievance that led to union organization are also considered particularly effective.[231] Finally, and most significantly, the vast majority of bargaining order cases involve a series of unfair labor practices rather than a single act of illegality.[232]

Although the bargaining order was described in *Gissel* as an unusual remedy and is so referred to in subsequent Board and court cases, the Board's willingness to grant such relief became so routine during the late 1970s that a study of post-*Gissel* decisions between 1979–1980 found that the issuance of a bargaining order had become customary whenever the union had achieved a majority of cards.[233]

As already suggested, the courts of appeals were far less willing than the Board to accept the routine issuance of bargaining orders remedies. The courts of appeals are, however, obviously in no better position than the Board to draw conclusions about the lasting impact of unfair labor practices. Court opinions, like those of the Board, reveal no easy basis for prediction. If the unfair labor practice seem to the court as particularly reprehensible, a bargaining order will be sustained; otherwise it will not. Thus the law is and is almost certain to remain confused and contradictory with respect to bargaining orders. Despite the unsatisfactory nature of the law, it serves a significantly useful deterrent effect. The possibility of a bargaining order serves to severely inhibit the commission of flagrant unfair labor practices by employers during an election campaign.

b. The Issuance of a Bargaining Order Where the Union Had Not Obtained a Card Majority

For years the Board had been unwilling to issue bargaining orders in the absence of a showing that the union had at one time achieved a card majority,[234] a reluctance that seemed inconsistent with the Board's previous willingness to issue such orders if a majority existed at one time.

The Board did eventually decide, however, that a bargaining order might be appropriate in such a case. In *United Dairy Farmers Cooperative Assn.*[235] and then in *Conair Corporation*,[236] the Board issued bargaining orders to remedy conduct deemed outrageous and pervasive despite the fact that at no point could the union demonstrate that it had majority support. The first nonmajority bargaining order was suggested by the Third Circuit in its remand of a Board decision in which only two Board members had firmly committed themselves to a view that the Board had authority to issue nonmajority bargaining orders.[237] The Third Circuit held that the Board did have such authority and remanded for Board consideration of whether the conduct in the context of that case met the requirements for issuance of a bargaining order. On remand the order was issued, but one of three votes for issuance was based on the Board's obligation to abide by the Third Circuit's holding.

In *Conair,* a three-member panel of the Board issued a "nonmajority" bargaining order, which was not enforced by the D.C. Circuit.[238] The thrust of the D.C. Circuit's reasoning was that granting a nonmajority bargaining order is impermissibly at odds with the concept of freedom of choice. Free choice is a statutory priority that should not be abrogated in the absence of a clear legislative directive; a nonmajority bargaining order replaces that free choice with an agency's guess at what is desirable for employees. The Board specifically adopted this reasoning in *Gourmet Food, Inc.,*[239] in which it overruled its earlier decision in *Conair Corp.* over a strong dissent by Member Zimmerman, who argued that the bargaining order was the best way to vindicate the employee's right of self organization. Otherwise, he argued, in such cases employees could be denied their basic statutory rights by outrageous employer conduct. The discussion in *Gourmet Food* was the one in which the conflicting priorities of the current Board and that of its predecessor were most clearly set out. Because both sides have cogent arguments, it is likely that this will continue to be an area of disagreement within the Board.

2. Bargaining Orders to Remedy Runaway Shops

In those rare cases in which the Board found that plant relocation violated the Act, it was faced with a difficult question of remedy. It was clear that the Board could order the employer to award the employees back pay from the time of the closing until they were offered jobs at the new location. It was also clear that the Board could order the employer to offer jobs at the new location, but since most of the employees were unwilling to avail themselves of the reinstatement remedy, it was of little effect. The most potent remedy available in such situations is to impose a back-pay obligation until such time as the employees have obtained comparable employment elsewhere. The Board has on occasion attempted as a remedy to order the employer to bargain with the union at the new location. However, this approach was rejected in the *Garwin* case in an opinion by then circuit Judge Burger who took the position that the Board could not order the employer to bargain with the union absent an election.[240] He argued that such a remedy would violate the free choice of the employees at the new location. It is highly likely that should the current Board find a section 8(a)(3) violation in a plant relocation, it would follow Justice Burger's opinion. To do otherwise would be inconsistent with the current Board's stress on the right to refrain from concerted activity. Moreover, imposing a bargaining remedy on a work force strange to the union would probably prove ineffective.

C. Union Access to Company Premises as a Remedy for Employer Unfair Labor Practices

On rare occasions the Board has sought to remedy employer unfair labor practices by granting unions greater access to the employees than they would otherwise be entitled to. This greater access has included rights to reply to captive audience speeches and the right of union organizers to enter company premises in order to meet with employees.[241] Such a remedy has much to commend it. It seems far more potent than the Board's normal remedy of setting aside the election, without involving the potential destruction of free choice involved in a bargaining order. The only significant interest adversely affected is the employer's property interest. Whatever weight this interest is normally given by the Board and the courts, it seems legitimate to weigh it less heavily where the employer has shown a willingness to interfere with employee rights under the Act. The data suggest that such a remedy would have an impact because familiarity with the union's campaign is positively associated with voting for the union.[242] Because imposed bargaining orders may not lead to contracts, it may well be that an access remedy would actually be more valuable as a way of overcoming the effect of employer unfair labor practices. Given the obvious advantages of access remedies, it is difficult to understand why the Board has been so reluctant to use them, and it is difficult to understand why the courts have struggled so much before enforcing those few which the Board has issued.

FOOTNOTES

1. NLRA Sections 7 and 8.

2. 29 U.S.C. § 152(3) (1976).

3. 322 U.S. 111 (1944).

4. 93 Cong.Rec. 6441–6442, 1947; H.R.Rep. No. 245, 80th Cong., 1st Sess. 18 (1947) See *NLRB v. United Insurance Co.*, 390 U.S. 254, 67 L.R.R.M. 2649 (1968).

5. 390 U.S. 254 (1968).

6. Restatement of Agency Section 220 (1939), Restatement of Agency 2nd Section 220 (1958) *NLRB v. United Insurance Co.*, 390 U.S. 254, 256–58, 67 L.R.R.M. 2649 (1968).

7. See, e.g., *A. Paladini, Inc.*, 168 N.L.R.B. 952, 67 L.R.R.M. 1022 (1967) (fishing boat captains not independent contractors where little opportunity to make decisions which affect profit and loss, and where employer exercised extensive control over operation of boats.) In this case the Board cautioned against mechanical application of the "right of control" test, stating that the test must be applied in light of the economic realities of a particular situation.

For Board's reference to the "right of control" test see, e.g., *Pulitzer Publishing Co.*, 146 N.L.R.B. 302 (1964); *National Freight, Inc.*, 146 N.L.R.B. 144, 55 L.R.R.M. 1259 (1964); and *Beacon Journal Publishing*, 188 N.L.R.B. 218, 220, 76 L.R.R.M. 1228 (1971).

8. See *A. Paladini, Inc.*, supra.

Other factors looked at are the relationship of the worker's work to the business of the employer, including the centrality of the employee's efforts to the principal business of the employer, the length of the worker's employment and the right of the employer to unilaterally set terms and conditions of employment. See also *Air Transit Inc.*, 248 N.L.R.B. 1302, 104 L.R.R.M. 1076 (1980), *enforcement denied, Air Transit Inc. v. NLRB*, 679 F.2d 1095, 110 L.R.R.M. 2630 (4th Cir.1982). The Fourth Circuit's disagreement was not framed in terms of disagreement with these three factors but rather involved a different analysis of the facts concerning control over the manner and means of performing the work. An excellent example of the Board's emphasis on the relationship of the worker's work to the business is contained in *Michigan Eye Bank*, 265 N.L.R.B. 179, 112 L.R.R.M. 1181 (1982). See also *Mitchell Bros. Truck Lines*, 249 N.L.R.B. 476, 104 L.R.R.M. 1134 (1980). However the centrality factor has been rejected as irrelevant by some courts. See *NLRB v. Associated Diamond Cabs, Inc.*, 702 F.2d 912, 113 L.R.R.M. 2001, 2007 (11th

Cir.1983), and *Seafarers Local 777 v. NLRB,* 603 F.2d 862 (D.C.Cir.1978), 101 L.R.R.M. 2628, 2634 (D.C.Cir.1979) (denying rehearing of 603 F.2d 862).

The Board in *Air Transit* at note 25 made clear that permanence in a relationship is indicative of employee status. The Board clarified this point in response to the Court's comment in *Seafarers Local 777,* supra, 101 L.R.R.M. 2628 at 2635. In contrast, use of the "length of employment" factor seems to have been rejected in *Yellow Taxi of Minneapolis v. NLRB,* 721 F.2d 366, 114 L.R.R.M. 3060 (D.C.Cir.1983), denying enforcement of a Board order. In the Board's *Air Transit* decision, the right unilaterally to impose terms and conditions resulted in a finding of employee status. See also *Standard Oil Co. of Ohio,* 241 N.L.R.B. 1248, 101 L.R.R.M. 1108 (1979). The evident absence of unilateral imposition of terms demonstrated independent contractor status in *Tarheel Coals Inc.,* 253 N.L.R.B. 563, 566, 106 L.R.R.M. 1042 (1980). (No adverse consequences experienced by truckers who refused to sign agreement incorporating changes.) Some courts have rejected the distinction, characterizing the unilateral imposition as demonstrating superior bargaining power rather than an employer-employee relationship.

NLRB v. Associated Diamond Cabs, 702 F.2d 912, 113 L.R.R.M. 2001 at 2007 (11th Cir.1983), *Seafarers Local 777 v. NLRB,* 603 F.2d 862, note 22, 99 L.R.R.M. 2903 (D.C.Cir. 1978) opinion accompanying denial of rehearing 603 F.2d 891, 101 L.R.R.M. 2628 (D.C.Cir. 1979).

9. Feerick, Baer & Arfa, *NLRB Representation Elections,* see 2.26, 1979–80.

10. See e.g., *Columbus Green Cals, Inc.,* 237 N.L.R.B. 176 (1978); *Tri–State Transp. Corp.,* 245 N.L.R.B. 1030 (1979).

11. A brief categorization of the Circuit's approaches is found in O'Connor, Fourth Circuit Review, Section 2(3) of the NLRA and the "Right to Control Test," 35 Washington & Lee L.Rev. 768, 770 n. 778–780 notes 81 and 82 and related text (1982).

12. Two other groups excluded from the Act's coverage are agricultural laborers and government employees. The exclusion of agricultural laborers was largely political and the exclusion of public employees rested on the notion, unquestioned at the time of the Act's passage, that unionization of public employees was potentially too disruptive of necessary governmental services to be encouraged or even permitted.

See Getman & Blackburn, Labor Relations Law, Practice and Policy, (1983) (p. 540 at 509).

13. H.R.Rep. No. 245 at 13 and 14, 80th Cong., 1st Sess. 4, reprinted in I NLRB, Legislative History of the Labor Management Relations Act, 1947 at 304–305.

14. Id., H.R.Rep. 16 and 17, Legislative History at 307–308.

15. See *Beasley v. Food Fair of North Carolina Inc.,* 416 U.S. 653 (1974), citing *NLRB v. Bell Aerospace Co.,* 416 U.S. 267 (1974); *Florida Power & Light Co. v. Electrical Workers (BEW), Local 641,* 417 U.S. 790 (1974), citing Senate Report No. 105 at 5, I Leg. Hist. 411 and House Report 245 at 14–17, I Leg.Hist. 305–308. See also *United Food and Commercial Workers Union v. NLRB (Parker Robb Chevrolet),* 711 F.2d 383, 113 L.R.R.M. 3175 in which the court, affirming a Board decision permitting the discriminatory supervisors stressed the importance of and re-emphasizes the concept of loyalty between its supervisors and management generally. The notion of separate zones for management and labor recurs with some frequency under the National Labor Relations Act.

16. Section 2(11) of the NLRA, 29 U.S.C. § 152(11) (1976).

17. The general rule is that supervisory status is determined by the existence of the authority, not the exercise of it. *New Jersey Famous Amos Chocolate Chip Corp.,* 236 N.L. R.B. 1093 (1978). See also *Southern Indiana Gas and Electric Co. v. NLRB,* 657 F.2d 878 (7th Cir.1981) and *James H. Matthews & Co. v. NLRB,* 354 F.2d 432, 434, 61 L.R.R.M. 2070 (8th Cir.1965). However, in contrast to the above cases is a line of precedent holding that if an employee who ordinarily is nonsupervisory occasionally or sporadically substitutes for a supervisor he does not thereby become a supervisor. See *Quik Pik Food Stores Inc.,* 252 N.L.R.B. 506, 105 L.R.R.M. 1523 (1980) (assistant manager not a supervisor), and *Complete Auto Transit Inc.,* 214 N.L.R.B. 425, 87 L.R.R.M. 1352 (1974).

18. *Ford Motor Company,* 66 N.L.R.B. 1317, 1322 (1946).

19. *North Arkansas Electric Cooperative Inc.*, 185 N.L.R.B. 550, 75 L.R.R.M. 1068 (1920) (managerial employees protected by Act unless that role involved employee relations matters), *enforcement denied*, 446 F.2d 602 (1972).

20. 416 U.S. 267, 275 (1974).

21. 444 U.S. 672 (1980) at 689–90.

22. *Duquesne University of the Holy Ghost*, 261 N.L.R.B. 587 (1982); *New York Medical College*, 263 N.L.R.B. 903 (1982).

23. *Boston University*, 281 N.L.R.B. 115 (1986) and cases cited *Loretto Heights College*, 264 N.L.R.B. 1107 (1982), *reversed*, 742 F.2d 1245 (10th Cir.1984).

24. See, e.g., *Thiel College*, 261 N.L.R.B. 84 (1982); *Duquesne University of the Holy Ghost*, 261 N.L.R.B. 85 (1982).

25. *New York Medical College*, 263 N.L.R.B. 903 (1982).

26. See E.G. Angel, *Professionals and Unionization*, 66 Minn.L.Rev. 383 (1982); See, e.g., Finken, The Yeshiva Decision a Somewhat Different View, 7 Journal of College and University Law 321 (1980–81).

27. 274 N.L.R.B. 168 (1985).

28. Note that these groups are routinely excluded from almost all units. The first for tactical reasons the latter two for statutory reasons. Section 9(b)(1) provides that professional employees are not to be included with nonprofessionals unless the professionals specifically so choose in a self-determination election. Section 9(b)(3) of the National Labor Relations Act forbids the board from including guards in the same bargaining unit as other employees and from certifying as the representative of a guard unit a union which has nonguard members or is affiliated with a nonguard union.

29. Petitions will be processed even if the union previously has not demanded recognition, as long as the employer declines to recognize the union at the representation hearing. *"M" Sys., Inc.*, 115 N.L.R.B. 1316, 38 L.R.R.M. 1055 (1956).

30. *Linden Lumber Div., Summer & Co. v. NLRB*, 419 U.S. 301, 87 L.R.R.M. 3236 (1974).

31. This commenced in 1961 with the amendment of the statute to permit such delegation.

32. Section 9(b) of the NLRA provides:

"The Board shall decide in each case whether, in order to assure to employees the fullest freedom in exercising the rights guaranteed by this Act, the unit appropriate for the purposes of collective bargaining shall be the employer unit, craft unit, plant unit, or subdivision thereof . . ."

33. *Morand Bros. Beverage Co.*, 91 N.L.R.B. 409, 418, 26 L.R.R.M. 1501 (1950), "*enforced*", 190 F.2d 576, 28 L.R.R.M. 2364 (7th Cir.1951) (emphasis in original); accord, *Saint Francis Hospital*, 265 N.L.R.B. 120, 109 L.R.R.M. 1153, 1158 (1976).

34. 3 NLRB Annual Report 174 (1938).

35. *Continental Baking Co.*, 99 N.L.R.B. 777, 782 (1952), 15 N.L.R.B.Ann.Rep. 39 (1950).

36. *Kalamazoo Paper Box Corp.*, 136 N.L.R.B. 134, 49 L.R.R.M. 1715 (1962). This case is representative—the factors are dealt with singly and in various combinations through thousands of cases.

37. See Abadeely, *The NLRB and the Appropriate Bargaining Unit*, 1971; Weber, Stability and Change in the *Structure of Collective Bargaining*, Prentice Hall, Inc., Englewood Cliffs, N.J. at 13 in Ullman, ed., Challenges to Collective Bargaining, 1967.

38. Feerick, et al., supra, sections 8.1 to 8.9.

39. Bargaining history is given substantial weight largely because continuing an established unit structure is viewed as promoting stability, one of the purposes of the NLRA, *Buffalo Broadcasting Co., Inc.*, 242 N.L.R.B. 1105 (1979), *Marion Power Shovel Company, Inc.*, 230 N.L.R.B. 576 (1977). There are, however, many categories of cases when the "substantial weight" is outweighed, e.g., where a group has had an ongoing objection to its inclusion in a unit, *Rainbow Lithographing Co.*, 69 N.L.R.B. 1383, 18 L.R.R.M. 1317 (1946); where the established unit is contrary to Board policy, *Manufacturing*

Woodworkers Association of Greater New York, Inc., 194 N.L.R.B. 1122 (1972) (union members only); lack of community interest, *A.L. Mechling Barge Lines Inc.,* 192 N.L.R.B. 1118, 1120 (1971), and *Crown Zellerbach Corp.,* 246 N.L.R.B. 203, 102 L.R.R.M. 1435 (1979).

40. *New England Power Company (Western Division),* 120 N.L.R.B. 666 (1958). See, e.g., *Consolidated Papers,* 220 N.L.R.B. 1280, 1283 (1957) (used as one of the factors).

41. *A. Harris & Co.,* 116 N.L.R.B. 1628 (1957).

42. *Temco Aircraft Corp.,* 121 N.L.R.B. 1085, 1088, 42 L.R.R.M. 1538 (1958), *Penn Color Inc.,* 249 N.L.R.B. 1117, 104 L.R.R.M. 1229 (1980). See also *Hegins Corporation,* 255 N.L.R.B. 1236 (1981), cf. *Pickering & Co.,* 248 N.L.R.B. 772 (1980) (presumption rebutted).

43. *Haag Drug Co.,* 169 N.L.R.B. 877, 67 L.R.R.M. 1289 (1968). *Big Y Foods, Inc.* 238 N.L.R.B. 860, 9 L.R.R.M. 1366 (1978). Cf. *Petrie Stores,* 266 N.L.R.B. 13, 112 L.R.R.M. 1233 (1983) (presumption rebutted), *ITT Continental Baking Co.,* 231 N.L.R.B. 326, 96 L.R. R.M. 102 (1977), *White Castle System,* 264 N.L.R.B. 43, 111 L.R.R.M. 1280 (1982).

44. *Metropolitan Life Ins. Co. (Woonsocket, R.I.),* 156 N.L.R.B. 1408, 1414–15, 61 L.R. R.M. 1249 (1966); *Empire Mut. Insurance Co.,* 195 N.L.R.B. 284, 79 L.R.R.M. 1348 (1972), cf. *Farmers Ins. Group,* 187 N.L.R.B. 844, 76 L.R.R.M. 1133 (1971) (finding regional unit rather than district office unit).

45. 269 N.L.R.B. 553 (1984). See generally Barford, *The New Dotson Majority Bargaining Units and Organizing Rights, A Return to Balance,* LIX Fla.B.J. 77 (1985).

46. *St. Francis Hospital,* 271 N.L.R.B. 948 (1984). *St. Lukes Memorial Hospital,* 274 N.L.R.B. 202 (1985).

47. *Samaritan Health Servs. Inc.,* 238 N.L.R.B. 629, 99 L.R.R.M. 1551 (1978). There are several versions of self-determination elections, the prototype arising in *Globe Machine and Stamping Co.* Under the *Globe* case, as is often true, the smaller group was a craft unit and the broader group was an industrial unit. In such cases, the craft group chooses between the craft union, the industrial union, or no representation. The larger group has two ballot choices: the industrial union, or no representation. If in the craft group a majority opts for the craft union, then the group constitutes a separate unit represented by the craft union. If the craft union does not get a majority, then the votes of the first group are pooled with the votes of the second group to determine if the industrial union gained a majority of all the votes cast. For this determination all the votes cast by both groups are counted; but those cast for the craft union are accorded no weight. If neither the industrial union nor the 'no representation' have a majority in the broader unit, then a run off election is held.

48. Employee preferences have also been polled in self-determination elections when only one union is seeking status as representative but where either a large all inclusive unit or smaller "subgroup" unit is appropriate. *Underwood Machinery Co.,* 59 N.L.R.B. 42, 15 L.R.R.M. 109 (1944); *NLRB v. Underwood Machinery Co.,* 179 F.2d 118 (1st Cir. 1949). See, e.g., *Union Carbide Corporation Chemical Division,* 156 N.L.R.B. 634 (1966).

49. *Rostone Corporation,* 196 N.L.R.B. 467 (1972).

50. Jurisdiction will also extend to non-profit organizations which operate like an industrial facility. See, *Arkansas Lighthouse for the Blind,* 289 N.L.R.B. 110 (1987). Jurisdiction will not extend to church operated schools due to risk of infringement of first amendment rights. *Trustees of St. Joseph's College,* 123 L.R.R.M. 1281 (1986). However, child care workers at a Catholic residential school *are* entitled to join a union, the NLRB recently found, despite the Supreme Court's 1979 decision in *NLRB v. Catholic Bishops of Chicago,* 440 U.S. 490 (1979). In *Hanna Boys Center,* 284 NLRB No. 121 (1987), the Board found that "the . . . first amendment issues surrounding the assertion of jurisdiction over teachers noted by the Court in *Catholic Bishop* are not involved" here even though the child care workers took the boys to chapel, oversaw their homework (including religious studies) and saw that their prayers were said.

51. Section 9(c)(1) provides for Board conduct of a hearing "if it has reasonable cause to believe that a question of representation 'affecting commerce' exists" (emphasis added); Section 10(a) provides The Board empowered . . . to prevent any person from engaging in any unfair labor practice . . . affecting commerce; Section 2(7) provides that the term "affecting commerce" means "in commerce, or burdening commerce or the free flow of commerce or having led or tending to lead to a labor dispute burdening or obstructing commerce." Section 2(b) further defines commerce.

52. Provided that the Board shall not decline to assert jurisdiction over any labor dispute over which it would assert jurisdiction under the standards prevailing upon August 1, 1959; 29 U.S.C. 164(c).

53. Provisions for an employer's so-called RM petition are contained in Section 9(c)(1)B, 29 U.S.C. § 59(c)(1)(B) (1976) as part of the 1947 Taft–Hartley amendments. Such a petition can only be filed by an employer who has actually been confronted with a demand by a union for either initial or continued recognition.

54. *NLRB v. J.I. Case Co.,* 201 F.2d 597 (9th Cir.1953), *O.D. Jennings & Co.,* 68 N.L.R.B. 516, 518, 18 L.R.R.M. 1133 (1946).

55. Feerick, et al., section 6.311. See *NLRB v. Martins Ferry Hospital Ass'n,* 649 F.2d 445, 107 L.R.R.M. 2569 (6th Cir.1981).

56. Section 9(c)(3), 29 U.S.C. § 159(c)9(3) (1976). A valid election is a final one which has been conclusive. Where election objections have been upheld and the election set aside there is no "one year" bar, nor a bar where there is a runoff election. *Nappa New York Warehouse Inc.,* 76 N.L.R.B. 840, 21 L.R.R.M. 1251 (1948). See also *Foreman & Clark Inc.,* 105 N.L.R.B. 333, 335 (1953).

57. The Blocking Charge Rule is set forth in the NLRB Field Manual § 11.730. However it is discretionary and not statutorily required. See *American Metal Prods. Co.,* 139 N.L.R.B. 601, 51 L.R.R.M. 1338 (1962). The courts have recognized the rule as within the Board's authority but on occasion they have objected to the Board's unthinking application of it. See, e.g., *Templeton v. Dixie Color Printing Co.,* 444 F.2d 1064 (5th Cir. 1971).

The courts have been more tolerant of the Board's use of discretion to prevent abuse of the blocking charge policy, where employees are being deprived of representation rights for undue periods, *Columbia Pictures Corporation,* 81 N.L.R.B. 1313, 23 L.R.R.M. 1504, (1949), where it is perceived that the filings are calculated to induce delay, see *Columbia,* supra, and *West Gate Sun Harbor Co.,* 93 N.L.R.B. 830, 27 L.R.R.M. 1474 (1951) or where under Section 9(c)(3) of the Act strikers will lose their voting rights after twelve months of an economic strike, *American Metal Prods. Co.,* supra.

58. See *Louis–Allis Co. v. NLRB,* 463 F.2d 512, 516, 80 L.R.R.M. 2864 (7th Cir.1972). The "request to proceed" is described in the NLRB Field Manual 11730.4. *General Cable Corp.,* 139 N.L.R.B. 1123, 51 L.R.R.M. 1444, 1450 (1962).

59. *Joy Silk Mills,* 85 N.L.R.B. 1263 (1949), enforced, 185 F.2d 732 (D.C.Cir.1950).

60. 419 U.S. 301 (1974).

61. 395 U.S. 575 (1969).

62. Only 4% of card signers questioned after the election said that they did not support the union at the time they signed the card; 82% said they did. Getman, Goldberg, Herman, Union Representation Elections Law and Reality (1976).

63. *Brooks v. NLRB,* 348 U.S. 96 (1954). The Board also bars an election for a reasonable period after informal recognition, which may be less than one year.

64. The employer and a certified union will both be barred from filing any form of petition by their own contract even if it is for a term longer than three years. *Montgomery Ward & Co.,* 137 N.L.R.B. 346, 50 L.R.R.M. 1137 (1962).

65. *Leonard Meats Co.,* 136 N.L.R.B. 1000, 49 L.R.R.M. 1901 (1962). The open period in the health care industry is ordinarily 120 to 90 days before termination, *Trinity Lutheran Hospital,* 218 N.L.R.B. 199, 89 L.R.R.M. 1238 (1975).

66. *Deluxe Metal Furniture,* 121 N.L.R.B. 995, 42 L.R.R.M. 1470 (1958). For the contract to act as a bar, certain conditions must be met. It must be in writing. It must cover base wages and working conditions, and it must not contain an illegal union security agreement or certain other illegal clauses. A contract will not necessarily operate as a bar when major changes in the structure of the company or of the current work force take place after it is negotiated, or if the contracting union becomes defunct. [However, the doctrine operates to discourage a local union from disaffiliating with the International which is a party to the agreement. The International will, under the doctrine, continue as bargaining representative unless it or its local affiliate becomes defunct or there is a schism at the highest levels of the International Union.]

67. *Crampton Co., Inc.,* 260 N.L.R.B. 69 (1982).

68. Detailed rules are set forth in *Deluxe Metal Furniture Co.,* 121 N.L.R.B. 995, 42 L.R.R.M. 1470 (1958).

69. *Mallinkrodt Chemical Works, Uranium Division,* 162 N.L.R.B. 387, 64 L.R.R.M. 1101 (1966).

70. They are as follows: (1) whether or not the proposed unit consists either of a distinct and homogenous group of skilled journeymen craftsmen performing the functions of their craft on a non-repetitive basis or of employees constituting a functionally distinct department working in trades or occupations for which a tradition of separate representations exist; (2) The history of collective bargaining of the employees sought and at the plant involved . . . with emphasis on whether the existing patterns of bargaining are productive of stability in labor relations and whether such stability will be unduly disrupted by the destruction of the existing patterns; (3) The extent to which the employees in the proposed unit have established and maintained their separate identity . . .; (4) The history and pattern of collective bargaining in the industry; (5) The degree of integration of the employer's production processes including the extent to which the normal operation of the production processes is dependent upon the performance of the assigned function of the employees in the proposed unit; (6) The qualifications of the union seeking to "carve out a separate unit including that union's experience in representing employees like those involved in the severance action."

71. *Mallinkrodt,* at 397.

72. See *Radio Corporation of America,* 173 N.L.R.B. 440, 448 (1968).

73. *Boaz Carpet Yarns,* 280 N.L.R.B. 4 (1985).

74. 252 N.L.R.B. 159 (1980).

75. *National Car Rental,* 237 N.L.R.B. 23, 99 L.R.R.M. 1027 (1978).

76. See, e.g., *New York Printing Pressmen v. NLRB,* 538 F.2d 496 (2d Cir.1976); *Western Distributing Co. v. NLRB,* 608 F.2d 397, 102 L.R.R.M. 2510 (10th Cir.1979).

77. — U.S. —, 107 S.Ct. 2225 (1987).

78. Id., at 2233.

79. — U.S. —, 107 S.Ct. 2225 (1987) at 2233–2234.

80. 417 U.S. 249 (1974).

81. Phelps Dodge Corp. v. NLRB, 313 U.S. 177 (1941).

82. Section 10(f), 29 U.S.C. 160(f) (1976).

83. *American Federation of Labor v. NLRB,* 308 U.S. 401 (1940). An employer who seeks to contest the unit determination, however, has a statutory method for doing so after an election won by the union. (Presumably, if the union loses, the employer's concern has been obviated.) He simply refuses to bargain with the union. The Board which has certified the union will find an unfair labor practice, and order the employer to bargain, which determination is a final order is subject to review. The record of the representation proceeding will be part of the unfair labor practice record. Indeed that record and the fact of the employer's refusal to bargain are likely to constitute the entire transcript, since the parties are not permitted to relitigate the representation issue in the unfair labor practice proceeding. Section 9d, 29 U.S.C. 159(d). See, e.g., *Trinity Memorial Hospital of Cudahy, Inc.,* 242 N.L.R.B. 441, 443, 101 L.R.R.M. 1190 (1979), applying principle that "It is well settled that in the absence of newly discovered or previously unavailable evidence or special circumstances, a respondent in a proceeding alleging a violation of Section 8(a)(5) is not entitled to relitigate issues which were or could have been litigated in a prior representation proceeding." See Rules and Regulations of the Board Section 102.67(f) and Section 102.69(c). If the Court concludes that the Board abused its discretion in the unit determination, it will deny enforcement of the Board's bargaining order.

84. Id., at 409, footnote z; See *NLRB v. International/California Medical Group Health Plan, Inc.,* 678 F.2d 806, 110 L.R.R.M. 2745 (9th Cir.1982).

85. Theoretically where a union feels that employees have been improperly included in a unit which it has been certified to represent, it could refuse to bargain for those employees, prompting an unfair labor practice charge in which it could then, through court appeal, dispute the unit determination. The avenue is described in *Bullard Co. v. NLRB,* 253 F.Supp. 391, 61 L.R.R.M. 2670, 2673 (D.C.1966). The uncertainty of an approach dependent on another party filing an unfair labor practice charge is emphasized by the court in *NLRB v. Interstate Dress Carriers, Inc.,* 610 F.2d 99 (3d Cir.1979).

After an election a union might picket in contravention of Section 8(b)(7)(B)'s prohibition of picketing within twelve months of a valid election. This would provide a route to challenge Board representation decisions through the union's defense to an unfair labor practice charge, i.e., by asserting the lack of validity of the election. *United Federation of College Teach., Local 1460 v. Miller,* 479 F.2d 1074 (2d Cir.1973). But see *NLRB v. Interstate Dress Carriers,* supra at 108–9, in which the Court questions the wisdom of such a route and refuses to treat the possibility of that approach as an available statutory means for seeking post-election judicial review.

86. 358 U.S. 184, 188 (1958). The Board admittedly had not followed the requirement of Section 9(b)(1) of the NLRA when it included a small number of professionals in a nonprofessional unit without a separate vote by the professionals.

87. 372 U.S. 10, 52 L.R.R.M. 2425 (1963).

88. There is also dictum, which is probably unreliable to the effect that judicial review may be exercised where significant constitutional rights are involved. *Fay v. Douds,* 172 F.2d 720 at 723, 23 L.R.R.M. 2356 (2d Cir.1949). This dictum has had a mixed reception and has been rejected or treated with skepticism by many circuits. See, e.g., *NLRB v. Interstate Dress Carriers, Inc.,* 610 F.2d 99, 107–109 (3d Cir.1979); *National Maritime Union v. NLRB,* 375 F.Supp. 421, 86 L.R.R.M. 2510 (E.D.Pa.1974), *cert. denied,* 421 U.S. 963, 89 L.R.R.M. 2248 (1975).

89. 376 U.S. 473, 481 (1964). The Court also noted that the issue therein was one of fact in contrast to the issue of statutory construction in *Leedom v. Kyne.* The limits of this narrow exception have not been established clearly or consistently by the lower courts. Summary analysis of cases involving *Leedom v. Kyne* appears in Morris, The Developing Labor Law, 2nd edition 1983 Volume II at p. 1717–18, an analysis which reflects that there have been only a few successful challenges based on *Leedom v. Kyne.*

90. NLRB Rules and Regulations.

91. *NLRB v. Gissel Packing Co.,* 395 U.S. 575 (1969).

92. *NLRB v. Drivers, Local 639,* 362 U.S. 274 (1960).

93. This economic power is discussed generally in Getman & Goldberg, NLRB Regulation of Campaign Tactics: The Behavioral Assumptions on which the Board Regulates, 27 Stan.L.Rev. 1465 (1975).

94. *General Shoe Corp.,* 77 N.L.R.B. 124, 21 L.R.R.M. 1337 (1948). See also discussion in R. Williams, P. Janus & K. Huhn, NLRB Regulation of Election Conduct, 19–23, 93–99 (1974); *Peerless Plywood Co.,* 107 N.L.R.B. 427, 429 (1953).

95. 324 U.S. 793, 798 (1945). The employer's interest was seen as a property right in the Board's opinion in the companion case to *Republic Aviation LeTourneau Company,* 54 N.L.R.B. 1253, at 1259–60, cited by the Court. There are perhaps really two interests, one in discipline and the other in property rights. Property rights are more at issue where the distributors are non-employees. See *NLRB v. Babcock & Wilcox Co.,* 351 U.S. 105, 38 L.R.R.M. 2001 (1956).

96. *TRW, Inc.,* 257 N.L.R.B. 442 (1981).

97. *Our Way, Inc.,* 268 N.L.R.B. 394 (1983). The current Board also declines to attribute significance to casual employer statements, as opposed to official rules. See, *Super–H Discount,* 123 L.R.R.M. 1177 (1986) where the Board held that an employer's orders to employees not to "talk union on the clock was lawful and so transitory as to have no impact on anyone."

98. *Beth Israel Hospital v. NLRB,* 437 U.S. 483, 98 L.R.R.M. 2727 (1978) (approving Board standard that hospitals can prohibit solicitation in immediate patient case areas, but if the prohibition extended beyond that there was a presumption of illegality "absent a showing that disruption of patient care would result.") *NLRB v. Baptist Hosp., Inc.,* 442 U.S. 773, 101 L.R.R.M. 2556 (1979).

99. See, e.g., *Times Publishing Co. v. NLRB,* 605 F.2d 847, 102 L.R.R.M. 2710 (5th Cir.1979), *enforcing* 240 N.L.R.B. 1158 (1979).

100. *Farah Manufacturing,* 187 N.L.R.B. 601, 602, 76 L.R.R.M. 110 (1970), enforced per currium, 450 F.2d 942 (5th Cir.1971).

101. There is much discussion in the cases about what evidence demonstrates discriminatory promulgation. There is some variation in the perception of rules whose timing (e.g., "precipitous promulgation") demonstrates their issuance in response to union activity. Often the timing appears as one factor which coupled with other factors demonstrates a "purpose to impede union organization." *William L. Bonnell Co. v. NLRB,* 405 F.2d 593, 70 L.R.R.M. 2255 (5th Cir.1969). In *NLRB v. Roney Plaza Apartments,* 597 F.2d 1046 (5th Cir.1979), the Court commented that "reasonable restrictions upon solicitation are not *per se* invalid because imposed during an organizational campaign . . . but commented further that "initial promulgation of a no solicitation policy upon the commencement of a union organization campaign is strong evidence of discriminatory intent."

However, in other cases the importance of timing has been minimized. *Serv–Air, Inc. v. NLRB,* 395 F.2d 557 at 560, 67 L.R.R.M. 2337 (10th Cir.1968), *cert. denied,* 393 U.S. 840, 69 L.R.R.M. 2435 (1968) (reversing Board). See also *F.P. Adams Co.,* 166 N.L.R.B. 967, 967–68 (rule instituted following demand for recognition valid where nature of operations indicated rule established to serve production, order and discipline.)

102. See Williams, Janus & Huhn, NLRB Regulation of Election Conduct, pp. 273, et seq. (1974).

103. *NLRB v. Olympic Medical Corp.,* 608 F.2d 762, 102 L.R.R.M. 2904 (9th Cir.1979) (union discussion forbidden by rule, other discussions allowed) *NLRB v. Electro Plastic Fabrics, Inc.,* 381 F.2d 374, 65 L.R.R.M. 3127 (4th Cir.1967) (union solicitation barred but other solicitation (including anti-union) still carried on). *NLRB v. Olympic Medical Corp.,* 608 F.2d 762, 102 L.R.R.M. 2904 (9th Cir.1979) (discussion of union issues forbidden, of other issues allowed); *Road Sprinkler Fitters Local 669 v. NLRB, (John Cuneo, Inc.),* 681 F.2d 11, 110 L.R.R.M. 2845 (D.C.Cir.1982) (discriminatory application of rule against talk about union—applied only to pro-union discussion.)

104. *Woonsocket Health Centre,* 245 N.L.R.B. 652, 657–658 (1980) (crackdown concerning access of off-duty employees), *NLRB v. Roney Plaza Apts.,* 597 F.2d 1046, 1049 (5th Cir.1979) (state's general principle that "A new rule or a tighter enforcement policy will however be invalid if imposed with discriminatory intent (citation omitted)." *Saint Vincents Hospital,* 265 N.L.R.B. 6, 111 L.R.R.M. 1349 (1982) (discriminatory enforcement), *Daniel International Corp.,* 266 N.L.R.B. 194, 113 L.R.R.M. 1098 (1983).

105. See *Serv–Air Inc.,* 175 N.L.R.B. 801 (1969), the Board interpreted a Court order (which concluded that the employer's indulgence of 2–3 solicitations for family of employees and hospitalization were beneficent acts not demonstrating discrimination) as simply showing *quantum* of incidents—rather than their charitable nature failed to establish discrimination. See also *Sequoyah Spinning Mills,* 194 N.L.R.B. 1175, 1176 (collecting for funeral flowers not demonstrating discriminatory application of no solicitation rule.) See also *William L. Bonnell Co. v. NLRB,* 405 F.2d 593, 70 L.R.R.M. 2255 at 2257 (5th Cir.1969) (referring to "minor well-defined exceptions for charitable or other purposes). However, for what would seem to be a less minor exception see *Montgomery Ward,* 227 N.L.R.B. 1172 (1977) in which the Employer did have a United Fund drive and the ALJ, citing *Sequoyah* and *Serv–Air,* emphasized the proposition that discrimination is not established by an "employer's limited allowances of work time for charitable solicitations."

106. *Stoddard Quirk Mfg. Co.,* 134 N.L.R.B. 615 (1962).

107. See *NLRB v. United Steelworkers of America (Nutone),* 357 U.S. 357, 42 L.R.R.M. 2324 (1958), *St. Francis Hospital,* 263 N.L.R.B. 834, 835 (1982).

108. The only significant exception is where the employer has a privileged broad solicitation rule. In *May Department Stores Co.,* 136 N.L.R.B. 797, 53 L.R.R.M. 2172 (6th Cir.1963), the Board concluded that there was a "glaring imbalance in opportunities for organizational communication" in the face of both a "privileged broad no solicitation rule" and anti-union speeches. The Board's order specified that if the employer, while enforcing a privileged broad no solicitation rule, made anti-union speeches during company time, it had to honor a union's request for a similar opportunity to address employees. The Sixth Circuit's denial of enforcement centered on "inadequate weight" given by the Board to other available avenues of communication. The Board reaffirmed its *May* doctrine in *Montgomery Ward & Co.,* 145 N.L.R.B. 846, 55 L.R.R.M. 1063 (1964), *enf. as modified,* 339 F.2d 889, 58 L.R.R.M. 2115 (6th Cir.1965). Board found "glaring imbalance" in communication opportunities in face of unlawful no solicitation rule, and "captive audience" speeches whose content was illegal. The Court, relying on the latter features to distinguish the case from its decision in *May,* enforced the Board's order. Note, however, that this principle applies solely to union access prior to election. The parties can bargain whether union reps may have access to the company, and include an access provision in the collective bargaining agreement. See, *Gilliam Candy Co.,* 282 NLRB No. 89 (1987).

109. *NLRB v. Babcock & Wilcox Co.,* 351 U.S. 105, 112, 173 (1956).

110. See generally, Note, Property Rights and Job Security: Workplace Solicitation by Non–Employee Union Organizers, 94 Yale L.J. 374 (1984).

111. *United Steelworkers v. NLRB (Florida Steel),* 646 F.2d 616, 629, 106 L.R.R.M. 2573 (D.C.Cir.1981).

112. *NLRB v. S. & H. Grossinger's Inc.,* 372 F.2d 26, 30, 64 L.R.R.M. 2295 (2d Cir. 1967).

113. *NLRB v. Kutsher's Hotel & Country Club, Inc.,* 427 F.2d 200, 201–202 (2d Cir. 1970).

114. 451 F.2d 794 (3d Cir.1971), *cert. denied,* 409 U.S. 1012 (1972).

115. *Sabine Towing & Transp. Co., Inc. v. NLRB,* 599 F.2d 663, 665 (5th Cir.1979).

116. *Hutzler Bros. Co. v. NLRB,* 630 F.2d 1012, 1017 (4th Cir.1980). This was the premise of the Court in *NLRB v. Tamiment, Inc.,* 451 F.2d 794 (3d Cir.1971). *See also* comments of dissenting Board members in *Ameron Automotive Centers,* 265 N.L.R.B. 58, 111 L.R.R.M. 1614, 1645 n. 29 (1982).

117. 436 U.S. 180, 205 (1978).

118. *Sears, Roebuck & Co. v. San Diego County,* 436 U.S. 180, 205, 98 L.R.R.M. 2282 (1978).

119. *Fairmont Hotel,* 282 N.L.R.B. No. 27 (1986).

120. Id., slip op. at 10.

121. 286 N.L.R.B. 32 (1987).

122. Id., slip op. at 3.

123. *Excelsior Underwear, Inc.,* 156 N.L.R.B. 1236, 1244 (1966).

124. 394 U.S. 759, 70 L.R.R.M. 3345 (1969).

125. 156 N.L.R.B. 1247, 1251, 61 L.R.R.M. 1222 (1969).

126. Getman, Goldberg and Herman at 90–104.

127. See generally Getman, Goldberg and Herman, NLRB Regulation of Campaign Tactics: the Behavioral Assumption on which the Board Regulates, 27 Stan.L.Rev. 1465 (1975).

128. For the majority view, see Report of the House Labor Committee, The Failure of Labor Law; A Betrayal of American Workers (1985) and the Authorities cited therein. For the minority viewpoint, Getman, Goldberg and Herman, supra, Cooper Authorization Cards and Union Representation Election Outcomes: An Empirical Assessment (1983). For an excellent personal statement of the minority view see Organizing in the 80's, Statement by Vincent J. Sirabella, Director of Organization Hotel Employees and Restaurant Employees International Union (AFL–CIO) to the Labor Conference on Organizing in the 80's, Albany New York (1985).

129. *NLRB v. Alco Mining Co.,* 425 F.2d 1128 (5th Cir.1970).

130. *NLRB v. Gissel Packing Co.,* 395 U.S. 575 (1969).

131. This point was made by Judge Posner in *NLRB v. Village IX Inc.*, 723 F.2d 1360 (7th Cir.1983). Although his point was directed to whether the employer's statement was a threat under *Gissel* its clear implication is that the Supreme Court in *Gissel* was guilty of underrating the argument in favor of employer discussion of the plant closing issue, absent a direct threat. See generally Getman, Labor Law and Free Speech: The Curious Policy of Limited Expression (43 Univ. of Md.L.Rev.) 4 (1984).

132. Getman and Blackburn, Labor Relations: Law Practice and Policy (1982).

133. See Getman and Goldberg, supra.

134. 388 F.2d 921 (2d Cir.1967).

135. 439 F.2d 876, 878 (6th Cir.1971).

136. 438 F.2d 1102 (9th Cir.1971) a supervisor "predicted" that if the union won, the employees' coffee breaks and lunch hours would be restricted, sick leave would be curtailed, certain amenities—like free laundry—would be eliminated, and some older employees approaching retirement might lose their pensions. He also predicted layoffs. The comments were based primarily on the belief that the union involved in the organization effort at hand would behave as the other unions at the plant behaved and would insist upon certain demands that the company would be forced to grant. Returning to the pre *Gissel* cases, the Ninth Circuit examined these comments in view of the totality of the campaign and found that the statements were not threats but "at most predictions of possible disadvantages which might arise from economic necessity or because of union demands or union policies." The Ninth Circuit seemed to ignore *Gissel's* quest for proof and considered instead whether all of the disputed communications were rooted in objective fact, and whether the predictions were of consequences which might well result if the union were chosen. The language quoted above was cited among others in *Beaunut Corp. v. NLRB*, 447 F.2d 112 (2d Cir.1971).

137. 723 F.2d 1360 (7th Cir.1983). See also *Midwest Stock Exchange v. NLRB*, 635 F.2d 1255, 105 L.R.R.M. 3172 (7th Cir.1980).

138. Id., at 1367.

139. 198 N.L.R.B. 20 (1972).

140. See *Ohio New & Rebuilt Parts*, 267 N.L.R.B. No. 66, *Panel Construction*, 246 N.L.R.B. 569 (1982). In *Island Holidays, Ltd.*, 208 N.L.R.B. 145, 85 L.R.R.M. 1225 (1974), the employer stated during the campaign that if the union were selected the employer would have to enforce the work rules more strictly since the union contract at other hotels in the area called for an employee's termination for their violation. The Board held that this prediction of stricter dress codes and other minor irritations was permissible:

> It is well established law that an employer has the right to express opinions or predictions or unfavorable consequences which he believes may result from unionization. Such predictions or opinions are not violations of the National Labor Relations Act if they have some reasonable basis in fact and provided that they are in fact predictions or opinions rather than veiled threats.

One recent study shows that the number of Court cases protecting employer speech have more than doubled since 1977, Marguiles, Gissel, A Standard Without a Following (Forthcoming); the same author also detected a "noticeable loosening up" by the Board.

141. See, e.g., *NLRB v. Lorben Corp.*, 345 F.2d 346 (2d Cir.1965).

142. 165 N.L.R.B. 1062 (1967).

143. *NLRB v. J.M. Machinery Corp.*, 410 F.2d 587 (5th Cir.1969); *NLRB v. Historic Smithville Inn*, 414 F.2d 1358 (3d Cir.1969).

144. *Retired Persons Pharmacy v. NLRB*, 519 F.2d 486 (2d Cir.1975); *General Mercantile & Hardware Co. v. NLRB*, 461 F.2d 952 (8th Cir.1972).

145. *Rossmore House*, 269 N.L.R.B. 198 (1984) specifically overruling *PPG Industries Inc.*, 251 N.L.R.B. 1146 (1980).

146. *Columbus Maintenance and Service Co., Inc. v. NLRB*, 758 F.2d 1125 (6th Cir. 1985).

147. In *Restaurant Corp.*, 271 N.L.R.B. 1080, 171 (1984), the Board rules that a conversation between a supervisor and an employee in which the employee mentioned certain areas of dissatisfaction and the supervisor said that the company was investigating them was not the solicitation of grievances or an implied promise conditioned on the rejection of the union.

148. 375 U.S. 405, 409 (1964).

149. *Texas Transport & Terminal Co.,* 179 N.L.R.B. 466 (1970).

150. *Jim Sandy Chevrolet,* 270 NLRB No. 156 (1984); *Flatbush Medical Center,* 270 NLRB No. 136 (1984); *Cardivan Co.,* 271 NLRB 563 (1984).

151. 414 U.S. 270, 281 (1973).

152. 77 N.L.R.B. 124, 127 (1948).

153. For a recent case where the Board has invoked the laboratory conditions standards, see, *Black and Decker Corp.,* 124 L.R.R.M. 1210 (1987) where the Board held that an employer interfered with an election by its distribution of various pieces of literature which made it clear that unionization would threaten job security and the development of new product lines. See also, *Sequatchie Valley Coal,* 281 NLRB No. 108 (1986), where the Board overturned an election when pro-union employees made a series of threats against a co-worker including death threats. The Board noted that the threats occurred throughout the pre-election period and were disseminated among a significant number of workers. Significantly, the union was found to have interfered with the election, even though the Board did not find that the employees were the agents of the union. The Board distinguished two recent election violence cases in which it had reached a contrary result.

154. 77 N.L.R.B. 124 (1948).

155. 119 N.L.R.B. 634, 635, 638 (1957).

156. *Peoria Plastics Co.,* 117 N.L.R.B. 545, 547 (1957).

157. *Peerless Plywood Co.,* 107 N.L.R.B. 427, 429 (1953).

158. *Sewell Mfg. Co.,* 138 N.L.R.B. 66, 70, 71 (1962).

159. *Archer Laundry Co.,* 150 N.L.R.B. 1427 (1965).

160. See *NLRB v. Schapiro & Whitehouse, Inc.,* 356 F.2d 675 (4th Cir.1966), in which the court denied enforcement of a Board bargaining order based on the union's suggesting that black employees had a special reason for voting for it.

161. *Universal Mfg. Corp.,* 156 N.L.R.B. 1459, 1466 (1966).

162. For a good discussion of this issue see Williams, Janus and Huhn, NLRB Regulation of Election Conduct 218–222 (1974).

163. A union did not interfere with an election despite threats of physical injury made by three pro-union employees. Board held that the employees were not agents of the union, and the threats were not intended to influence their co-workers to vote for the union. *Pony Express,* 123 L.R.R.M. 1324.

164. See *James Lee & Sons Co.,* 130 N.L.R.B. 290 (1961); *The Falmouth Co.,* 114 N.L.R.B. 896 (1955).

165. This early evolution is described in Williams et al., pp. 17–25.

166. 140 N.L.R.B. 221, 224 (1962).

167. *NLRB v. Houston Chronicle Publishing Co.,* 300 F.2d 273 (5th Cir.1962); *Cross Baking Co. v. NLRB,* 453 F.2d 1346 (1st Cir.1971).

168. The part of the study dealing with campaign misrepresentations is reported in Getman and Goldberg, The Behavioral Assumptions Underlying NLRB Regulation of Campaign Misrepresentation: An Empirical Evaluation, 28 Stan.L.Rev. 263 (1976).

169. 228 N.L.R.B. 1311 (1977).

170. 239 N.L.R.B. 619 (1978).

171. 263 N.L.R.B. 127 (1982).

172. See W. Dickens, The Effects of Company Campaigns or Certification Elections: Law and Reality Once Again, 36 Indus. & Lab.Rel.Rev. 560 (1983).

173. Weiler, "Promises to Keep: Securing Workers' Rights to Self–Organization Under the NLRA," 96 Harvard L.Rev. 1769 (1983).

174. See Cooper, "Authorization Cards and Union Representation Election Outcome: An Empirical Assessment of the Assumptions Underlying the Supreme Court's *Gissel* Decision," 79 Northwestern Univ.L.Rev. 507 (1984).

175. Many of the cases in this area addressed discharges of employees for anti-union activity. However, the statutory language obviously encompasses more than discharge. For an interesting case, see *David's Kosher Deli,* 282 NLRB No. 107 (1987), where the Board held that an employee who quit her job because her employer threatened to reveal that her daughter had an abortion unless the employee's mother ceased her union activity, was constructively discharged in violation of the Taft–Hartley Act.

176. See *Radio Officers v. NLRB,* 347 U.S. 17 (1954).

177. Professor Weiler, has argued that there has been a dramatic increase Weiler, Promises to Keep: Securing Workers' Rights to Self–Organization Under the NLRA, 96 Harv.L.Rev. 1769 (1983).

178. Because the question of motive is crucial to cases of discriminatory discharge, and because such cases make up a high percentage of the 8(a)(3) cases it has sometimes been argued that an 8(a)(3) violation requires a finding that the employer acted for the purpose of discouraging union membership. Although there is some language to this effect in court cases the Supreme Court finally rejected this position in *NLRB v. Great Dane Trailers, Inc.,* 388 U.S. 26 (1967); See Getman, Section 8(a)(3) of the NLRA and the Effort to Insulate Free Employee Choice, 32 U.Chi.L.Rev. 735 (1965).

179. See *Universal Camera Corp. v. NLRB,* 340 U.S. 474 (1951); Note, Proving an 8(a)(3) Violation: The Changing Standard, 114 U.Pa.L.Rev. 866 (1966).

180. See, e.g., *Mueller Brass Co. v. NLRB,* 544 F.2d 815 (1977).

181. See, for example, *Washington Materials, Inc. v. NLRB,* 803 F.2d 1333, 123 L.R. R.M. 2774 (4th Cir.1986).

182. *Frosty Morn Meats, Inc. v. NLRB,* 296 F.2d 617 (5th Cir.1961); *NLRB v. Sacramento Clinical Laboratory, Inc.,* 623 F.2d 110, 105 L.R.R.M. 2054 (9th Cir.1980); *Edgewood Nursing Home v. NLRB,* 581 F.2d 363 (3d Cir.1978).

183. 251 N.L.R.B. 150 (1980).

184. 429 U.S. 274 (1977).

185. 462 U.S. 393 (1983).

186. *Chromalloy Mining and Minerals v. NLRB,* 620 F.2d 1120 (5th Cir.1980).

187. 284 F.2d 781 (6th Cir.1960); See also *NLRB v. Rapid Bindery, Inc.,* 293 F.2d 170 (2d Cir.1961); *NLRB v. Adkins Transfer Co.,* 226 F.2d 324 (6th Cir.1955).

188. 380 U.S. 263 (1965).

189. 168 N.L.R.B. 1082 (1968).

190. 177 N.L.R.B. 591 (1969), *enf'd,* 431 F.2d 254 (8th Cir.1970).

191. 193 N.L.R.B. 10 (1971).

192. 204 N.L.R.B. 50 (1973).

193. Great Chinese American Sewing Company; Esprit De Corp., 227 N.L.R.B. 1670 (1977) and Gray–Grimes Tool Company, Inc., 221 N.L.R.B. 736 (1975).

194. *Local 57, International Ladies Garment Workers' Union v. NLRB,* 374 F.2d 295 (D.C.Cir.1967).

195. 324 U.S. 793 (1945).

196. Getman, *Section 8(a)(3) of the NLRA* supra.

197. *NLRB v. Fansteel Metallurgical Corp.,* 306 U.S. 240 (1939).

198. Bethel, The NLRB and the Discharge of Supervisors: Accommodating Employee Rights and Congressional Intent.

199. See, *Consumer's Power Company,* 282 NLRB No. 24, 123 L.R.R.M. 1305 (1986). A divided Board held that a meterman who complained that his supervisor failed to provide police protection to a co-worker had engaged in concerted activity thereby.

See also, *NLRB v. Coca Cola Bottling Co.,* 811 F.2d 82, 124 L.R.R.M. 2585 (1987), in which the Seventh Circuit held that an employee's testimony at a criminal trial on the behalf of a co-worker who was criminally charged for misconduct during a strike was "concerted" activity within the meaning of section 7.

An employer unlawfully threatened to close its plant if an employee reported safety violations to OSHA. A call to OSHA by the employee in question would not be protected by Taft–Hartley Act. But since threat was made when there were "lots of people around," it was. *Unico Replacement Parts,* 286 NLRB No. 70 (1986).

200. 221 N.L.R.B. 999 (1975).

201. Some recent cases from the 6th and 3rd Circuits indicate a slightly broader approach. The U.S. Court of Appeals for the 6th Circuit found protected concerted activity on the part of employees who gave affidavits to a sheriff stating that their employer's vice president had embezzled company funds. The court found that the employees' overriding concern was for their job security, and that the possibility of unionizing to protect their jobs was brought up at the same meeting that produced the statements to the sheriff. *Squier Distributing Co. v. Teamsters Local 7,* 801 F.2d 238 (6th Cir.1986). In the 3rd Circuit, the court held that an employee who discussed wage rates with two co-workers and the desirability of making contact with a union if the next raise was disappointing was engaged in concerted activity. *D & D Distribution Company v. NLRB,* 801 F.2d 636 (3d Cir.1986).

202. 268 N.L.R.B. 473 (1984).

203. *Prill v. NLRB,* 755 F.2d 941 (D.C.Cir.1985), cert. denied, 474 U.S. 948 (1985).

204. *NLRB v. City Disposal Sys. Inc.,* 465 U.S. 822 (1984).

205. See footnote 199.

206. Dreis & Krump Mfg., Inc., 221 N.L.R.B. 309 (1975).

207. Roadway Express, Inc., 257 N.L.R.B. 1197 (1981).

208. *Phelps Dodge Corp. v. NLRB,* 313 U.S. 177 (1941).

209. Isis Plumbing Co., 138 N.L.R.B. 716 (1962).

210. *General Shoe,* supra.

211. Weiler, *Promises to Keep,* supra, *Dodge Corp. v. NLRB,* 313 U.S. 177 (1941).

212. 395 U.S. 575 (1969).

213. Id., at 614.

214. Id., at 614–615.

215. *First Lakewood Associates v. NLRB,* 582 F.2d 416, 99 L.R.R.M. 2192 (7th Cir. 1978). *NLRB v. Marion Rohr Corp., Inc.,* 714 F.2d 228, 114 L.R.R.M. 2126, at 2128 (2d Cir.1983).

216. *NLRB v. Village IX, Inc. d/b/a Shenanigans,* 723 F.2d 1360 (7th Cir.1983) and cases and sources cited therein (caustic criticism of Board's approach.)

First Lakewood Associates v. NLRB, 582 F.2d 416, 99 L.R.R.M. 2192 (7th Cir.1978) (refers to Board's "cavalier treatment" of necessary *Gissel* findings.) *NLRB v. Jamaica Towing, Inc.,* 602 F.2d 1100, 101 L.R.R.M. 3011 (2d Cir.1979) (notes appearance of *ad hoc* decisions by Board, and lack of standards.) *NLRB v. Marion Rohr Corp.,* 714 F.2d 228, 114 L.R.R.M. 2913 (5th Cir.1970), *cert. denied,* 400 U.S. 997 (1971). See *NLRB v. General Stencils, Inc.,* 438 F.2d 894 (2d 1971) where the court recommended that the Board set out hierarchy of unfair labor practices that were unlikely to be eased by traditional remedies and would call for a bargaining order.

217. *NLRB v. American Cable Systems Inc.,* 427 F.2d 446, 449, 73 L.R.R.M. 2913 (5th Cir.1970), *cert. denied,* 400 U.S. 957 (1970).

218. See, e.g., *United Services for Handicapped v. NLRB,* 678 F.2d 661, 110 L.R.R.M. 3231 (6th Cir.1982), dissenting opinion in *Southern Moldings, Inc. v. NLRB,* 715 F.2d 1069, 114 L.R.R.M. 2100 at 2106 (6th Cir.1983).

219. *NLRB v. Rexair, Inc.,* 646 F.2d 249, 107 L.R.R.M. 3081 (6th Cir.1981). See also *United Services for Handicapped v. NLRB,* 678 F.2d 661, 110 L.R.R.M. 3231 (6th Cir.1982).

220. *Bandag, Inc. v. NLRB,* 583 F.2d 765, 99 L.R.R.M. 3226 (at 3232–33) (5th Cir. 1978) (bargaining orders always remedial, not punitive). *NLRB v. Marion Rohr Corp.,*

Inc., 714 F.2d 228, 114 L.R.R.M. 2126 at 2128 (reference to preference for election remedy as reflection of policy that representation not be forced on employees).

221. *United States v. United Dairy Farmers Cooperative Ass'n,* 611 F.2d 488 (3d Cir. 1979). (Board notes that risk of imposing union on nonconsenting employees is only justified if it serves substantial remedial interests.).

222. *Southern Moldings Inc. v. NLRB,* 715 F.2d 1069, 114 L.R.R.M. 2100 (6th Cir. 1983) and cases cited therein (vacated and petition for rehearing granted 719 F.2d 858) 114 L.R.R.M. 3135 (1983).

223. *NLRB v. Rexair, Inc.,* 646 F.2d 249, 107 L.R.R.M. 1081 (6th Cir.1981), *United Services for Handicapped v. NLRB,* 678 F.2d 661 at 664, 110 L.R.R.M. 3231 (6th Cir.1982), *Southern Moldings Inc. v. NLRB,* 715 F.2d 1069, 114 L.R.R.M. 2100 (6th Cir.1983), vacated and petition for rehearing granted see notes 9 and 11 above. *Peerless of America, Inc. v. NLRB,* 484 F.2d 1108, 83 L.R.R.M. 3000 (7th Cir.1973), *First Lakewood Associates v. NLRB,* 582 F.2d 416, 99 L.R.R.M. 2192 (7th Cir.1978).

224. Miller, dissent in *General Stencils Inc.,* 195 N.L.R.B. 1109 at 111, 79 L.R.R.M. 1608 (1972); *enf. denied,* 472 F.2d 170, 82 L.R.R.M. 2081 (2d Cir.1972).

225. *Gibson Prods. Co.,* 185 N.L.R.B. 362, 75 L.R.R.M. 1055 (1970), on remand from 73 L.R.R.M. 2913 (5th Cir.1970) principle and related order in 172 N.L.R.B. 794, *enforcement denied,* 494 F.2d 762 (1974). See also *American Cable Sys. Inc.,* 179 N.L.R.B. 846, 72 L.R.R.M. 1524 (1969), *enforcement denied and remanded,* 427 F.2d 446, 73 L.R.R.M. 2913 (5th Cir.1970), *Marion Rohr,* 261 N.L.R.B. No. 138, 110 L.R.R.M. 1149 (1982), *enforcement denied,* 714 F.2d 228, 114 L.R.R.M. 2126 (2d Cir.1983) (Board states that ALJ properly held irrelevant the passage of time and employee turnover).

226. It should be noted in assessing the following cases that in many circuits the issue has evolved from whether changed circumstances and turnover are relevant to at what point in proceedings (preorder, postorder, enforcement etc.) they are relevant. Rejecting Board view, in whole or significant part: 2nd circuit: *NLRB v. Knogo Corp.,* 727 F.2d 55, 115 L.R.R.M. 2756 (2d Cir.1984) (enforcement of bargaining order denied in context of three year lapse since signing of cards and turnover of employees). *NLRB v. Jamaica Towing, Inc.,* 602 F.2d 1100, 101 L.R.R.M. 3011 (2d Cir.1979) (enforcement of bargaining order denied based on coupled factors—passage of time and substantial change in work force.) See also *NLRB v. MSL Industries, Heads and Threads Div.,* 724 F.2d 282, 115 L.R.R.M. 2084 (2d Cir.1983) (post unfair labor practice events relevant to possibility of free and fair election, appropriateness of bargaining order to be assessed at time issued) and *NLRB v. Marion Rohr Corp., Inc.,* 714 F.2d 228, 114 L.R.R.M. 2126 (2d Cir.1983) consider effects of time and change in employee complement, 5th Circuit: *Bandag, Inc. v. NLRB,* 583 F.2d 765, 99 L.R.R.M. 3226 (5th Cir.1978), *NLRB v. American Cable Systems, Inc.,* 427 F.2d 446, 73 L.R.R.M. 2913 (5th Cir.1978) (consider subsequent events). However, in *Chromalloy Min. and Minerals v. N.L.R.B.,* 620 F.2d 1120 (5th Cir. 1980) the Court summarizes and elaborates on its position indicating limits to the consideration of subsequent events. *D.C. Circuit Pedros, Inc. v. NLRB,* 652 F.2d 1005, 107 L.R.R.M. 2023 (D.C.Cir.1981) requirement that on remand Board assess current conditions. *At least partially accepting Board View:* Ninth Circuit: *NLRB v. L.B. Foster Co.,* 418 F.2d 1, 72 L.R.R.M. 2736 (9th Cir.1969), *cert. denied,* 397 U.S. 990, 73 L.R.R.M. 2791 (1970). However, the Ninth Circuit later held that "the board must consider changes occurring before the administrative hearing"; *NLRB v. Western Drug,* 600 F.2d 1324, 1326, 101 L.R.R.M. 3023 (9th Cir.1979). See also *NLRB v. Peninsula Association for Retarded Children and Adults,* 627 F.2d 202 (9th Cir.1980) (court distinguishes lapse of time due to adjudication from relevancy of lapse between violation and holding of election). Seventh Circuit: *New Alaska Development Corp. v. NLRB,* 441 F.2d 491, 76 L.R.R.M. 2689 (7th Cir.1971), and *NLRB v. Drives, Inc.,* 440 F.2d 354, 76 L.R.R.M. 2296 (7th Cir.1971), *cert. denied,* 404 U.S. 912, 78 L.R.R.M. 2585 (1971). However, now the Seventh Circuit also distinguishes between pre- and post-order turnover. *Red Oaks Nursing Home, Inc. v. NLRB,* 633 F.2d 503, 105 L.R.R.M. 3028, 3032 (7th Cir.1980) (preorder turnover one factor in denying enforcement of Board's bargaining order.) Eighth Circuit: *NLRB v. Dixisteel Bldgs., Inc.,* 445 F.2d 1260, 1265 (8th Cir.1971) (limits situations where employee turnover a relevant consideration). Sixth Circuit: *Exchange Bank v. NLRB,* 115 L.R.R.M. 3692 (6th Cir.1984), (Board in issuing its order must consider present effects of past unfair labor practices in deciding whether fair election can be held, but Court summarizes circuit's position in prior cases with statement that bargaining orders are rarely effected by events, occurring after issuance, and that Board need not look at employee turnover in making decision about seeking enforcement of bargaining order. See also *United Services for Handicapped v. NLRB,* 678 F.2d 661, 110 L.R.R.M. 3231 (1982) (stressing need to assess present effects of past ULP). *NLRB v. Arrow Molded Plastics, Inc.,* 653 F.2d 280, 107 L.R.R.M. 3332 (6th Cir.1981) (enforcement of bargaining order denied due to nature of ULP's lapse of time). *NLRB v. Frederick's Foodland, Inc.,* 655 F.2d 88, 107 L.R.R.M. 3216 (6th Cir.1981) (fair election possible in view of passage of time, since first election large increase in number of employees and nature of ULP's) (*Arrow* and *Frederick's* apparently did not involve post-order changes).

227. *First Lakewood Associates,* 231 N.L.R.B. 68, 96 L.R.R.M. 1316 (1977) ("serious and pervasive" unfair labor practices, minimal explanation of significance).

228. *Ohio New and Rebuilt Parts Inc.,* 267 N.L.R.B. 66, 114 L.R.R.M. 1053, at 1055 (1983) (action part of the general company plan to destroy employee support of Union). *Arthur Briggs,* 265 N.L.R.B. 38, 112 L.R.R.M. 1302 (1982) (several violations supporting bargaining order, including surveillance deliberately designed to discourage Union activities).

229. *Piggly Wiggly (Tuscaloosa Div.),* 258 N.L.R.B. 1081, at 1082 (1981), *enforced,* 705 F.2d 1537 (11th Cir.1983) (discussing impact of discharges, suspensions), citing *Devon Gables Nursing Home,* 237 N.L.R.B. 775, 776–777 (1978) and *Shop Rite Supermarket Inc.,* 231 N.L.R.B. 500, at 507–508. *Ohio New and Rebuilt Parts Inc.,* 267 N.L.R.B. 66, 114 L.R. R.M. 1053 at 1055 (1983). *Pace Oldsmobile, Inc.,* 265 N.L.R.B. 101, 112 L.R.R.M. 1186, 1188 discharge and threat of closure "hallmark" violations). *Larid Printing,* 264 N.L. R.B. 40 at 370 (1982). *Penn Color Inc.,* 261 N.L.R.B. 394, 396, (1982).

230. See *NLRB v. Wilhow Corp.,* 666 F.2d 1294 at 1305 (10th Cir.1981) (difficulty in erasing effects of ULP's).

231. *Penn Color Inc.,* 261 N.L.R.B. 394 (1982) solicitation of grievances and correction of problems. *Piggly–Wiggly (Tuscaloosa Div.),* 258 N.L.R.B. 1081 (1981), *enforced,* 705 F.2d 1537 (11th Cir.1983) (promises of economic benefit).

232. See *Ohio New and Rebuilt Parts, Inc.,* 267 N.L.R.B. 66, 114 L.R.R.M. 1053, at 1055 (1983); *Larid Printing Inc.,* 264 N.L.R.B. 368, 370, numerous hallmark violations. *Penn Color Inc.,* 261 N.L.R.B. 394 (1982).

233. Hood, *Bargaining Orders: The Effect of Gissel Packing Company,* 32 Labor L.J. 203 (1981); see also comments of court in *Red Oaks Nursing Home v. NLRB,* 633 F.2d 503, 105 L.R.R.M. 3028, 3031 (7th Cir.1980).

234. *Loray Corporation,* 184 N.L.R.B. 557 (1970) (Board emphasized lack of majority status in reversing trial examiner's bargaining order which was based on outrageous and pervasive violations (threats, discharge, layoffs).

235. 257 N.L.R.B. 129 (1981).

236. 261 N.L.R.B. 178 (1982).

237. 242 N.L.R.B. 1026 (1979) remanded for consideration of bargaining order issue, *United Dairy Farmers Cooperative Ass'n v. NLRB,* 633 F.2d 1054 (3d Cir.1979).

238. *Conair Corp. v. NLRB,* 721 F.2d 1355 (D.C.Cir.1983).

239. *Gourmet Foods Inc.,* 270 N.L.R.B. 113 (1984).

240. *Local 57, International Ladies Garment Workers' Union v. NLRB,* 374 F.2d 295 (D.C.Cir.1967).

241. See Note, *NLRB Orders Granting Unions Access to Company Property,* 68 Cornell L.Rev. 895 (1983); *NLRB v. Marion Rohr Corp., Inc.,* 714 F.2d 228, 114 L.R.R.M. 2126 (1983). *NLRB v. Village IX Inc. d/b/a/ Shenanigans,* 723 F.2d 1360, 115 L.R.R.M. 2297, 2303–4 (7th Cir.1983) (discusses Board's general history of inadequate findings). See also other Seventh Cir. cases including *First Lakewood Associates v. NLRB,* 582 F.2d 416, 99 L.R.R.M. 2192 (7th Cir.1978) and *Red Oaks Nursing Home, Inc. v. NLRB,* 633 F.2d 503, 105 L.R.R.M. 3028 (7th Cir.1980) (refers to lack of enforcement if Board makes no findings and detailed analysis concerning "residual impact . . . or the likelihood of recurrence" of any of the ULP's or if Board makes only conclusory statements.) A similar case is *NLRB v. Armcor Industries, Inc.,* 535 F.2d 239, 92 L.R.R.M. 2374 (3d Cir. 1976) (requires reasoned analysis by Board of factors including impact of ULP on election processes).

242. J. Getman, S. Goldberg & J. Herman, Union Representation Elections: Law and Reality (1976).

Relevant Books, Articles, and Suggested Reading

BOOKS:

Feerick, Baer & Arfa, NLRB Election Law Practice & Procedure (1979).

Getman, Goldberg, & Herman, Union Representation Elections: Law and Reality (1976).

Modjeska, NLRB Practice (1983).

Schlossberg, Organizing & the Law (1967).

Williams, Janus & Huhn, NLRB Regulation of Election Conduct (1974).

ARTICLES:

Angel, "Professional and Unionization," 66 Minn.L.Rev. 383 (1982).

Bok, "The Regulation of Campaign Tactics in Representation Elections Under the National Labor Relations Act," 78 Harvard L.Rev. 38 (1964).

Cooper, "Authorization Cards and Union Representation Election Outcome: An Empirical Assessment of the Assumptions Underlying the Supreme Court's *Gissel* Decision," 79 Northwestern Univ. L.Rev. 87 (1984).

Farber & Saks, "Why Workers Want Unions: The Role of Relative Wages and Job Characteristics," 88 Jour. of Political Economy 349 (1980).

Flanagan, "NLRA Litigation and Union Representation," 38 Stanford L.Rev. 957 (1986).

Getman, "Ruminations on Union Organizing in the Private Sector," 53 Univ.Chicago L.Rev. 45 (1986).

Getman, "Section 8(a)(3) of the NLRA and the Effort to Insulate Free Employee Choice," 32 Univ.Chicago L.Rev. 735 (1965).

Leslie, "Labor Bargaining Units," 70 Virginia L.Rev. 353 (1984).

Note, "Property Rights and Job Security Workplace Solicitation by Nonemployee Union Organizers," 94 Yale L.Journal 374 (1984).

Oberer, "The Scientific Factor in Sections 8(a)(1) and (3) of the Labor Act: Of Balancing, Hostile Motive, Dogs and Tails," 52 Cornell L.Q. 491 (1967).

Pogrebin, "NLRB Bargaining Orders Since Gissel, Wandering From a Landmark," 46 St. John's L.Rev. 193 (1972).

Symposium, "Four Perspectives on Union Representation Elections—Law & Reality," 28 Stan.L.Rev. 1161 (1976).

Suntrup, "NLRB v. Yeshiva University and Unionization in Higher Education," Indus.Rel.L.Jour. 287 (1981).

Weiler, "Promises to Keep: Securing Workers' Rights to Self–Organization Under the NLRA," 96 Harvard L.Rev. 1769 (1983).

Chapter II

COLLECTIVE BARGAINING

Part I. Exclusivity

A. The Statutory Scheme

Section 8(a)(5) makes it an unfair labor practice for an employer "to refuse to bargain collectively with the representatives of his employees. . . ."[1] The nature of the obligation is further articulated by section 9(a) and section 8(d), which sections as interpreted, define the role of an incumbent union through two significant legal doctrines: "exclusivity" and "good faith bargaining." Exclusivity is partially defined by section 9(a)(1), and good faith bargaining is partially defined by section 8(d). Exclusivity refers to the preeminent role of the union selected in accordance with the procedures described in Chapter One. It severely limits an employer's ability to deal with individual employees or other groups of employees once a union is selected. Good faith bargaining refers to the obligations to negotiate a collective agreement that an employer owes to an incumbent union. Section 8(b)(3) imposes a parallel obligation upon the union.

Exclusivity is referred to but not defined by section 9(a), which states that "[r]epresentatives designated . . . by the majority of employees in a unit appropriate for such purposes, shall be the exclusive representatives of all the employees. . . ."[2]

The contours of exclusivity have been developed in a series of Board and court decisions that have employed the doctrine to foster collective bargaining by eliminating other techniques that the employer might use to establish wages, hours, or conditions of employment. These are the matters with respect to which the employer is required to bargain with an incumbent union under section 8(d). Exclusivity not only prevents the employer from dealing with other groups or unions but also precludes individual contracts and unilateral employer action. The doctrine of exclusivity thus places the union between the employer and his labor relations goals requiring him to negotiate with the union in order to achieve his goals.

B. The Role of Exclusivity in Limiting Employer Conduct

1. Unilateral Action

Once a union has been selected in accordance with the procedures described in Chapter One, an employer is prohibited from taking unilateral action with respect to the matters covered by section

9(a) ("rates of pay, wages, hours of employment or other conditions of employment") until he has bargained in good faith with the union with respect to such matters. More than any other, it is this section, as interpreted, that gives a designated union a significant voice in establishing working conditions. Thus union voice is directly related to the breadth given to the statutory language quoted above. The employer's duty to bargain, however, does not mean that it is required to get the union's agreement prior to acting, but only to bargain with the union. Once impasse is reached he may unilaterally establish changes that he earlier proposed to the union. Accordingly, the requirement of bargaining to impasse (as will be developed more fully below) is a significant one.

2. Direct Bargaining Between the Employer and Individual Employees

The most fundamental of the changes that selection of a union entails, is that it prohibits the employer from dealing with individual employees independently of the union or of changing wages or working conditions unilaterally. The employer can no longer select individuals to reward or to punish by making changes in their salary or working conditions.[3] He must bargain with the union, which will almost always insist on dealing on the basis of general categories, seeking to establish wage rates, job duties, and working conditions for designated classes of employees. Indeed, under the duty of fair representation, it would generally be an unfair labor practice for a union to negotiate for individuals rather than in terms of job classifications.[4]

The prohibition against individual dealing does not apply to disciplinary action, although any departure from preexisting policy with regard to discipline would constitute improper unilateral action unless preceded by adequate bargaining.[5] Indeed not only is the establishment of new rules unlawful, but so is more stringent enforcement of existing rules. Thus, for example, in *Master Slack*,[6] the Board found that respondent's unilaterally adopted policy of more rigid enforcement of tardiness and absenteeism rules was a unilateral change in terms and conditions of employment.

A proviso to section 9(a) provides that any "individual or group of employees shall have the right at any time to present grievances to their employer without the intervention of the bargaining representative as long as the adjustment is not inconsistent with the terms of a collective-bargaining agreement then in effect. . . ."[7] This proviso was originally considered a significant exception to exclusivity, justified by the need to protect the interests of individual employees. However, the proviso has been rendered much less important than it was originally thought to be by two related developments: the judicial decision to utilize the duty of fair representation as the major vehicle for protecting individual rights under collective agreements and the very narrow construction given to the proviso. Thus, despite the proviso's seemingly absolute language, the Supreme Court held in *Vaca v. Sipes*[8] that an individual employee could not insist upon presenting his grievance individually when the collective-bargaining agreement provided that the employee was required to go through the grievance procedure controlled by the union. The Court acknowledged the union's right to settle or waive the grievance or refuse to process it to arbitration. Despite the proviso to section 9(a), the individual was bound by action of the union unless "the employee can prove that the union as bargaining agent breached its duty of fair representation in its handling of the employee's grievance," which could be proved by showing that the union's action was "arbitrary, discriminatory, or in bad faith."[9]

The opinion in *Vaca v. Sipes* reduced the significance of the legislatively established statutory proviso and increased that of the judicially created duty of fair representation. "Nor do we see substantial danger to the interests of the individual employee if his statutory agent is given the contractual power honestly and in good faith to settle grievances short of arbitration."

3. Dealing Between the Employer and Groups of Employees

a. RIVAL UNIONS

Under the doctrine of exclusivity, rival labor organizations have almost no right to deal with the employer. They may not bargain with the employer,[10] may not use economic pressure against him,[11] and may not take advantage of the proviso to section 9(a), which states that "a group of employees shall have the right at any time to present grievances to their employer" to play an active role in resolving grievances for their adherents.[12] The term "groups" of employees referred to in the proviso does not give rights to labor organizations but only to a number of employees who have the same grievance. In short, the only activity in which the rival union may engage is to communicate to the employees the case for changing their representative. In order to facilitate free choice in this regard, the doctrine of exclusivity does not give the incumbent union sole access to the employees. The Board and courts have been careful to prevent the incumbent union from using its status as exclusive representative to prevent rival unions from getting their organizing message heard.[13] This approach has had the result of preventing the incumbent union from bargaining away its own access rights or those of its adherents.

In *Magnavox Co. of Tennessee*,[14] the employer had been authorized by the collective-bargaining agreement to issue rules for the maintenance of orderly conditions on plant property. Pursuant to this general grant of authority, the employer had adopted a rule prohibiting the distribution of literature in non-working areas on non-work time. The NLRB held that the no-distribution rule was invalid, notwithstanding the fact that those who sought to distribute literature were supporters of the incumbent: "[W]e find nothing in the statute, to suggest that employees who wish to exercise their section 7 right to *reject* a union representative are entitled to more protection than employees who wish to exercise the same section 7 right to *support* a union representative." Following reversal by the Sixth Circuit,[15] the Board appealed to the Supreme Court, which upheld the Board's determination.[16] In his majority opinion, Justice Douglas distinguished a waiver of economic rights (e.g., the right to strike) from the waiver that was involved in the present case.

> "[A] different rule should obtain where the rights of the employees to exercise their choice of a bargaining representative [are] involved—whether to have no bargaining representative, or to retain the present one, or to obtain a new one. When the right to such a choice is at issue, it is difficult to assume that the incumbent union has no self-interest of its own to serve by perpetuating itself as the bargaining representative. (Citation omitted.) The place of work is a place uniquely appropriate for dissemination of views concerning the bargaining representative and the various options open to the employees. So long as the distribution is by employees to employees and so long as the in-plant solicitation is on non-working time, banning of that solicitation might seriously dilute Section 7 rights."

Justice Douglas went on to argue that it would be unfair to limit the right of in-plant distribution to opponents of the incumbent union. Therefore, he concluded that *all* employees had a nonwaivable section 7 right to distribute literature relative to the selection of a bargaining representative.

The holding in *Magnavox* has since been expanded so the general rule is now that the union may not limit the rights of any subgroup to influence the employees in any matter relating to the exercise of section 7 rights. Thus, exclusivity severely limits the right of groups other than the union to communicate with the employer, but their ability to communicate with employees is protected. For example, in *Ford Motor Co.,* several employees who belonged to a UAW splinter group had been disciplined for handing out literature that demanded a strike vote concerning impending layoffs and derided the UAW's "Henry Have A Heart" campaign. The NLRB held that the employer had committed an unfair labor practice notwithstanding the presence of a broad no-distribution rule in the collective-bargaining agreement, because the employees had a nonwaivable right to distribute "literature which pertains to the employee's selection or rejection of a labor organization as their collective-bargaining representative, or other matters related to the exercise by employees of their section 7 rights." [17]

b. EXCLUSIVITY AND EMPLOYER COMMUNICATION WITH EMPLOYEES IN THE BARGAINING CONTEXT

While it is clear that employers may not negotiate with rank-and-file employees, it is not clear what constitutes bargaining for these purposes. In particular, what forms of employer communication to the rank and file will be characterized as an effort to avoid bargaining with the union? Under present case law, employer communications to unit workers during collective bargaining are not automatically violative of section 8(a)(5). In the absence of an explicit bargaining offer, the Board attempts to determine whether the employer intended to circumvent the union. Such determinations necessarily require examination both of the content of the communications and the context in which they are expressed. The best known case applying this approach is *NLRB v. General Electric Co.,*[18] in which the Second Circuit outlawed a bargaining strategy known as "Boulwareism." This technique had been widely publicized as a new and powerful management bargaining strategy that avoided the "bazaar haggling" of traditional contract negotiations. Under this approach, management would seize the bargaining initiative by putting on the table "a firm, fair offer," reinforced by a massive public relations campaign aimed at the rank and file, and utilizing media as well as personal contacts. While the company announced that union proposals would be considered to see whether the company overlooked anything in formulating its position, it made clear that it anticipated an extremely minor role for the union in that regard. Indeed, if the company had prepared adequately there should be no role at all for the union, since the give and take of "auction bargaining" was specifically disavowed.

The Second Circuit affirmed the NLRB's finding that General Electric's conduct violated section 8(a)(5). It held that the company's take-it-or-leave-it bargaining methods, when combined with a widely publicized stance that its positions once taken were unalterable, constituted "a refusal to bargain in fact." Although the court did not specifically find that General Electric's communications violated section 8(a)(5), it asserted that the publicity campaign denigrated the union's status because it portrayed the company as the true defender of employee interests. Moreover, the court noted that General Electric's refusal to withhold communications until the union had a chance to propose changes was indicative of the company's desire to "deal with the Union through the employees rather than with the employees through the Union." [19]

The Second Circuit decision seemed to mark the end of Boulwareism as a bargaining technique, although Boulwareism is frequently charged by unions and denied by management. It is not clear that the strategy was a casualty of law rather than of its own limitations as a method of bargaining. A relatively high initial offer is a risky technique because it generally signals the union that there is more to be had if the employees remain united. To hold to a bargaining position throughout negotiations at the minimum end of what is acceptable to the union requires a firm committed management and a divided union. Among the aftereffects of General Electric's use of this technique were a shake-up of union leadership, the development of a coalition strategy by several of the unions with whom General Electric dealt, and a major effort by one of the unions to win back the allegiance of its rank and file. These tactics proved successful and convinced many people in General Electric management that a new, less confrontational approach was called for. Had General Electric officials remained committed to Boulwareism, they could have legally developed a policy that incorporated its basic features: a management proposal close to the eventual terms of agreement and a series of communications setting out and justifying management's bargaining position.

In *Proctor and Gamble Mfg. Co.,*[20] the company through letters, bulletins, and meetings conveyed the following messages to employees during bargaining sessions: (a) information on the status of negotiations, (b) explanations of its bargaining table and grievance positions, (c) refutation of charges made by the union, and (d) criticism of the union leadership's bargaining tactics, which were purported to be the reasons for the current deadlock. The Board found that these messages did not manifest an unlawful intention to undermine or bypass the union as bargaining representative:

> "The fact that an employer chooses to inform employees of the status of negotiations, or of proposals previously made to the Union, or of its version of a breakdown in negotiations will not alone establish a failure to bargain in good faith."

The Board distinguished the Proctor and Gamble campaign from that used in the General Electric case by asserting that Proctor and Gamble's communications were not coupled with a fixed position at the bargaining table—the company's unambiguous willingness to actively engage in give and take bargaining showed that it was not attempting to undermine the union. Moreover, the Board noted that all of the company's literature had been sent to the union and did not exceed the terms that the company had offered at the bargaining table.[21] It takes very little compromise to overcome the claim of a fixed position.

The question of whether an employer is seeking to bypass a union frequently arises in a strike situation when the employer tries to convince striking workers to return to work. In general, communications for this purpose are lawful.[22]

It is well-established law that employer communications constitute an unfair labor practice if they include an offer of terms that are different or superior to those offered the union.[23] One possible exception to this rule is when the employer specifically ties the new proposal to a union contract, which will be negotiated if the employees return to work. In *Hoffman Beverage Co.,*[24] the Board found no section 8(a)(5) violation where an employer promised to rehire striking drivers if they would prevail upon the union through mass petitions or demonstrations to abrogate the wage provision in the current collective agreement and accept an incentive plan similar to that which had been offered to another drivers' union. According to the Board, the company "was not trying to bargain individually with employees about substituting an incentive pay plan for the existing pay system, but was seeking to enlist the aid of the employees in bringing [the union] to the bargaining table."[25]

Such decisions seem to be inconsistent with the General Electric case and to take a very limited definition of bargaining. Perhaps they stand for the proposition that a limited amount of indirect pressure on the union through individual bargaining will be permitted after good faith negotiations have reached impasse.

In strike situations, however, explicit employer offers to deal with individuals as opposed to the union are uniformly prohibited. In *Safeway Trails, Inc. v. NLRB,*[26] for example, the company sent strikers a letter blaming the union representative for the company's failure to reach agreement with the union. It urged that each employee should now act in the interest of his own personal welfare and aid in getting an early settlement. A second letter stated that it was puzzling why the strikers would allow a representative with so little seniority to control their interests. Three months after the second letter was sent, the company president told an employee's wife that he could settle the strike if he were allowed to meet with any three employees other than the union representative; he also told a senior employee that he couldn't understand why the older men in the unit couldn't do something to get the strike settled. The D.C. Circuit affirmed the Board's finding that the company had attempted to undermine the authority of the union negotiator and had thus violated section 8(a)(5). It also affirmed the Board's holding that such a violation could be found even where the employer had manifested good faith at the bargaining table, a question which had been left open in prior employer communication decisions such as *General Electric Co.*[27]

If the strike itself is an unfair labor practice or otherwise unprotected activity, employer solicitations that would normally violate the Act will be permitted. For example, in *California Cotton Cooperative*

Association,[28] an employer communicated to strikers, *inter alia,* that it would recognize neither the union nor the collective agreement. The Board found no section 8(a)(1) violation because the employees' walk-out breached a no-strike clause in the contract and was unprotected. Similarly, in *Publicity Engravers Inc.,*[29] an employer's offer to strikers of more money than the current salary rate was held not to violate section 8(a)(1) because the union did not timely inform the state mediation board of its strike pursuant to section 8(d) of the Act. It is not at all clear why the reach of exclusivity should be limited simply because the union has violated the Act but where its transgression did not involve an unwillingness to continue bargaining with the employer. It should be noted that the employer has other remedies available in such cases, including self help and the Board's unfair labor practice processes. These cases represent an unnecessarily legalistic and unfortunate approach in that they permit basic rights under the Act to be forfeited because of technical violations, and they treat offending unions as outlaws, a policy hardly conducive to industrial rationality.

As the above discussion makes clear the doctrine of exclusivity varies somewhat in the extent to which it prevents (a) individual bargaining, (b) dealing with other organizations or groups, and (c) unilateral action. Dealing with other groups is given the least leeway because it is almost totally inconsistent with the employees' choice of the union. Individual bargaining is given some scope as a way of protecting individual contract interests or to recognize differences in bargaining power within the unit. Unilateral action is permitted under some circumstances to insure the possibility of needed change and sometimes in deference to traditional concepts of ownership.

C. Impasse

The impact of exclusivity on management decision making is limited by the ability of an employer to make unilateral changes after bargaining to impasse over them.

The concept of impasse is quite important under the Act. It determines when an employer may lock out or take unilateral action. It determines when insisting upon a permissive subject becomes an unfair labor practice and it marks the point at which the parties are free to discontinue bargaining. According to Board doctrine, an impasse exists when the possibility of agreement through continued discussion has been exhausted. It is difficult to tell when this occurs. Part of a party's strategy in bargaining will often be to convince the other side that it has gone as far as it can making compromises. This strategy may serve one of two legitimate goals. First, it may convince the other side that it must accept the terms currently on the table or at least make a significant new offer in order to stimulate movement. Second, it can underline the importance of any change in position, thus increasing the impact of minor compromise. The rhythm of collective bargaining is such that significant movement is often preceded by a mood of hopeless deadlock purposely created by either side.

Legally, it will usually be in the union's interest to argue that no impasse in fact exists. Thus, a well counseled union may be trying to convey that its position is fixed for bargaining purposes while leaving open enough suggestion for change to avoid impasse for legal purposes. Because an impasse relieves the employer of his duty to bargain, an employer too eager to reach impasse may be found to have bargained in bad faith.

1. When Is Impasse Reached

Impasse occurs only when both sides have firmly reached contrary positions on issues that could prevent an agreement. The Board's determination of impasse requires a prediction of the future willingness of either side to "move"—to sign an agreement less favorable to it than its last demanded version. The Board makes such a prediction based on its own analysis of "objective indicators" of the states of mind of the parties.

In *Carpenter Sprinkler Corp. v. NLRB*,[30] the Second Circuit upheld a Board finding that no impasse in contract negotiations existed and upheld section 8(a)(5) charges against an employer attempting to use "impasse" as a justification for unilateral changes. The facts in that case were that after three negotiating sessions in which the parties remained far apart, the union representative told the company they were at "impasse." Four days later, the company stated that it "agreed" with the union that impasse existed and the company proceeded to unilaterally change wages and benefits. When charges were filed, the critical issue was whether both parties were right when they said they had reached impasse. The Board and court concluded that they were wrong.

According to the Board, citing an earlier decision, impasse results from "[ir]reconcilable differences in the parties' positions reached after exhaustive, good-faith negotiations."[31] Statements by either party may be evidence of impasse, but do not establish it; unilateral action cannot be justified by a good-faith, but mistaken belief that impasse exists. Whether "irreconcilable differences" exist is a substantive question, involving a state-of-mind evaluation. However, a procedural requirement of "sufficiently exhaustive" negotiations must also be met. The criteria are vague and a well-counseled union can generally forestall a finding of impasse for some time by offering modifications.

2. Impasse and Bad Faith Bargaining

An employer that causes an impasse (or a "breakdown in negotiations") by bad faith bargaining cannot then take advantage of the results of this violation to impose a unilateral change. In several cases, an employer's unilateral change in wages or other conditions of employment has been found violative of section 8(a)(5) when the impasse resulted from the employer's bad faith bargaining.[33] Union bad faith on the other hand will justify unilateral action without going through "exhaustive negotiations."

3. Unilateral Action After Impasse

When impasse occurs, the employer may act unilaterally. The changes that the employer implements must be those that the union rejected. An employer is not permitted to bargain to impasse and then initiate changes more favorable to the employees.[34] He may make changes clearly more favorable to himself on the theory that this has already been rejected.[35]

Upon genuine impasse on the issue of wages, an employer is free not only to raise wages but to lower them as well. Impasse must be on the issue of wages itself before a unilateral change in wages is allowable. If impasse exists on this issue alone, with the parties continuing to negotiate on other issues, the impasse will be sufficient to allow a unilateral reduction in wages by the employer.[36]

D. The Role of Exclusivity in Limiting Actions by Employees

1. Implications of Exclusivity for the Protected Status of Economic Pressure

Another major implication of exclusivity is that the protection of section 7 does not extend to economic pressure directed against the employer in support of bargaining demands by individuals or groups other than the incumbent union. Given that the employer commits an unfair labor practice if he bargains with subgroups or individuals, it would be unfair to deny him the right to self help to prevent or lessen the impact of such pressure. Even where employees have used independent economic pressure in order to support the union's bargaining position, the courts have generally held their action unprotected by section 7.[37] The reasons for this are not clear. The courts have justified this conclusion in terms of exclusivity but they have not really explained why actions that support the union's bargaining demand and that the union does not object to are in any way threatening to the union's status. Indeed, such pressure is often quite helpful to the union whose negotiators are then able to argue that unless their demands are met, the union will not be able to control its more militant members. It may be that the explanation for this phenomenon lies in the unarticulated premise that the employer who is now required to deal with the union in all major labor relation matters is entitled in return to have only a single ascertainable source of economic pressure. The employer can generally tell from the progress of negotiations whether a union-called strike is near and it can shape its conduct accordingly. It is arguable that the employer should be able to rely on this information particularly since he is limited in his ability to communicate directly with rank-and-file employees in a bargaining situation.

2. Exclusivity and Efforts to Combat Discrimination

In *Emporium Capwell Co. v. Western Addition Community Organization (WACO),*[38] the Supreme Court rejected the argument that an exception to the doctrine of exclusivity should be made for efforts by minority employees to negotiate with their employer concerning an end to racial discrimination.

In that case, a number of minority employees claimed that their employer was denying blacks promotions and good assignments. The workers were informed by both the union and the California Fair Employment Practices Committee of the availability of a contractual grievance procedure, which they were advised to follow. These employees refused to do so, claiming that it was inadequate to handle a systematic grievance of this kind. They held a press conference during which they denounced the store's employment policy as racist and then picketed it on successive Saturdays. They simultaneously distributed handbills urging customers not to patronize the store, refused to listen to the employer's warnings, ignored the advice of a union official that they rely on the grievance procedure called for in the collective bargaining agreement, and instead pressed their demands directly to the company president, who refused to "be drawn into such a matter." As a result of these activities, the two employees were discharged. The Court characterized the employees' behavior as the "decision by a handful of employees to bypass the grievance procedure in favor of attempting to bargain with their employer. . . ."[39]

The Court stated that efforts to bargain independently on any issue were inconsistent with the union's role of providing a forum in which employee positions were coordinated and were ultimately divisive of worker unity. "An employer confronted with bargaining demands from each of several minority groups would not . . . be able to agree to remedial steps satisfactory to all at once. Competing claims on the employer's ability to accommodate each group's demands . . . could only set one group against the other. . . ."

The Court rejected the argument that its decision left the minority employees vulnerable to domination by the union's majority, pointing out that under the duty of fair representation, the union was legally obliged to advance the interest of minority employees under the contract. The accommodation between the interests of the minority employees and the doctrine of exclusivity thus reached is inevitably a tenuous one, which might become too burdensome to the union or inadequate to protect the rights of minority employees depending upon the breadth given to the duty of fair representation. (This is discussed more fully in chapter three.) The doctrine of exclusivity does not prevent minority employees from seeking support within the unit, however, so long as no effort is made to bargain independently.

In *Dreis & Krump Mfg. Co., Inc. v. NLRB*,[40] an employee named Mayer with a pending grievance had been fired after distributing a message among his co-workers concerning his grievance. The Court said, "Mayer's grievance was pending, in accordance with established contractual procedures, and . . . the message he distributed to his fellow employees was consistent with orderly resolution of that grievance. Mayer sought no separate pact or negotiations with his employer; rather his activity was directed toward eliciting the support of his co-workers in the resolution of his grievance." The court characterized the purpose of Mayer's actions as being in furtherance of the contract grievance system, while noting that the purpose behind the actions of the employees in *Emporium Capwell* was to use economic pressure to compel the employer to bargain separately with the minority group.[41]

Similarly, in *NLRB v. Owners Maintenance Corp.*,[42] two Puerto Rican employees, Soto and Veve, were discharged for allegedly falsifying information on their employment applications. The Court held that post-discharge public leafletting before arbitration of their grievance concerning their discharge was a concerted activity protected under section 7. In its reasoning, the Court stated that the goal of leafletting was the enlistment of support for the employees' rights in the grievance proceedings and did not constitute separate bargaining as in *Emporium Capwell.* "Soto and Veve did not seek to undermine the established contractual grievance mechanism, but rather to make effective use of it."

One difficult question that remains concerns the ability of plaintiffs in class actions under Title VII to achieve special treatment for minority employees or job applicants. In some cases this has been permitted; in other cases it has been rejected on the basis of *Emporium Capwell.*[43]

E. Limits on Exclusivity Based on the Duty of Fair Representation

1. The Development of the Doctrine

In *Steele v. Louisville & Nashville R.R.*,[44] a case involving construction of the Railway Labor Act, the United States Supreme Court held that implicit in the concept of exclusivity was the obligation to represent all employees in the unit fairly and in good faith. "The exercise of the granted power to act on behalf of others involves the assumption toward them of the duty to exercise the power in their interest and behalf. . . ." The case involved an effort by a white union of railway workers to eliminate through negotiations the jobs of black workers who were represented by the union but who were not admitted to membership. The cases arose when there was no fair employment act under which this behavior could be remedied, and the Court plainly indicated that any other conclusion would render the basic scheme of the Railway Labor Act unconstitutional. In a case decided the same day as *Steele*,[45] the Court made clear that such a duty similarly existed under the NLRA even though neither the duty nor provision for its enforcement was spelled out. Initially the duty under the NLRA was enforced exclusively through litigation in the courts but after passage of the Taft–Hartley Amendments to the NLRA the Board held that breach of the duty violated sections 8(b)(1)(a), and (2) of the Act. The Supreme Court eventually held that violation of the duty under the NLRA could be remedied either through an unfair labor practice charge or through a section 301 action in court.

Although most of the early cases involved allegations of racial discrimination, the Court's language in describing the duty was never limited to such cases, and it was clear from the beginning that other forms of "invidious" discrimination were prohibited. It is well established that a union in its bargaining may not act to disadvantage employees based on race, gender, political opinions, or union activity, but in the context of negotiation it is still unclear how far beyond this the duty extends.

2. Affirmative Union Obligations to Overcome Unlawful Discrimination [46]

A union cannot acquiesce in unlawful employer discrimination based on race, ethnicity, or gender. Indeed, under the duty of fair representation a union is probably required to propose standards for overcoming past discrimination. It is not clear, however, how extensive this obligation is. It is settled that a union may propose a system of preference for women or minority group members to overcome the effects of past discrimination,[47] and it is arguable that a union that is aware of past unlawful discrimination against a portion of its membership is obliged to propose a significant remedy such as quotas or preferential treatment to remedy it. Neither the Board nor the courts have so held, however. If such an obligation existed, there would be the further question of whether the union was required to bargain to impasse in support of its proposal. It is likely that if a duty to propose significant remedies was included under the NLRA a union would be required either to bargain to impasse, or to take some legal action against the employer on behalf of the aggrieved employees.[48]

One important way to ensure that a union represents all employees fairly is to monitor the makeup of the union's bargaining committee. The bargaining committee generally plays a crucial role in deciding which proposals to insist on and which to withdraw. As a member of the negotiating team, an individual employee can influence the process by taking an active part in support of favored positions during union caucuses. The process by which employees are selected for membership on a bargaining team is complex, political, and delicate. It would probably place too heavy a burden on the process to insist that negotiating teams mirror the ethnic diversity and sexual make-up of the work force. However, if a union's bargaining committees has, over time, not included women or minority members in anywhere near their proportion in the work force, such an omission probably reflects either conscious or unconscious bias and has probably also affected the bargaining process in subtle but significant and harmful ways. In such a case, judicial supervision of the process of selection under the duty of fair representation would be appropriate.[49]

3. The Duty of Fair Representation and the Choice Between Competing Interests

Sooner or later in the bargaining process, a union must choose among competing employee interests. In formulating initial proposals, for example, the union generally will favor more experienced employees through clauses expanding the use of seniority as a basis for allocating benefits, selecting employees for promotion, and ordering layoffs. If the union chooses to seek percentage raises, it favors the more highly paid. If it seeks flat across-the-board increases, it aids the lower paid. Similar choices are made in the choice of the unit in which seniority is held. During the initial period of formulating proposals, this role may be masked by including something for everyone, in which case the painful choices concerning preferences are made when proposals are abandoned or altered in order to achieve agreement. A Chinese menu approach of something for everyone makes agreement more difficult, but it permits the union to blame the employer for the rejection of proposals favored by significant numbers of employees. In almost every union the process by which proposals are abandoned or reinforced is essentially a political one, and in almost every union during the course of negotiation disagreements arise that are settled through a complex internal negotiating process. Often this process is the most emotional and difficult part of the overall negotiations for union representatives. The result of the internal bargaining turns on such things as: (a) the number of members committed to a position (this gives an advantage to the rank and file); (b) the need for the support of particular members in the event of a strike (this gives preference to the more highly skilled—quarterbacks over linemen, sergeants over foot cops;) and (c) the ability of the directly effected groups to convince others, which may turn on the eloquence of their spokespeople and what is provided for in other contracts in the same industry. For the most part, this process of internal negotiation has proceeded without Board or judicial oversight through the duty of fair representation, which given the nature of the process seems a highly desirable result. There is, however, some authority suggesting that under certain circumstances selection of union bargaining positions might breach the duty of fair representation if the selection is made on the grounds of political expediency.

In *Barton Brands, Ltd. v. NLRB*,[50] an employer acquired a new facility, the employees of which had previously been members of a different local of the same union. The union initially proposed dovetailing the seniority rosters of the two units and the employer acquiesced. Thereafter the employees of the larger, acquiring unit became dissatisfied and during the next negotiation the union leadership canvassed the unit and on this basis proposed an endtailing system under which the employees who had worked for the acquired unit would be accorded less seniority than those of the larger unit "for the purposes of layoff and recall." The Board found and the Seventh Circuit agreed that the union's shift in proposal violated the duty of fair representation. The Court stated:

> "The record suggests that the union acted solely on grounds of political expediency in reducing the former . . . employees' seniority. While a union may make seniority decisions within a wide range of reasonableness . . . such decisions may not be made solely for the benefit of a stronger more politically favored group over a minority group. To allow such arbitrary decision making is contrary to the union's duty of fair representation which compensated employees for the opportunity to bargain for themselves."

The Court indicated that on remand the union could be "absolved of liability . . . [if it could] show some objective justification beyond that of placating the desires of the majority of the union employees at the expense of the minority."

The Court's use of the term "arbitrary" to describe union action based on canvassing the wishes of its members demonstrates the potential of legal terms to take on meanings far removed from their customary usage. It is difficult to understand the Court's casual, apparently unqualified, statement that it is "arbitrary" for a union to advance positions that might disadvantage some of the employees it represents because a majority of those in the union think it would be desirable from the standpoint of their own self-interest. The Court describes such a choice as "political" and demands justification on some more principled basis. Yet it is difficult to imagine a more or better principled basis for a democratic union than majority will. This is precisely the standard unions are expected to use. The fact that the majority is deciding on the basis of its own self-interest is neither unusual or improper. Unions use this standard regularly in favoring such things as minimum standards over merit pay. Indeed, the invariable use of seniority in promotions and layoffs is proposed by unions in part because it is favored by a majority of employees who recognize that it will give them an advantage over later hirees. It also will give senior rank-and-file employees an advantage over those in the work force who would do better under another system such as merit or skill. It is of course true that seniority provides an objective standard as a basis of preference, but seniority on the basis of time working for the contracting employer was the very standard urged for layoffs by the union in *Barton Brands.* It should also be noted that the union in *Barton Brands* was not seeking to sacrifice some employees to bring benefit to others. It was advocating a system for allocating the burdens if the employer decided that layoffs were necessary. It is difficult to know what standard the court would prefer. Normally when a union disfavors the interests of the majority, it is to win the support of an elite, specially skilled group (the quarterback and skilled trades people). Surely the courts would not require that unions adopt a principle favoring the skilled minority or one holding that the union does something improper when it chooses the interests of the unskilled rank and file. Imagine a union that opposes the introduction of new machinery because it would require special trained employees and might cost its members jobs. If the union sought to prevent the use of the new machinery, its actions would be lawful. The union could also lawfully oppose hiring new employees to work the machine. If the union proposed a clause that gave existing employees a preference over those hired to work the new machinery, such an approach would probably be viewed as a laudable effort to accommodate new technology while protecting the union's members. The difference in *Barton Brands* was that the employees of the acquired concern had already acquired seniority based on dovetailing and were already members of the unit with seniority represented by the union at the time that the entailing was decided upon. That was the basis of the decision. If so, however, the union and probably the old Barton employees were penalized because they made an initial effort to be generous in the allocation of seniority to the new employees— generosity that the employer's subsequent conduct made them regret. The message of the case to unions might therefore be to avoid the mistake of attempting to dovetail initially.

The reach of *Barton Brands* is not clear. Its language suggests that the duty of fair representation breached whenever a union chooses to advance the interests of the majority at the expense of other employees. As already noted, such choices are made regularly in collective bargaining. While the Board continues to rely on *Barton Brands* in similar situations, the courts have not. Neither the Board nor the courts have thus far shown any inclination to extend *Barton*

Brands and to use the concept of political decision-making to sit in judgment on the collective bargaining process, unions have been permitted to use either entailing or dovetailing of seniority rosters in member and acquisition cases without violation of the duty of fair representation being found.[51]

Part II. The Distinction Between Mandatory and Permissive Bargaining Topics

A. The Statutory Scheme as Developed by the Board and Courts

1. The Basic Distinction

Section 8(d) of the NLRA defines the duty to bargain as the obligation to "confer in good faith with respect to wages, hours, and other terms and conditions of employment. . . ."[52] The conference committee in adopting this language rejected a House version that attempted to specifically limit the subject matters appropriate for collective bargaining, adopting instead the view of the House minority report that the duty "cannot and should not be straitjacketed by legislative enactment."[53]

In *NLRB v. Wooster Division of Borg–Warner Corp.,*[54] the Supreme Court accepted the Board's distinction between mandatory and permissive subjects of bargaining.[56] The Court found that the company had bargained in good faith about statutorily required subjects, but that it had violated the Act since it refused to sign an agreement without two clauses that did not deal with wages, hours, or condition of employment. The Board concluded and the Court affirmed that

> "[s]uch conduct is, in substance, a refusal to bargain about the subjects that are within the scope of mandatory bargaining. This does not mean that bargaining is to be confined to the statutory subjects. Each of the two controversial clauses is lawful in itself. Each would be enforceable if agreed to by the unions. But it does not follow that, because the company may propose these clauses, it can lawfully insist upon them as a condition to any agreement."

The Court later described the general parameters of mandatory topics in *Allied Chemical Workers v. Pittsburgh Plate Glass*[57] as "issues that settle an aspect of the relationship between the employer and the employees."

2. The Concept of Non–Mandatory (Permissive) Topics

Topics of bargaining that are permissive (not illegal) but not mandatory tend to fall into three distinct spheres: those that concern employer-third party relations and are classified as outside the scope of union concerns; those that deal with union-employee relations, which are generally regarded as outside the scope of management concerns;

and efforts to change the Board determination as to the appropriate unit for collective bargaining, which are protected against both parties. Within the statutory area, triviality does not appear to be a valid objection to classifying issues as mandatory subjects. Thus, in *Ford Motor Co. v. NLRB*,[58] the Supreme Court held that in-plant food services and prices were a mandatory subject of bargaining. Food services and prices are plainly an aspect of the working environment, said the Court. This being the case, it was not a legitimate argument that the issue was not important enough to trigger the mandate to bargain. When the issue primarily implicates the employment relationship, it is for the parties to determine through collective bargaining how important the issue is to them.[59]

B. The Role of Management Prerogatives in Defining the Distinction

1. Limiting Statutory Language

The Act requires an employer to bargain with an incumbent union with respect to "wages, hours and conditions of employment." The reach of this language sets the boundaries protected by the concept of exclusivity. The question that has recurred most frequently in its interpretation concerns the impact of this language on investment decisions. The Board has historically applied a broad definition of "terms and conditions," imposing a duty to bargain over those economic decisions affecting the job security of workers. Decisions to mechanize,[60] to "consolidate" operations,[61] to discontinue product lines and departments,[62] to partially close down operations,[63] and to subcontract out work,[64] have all been held by the Board to be mandatory subjects of bargaining, even where economically motivated. The clearest statement of this rationale occurs in *Ozark Trailers*,[65] a plant closing case:

> "For, just as the employer has invested capital in the business, so the employee has invested years of his working life, accumulating seniority, accruing pension rights, and developing skills that may or may not be salable to another employer. And, just as the employer's interest in the protection of his capital investment is entitled to consideration in our interpretation of the Act, so too is the employee's interest in the protection of his livelihood."

The approach received a mixed reception, at best, by the courts of appeals. Several circuits limited the duty to bargain to decisions that did not involve basic changes in operations. They reversed the Board's imposition of a duty to bargain where they found that "economics reasons" motivated a partial or complete cessation of operations.[66]

The Fifth Circuit, on the other hand, at one time approved Board findings of a duty to bargain over partial plant closings despite "sound business reasons" for such decisions.[67] The decision, however, revealed the court's ambivalent approach. Because the court found that the company would undoubtedly refuse "for good and sufficient reasons" to reestablish the closed operations, it viewed negotiations as an "exercise in futility" and refused to enforce the Board's order to bargain despite its agreement with the Board's holding.

The Supreme Court, which at one time seemed to favor collective bargaining in situations in which basic job rights were at stake, more recently has carved out upon an extensive area for unilateral management action. The Court, without either empirical evidence or sophisticated economic analysis, has assumed that greater efficiency is achieved in this way.

2. From *Fibreboard* to *First National Maintenance*

The Court's first major decision, defining the bargaining obligation of employers with respect to decisions affecting job rights, was *Fibreboard v. NLRB*,[68] which dealt with a decision to subcontract out maintenance work previously done by unit employees. The Court held this to be a mandatory bargaining topic: "The words [terms and conditions of employment] . . . plainly cover termination of employment which, as the facts of this case indicate, necessarily results from the contracting out of work performed by members of the established bargaining unit."

The holding was a narrow one, imposing a duty to bargain over "the replacement of employees in the existing bargaining unit with those of an independent contractor to do the same work under similar conditions of employment." Some of the Court's language suggested a broader reach for the language of section 8(d), which led Justice Stewart to write a special concurrence stressing that '[N]othing the Court holds today should be understood as imposing a duty to bargain collectively regarding managerial decisions, which lie at the core of entrepreneurial control. Decisions concerning the commitment of investment capital and the basic scope of the enterprise are not in themselves primarily about conditions of employment."[69]

The strongly contrasting strains in *Fibreboard* (one stressing the breadth of section 8(d), the other focusing on the interests of management) allowed the Board and the courts wide latitude in applying *Fibreboard* to subsequent cases. The *Fibreboard* decision was a source of disagreement for the courts of appeals, particularly with respect to the question of plant closing.

In *Brockway Motor Trucks v. NLRB*,[70] the Third Circuit concluded that there was a presumption of a duty to bargain over plant shutdowns where the employer has more than one plant. The presumption could be rebutted by evidence of dire economic necessity or the actions of a third party that would make bargaining an "exercise in futility." [71]   The Supreme Court rejected this approach in *First National Maintenance Corp. v. NLRB.* [72]

In considering whether the scope of the duty to bargain should include a management decision to close part of its operation, the Court noted the importance of these decisions for workers, but it stated: "Nonetheless, in view of an employer's need for unencumbered decisionmaking, bargaining over management decisions that have a substantial impact on the continued availability of employment should be required only if the benefit, for *labor-management relations and the collective bargaining process,* outweighs the burden placed on the conduct of the business." The Supreme Court distinguished three kinds of management decisions. Some decisions are "almost exclusively an aspect of the relationship between employer and employee" and are mandatory subjects of bargaining. Other decisions "have only an indirect and attenuated impact on the employment relationship" and thus are clearly permissive subjects of bargaining. Finally, other decisions directly affect the very existence of jobs and yet may involve "a change in the scope and direction of the enterprise." Regarding these decisions, the majority concluded that "Congress had no expectation that the elected union representative would become an equal partner in the running of the business enterprise in which the union's members are involved." The benefit to the process of collective bargaining was to be measured by the extent to which it served the main aim of the Act of maintaining industrial peace.

The Court then balanced the benefit to the process of bargaining against the employer's interest in unfettered discretion, and found that there was no duty to bargain over decisions to close part of the employer's operations.

"We conclude that the harm likely to be done to an employer's need to operate freely in deciding whether to shut down part of its business purely for economic reasons outweighs the incremental benefit that might be gained through the union's participation in making the decision, and we hold that the decision itself is not part of § 8(d)'s 'terms and conditions,' . . . over which Congress has mandated bargaining."

The majority opinion concluded that the interests of the union were adequately protected by requiring bargaining over the "effects" of the company's decision which bargaining, the Court stated, "must be conducted in a meaningful manner in a meaningful time." What is striking about this opinion is the Court's purporting to find a commitment to economic efficiency in an Act historically supported on other grounds and its equation of efficiency with unilateral management decision.

Although the Court purported to "intimate no view as to other types of management decisions, such as plant relocations, sales, other kinds of subcontracting automation, etc. . . . ," the rationale is a general one resting on the conclusion that "[m]anagement must be free from the constraints of the bargaining process to the extent essential for the running of a profitable business," and the rationale easily extended beyond the already wide range of decisions characterizable as "partial closings."

The Court reasoned that the union's efforts in bargaining would be directed toward overturning the decision. Where labor costs were a significant factor and union concessions might therefore have some impact, management would have an incentive to bargain voluntarily. Where labor costs were not a significant factor, bargaining would be an exercise in futility, since the employer is not required to make any concessions. The Court concluded that the process was not served by compelling fruitless discussions that might burden employer decision-making without the likelihood of changing or improving it.

3. The Board's Application of *First National Maintenance*

In *Otis Elevator Co.,*[73] the current Board made clear that it would follow the Supreme Court's lead in restricting the area of mandatory bargaining under section 8(d) in order to permit unilateral, economically motivated management decisions. The case involved an employer's decision to transfer work from its New Jersey to its Connecticut facility. The Board found that the decision was not based on labor costs and thus even though labor costs were one of the factors stimulating the original consideration, the decision was not one amenable to change through collective bargaining. The Board sought to draw a sharp distinction between decisions based on labor costs and those based upon either technological or entrepreneurial considerations. It therefore announced that henceforth "all decisions affecting the direction, scope, or nature of a business will be treated as nonmandatory topics unless they turn upon labor costs, and the employer will be free to make such decisions without bargaining with the union about them. The employer will however be required to bargain about the effects of its decision." It is difficult to imagine a managerial decision that an employer is not free to make unilaterally after this opinion, whether a decision about subcontracting, consolidating, terminating a part of a business, or merging lines of production, because virtually all managerial decisions can be explained as based on considerations other than labor costs. In order to protect the jobs of its members, unions will be required to seek contract clauses limiting employer discretion even though insisting upon such clauses would under current doctrine probably constitute an unfair labor practice.

Both *Otis Elevator* and *First National Maintenance* may be seen as part of a retreat by the Board and the courts from their original approach under the Act of broad support for collective bargaining to a new position whereby collective bargaining is seen as a form of interference with managerial efficiency.

C. Decision Bargaining vs. Effects Bargaining

The practical significance of the *First National Maintenance* decision turns in large part on the difference between decision bargaining and effects bargaining, a distinction that has not yet been clearly defined.

1. The General Concept

As stated by the Third Circuit in *NLRB v. Royal Plating and Polishing Co.*,[74] the purpose of effects bargaining was to give the union "an opportunity to bargain over the rights of the employees whose employment status will be altered by the managerial decision." The court observed that "issues such as severance pay, seniority and pensions, among others, are necessarily of particular relevance and importance" in bargaining over effects. The Board has long maintained an analogous position.[75] As these authorities themselves indicate, effects bargaining is not limited to the issues enumerated above, but encompasses "any and all" effects of the decision.[76] The most important of these effects are opportunities for continued employment at the employer's other facilities. As the Second Circuit observed in its opinion in *Cooper Thermometer Co. v. NLRB*:[77]

> "[T]he Board may reasonably interpret § 8(a)(5) as explicated in § 8(d), as requiring an employer relocating his plant not merely to give reasonable notice to a recognized union and to negotiate the terms of the shutdown, but also to discuss with it the basis on which employees may transfer and, in that connection, to give information as to jobs in the new plant essential to the intelligent formulation of the union's requests. The most important interest of workers is in working; the Board may reasonably consider that an employer does not fulfill his obligations under § 8(a)(5) if he refuses even to discuss with employees' representatives on what basis they may continue to be employed."

The employer's duty to furnish necessary information attaches in the context of effects bargaining and the same tests outlined for imposition of the duty apply.[78] Accordingly, through a carefully framed request, the bargaining agent has the right of access to a broad scope of information.

2. When the Duty Attaches

The key to the distinction between "effects bargaining" and "decision bargaining" is the issue of timing. At what point must the employer notify the union of its intent to close down. If a union learns of the employer's plan before definitive action has been taken, it is in a position to raise counter proposals, seek to participate in a buy out, offer to reduce labor costs, or apply economic pressure in an effort to get the employer to change its mind. Theoretically, the employer may respond differently to union proposals under the two types of bargaining. It must discuss the alternatives under decision bargaining but may refuse to do so under effects bargaining. Whatever the standard, however, an employer is likely to explain the basis for its decision and to consider any union counterproposal seriously if there is a realistic chance of a union concession changing it. Under decision bargaining an employer whose mind is made up need only respond seriously to the union to meet his obligation, an approach he is almost certain to take under effects bargaining.

The duty to decision bargain requires that the employer give the union "advance notice of its intention to close and provide the Union with a fair opportunity to bargain." [79] How much advance notice is required is unclear. The cases seem to indicate the duty arises when the decision "is under active consideration and [is] imminent." [80] The cases also indicate that the determination is to be on a case-by-case basis. Thus, in *Royal Typewriter Co.,*[81] for example, the Board concluded that the respondent had failed to bargain in good faith where it gave the union only eight days notice before announcing its decision to partially terminate operations.

In *Town and Country,*[82] the Board stated that "[n]o genuine bargaining . . . can be conducted where [the] decision has already been made and implemented." The Sixth Circuit, in *Weldtronic Co. v. NLRB,*[83] stated that "[t]he duty to bargain came into play prior to removal of the work." [84]

As with the duty to decision bargain, the effects bargaining cases announce no set time for notification, but require that it be delivered sufficiently in advance of the effectuation of the decision "to give the union a meaningful chance to offer counter-proposals and counter-arguments." [85] As in the decision bargaining context, "when a union has sufficiently clear and timely notice of the employer's plan" it waives its rights if it fails to request bargaining.[86] Thus, the cases do not show a clear difference between decision and effects bargaining with regard to timing.

Under either system, the employer has the duty to give the union advance notice of its intention to cease operations and must provide it with an opportunity to bargain. The cases indicate that the employer's notice of intent must be specific: "An employer has not met its duty where, during negotiations, it merely makes a limited reference to the possibility of a closing." [87] Once such notice has been given, however, the burden is upon the union to demand bargaining.

In sum, the differences between "effects" and "decision" bargaining are unclear and fairly subtle and litigation may be expected, particularly over the question of the timing of notice necessary for adequate effects bargaining. In the meantime, it is not clear what the practical significance of the distinction will be.

D. Bargaining for Retired Employees

The Supreme Court in *Allied Chemical Workers v. Pittsburgh Plate Glass Co.,* eliminated from the range of mandatory bargaining topics changes in the benefits to be given retired employees. It stated that the duty to bargain "extends only to the terms and conditions of employment of the employers' 'employees' in the unit appropriate for such purposes' which the union represents." [88] The Court held that this excluded retirees from those "whose ongoing benefits are embraced by the bargaining obligation of § 8(a)(5)."

The decision in *Pittsburgh Plate Glass* did not affect bargaining over pension benefits for current members of the unit, which is a mandatory bargaining subject. Once an employee retires, however, the union can no longer insist upon bargaining on his behalf. The Court rejected the argument made by the Board that "the benefits granted retired employees are mandatory subjects of bargaining because they vitally affect . . . active employees;" the Court described the impact on current employees as "speculative and unsubstantiated at best." The technical nature of the opinion makes it difficult to understand the policy basis which must have been crucial to the conclusion. Certainly the Court easily could have accepted the Board's conclusion concerning the nexus between the interests of current and retired employees. Perhaps the opinion was motivated by concern that the interest of retired employees would be sacrificed by the union on behalf of current members who vote in union elections. If such a concern lies behind the decision, it is shortsighted. It ignores the legal protection available for retired employees through the law of contracts (ERISA) and the duty of fair representation, and it ignores the realities of labor relations. A union could not break faith with its retired members without creating unhappiness and anxiety among current members. Current members who anticipate retirement in the near future would necessarily be unwilling to accept a program that jeopardized the security of their retirement benefits. Furthermore, the Court's opinion ignores the sense of community and concern that in almost all unions bind current and retired members.

E. Protecting the Autonomy of Union–Employee Relations

In *NLRB v. Borg–Warner,*[89] the Supreme Court employed the newly-elaborated distinction between mandatory and permissive subjects for the first time to preserve the capacity of the union to act autonomously within the collective bargaining process. The employer had insisted successfully on two clauses: a ballot clause, requiring a strike vote on the employer's last offer; and a recognition clause, substituting the union local as the bargaining agent for the Board-certified international union. Because these clauses did not deal with the employer-employee relationship and could only have the effect of reducing the capacity of the union to negotiate with the employer, the Court held they were outside section 8(d)'s list of mandatory subjects.

Borg–Warner has been extended to render non-mandatory any employer demand that interferes with the ability of union officials to negotiate independently of the membership. The Sixth Circuit, in holding an employer's insistence on a ratification clause violative of 8(a)(5) in *Houchens Market v. NLRB*,[90] noted that

> "the Company . . . was attempting to bargain . . . with respect to a matter which was exclusively within the internal domain of the Union. Members of a Union have the right to determine the extent of authority delegated to their bargaining unit. . . . It is not an issue which the Company can insist upon without mutual agreement by the Union, any more than the Union can insist that the contract be submitted to the Board of Directors of the shareholders of the Company."

Similarly, the employer cannot insist that bargaining be contingent on a union committee acceptable to the employer, and thus exclude representatives of other unions from observing negotiations with the union representing its employees. In *General Electric Co. v. NLRB*,[91] Judge Feinberg observed that the "right of employees . . . to choose whomever they wish to represent them in formal labor negotiations is fundamental to the statutory scheme. . . . There have been exceptions to the general rule that either side can choose bargaining representatives freely, but they have been rare and confined to situations so infected with ill-will . . . or conflict of interest as to make good faith bargaining impracticable." Absent some "clear and present danger" to the bargaining process posed by the union's choice of representatives, the statutory concern for union autonomy precludes employer interference with this choice. Nor can the union insist upon influencing the employer's choice.

Another aspect of the Board's solicitude for union autonomy is its unwillingness to allow the employer to condition bargaining on the financial solvency of the union. Thus, demands for performance bonds, liquidated damages clauses, and indemnity provisions for violation of no-strike pledges have consistently been held to be permissive subjects only.[92] As the Board stated in *Excello Dry Wall Co.*,[93] "The statutory obligation to bargain is not limited and cannot be limited to financially responsible parties, whether employer or labor union." [94]

F. Clauses Affecting the Integrity of the Bargaining Unit

The mandatory/permissive distinction has been used to protect section 9(b) unit determinations. Judge Bazelon articulated the policy considerations behind this conclusion in *Oil Chemical and Atomic Work-*

ers Int'l Union v. NLRB,[95] which held that an oil company could not be required to meet at a single time and place with nineteen independently certified locals to bargain about company-wide fringe benefits: "Under Section 9(b), the task of designating the appropriate unit for the purposes of collective bargaining belongs exclusively to the National Labor Relations Board. While it has been held that the parties may agree to consolidate units for purposes of collective bargaining, respect for the stability of industrial relations imported by the Board's determination has led to the rule that a party may not be forced to bargain on other than a unit basis."[96]

If each unit is strong enough in isolation to insist on its demands, coordination can be achieved by pressing identical demands. Thus, the Fifth Circuit allowed three units to insist on common contract expiration dates in order to strengthen their bargaining position.[97]

Unions have tried to condition their acceptance of the employer's offer on receiving similar proposals from another employer, usually a subsidiary. The circuits appear divided on this tactic. The Third Circuit held the union could condition settlement on simultaneous, satisfactory settlements elsewhere, reasoning that separate negotiations had been held in all locations and that parallel action is not an attempt to merge units: "The fact that a demand may have extra-unit effects does not alter its status as a mandatory subject of bargaining."[98] The Sixth Circuit agreed with the Board, however, that where a union withheld consideration of all offers from each of three subsidiaries until they got identical offers from all, it violated its duty to bargain by insisting on the permissive subject of multi-unit bargaining.[99]

G. The Practical Significance of the Mandatory/Permissive Distinction at the Bargaining Table

1. What Constitutes Unlawful Insistence

It is clearly unlawful to explicitly condition either an agreement or the willingness to negotiate on acceptance of a non-mandatory demand. It is also unlawful to tie the acceptance of a single mandatory proposal to the acceptance of a party's position on a permissive topic. It is unclear what conduct short of this explicit conditioning will be found unlawful by the Board and courts.

In general, the further the parties are from agreement on mandatory issues, the more insistent they may be on permissive demands. The closer they come to an agreement, the more likely they are to violate the law by maintaining their position on a nonmandatory topic. In *Union Carbide,*[100] the company stated that its "final offer" was "not to be juggled, would not pull out anything or put in something else (sic)."[101] The "final offer" contained an important non-mandatory demand. The Board reversed the trial examiner's conclusion of unlawful insistence on a permissive topic

based on its finding of total irreconcilability of the parties. Then–
Judge Burger for the D.C. Circuit enforced the Board's decision,
agreeing with the irreconcilability, finding and emphasizing the company's good faith in attempting to reach an agreement. He found that
given this good faith, the company's "less than subtle emphasis" on
the permissive demand did not constitute a violation.[102] No mention
was made of the *Borg–Warner* majority's holding that the subjective
good faith of a party does not justify its insistence on a permissive
bargaining topic.

Similarly, in *GIA, Inc.,*[103] the parties were engaged in their first
bargaining attempt after an NLRB election. One of the company's
demands was for a "no strike clause," which included unfair labor
practice strikes and a binding arbitration provision, which the trial
examiner and Board assumed (without finding) was a non-mandatory
bargaining topic. After many sessions, thirty items remained open,
including all economic issues, and the parties made an attempt to
salvage the situation through mediation, which failed. The union
suggested to the mediator that it would accept all of the company's
non-economic proposals except the non-mandatory bargaining topics.
The company responded that there were too many open issues and so
it couldn't understand what the suggestion meant. The Board's
conclusions about the significance of these transactions were as follows:

> "The evidence is clear that at the last negotiation session
> which occurred on April 5, 1977, the Union made an attempt to
> offer to Respondent an acceptance of all noneconomic items
> which were contained in Respondent's proposal, in trade for
> withdrawal of Respondent's no-strike clause. It appears that this
> offer was presented to the Federal mediator. However, the
> uncontradicted evidence is that the Federal mediator never pre
> sented the offer as such to Respondent, nor did Respondent
> refuse said offer. What the Federal mediator communicated to
> Respondent's representative privately was certainly not compre
> hended as an offer by Respondent.

> The parties are in complete accord that the Union represen
> tative never attempted to present his offer directly to Respondent,
> nor did Respondent communicate any refusal of any offer directly
> to the charging party. It is clearly established in this record that
> there were no face-to-face negotiations between the parties of any
> kind, in any way, shape or form, during this last session. In fact
> the Union, Respondent, and the mediator acknowledged that
> there were too many open items existing."

Given mediators' uniform practice of protecting confidentiality and
general willingness to test proposals informally, this case and the cases
dealing with package proposals create usable strategies for signaling

the insistence upon a non-mandatory topic without bargaining to impasse. The cases currently suggest that to be guilty of unlawful insistence on a non-mandatory topic, a party either must insist on the permissive demand explicitly or must refuse an offer that is essentially identical to its last offer, minus the non-mandatory topic. Thus the impact of the distinction on the bargaining process is to create an obstacle for the uninformed, but not for the skillfully counseled.

2. Discussion of Permissive Topics

If acceptance of a non-mandatory proposal is of importance to either side, it generally is easy to signal that fact to the other side without violating the law. In mature relationships, an important part of the process of collective bargaining takes place through informal, off-the-record discussions between the chief negotiators or high level officials. It is understood and respected that these conversations are not to be used as the basis for filing charges. During the course of such discussions, it is important for each side to find out what the other will give up in order to get one of its key proposals accepted. If a management negotiator discovers that a union will lower its demands significantly in exchange for acceptance of a non-mandatory topic, she is obligated to discuss this with her principals and if they reject the concept to notify and explain the rejection to the union. If the parties are later formally at impasse over wages, the same informal, unofficial channels may be used to make clear that the union will change its posture if management makes a counterproposal dealing with the non-mandatory topic. Because it is easy enough to avoid the distinction in this way, in mature relationships it is sometimes explicitly ignored. Sometimes the negotiators will simply announce "we are not required to bargain, but this is what we are prepared to do," thereby preserving their legal position while bargaining over the issue. In sum, it is rarely the case that the distinction prevents discussion or even informal insistence. What it does do is provide a legal technique by which a subsequent strike may either be made unlawful (if a union insists on a permissive clause in which case the employees may be discharged) or be turned into an unfair labor practice strike (if management refuses to discuss a mandatory proposal, in which case the employees may not be permanently replaced).

Part III. The Role of Law in Insuring Good Faith Bargaining

A. Defining Good Faith

The terms "good faith" and "bad faith" are difficult to define. They do not easily correspond to the potential states of mind with which an employer may approach negotiations. Some courts have attempted to offer a seemingly straightforward distinction based on the employer's willingness to come to an agreement. Judge Magruder first articulated this standard in *NLRB v. Reed Prince,*[104] defining bad faith as the "desire not to reach an agreement." The simplicity of the definition is deceptive, however, unless it is limited to an employer who is determined not to sign an agreement regardless of the concessions that the union is prepared to make. Bargaining with the goal of not reaching an agreement is generally referred to as "surface bargaining." The vast majority of employers involved in surface bargaining cases make some proposals and there is some agreement which they would be willing if not eager to accept. Thus, if the mere willingness to accept some proposals would be enough, it would almost never be possible to prove bad faith bargaining. An employer can easily devise a contract proposal containing a very strong management-rights clause together with a no-strike clause, which would put the union in a weaker position and the employer in a stronger position than they would be in if no agreement was reached. Under such a proposal the union loses the right to strike and the employer is able to take unilateral action with respect to the matter covered by the management-rights clause. Much of the case law dealing with section 8(a)(5) addresses the question of what beyond a willingness to sign such an agreement is necessary in order to establish good faith for an employer. The cases have essentially focused on three questions which may be present separately or in combination:

1. Are there substantive limitations on how favorable to himself or unaccommodating to the union the contract that the employer is willing to sign may be?

2. Must the employer make concessions in bargaining?

3. Are there forms and procedures that must be adhered to in bargaining to avoid the risk of being found to have failed to bargain in good faith?

B. The Elements of Good Faith

1. Reasonableness of Proposals

Neither the Board nor the courts have been consistent in considering the relationships between substantive proposals and good faith. In general, both hold that the reasonableness of proposals is not relevant, but that the proposals may be looked to in determining whether evidence exists of a sincere desire to reach an agreement.

The issue of the Board's ability to find bad faith on the basis of employer proposals is much like the evaluation of employer speech in that there have been great differences within the Board, between the Board and the courts, and among the courts themselves. The Supreme Court has never ruled on this issue directly, although it has indirectly suggested both the legitimacy and impropriety of the Board's considering the reasonableness of employer proposals. Thus, in *NLRB v. American National Insurance Co.,*[105] the Court overturned the Board's finding that the employer's insistence upon a very broad management-rights clause was proof of bad faith. The Court instructed the Board not to pass upon the desirability of the substantive terms of an agreement. The Court has also stressed in other contexts the absence of the Board's power to insist upon reasonable bargaining behavior. At the same time, the Court itself in evaluating surface bargaining cases has considered whether the proposals contained clauses usually found in other contracts.[106]

The courts of appeals are also split. The First Circuit explicitly recognized the legitimacy of considering reasonableness in *NLRB v. Reed Prince,* in which Judge Magruder stated that "if the Board is not to be blinded by . . . surface notions of collective bargaining, it must take some cognizance of the reasonableness of the positions taken by an employer in the course of negotiations."

On the other hand, the Fifth Circuit has shown great reluctance to permit the Board to inquire into reasonableness, and it has regularly concluded that the breadth of the management-rights clause is not a valid indication of bad faith. The court has expressed the view that to do otherwise would be the first step towards permitting the Board to play the role of arbitrator in determining the outcome of negotiations. In *White v. NLRB,*[107] the Fifth Circuit overturned a Board ruling that had found sufficient evidence of bad faith bargaining in the company's insistence upon a management-rights clause that retained all power to make decisions, together with the company's unwillingness to yield on any substantial points. Subsequent Fifth Circuit decisions indicate a continued reluctance to impute bad faith on the basis of even very one-sided contract proposals in the absence of additional evidence.

Thus in *Chevron Oil Co. v. NLRB,*[108] the company insisted on a broad management-rights clause, a no-strike provision, and a grievance procedure that did not provide for arbitration. The Fifth Circuit found only a case of "hard bargaining between two parties who were possessed of disparate economic power" and no "substantial evidence on the record as a whole to support the Board's finding that the Company went through the motions of negotiation as an elaborate pretense with no sincere desire to reach an agreement."

In *NLRB v. United Clay Mines Corp.,* the Sixth Circuit took a similar position.[109] Noting that the company had met promptly and otherwise cooperated with the union in establishing bargaining procedures, the Court overturned the Board and held that the company's insistence both on a no-strike clause and on retention of the final decision on all grievances was not an indication of bad faith, but only of hard bargaining.[110] In *Kayser–Roth Hosiery Co. v. NLRB,*[111] however, the Sixth Circuit enforced without opinion a Board finding of bad faith that was based largely on the unreasonableness of the company's position.[112] Relying on Judge Magruder's opinion in *Reed & Prince,* the Board found that the company's insistence on a strong management-rights clause, a no-strike clause, and no arbitration was a proposal no self-respecting union could accept and was indicative of a "calculated intent to eliminate from any meaningful consideration the entire principle of union recognition."

Decisions in other circuits have also relied on the unreasonableness of employer proposals as evidence of bad faith. The Seventh Circuit in *NLRB v. Wright Motors, Inc.,*[113] upheld the Board's finding that the employer had insisted in bad faith on unreasonable positions to avoid negotiating on economic issues. Though it acknowledged the principle that the Board and the courts should not "sit in judgment on the substantive terms offered by parties negotiating in good faith," the court reasoned that "[s]ometimes, especially if the parties are sophisticated, the only indicia of bad faith may be the proposals advanced and adhered to."

Ninth Circuit decisions have also followed the *Reed and Prince* reasoning. Though indicating that the company's insistence on unilateral control of such basic subjects as wages and hours was not itself a violation, the court in *A.H. Belo Corp. (WFFA–TV) v. NLRB,* accepted such insistence as "a circumstance which may be considered by the Board in determining whether a party has bargained in good faith." [114]

2. Proper Forms and Procedures

The enforcement of section 8(a)(5) historically has been tied to the Board's conclusion that certain methods of negotiating are essential to good faith bargaining and certain others are highly correlated with it. A behavioral model of what constitutes good faith is implicit in the cases. While conformity with the model in all particulars is not crucial, any departure from it is likely to be closely scrutinized, and certain departures automatically constitute an unfair labor practice. The Board's model of the reasonable employer bargainer is as follows: the employer meets promptly and regularly with the union on company time, works through the union bargaining committee, and does not attempt to create division between it and the membership by making direct appeals to the rank and file. He responds to the union's proposals with counterproposals that are not so outrageous as to create animosity, but which he anticipates he will amend further during the course of negotiations. His positions are explained patiently by the company's negotiator, who has sufficient authority to conclude an agreement. When tentative agreements are reached during negotiations, they are not later withdrawn. When factual claims are made, any evidence bearing on them is made available to the union, as is other information necessary for the union to bargain successfully. There is a strong focus on reasoned, informed discussion.

a. Explanation and Counterproposals

Bargaining conduct by an employer will be held violative of 8(a) (5) if the employer refuses to explain his position or to set forth counterproposals embodying the terms and conditions of employment to which he would agree.[115] The Board has made it clear that good faith requires some kind of counteroffer from an employer, if only one proposing existing wages and working conditions.[116]

After some counterproposals have been made, the employer may usually stand fast. Thus in *Dierk Forests, Inc.*,[117] no violation was found because the "respondent submitted numerous counterproposals, discussed at length the Union's various proposals, and where the Respondent remained adamant on an issue, it gave the reasons for its position. . . ." Similarly, in *Philip Carey Mfg. Co.*,[118] the Board held there was no breach of 8(a)(5) where the employer made a firm, final offer subsequent to a lengthy process of negotiation involving offers and counteroffers. "That the Respondent regarded its offer as final is a matter of its own judgment. One need not listen to argument endlessly. There comes a point in any negotiation where the positions of the parties are set and beyond which they will not go."

b. Adherence to Agreement

In *Hartford Fire Ins. Co.*,[119] after three bargaining sessions characterized by offers and counteroffers, the employer refused to make any further counterproposals, although it alleged it had some. When Hartford retreated from previously agreed items, the Board found that these two tactics combined indicated that the employer had no intention of reaching an agreement and was in bad faith.

This latter tactic of engaging in negotiations and withdrawing previously made concessions when agreement is reached on other terms is frequently used by the Board as an indication of bad faith.[120] The courts, however, generally have held that withdrawal of concessions does not automatically constitute bad faith: "The withdrawal, without good cause, of previously agreed-to proposals can be strong evidence that the employer is merely stringing the Union along and that it is not bargaining with the good faith intent to reach an agreement. But we have recognized that the withdrawal of previous proposals . . . does not establish per se the absence of good faith. . . . The Employer's action must be viewed in the context of the negotiations in which they arose." [121]

There is, moreover, a line of cases holding that an employer's adamant insistence on a fixed position is perfectly consistent with the duty to bargain in good faith. In *NLRB v. Herman Sausage Co.*,[122] the Court noted that "[i]f the insistence on the inclusion or exclusion of a proposed contract term is genuinely and sincerely held, if it is not mere window dressing, it may be maintained forever though it produce a stalemate. Deep conviction, firmly held and from which no withdrawal will be made . . . may be both the right of the citizen and essential to our economic legal system, thus far maintained, of free collective bargaining."

Thus, the cases do not indicate with any consistency how far an employer may go in insisting upon its own proposals.

c. THE DUTY TO FURNISH INFORMATION

In general an employer is required to furnish the union with information necessary for the union to bargain effectively. Failure to do so automatically constitutes a violation of section 8(a)(5).

(1) When the Duty to Furnish Information Arises

Relevance is one of the most important factors in any case involving the duty to disclose. Certain types of information, such as wage and related data for members of the bargaining unit, have been held to be so important to the employer-employee relationship that they are presumptively relevant.[123] However, "[i]f the information requested has no relevance to any legitimate union collective bargaining need, a refusal to furnish it could not be an unfair labor practice."[124] In this area the burden of proof is on the employer to show a lack of relevance or to adequately explain why the employer cannot produce the information in good faith.[125] On the other hand, when a union requests information that is not ordinarily relevant to its role as bargaining agent, then the burden of proof is on the union.[126]

If an employer claims "inability to pay" higher wages or the need to remain "competitive," the court will enforce an order requiring the company to supply such information as would "substantiate the [company's] position of its economic inability to pay the requested wage increase."[127] Basically, it is the employer's contentions that establish the relevance of the financial information. This reliance on the employer's claims to trigger the supplying of financial information puts a premium on sophistication. It would seem that information as to the employer's financial wellbeing is relevant to intelligent bargaining and should be available as to salary information on demand.

The courts also consider the form of the information requested by the union. An employer may offer the necessary information in a form designed to protect its legitimate interests. Bona fide claims as to why the information would not be released in the requested form coupled with offers to supply the information in a different form will be honored.[128]

(2) Claims of Confidentiality

Historically, employer claims of confidentiality of information have been rejected. In *Aluminum Ore Co. v. NLRB*,[129] the employer, claiming confidentiality, refused to supply job classifications, job descriptions, and past wage data. The appellate court said, "if there be any reasonable basis for the contention that this may have been confidential data of the employer before passage of the Act, it seems to us it cannot be so held in the face of the expressed social and economic purposes of the statute." Similarly, claims of confidentiality of wage data were summarily rejected in *Electric Auto–Lite Co.*,[130] and in several newspaper cases where it was also argued that the information should be kept confidential to protect the privacy interests of highly salaried writers and to prevent pirating of talent by competitors if salaries were made known.[131]

The most important case upholding claims of confidentiality is *Detroit Edison Co. v. NLRB*.[132] The Supreme Court, in that case, established a new limitation on the scope of Board remedies in cases involving the duty to disclose information relating to a pending grievance. A standardized psychological testing program had been used by the company to determine the suitability of specific employees for openings in technical positions. Since none of the senior applicants had passed the test, the employer filled the six positions with junior employees from another plant who had passed the test. The employer, however, refused to release the test questions, the actual employee answer sheets, and the scores linked to the names of the employees, but it did offer to release the score linked with the name of the employee who signed a waiver releasing the employer's psychologist from his pledge of confidentiality (the union declined to seek the releases).

The Board[133] and the appellate court[134] rejected the employer's contentions that the union's need for information was outweighed by the employees' privacy interests, the ethical obligations of the employer's industrial psychologist to keep the information confidential, and the employer's interest in keeping the scores secret because disclosure could cause the tests to become invalid. The Board ordered the company to give the union the right to use the tests and other materials to "the extent necessary to process and arbitrate the grievances . . . but not to copy the tests, or otherwise use them, for the purpose of disclosing the tests. . . ."[135]

The Supreme Court held that the Board had abused its discretion in ordering the employer to turn over the tests and answer sheets directly to the union, and it held that the employer had satisfied his statutory duty to disclose relevant information as to the test scores by offering to disclose them for any employee who signed a release.

Agreeing with the company's concerns as to the deterioration of the test's validity that disclosure could cause, the Court rejected the Board's argument that the order adequately protected the security of the tests.

Detroit Edison marked a significant departure from the then existing approach to claims of confidentiality. First, the Court overrode the Board's determination in favor of disclosure despite the fact that the material sought was relevant to the union's collective-bargaining role and safeguards were provided to protect the employer's interest. This suggests a new judicially enforced balance giving greater weight to confidentiality in future cases and giving less deference to Board determinations and to the role of the union than had previously been the case. For the first time the Court recognized a claim by the employer on behalf of employees as against the union, thus drawing a distinction between the employees and the union that previous case law had rejected. It seems clear that this determination is a part of a series of cases in which the Court in interpreting the Act has given less weight to collective bargaining and more to competing values.

3. The Significance of Different Elements of the Model

Certain of the behavioral components of the Board's model of good faith bargaining are legally more significant than others. Thus refusal to supply information to support claims or permit the union to bargain intelligently is a *per se* violation, while appeals to the rank and file are only evidence of bad faith. The withdrawal of concessions once made is somewhere in between. There is no obvious reason in terms of bargaining significance or state of mind why these differences exist. If these forms of behavior were analyzed as indirect measures of the employer's state of mind, there would be little basis for picking among them. An employer who refuses to divulge information might do so for reasons of confidentiality or as a bargaining tactic despite his willingness to come to agreement with the union. The Supreme Court in *NLRB v. Truitt Mfg. Co.,*[136] which established the significance of refusals to make information available, never explained why this form of behavior should be treated as demonstrating bad faith. The Court merely stated that "[g]ood faith bargaining necessarily requires that claims be honest. . . . [I]f . . . an argument is important enough to present in the give and take of bargaining, it is important enough to require some proof of its accuracy"—a statement that would make many negotiators smile.

4. The Alternate Model

Despite the many cases describing him, the "rational bargainer" is inconsistent with another model, that of the "fighting bargainer," which emerges principally from court cases.

The "fighting bargainer" seeks to obtain the most favorable agreement possible through the use of economic pressure—either strikes or lockouts. He is willing to sign an agreement, but only on terms extremely favorable to himself.[137] He does not so much seek to convince the other side of the wisdom of his position as to convince them that failure to accept his terms will lead to serious economic harm. The "fighting bargainer" model was most clearly enunciated in *NLRB v. Insurance Agents' Intern. Union.*[138] The union in that case, simultaneously with negotiations, engaged in intermittent strikes and slow down tactics; the Board had held that the union was not bargaining in good faith.[139] The Board stated that the "[r]espondent's reliance upon harassing tactics . . . for the avowed purpose of compelling the Company to capitulate to its terms is the antithesis of the reasoned discussion it was duty-bound to follow. Indeed, it clearly revealed an unwillingness to submit its demands to the consideration of the bargaining table where argument, persuasion, and the free interchange of views could take place." The Supreme Court accepted the Board's premise that the conduct was unprotected, but it rejected the Board's conclusion that the union violated section 8(a)(5).

The Court stated that the Board's approach proceeded from "an erroneous view of collective bargaining." "It must be realized that collective bargaining, under a system where the Government does not attempt to control the results of negotiations, cannot be equated with an academic collective search for truth." The Court argued that such use of the rational bargaining model would undercut the scheme of the Act, which relied heavily on economic pressure, and it would also inject the Board too much into the bargaining process. "[I]f the Board could regulate the choice of economic weapons that may be used as part of collective bargaining, it would be in a position to exercise considerable influence upon the substantive terms on which the parties contract. . . . [T]he Government might have to enter even more directly into the negotiation of collective agreements. Our labor policy is not presently erected on a foundation of government control of the results of negotiations . . . Nor does it contain a charter for the National Labor Relations Board to act at large in equalizing disparities of bargaining power. . . ."

In subsequent cases the Court held that the fighting bargaining model restricted not only the Board's use of section 8(a)(5) to regulate economic pressure, but also its ability under section 8(a)(3) and 8(a)(1) to evaluate employer economic pressure in the bargaining context. In *American Ship Building Co. v. NLRB,*[140] the Court held that an employer could legitimately lock out his employees after an impasse had been reached in order to get them to accept his bargaining demands, and in *NLRB v. Brown*[141] the Court affirmed the right of an employer to lock out its employees who were members of a union that had struck another member of the employer's multi-employer bargaining group. In both opinions the Court used language that embraced the fighting bargaining model and that rejected any major role for the Board in regulating the bargaining process either directly or through developing categories of permissible and impermissible economic pressure. "[T]he Act also contemplated resort to economic weapons should more peaceful measures not avail. Sections 8(a)(1) and (3) do not give the Board a general authority to assess the relative economic power of the adversaries in the bargaining process and to deny weapons to one party or the other because of its assessment of that party's bargaining power."

The fighting bargaining model, if extended to the limits of its logic, would severely restrict the Board's application of section 8(a)(3), which has historically regulated the employer's ability to respond to union activity in such a way as to punish people for engaging in it. There is considerable language in the *American Shipbuilding* case openly suggesting that the fighting bargainer model limits application of section 8(a)(3) almost exclusively to cases where the employer is motivated by a specific desire to chill unionism rather than by legitimate business motives that include advancement of his bargaining positions. In subsequent cases the Court has had to back away from the application of the fighting bargainer model in section 8(a)(3) and 8(a)(1) cases. It has recognized that the Board can pick and choose among economic weapons in terms of their likely impact on union activity.[142] Thus the fighting bargainer model is limited both by the policies of section 8(a)(3) and by those areas in which the court has embraced the rational bargaining model such as *NLRB v. Turitt Mfg. Co.*[143] Where bargaining negotiations are involved, there is thus no easy way to tell which approach the courts will accept in a particular case. In general, the courts seem to favor the fighting bargainer model over the rational bargainer model especially where the question involves the use of economic pressure; the Board's preference is the reverse, particularly where the employer's action seems to challenge the union status in some significant way.

C. The Duty to Bargain During the Term of an Agreement

1. The Basic Concept

The Board has stated frequently that the "duty to bargain" continues during the term of an existing agreement.[144] This means that absent clear contractual provisions to the contrary: (a) the parties are required to discuss proposals made by the other about matters not covered by the agreement; (b) the employer may not take unilateral action with respect to matters not covered by the agreement; (c) the parties are obliged to attempt to resolve grievances through the existing system.

The duty to discuss new proposals is only rarely of practical significance. There are a variety of reasons why this is so. New proposals that normally would come from the union are generally prohibited by a specific term in the agreement, either one under which the parties agree not to propose new clauses or under a provision through which the parties agree that the duty to bargain has been satisfied for the term of the agreement. Moreover, unions do not like to propose new clauses during the term of an agreement partly because it is difficult to arouse the type of support necessary to make bargaining credible and partly because of the fact that strikes during the term of an agreement are always prohibited either by an express clause or by implication from the grievance system. Without its ability to strike in support of its proposal the union's bargaining position is obviously a weak one.

2. Possible Employer Breaches During the Terms of an Agreement

a. REFUSALS TO DISCUSS UNION PROPOSALS

A union may offer a new proposal about a mandatory topic that the employer refuses to consider, leading to a charge that the employer by failing to discuss the proposal is violating his duty to bargain in good faith about such topics. The employer is likely to defend on one of two grounds: (a) that the contract gives him the right to deal with this area either directly or through the management-rights clause. Such clauses contain general language acknowledging the employer's overall ability to "manage the enterprise" and to make decisions in a variety of areas such as scheduling discipline investment, etc.; or (b) on the grounds that the union has waived the right to bargain over such issues by virtue of a clause in the collective agreement stating that the signing of the contract fulfills the employer's duty to bargain during the period the contract is in effect. Such a clause is referred to as a "zipper clause." Both management-rights clauses and the zipper clauses constitute waivers of the duty to bargain. Both will be given effect by the Board against a union's desire to open the contract.[145] The Board and the courts are currently favorable to the argument that signing a contract basically fulfills the employer's obligations to consider union proposals. The Act's preference for industrial stability favors broad interpretation of zipper clauses for these purposes.

b. UNILATERAL EMPLOYER ACTION DURING THE TERMS OF AN AGREEMENT

Unilateral action by an employer might violate section 8(a)(5), either because the contract does not deal with the matter, or because the contract prohibits the employer from taking such action and his doing so therefore constitutes a "modification" of the contract for purposes of section 8(d)(4).

During the late seventies and early 1980s, the Board used section 8(d) to limit the ability of employers to make substantial changes during the term of an agreement. Absent language specifically permitting it, the Board read contracts as including an implied agreement not to relocate or substantially modify operations. The current Board, in *Milwaukee Spring Div. of Illinois Coil Spring Co.,*[146] reversed this approach and held that absent specific language prohibiting it, employers were free to make such changes so long as they met their obligation to bargain over them to impasse if they were based on labor costs or over their effects if they were not. Moreover, not every breach of contract constitutes a modification. Modification occurs only when the employer's interpretation of the contract has significant lasting consequences for its continued enforcement. The Board defined a modification as a unilateral act that "effects a change which has a continuing impact on a basic term or condition of employment." [147] It is possible to argue that most breaches of contract meet the definition and the line between breach and modification has historically been a hazy one.

Employer unilateral action that would violate section 8(a)(5), either because it modifies the contract or because of failure to negotiate may be legitimated either through the management-rights clause or else through a direct waiver of the right to bargain over it. Zipper clauses, if given literal effect, would generally permit unilateral management action with respect to items not covered by the agreement.

Both the management rights clause and the zipper clause may be understood as waivers by the union of management's duty to bargain over items not otherwise covered by the agreement. Because they involve a waiver of statutory rights, the Board historically has construed such clauses narrowly, holding that the management rights clause has only a limited scope and that zipper clauses function only to prevent the union from raising new items during the course of the agreement, unless otherwise stated in the clearest possible language.[148] As a result of its approach to contract interpretation through the concept of statutory rights, the Board has tended to reject the idea that a collective-bargaining agreement governs the entire relationship between the parties during its term. This approach is different from the approach taken by arbitrators, who generally assume that the management-rights clause applies by implication to matters not otherwise dealt with by the agreement.

When the union's claim is either that the employer's action violates the agreement or constitutes unlawful unilateral action under the *Collyer* doctrine.[149] (discussed in Chapter Three), the union is required to go to arbitration first. Only in rare cases will the Board either hear the case initially or overturn the arbitrator's award. Arbitrators almost never hold that a contract is inapposite with respect to an employer's ability to take action. Thus as a practical matter almost all unilateral action cases are handled through the grievance system and not by Board application of section 8(a)(5). The *Collyer* doctrine does not eliminate all Board jurisdiction over contract violations, however. Claims of union violation are frequently not covered by the grievance machinery. Moreover, the Board will not defer if it does not believe that a good faith dispute exists about the employer's ability to take the action in question or if the Board believes that the employer does not have an arguable case.[150]

3. The Grievance System as a Form of Bargaining

The Board has recognized that the grievance system is the major process by which the parties bargain during the term of an agreement. While this process takes place largely without Board interference, the Board and the courts have utilized section 8(a)(5) in various ways to strengthen the grievance system. Refusal to utilize or implement the grievance system constitutes a breach of the duty to bargain.[151] The parties are required to make available to each other information necessary to permit each of them to utilize the grievance machinery effectively.[152] Activity by employees in bargaining and processing grievances is protected by section 7 and interference or reprisals against employees for their behavior comes within the "ambit" of section 8(a)(1) and (3). The Board has utilized section 8(a)(5) to protect the status of union stewards.

a. The Presentation of Individual Grievances

As noted above, the Act in section 9(a) distinguishes between the presentation of grievances and bargaining. However, the term "grievance" is not defined. It might be argued that the term "grievance" under section 9(a) is essentially equivalent to its use in a collective agreement which would make it coextensive with claims of violation of a written contract. While such a definition would have the merit of moderately well-defined limits and relative simplicity, it is supported neither by existing precedent, nor by the language or policy of section 9(a).

The definition of a grievance under a collective agreement reflects the frequent use of the system to resolve major issues of policy left open either deliberately or through inadvertence by the collective-bargaining process. While grievances involving discipline or promotion may be particular to the individuals directly involved, the resolution of others—for example, those involving subcontracting, rates of pay or insurance coverage—may affect the employees generally. The grievance system provides a technique for bargaining about such issues, and if individuals could bring and settle their own claims of contract violation, it would detract from the ability of the exclusive agent to bargain on behalf of the employees generally. The legislative history suggests that the proviso is not intended to have so broad a scope, and the Board and the courts have similarly interpreted the reach of the proviso narrowly, essentially limiting it to matters that affect only the particular employees.[153] On the other hand the language of the proviso seems to contemplate individual complaints not necessarily based upon contract language. For example, an employee who is upset with her forewoman's language would probably not have a contractual grievance but would seem to have a perfect section 9(a) proviso grievance.

The Act does not define the implication of the right to present a grievance under the proviso. It imposes no duty upon the employer to listen or to attempt to resolve the grievance. As already noted, *Vaca v. Sipes* establishes that the employer is not obligated to hear an individual grievance if he agrees with the union not to do so. The question remains whether the employer is obliged to do so in the absence of an agreement to the contrary. It is probable that he may refuse to respond and insist upon working through the union.[154] This is consistent with *Vaca v. Sipes* and gives the employer protection against being caught in a crossfire in which the union and the individual each have conflicting, reasonable claims against her. Thus it seems likely that the proviso bestows neither a right upon employees nor an obligation upon employers. All it does is to give employers a limited defense to unfair labor practice charges based on exclusivity when they deal with an individual in resolving a grievance without working through the union.

4. The Impact of Bankruptcy

In *NLRB v. Bildisco,*[155] the Supreme Court held that an employer could be released from its obligations under a collective-bargaining agreement through bankruptcy. The bankruptcy code was thereupon amended[156] to require specific findings before a collective-bargaining agreement could be rejected. The amendment imposed an obligation upon the employer before rejecting to bargain with the union, to present the union with information, and to make a proposal which the union refused without good cause. Further, the proposed reorganization must be necessary and fair. It is still too early to tell how this process will work, but early indications suggest greater leniency by the bankruptcy courts towards the employer than the language of the statute would imply. Courts are bound to be lenient towards employers in financial trouble so long as the employer makes a proposal and attempts to bargain with the union about it.[157] Nevertheless, bankruptcy is not likely to become a widespread technique for midterm modification or for avoiding collective-bargaining obligations.[158] The potentially harmful economic consequences of bankruptcy to the employer are too great, and in any case, the duty to bargain continues.

5. Union Violations of Section 8(d)

Section 8(d) prohibits unions during the term of an agreement from modifying an agreement or seeking to do so by a strike.

Section 8(d) cases involving unions have risen in two contexts: first, when a union that is a party to a collective-bargaining agreement goes on strike in order to get the employer to agree to a modification; second, when the union modifies the agreement on its own. Typical of the first class of cases is *United Marine Division Local 333.*[159] The respondent union in that case represented the employer's tugboat employees. Another union represented the employer's barge employees. The respondent union had threatened the employer with work stoppages unless its barges were manned with two barge employees while being towed. An unfair labor practice charge was filed, and a three-member panel of the Board held that "the Respondent Union's insistence on a change in working conditions of the tugboat employees whom it represented, backed up by the threat to enforce this demand with work stoppages, was in effect an attempt to unilaterally change and modify the working conditions of the tugboat employees during the midterm of its contract covering tugboat employees and it thereby engaged in bad-faith bargaining in violation of section 8(b)(3) and (d) of the Act." The NLRB has drawn a distinction between strikes to secure a modification in a collective-bargaining agreement and strikes in support of a contract grievance. The former are forbidden by section 8(d); the latter are outside its scope. In *Teamsters Local 741*[160] drivers who had refused to cross a picket line were denied layover pay by the employer. The union filed a grievance and went on strike in support of its position on the grievance. A three-member panel of the Board held that the union's action did not constitute a violation of 8(b)(3) and 8(d). In his decision (which was adopted by the Board), the trial examiner had explicitly rejected the employer's argument that the strike constituted an unlawful attempt to modify the grievance procedures provided by the collective-bargaining agreement.

Part IV.　Bargaining and Strikes

A.　The Central Role of Strikes in the American System of Collective Bargaining—The Minor Role of Law in Negotiations

The most notable thing about the legal requirement that a party bargain in good faith is its minor role in shaping labor negotiations. This is because of the combination of limited substantive reach and weak remedies that have consistently marked the interpretation of this requirement. The legislative history and the statutory language both reflect the desire that section 8(a)(5) not become a rival avenue to negotiation for the creation of an agreement. Concerned that the Board, "in the guise of determining whether or not employers had bargaining in good faith," would seek increasingly "to control the terms of collective bargaining agreements," [161] Congress defined collective bargaining in section 8(d) as including the obligation "to meet at reasonable times and confer in good faith with respect to wages, hours and other conditions of employment . . ." but not as compelling "either party to agree to a proposal or requir[ing] the making of a concession." [162] Both labor and management have been fearful historically of governmental regulation of collective bargaining—management because of the belief that government involvement would inevitably create a minimum set of terms that an employer must accept, and the unions because of fear that such an approach would inevitably limit what could be achieved through negotiations. Many union leaders also believe that if the government sets wages and working conditions, the government's role would detract from that of the union and ultimately weaken the employee's commitment to the strike weapon that plays a crucial role in the process of negotiation under the present system. Currently, when the parties negotiate they are aware that the government will not establish an agreement for the parties if bargaining is not successful. The motive that ultimately persuades employers to accept union contract proposals is the fear of the consequences of a strike. What persuades the union to make compromise proposals is the potential harm to the union and its members that may accrue from a strike. Union members who strike are risking their jobs and are necessarily giving up their pay during the period of the strike. The system works as well as it does because the consequences of failing to reach agreement are potentially harmful to both sides.

B. The Protection of Economic Pressure by Section 7

1. The Concept of Protected Activity

In place of regulating the bargaining process to ensure agreements, the Wagner Act sought to protect the right of employees to strike in support of their bargaining demands. To this end, section 7 granted employees the right to engage in concerted activity, while section 8 limited the right of employers to respond. The right to use economic pressure was included in section 7 in order to prohibit employers from using participation in such activity as grounds for disciplinary action. It was not intended, however, that an employer be required to yield to his employees' demands. As already noted, the scheme of the Act contemplates that an employer may resist employee bargaining demands and subject the union to a test of economic power. A natural tension exists between the policy forbidding an employer to discipline employees using economic pressure and the policy permitting him to defend his own economic interests. The Board and the courts are often required to characterize particular employer responses as either unlawful labor practices or as legitimate steps to resist union pressure. The line between these concepts is a vague one. Accordingly, the extent to which employers may take action which imposes hardships on employees who engage in economic pressure has been a source of continual difficulty in the enforcement of the Act.

2. The Rights of Striking Employees

An employer may take a variety of steps in response to employee economic pressure without violating the Act. It need not pay employees for the time they spend engaged in such economic pressure activity. Employee absence for union activity may be taken into account in computing bonuses, and economic pressure by employees will justify a lockout or a unilateral subcontracting of work.[163] The most significant permissible response is the employer's ability to hire permanent replacements for striking employees. This employer prerogative was recognized by the Supreme Court, in dictum, in *NLRB v. MacKay Radio & Telegraph Co.*,[164] and since then has been largely unquestioned. The basis for the rule is not completely obvious. The Court in *MacKay* justified its conclusion in terms of the employer's right to "protect and continue his business." The validity of this justification turns on the accuracy of the assumption that underlies it— that without the ability to permanently replace strikers, employers will be unable to operate during strikes. While the assumption is doubtlessly valid in some instances, it is questionable that it is valid in enough cases to justify a blanket rule that imposes so great a risk on those who participate in activity "protected" by the National Labor Relations Act. It is unfortunate that a rule of such importance was adopted without any real effort to evaluate the factual assumption on which it is based. In view of the rule's long duration, it is most unlikely that such an evaluation will be undertaken in the future or that the *MacKay* rule will be abandoned in the interest of consistent application of sections 8(a)(1) and 8(a)(3). Such questions as exist concern the operation of the rule rather than its validity.

Theoretically, an employer's ability to permanently replace striking employees is limited to cases in which such action is taken for economic motives. An employer may permanently replace strikers in order to continue his business, but not in order to punish employees for engaging in protected activities.[165] In many situations it is impossible to categorize with any assurance the employer's conduct. Is he replacing for economic motives or discharging for punitive motives? This is not the type of determination that can be made readily with the fact-finding techniques used by the Board in the typical 8(a)(3) discriminatory discharge case. Generally there is little in the record other than the ambiguous act of replacement. An employer who hires replacements during a strike almost certainly is motivated in part by the desire to continue operations. He is probably also aware that his new employees are less likely to be union adherents than the strikers they replaced and that his action will have a deterrent effect on any future strike action. These are advantages that most employers will consider in evaluating whether to hire permanent replacements and that will be balanced against the risk of violence and permanent bad feelings and the prolongation of the strike over the issues of reinstatement of the strikers that such a move inevitably entails. In short, an inquiry into the employer's state of mind in such situations would be difficult and the probable results equivocal.

The Board, in fact, does not seek to evaluate the employer's state of mind in order to determine the legality of his conduct. Instead, it has devised a fairly mechanical test to distinguish between legal replacement and illegal discharge. Unless it can be demonstrated that the employer has singled out for replacement those whom he knows to be active union members, he is permitted to lay off permanently any striking employees, as long as they are not notified that they are replaced or treated as having been replaced before new employees are hired. Employees are improperly discharged if before replacements are hired, official action is taken to indicate that the old employees may not return to work after the strike. This test, which has been approved by the courts,[166] is related only occasionally to the employer's reasons for acting. It is more likely to indicate whether the employer had competent counsel. As long as the basic assumptions of the *MacKay* doctrine are accepted, however, the current rule is probably as good as any which can be devised. It prohibits flagrant attempts to punish protected activity and spells out what an employer may do with clarity.

The permanent replacement of a striker does not remove all his rights to claim his former job. In *NLRB v. Fleetwood Trailer Co.,*[167] the Supreme Court affirmed the Board's conclusion that an employer violated the Act by not rehiring strikers when it resumed full production some two months after the strike. The Court held that a striking employee remains an employee if she has not obtained "regular or substantially equivalent employment" and that during this period the employer had the burden of establishing a "legitimate and substantial business justification" for refusing to reinstate her. Subsequently, in *Laidlaw Corp. v. NLRB,* the Court held that economic strikers are entitled to priority in rehiring unless either the strikers have acquired equivalent employment or the employer can show that failure to reinstate was for a legitimate and substantial business reason.[168]

Until quite recently the right to permanently replace has not been widely used and striking employees have sometimes been unaware of their legal jeopardy. Practical rather than legal considerations have generally inhibited the use of this power. The hiring of permanent replacements is almost guaranteed to produce a violent response and it makes eventual settlement with the union problematic since a fundamental union demand in any settlement is the reinstatement of the strikers. The issue of what to do with the replacements is likely to become a stumbling block inhibiting successful completion of the negotiations. This issue has been complicated by the Supreme Court decision in *Belknap v. Hale* [169] holding that employees hired as permanent replacements could sue the employer in the event a strike settlement resulted in the loss of their jobs to strikers. The ruling makes the decision to employ permanent replacements an act of great significance. If strikers threatened with permanent replacement return, they are likely to be angry and uncooperative. Relations between returned strikers and permanent replacements may be strained long after the strike's end.

The subtlety of the law in this area is such that the right of permanent replacement does not include the right to give strike replacements greater seniority than that held by the strikers. [170] It is as though the law permits killing but not wounding.

Another obvious example of the vulnerability of protected activity is an employer lockout that is undertaken to exert pressure on employees because of their bargaining positions. The Board for a long time held that such conduct violates sections 8(a)(3) and (1). The Supreme Court rejected this conclusion in *American Ship Building Co. v. NLRB*, [171] holding that such conduct was within the Act's policy favoring the free use of economic pressure by both sides. On the other hand, the hiring of permanent strike replacements to take the jobs of those locked out is clearly illegal despite its potential effectiveness as a form of economic pressure. [172] However there are circumstances where the employer can lock out and continue operations with temporary employees. [173]

Another source of difficulty arises from the fact that the statutory scheme does not recognize economic pressure as a legitimate means of solving all disputes. The Act in section 8(b) specifically prohibits the use of strikes by unions under certain circumstances. Conduct held unlawful by section 8(b) has never been held protected by section 7. The Board and the courts have refused to protect economic pressure in other circumstances on the grounds that the nature of the dispute was such as to make its use unjustified. In some areas of traditional management concern such as the right to appoint supervisors it generally has been held that the employer should be able to make decisions without running the risk of economic combat. Alternatively, the employer's involvement in an issue that concerns his employees may be so slight that it is considered improper for the employees to cause him economic hardship in pursuing their own interests. [174]

From time to time the courts have also indicated that certain forms of economic pressure go beyond the purposes of the Act and inflict an unfair hardship upon the employer. Such tactics, which the Supreme Court characterized as "indefensible," are unprotected. It was accepted law for some time that intermittent work stoppages and other forms of partial strikes come under this rubric. However, the Supreme Court in *Lodge 76 Machinists v. WERC* gave to the Board the right to draw distinctions between different types of partial strike activity.[175] The Board has been loathe to exercise its discretion to hold partial strikes protected, and in general partial strikes probably still come under the category of indefensible economic pressure. It is far from clear why this should be so. In most situations in which unions use such tactics it is because they do not have the economic strength to engage in a traditional strike. Moreover, the employer may certainly respond to such action by locking out his employees.

The other generally cited area of indefensible union activity is disloyalty, which was first held by the Supreme Court to make strike activity unprotected in *NLRB v. Local Union No. 1229 IBEW*,[176] a case in which a group of TV station technicians were held to have engaged in unprotected activity because they passed out handbills that criticized their employer station's programming. While the precedent is generally old and the reasoning often unpersuasive, it is usually accepted that union activity attacking the employer's product, or other propaganda attacking the employer for reasons unrelated to its labor relations policies, is probably unprotected.

3. The Impact of a Protected Economic Strike on the Duty to Bargain

The duty to bargain continues during a strike,[177] but the contours of the duty are not clearly marked. Although an employer is still obliged to respond to union proposals, a union that goes on strike is rarely in a position to deny that impasse has been reached. Where a union makes new proposals, an employer is obliged to bargain, but considerable leeway is given to the employer in setting the time and nature of the meeting in the name of bargaining tactics. Unilateral employer action taken with respect to matters not presented to the union at the bargaining table may be divided into two basic types: (a) actions taken by the employer to lessen the effects of the strike or to put bargaining pressure on the union; (b) actions taken to change working conditions permanently.

As to actions to lessen the impact of a strike, considerable leeway is granted to the employer to take unilateral action, on the theory that to impose a bargaining obligation before an employer could respond to a strike would be meaningless except as a way for the union to delay the employer's response.[178] With respect to permanent changes unrelated to the strike, the duty to bargain continues and the employer must offer to bargain with the union before taking such action.[179] Most cases of unilateral change during a strike involve action that may be characterized as bargaining pressure that also has harmful effects on the members of the bargaining unit, as is the case where work is subcontracted or where permanent replacements are hired.[180]

Certain employer action is permitted without regard to its impact on union activity, without a requirement of prior bargaining. Such actions include withholding benefits during a strike, hiring permanent replacements, locking out, and hiring temporary replacements after impasse has been achieved.[181] Other actions, such as the grant of super-seniority to strikers and denying them benefits granted to other employees, are forbidden by sections 8(a)(3) and (1).[182] Action improving wages or changing general working conditions or permanently subcontracting work performed by strikers must first be presented to the union.[183]

One area which has been the subject of considerable confusion concerns the employer's obligation to bargain with the union over the wages and working conditions of strike replacements. Employers frequently seek to pay such replacements more than they paid the strikers. If the replacements are hired on a permanent basis and the rate applies only to replacement, the employer violates section 8(a)(3) based on the rationale of *Erie Registor* and *Great Dane Trailers.*[184] However, the employer may pay the replacements differently from the strikers without violating section 8(a)(3) under certain circumstances—the wage rate may be lower, it may be temporary, or it may constitute the implementation of a new general policy. In these circumstances, the issue becomes "Does an employer have an obligation to bargain with the union before instituting the new rates?" The Board's current authority suggests no obligation to bargain with the union over the wages of strike replacements under any circumstances.[185] This conclusion is based on the conclusion that the interests of the union and the replacements are inevitably in conflict. This is true for temporary replacements, but where the rate is intended to be permanent the issue becomes more complex because it affects the interests of strikers as well. It is not yet clear how either the Board or courts will treat such issues. The distinctions do not seem based either on statutory language or labor relations realities.

In *Hawaii Meat Co. v. NLRB*, 321 F.2d 397 [186] the Ninth Circuit held that no duty to bargain existed with respect to either permanent subcontracting or the hiring of replacements, on the grounds that bargaining would be meaningless and merely provide an excuse for delay. The decision is questionable because it seems inevitable that some unions faced with a serious statement of employer intent to take such drastic action would reassess or amend their position in an effort to get the employer to refrain. The seriousness of the consequences militates against ignoring the normal bargaining requirement. The realities of a strike situation should more logically decrease the amount of time before an impasse may be said to exist rather than totally abrogate the duty to bargain. The decision in *Hawaii Meat Co.* has been described narrowly as pertaining only to the strike period by the Seventh Circuit in *American Cynamid Co. v. NLRB.*[187] Its holding with respect to subcontracting has not been accepted by the Board [188] which has specifically refused to accept the equation of replacement and subcontracting adopted by the Court in the *Hawaii Meat Co.* case.

4. The Duty to Bargain During Illegal or Unprotected Strikes

It is generally held that a strike that violates section 8(b)(3) relieves the employer of his duty to bargain.[189] The reason for this conclusion is far from clear. It does not seem obvious that an employer be permitted to take unilateral actions that make permanent changes because a strike is partly over a permissive issue that the union mistakenly thought mandatory. The consequences of such a technical violation are already serious enough because the employees lose their reinstatement rights.

With respect to other unfair labor practices there may be even less reason to eliminate the employer's bargaining obligation. For example, suppose a union violates section 8(b)(4) by appeals to customers at the premises of a neutral employer, which appeals fall outside the scope of the proviso to section 8(b)(4)(B). In such a case the injured party is the neutral who is protected by the ability to obtain an injunction and by the right to collect money damages by virtue of section 303 of the NLRA. The primary employer is similarly protected and there seems little reason to give him the additional right to cease bargaining.

When a union engages in a strike that is unprotected because it breaches a no-strike clause, the cases are in conflict about the employer's ability to cease bargaining either during the period of the strike or permanently. There are some cases that hold that employers may refuse to bargain while such a strike is in process.[190] Professor Gorman suggests that such cases are "of dubious vitality," pointing out that "they run counter to the policy . . . that a strike in breach of a no strike clause does not . . . relieve the employer of its duty to arbitrate contract grievances." [191] His conclusion seems quite sensible.

In light of the questionable status of the employer's right to cease bargaining even temporarily, it is particularly remarkable that a body of authority exists for the proposition that an employer may permanently withdraw recognition of union that violates a no-strike clause.

In *Marathon Electric Mfg. Corp.,*[192] the Board concluded that an employer acted lawfully where, in response to a walkout in contravention of a no-strike clause, it withdrew recognition of the union and rescinded its agreement to the terms of the collective-bargaining agreement.

The D.C. Circuit, in enforcing the Board's decision, observed:

"It is general law that one party to a contract need not perform if the other party refuses in a material respect to do so. And that rule applies to labor contracts. Moreover, in cases where the breach is a strike in violation of a collective bargaining agreement . . . application of the rule is supported by the rationale underlying such agreements. The prevention of strike is one of the principle purposes of labor contracts and of the Act . . . The walkout [in the instant case] was a material breach which justified the subsequent rescission of the contract by the Company." [193]

The scope and current vitality of the *Marathon* doctrine is not clear. It has been cited favorably in a 1980 Third Circuit case,[194] but it has not been applied for some time, and it was rejected inferentially by the Supreme Court in *Carbon Fuel Co. v. UMW*,[195] which held that union liability for a wildcat strike could not be lightly assumed.

The issue of an employer's ability to respond to wildcat strikes is related to the question of union responsibility for employee walkouts. Where wildcat strikes occur it is often the case that no formal union vote is taken authorizing it. The issue of the union's responsibility has to be determined by the actions of its leadership. The courts generally have been willing to find local union responsibility wherever the union's leadership has taken part in a strike. Another question concerns the liability of an international union for the acts of the local. The courts of appeals have traditionally been quite severe in holding both the local and international union liable, on the grounds that masses of employees are unlikely to undertake such action without direction and leadership. The Supreme Court's most recent decision in *Carbon Fuel Co. v. UMW*, however, suggests that union responsibility should be limited solely to cases in which the union's institutional responsibility is quite clear and the breach is serious and clearly unlawful.

5. Replacement of Employees for Honoring Picket Lines

The Board and the courts are in general agreement with respect to the employer's ability to hire permanent replacements for striking employees. There is less agreement about the related problem of an employer's ability to respond when his employees refuse to cross a picket line at the premises of another employer. Confusion in this area stems from different interpretations of the Supreme Court's opinion in *NLRB v. Rockaway News Supply Co.*[196] In that case, an employee was discharged for refusing to cross a picket line. The employee's refusal was a violation of the applicable collective-bargaining agreement, but the Board held the agreement void.[197] It accordingly held the activity protected and the discharge illegal. The Board treated the refusal to cross the picket line as an economic strike and sought to apply the distinction between discharge and replacement. Since the employee had been told that he was "fired" at a time when no replacement had been hired, the Board concluded that he had been illegally "discharged," and ordered reinstatement. The court of appeals refused enforcement of the Board's order,[198] and the Supreme Court affirmed the court of appeals. The Court held valid the provision of the collective-bargaining agreement giving the employer the right to discharge the employee for such behavior. The employee's conduct was therefore unprotected. But the Court also analyzed the case on the assumption that the employee's conduct was protected, and it rejected the Board's attempt to distinguish between replacement and discharge "in this context" as "unrealistic and unfounded." Indeed, the Court acidly described the Board's analysis as "verbal ritual reminiscent of medieval real property law."

When the Board, after some seesawing, concluded once again that refusal to cross a lawful picket line was protected, it simultaneously rejected the tests previously employed to distinguish between discharge and replacement. In its opinion *Redwing Carriers, Inc.*[199] the Board stated:

> "[W]e are convinced that substance, rather than form, should be controlling. That is, where it is clear from the record that the employer acted only to preserve efficient operation of his business, and terminated the service of the employees only so it could immediately or within a short period thereafter replace them with others willing to perform the scheduled work, we can see no reason for reaching different results solely on the basis of the precise words, i.e., replacement or discharge, used by the employer, or the chronological order in which the employer terminated and replaced the employees in question."

The significance of this language depends upon the nature of the evidence necessary for an employer to demonstrate that he "acted only to preserve the efficient operation of his business." The Board has indicated, however, that a respondent can prove its case by establishing two propositions:

1. that the refusal to cross the picket line constituted a substantial interference with respondent's business which could not be overcome by merely assigning another employee to do the work; and

2. that replacements were in fact hired.[200]

The *Redwing* decision thus did not mean that the Board was completely prepared to abandon the distinction between replacement and discharge in this context. Not only did the fact of and need for replacement have to be established in order to prove the legitimacy of the employer's motive, but the timing of replacement continued to be significant as well.

The Board and the courts have continued to characterize refusals to cross stranger picket lines as protected activity; however, the degree of protection has neither been great nor easily ascertainable. Where the employees refusal has placed a significant burden on the employer, discharge has been permitted. As stated by Judge Posner in *NLRB v. Browning–Ferris Industries,*[201] ". . . concluding that conduct is protected does not make it sacrosanct but does require the employer to demonstrate good cause for suppression." This language was quoted with approval by Judge Friendly and a similar balancing approach applied in *Business Services By Manpower v. NLRB.*[202]

In general, the Courts have held that if the employer was able to manage merely by reassigning his personnel, then it should be permissible for the Board to conclude that the degree of interference with his economic interests was too small to justify punishing an employee for exercising his statutory right. Similarly, if the employee changes his mind and expresses a willingness to do the job before the employer has committed himself to another, there is no legitimate reason why his reinstatement should be denied. The analogy to an economic striker in this context is apt. Once such an employee expresses a willingness to work, there is no legitimate interest that the employer can invoke to refuse him employment unless his place has been filled. Neither the employer's displeasure with his actions nor the possibility of similar conduct in the future should afford a basis for discharging him. The only permissible employer justification for dismissing an employee who is engaged in protected conduct should be the desire to avoid interference with current operations.

Part V. Remedies for Refusals to Bargain

A. Failure to Bargain in Good Faith

In *H.K. Porter Co. v. NLRB,*[203] the Supreme Court held that the Board did not have the authority to order an employer to accept a contract clause that the employer had in bad faith refused to accept. The Court held such a remedy would "violate the fundamental premise" of the Act—"freedom of contract." The Board has since taken the position that the *H.K. Porter* case denies the Board the authority to issue a make whole remedy under which the employees would be compensated for what they lost economically by virtue of the employer's bad faith.[204] The necessity of equating these two remedies is not obvious because one remedy controls the future relationship of the parties while the other remedy merely calculates the cost of a past violation. The Board has justified its refusal to issue a make-whole remedy for refusals to bargain in good faith by pointing out that under the statute an employer is required to refuse to bargain as a way of getting judicial review of the propriety of the Board's unit determination. However, it would be possible to distinguish violations based on an unreasonable claim of inappropriate unit from those based on surface bargaining. In certain cases the Board has awarded litigation and organizing expenses to a union, but this has been rare and restricted to cases of repeated and flagrant violations.[205]

1. Insisting Upon a Permissive Subject

There is some authority for the proposition that if a party has illegally and successfully insisted upon a permissive subject of bargaining, which is included in the contract, the Board may order the offending clause stricken from the contract.[206] The use of such a remedy seems basically inconsistent with *H.K. Porter* because the parties are left with a contract that they did not negotiate. The party that obtained the permissive clause could undoubtedly have been able to obtain some other mandatory concession instead. In view of this problem, a clause reopening a contract, if the permissive clause is stricken should be honored.

By far the main significance of the mandatory/permissive distinction has been in terms of reinstatement rights. If a union strikes illegally because it is insisting upon a permissive subject, then the strike is unprotected and the employees can be discharged. On the other hand, if the strike is caused by the employer's insistence upon a permissive subject and by his refusal to discuss a mandatory proposal in good faith, the strike is an "unfair labor practice strike" (a strike caused or prolonged by an unfair labor practice), and the employer has lost the ability to permanently replace the striking employees.[207]

B. Midterm Modification

1. Union Violations

Where the union has gone on strike, or otherwise exerted economic pressure in an attempt to modify the collective-bargaining agreement, a cease-and-desist order is issued.[208] But where the union actually *modifies* the collective-bargaining agreement, make-whole remedies are awarded.

In recent cases the Board has awarded make-whole remedies where the union actually succeeded in modifying the collective-bargaining agreement. For example, in *Plumbers, Local Union No. 420*,[209] a local had first accepted the National Construction Agreement and then "coerced" the employer into signing a local agreement by means of a strike in violation of 8(d). The Board ordered the local to make the employer whole "for any expenditures that it incurred pursuant to the local agreement unlawfully imposed upon it, which it would not have incurred under the National Construction Agreement." The administrative law judge had simply ordered rescission of the new agreement and restoration of the old one; the Board overruled him and held that a make-whole remedy was appropriate.

Both *Systems Council T-6* [210] and *Communications Workers of American, Local 1122* [211] involved union bans on members' acceptance of temporary supervisory assignments. In both cases the unions were held to have violated 8(b)(3). In *CWA, Local 1122*, the union was ordered to pay back pay to any unit employee who had accepted an appointment as a temporary supervisor and had been forced to relinquish the position as a result of the ban. In *Systems Council T-6*, the Board held this remedy inadequate and directed back pay "for all employees who refused temporary supervisory positions because of the ban as well as to those who relinquished such positions."

Although the precedents are scanty, the Board's "make-whole" approach seems to have been endorsed by the courts. The Board's order in *CWA, Local 1122* was enforced by the Second Circuit without opinion,[212] and in *Systems Council T-6* the Board's order was enforced with only a brief comment on remedy: "With regard to respondents' challenge to the Board's back pay order, we note only that we find no abuse of the Board's substantial remedial discretion, and that uncertainty as to the application of the order may be resolved in subsequent compliance proceedings." [213]

2. Company Violations—Unilateral Action

Where unlawful midterm modification of a contract by an employer is found, the Board will rescind the unilateral changes, order a return to the status quo ante, and order the affected union or employees or both made whole for any damages suffered as a result of the changes. The Board's theory as to the appropriateness of this remedy was expressed in *John W. Bolton & Sons, Inc.*,[214] a frequently cited case on the issue of remedy for midterm contract changes. In the case the employer instituted a new wage incentive plan unilaterally and without prior discussion with the union. The Board, finding failure to bargain and unlawful modification of the contract in violation of 8(d), ordered the plan revoked and the old salary plan restored. In so doing the Board said:

> "To permit the incentive bonus plan to remain in effect in the face of the clear mandate of the Act would enable Respondent to retain the fruits of its unfair labor practice and thereby give it an advantage at the bargaining table when and if the issue of the plan was properly raised at the appropriate time."

This same reasoning and remedy was employed in subsequent midterm modification of contract cases. In *Standard Oil Co.*,[215] for example, all modifications made by an employer inconsistent with the existing bargaining agreement were ordered revoked and rescinded. And in *Kinard Trucking*,[216] where a unilateral wage reduction was found to constitute unlawful modification of the contract, the employer was ordered to revoke the reduction, restore the status quo ante, and make the employees whole.

The conclusion that an employer should not be allowed to come to the table at the appropriate bargaining time with unfair advantages that have accrued to him as a result of unlawful changes is accepted throughout the failure to bargain cases. This is especially true where the employer makes a change in established employee benefits without first consulting the union. The appropriate remedy for such a situation was set out in *Southland Paper Mills, Inc.*[217] There the employer discontinued a hunting privilege that employees had long enjoyed. The privilege was not covered by the collective-bargaining agreement and was not discussed in negotiations. Nevertheless, the Board found that the privilege was regarded by both the employer and employees as a fringe benefit of substantial value and thus the employer had an obligation to discuss the matter with the union. In fashioning the remedy the Board said:

> "In circumstances involving violations of Section 8(a)(5) by unilaterally depriving employees of established employment benefits, it is the Board's policy to order restoration of the status quo ante to the extent feasible and in the absence of evidence establishing that to do so would impose an undue or unfair burden upon the respondent."

Although the Board generally orders rescission of unilateral changes made without discussion and a return to the extent feasible of the status quo ante, it does not always do so. In *Herman Sausage Co., Inc.,* the employer unilaterally granted a wage increase and concurrently effectuated a decrease in benefits without consulting the union. Finding a failure to bargain, the Board began its discussion of remedy by saying that its customary policy was to direct an employer to restore the status quo whenever it has taken unlawful unilateral action to the detriment of its employees. The Board went on to say, however, that where it is unclear whether the overall effect of the unilateral changes has been detrimental to employees, it will make the matter of the remedy turn on "the affirmative desire of the affected employees . . . as expressed through their collective-bargaining representative."[218] In short, does the union seek restoration?

In sum, the Board's remedial approach in 8(a)(5) cases varies depending upon the nature of the violation. The crucial factor in determining remedy is the potential impact on free collective bargaining, not the seriousness of the violation nor the degree of moral turpitude involved.

FOOTNOTES

1.	29 U.S.C. § 158(a)(5) (1976).

2. Id. at § 159(a).

3. See, e.g., *J. Zembrodt Express Inc.*, 193 N.L.R.B. 126 (1971); *Teledyne Rental Products Corp.*, 210 N.L.R.B. 435 (1974).

4. *Bennett Packaging Company*, 285 N.L.R.B. 80 (1987).

5. See, e.g., *Wilkinson Mfg. Co.*, 791, 796 (1971).

6. 230 N.L.R.B. 1054 (1977).

7. 29 U.S.C. § 159(a) (1976).

8. 386 U.S. 171 (1967).

9. Id. at 186, 190.

10. See, e.g., *NLRB v. National Motor Bearing Co.*, 105 F.2d 652 (9th Cir.1939).

11. *Emporium Capwell Co. v. Western Addition Community Organization*, 420 U.S. 50 (1975).

12. See, e.g., *Federal Telephone and Radio Co.*, 107 N.L.R.B. 649 (1953). *But see Douds v. Retail Union Local 1250*, 173 F.2d 764 (2d Cir.1949).

13. See, e.g., *NLRB v. Mid–States Metal Products, Inc.*, 403 F.2d 702 (5th Cir.1968).

14. 195 N.L.R.B. 265 (1972).

15. *Magnavox Co. of Tennessee v. NLRB*, 474 F.2d 1269 (6th Cir.1973).

16. *NLRB v. Magnavox*, 415 U.S. 322 (1974).

17. Ford Motor Co., 233 N.L.R.B. 618 (1977).

18. 418 F.2d 736 (2d Cir.1969), *cert. denied*, 397 U.S. 965 (1970). The approach was named after its founder, Lemuel R. Boulware; See Northrup, *Boulwareism* (1964).

19. Id. at 759.

20. 160 N.L.R.B. 334 (1966).

21. See also *NLRB v. Movie Star, Inc.*, 361 F.2d 346 (5th Cir.1966) (employer's communication of final bargaining offer to employees held not an 8(a)(5) violation); *Wantaugh Auto Sales*, 177 N.L.R.B. 150 (1969) (employer's communication with locked out employees ruled not on 8(a)(5) violation).

22. Thus, in *NLRB v. Penokee Veneer Co.*, 168 F.2d 868, 4 ALR2d 1350 (7th Cir.1948) an employer sent a letter to strikers asking them if they would desire to return to work under the conditions proposed by at its last meeting with the union, conditions which the union had both rejected and refused to convey to its constituents. The Seventh Circuit denied enforcement of the NLRB's § 8(a)(1) finding, rejecting the conclusion that the company had attempted to bypass the union in favor of individual dealing. The court asserted that in view of the fact that the company had never been charged with a failure to bargain in good faith in its dealings with the union, the Board's conclusions were unjustified.

23. For example, in *American Steel Building Co.*, 208 NLRB 900 (1974), a shipping supervisor offered a striking employee a higher wage and better clothes to wear if he would return to work. The NLRB found a § 8(a)(5) violation, noting that while noncoercive solicitation of individual workers was not *per se* a violation of the Act, a violation will be found where the solicitation was accompanied by a promise of benefit.

See also *NLRB v. J.H. Bonck Co.*, 424 F.2d 634 (5th Cir.1970) (employer's communication with employees announcing pay increase held to violate 8(a)(5) and 8(a)(1), where there had been no meaningful wage negotiations with union); *Glazers Wholesale Drug Co.*, 211 N.L.R.B. 1063 (1974) (employer's offer of higher wages to strikers not justified by economic necessity).

24. 163 N.L.R.B. 981 (1967).

25. Id. at 982. See also *White Sulphur Springs Co. v. NLRB*, 316 F.2d 410 (D.C.Cir. 1963).

26. 641 F.2d 930 (D.C.Cir.1979), *cert. denied*, 444 U.S. 1072 (1980).

27. See also *Federal Dairy Co.*, 130 N.L.R.B. 1158 (1961) (employer's urging striking employees to abandon union ruled 8(a)(1) and 8(a)(5) violation).

28. 110 N.L.R.B. 1494 (1954).

29. 161 N.L.R.B. 221 (1966).

30. 605 F.2d 60 (2d Cir.1979).

31. *Carpenter Sprinkler Corp.*, 238 N.L.R.B. 974, 982 (1978).

33. See, e.g., *United Contractors, Inc.*, 244 N.L.R.B. 72 (1979); *Meltox Mfg. Co.*, 225 N.L.R.B. 1317 (1976).

34. See *NLRB v. Crompton-Highland Mills, Inc.*, 337 U.S. 217 (1949).

35. See, e.g., *Dallas General Drivers, Intern. Bro. of Teamsters, Local 745 v. NLRB*, 355 F.2d 842 (D.C.Cir.1966) (Burger, J.); *Empire Terminal Warehouse Co.*, 151 N.L.R.B. 1359 (1965). Nevertheless, see, *Cuyamaca Meat's Inc. v. San Diego and Imperial Counties Butchers' & Food Employers' Pension Trust Fund*, 827 F.2d 491 (9th Cir.1987). Employer continued to contribute to employee trust fund after reaching impasse in negotiating a new collective bargaining agreement with incumbent union. Five months after impasse was reached employer ceased contributions to fund. Held: employer's unilateral continuation of contributions which was "reasonably comprehended in its pre-impasse offer," imposed a legal obligation on employer which precluded employer from ceasing contributions unilaterally at a later date.

36. *Highway Billboards*, 206 N.L.R.B. 22 (1973).

37. See, e.g., *NLRB v. Draper Corp.*, 145 F.2d 199 (4th Cir.1944); *Lee A. Consaul Co., Inc. v. NLRB*, 469 F.2d 84 (9th Cir.1972).

38. 420 U.S. 50 (1975).

39. Id. at 67.

40. 544 F.2d 320 (7th Cir.1976).

41. Id.

42. 581 F.2d 44 (2d Cir.1978).

43. See, e.g., *Myers v. Gilman Paper Corp.*, 544 F.2d 837 (5th Cir.1977). "[A] court may not allow the substitution of a solution for past discrimination negotiated between the employer and the plaintiffs for that achieved through collective bargaining unless it first determines that the collectively bargained solution either violates Title VII or is inadequate in some particular to cure the effects of past discrimination." Id. at 858.

44. 323 U.S. 192 (1944).

45. *Wallace Corp. v. NLRB*, 323 U.S. 248 (1944).

46. See generally, Malin, *Individual Rights Within the Union*, BNA 1984, p. 410 et seq.

47. *Steelworkers v. Weber*, 443 U.S. 193 (1979); *Bell & Howell*, 230 N.L.R.B. 420 (1977).

48. In the absence of past discrimination, such a proposal risks a finding that the union breached its duty to its white or male members.

49. For a somewhat different view of the overall issue see Silverstein, Union Decisions on Collective Bargaining Goals: A Proposal for Interest Group Participation, 77 Mich.L.Rev. 1485 (1979).

50. 529 F.2d 793 (7th Cir.1976).

51. See *Balor v. Newspaper & Graphic Communications Union Local 6*, 628 F.2d 156 (D.C.Cir. 1980). The Board has recently reaffirmed its acceptance of the *Parton Brand* case reasoning in this regard Teamsters Local 42, 281 NLRB No. 132 (1987).

52. 29 U.S.C. § 158(d) (1976).

53. H.R.Rep. No. 245, 80th Cong., 1st Sess. 71 (1947).

54. 356 U.S. 342 (1958).

56. Prior to *Wooster Division of Borg-Warner*, the Board held on numerous occasions that although a union might agree to certain proposals, it could not be required to bargain with respect to them. See *Wooster Division of Borg-Warner Corp.*, 113 N.L.R.B. 1288, 1292 (1955) (and cases cited therein).

57. 404 U.S. 157 (1971) (footnote omitted).

58. 441 U.S. 488 (1979).

59. See also, Owens–Corning Fiberglas Corp., 282 NLRB No. 85 where the Board decided that the continued availability of a "company store" where employees could buy company products at a discount was a mandatory topic of bargaining.

60. *Doug Neal Management Co.*, 226 N.L.R.B. 985 (1976), *enforcement denied, NLRB v. Doug Neal Management Co.*, 620 F.2d 1133 (6th Cir.1980).

61. *Aerospace Supply, Inc. (d/b/a Anadite Industrial Supply Co.)*, 238 N.L.R.B. 1291 (1978).

62. *W.R. Grace & Co.*, 421 U.S. 757 (1983).

63. *Winn–Dixie Stores*, 147 N.L.R.B. 788 (1964), *enforcement denied on other grounds*, 361 F.2d 512 (5th Cir.1966).

64. *Empire Dental Co.*, 211 N.L.R.B. 860 (1974).

65. 161 N.L.R.B. 561 (1966).

66. *Royal Typewriter Co. v. NLRB*, 533 F.2d 1030, 1038–39 (8th Cir.1976) (and cases cited therein).

67. *NLRB v. Winn–Dixie Stores, Inc.*, 361 F.2d 512 (5th Cir.1966); *NLRB v. American Manufacturing Co.*, 351 F.2d 74 (5th Cir.1965).

68. 379 U.S. 203 (1964) at 210.

69. Id. at 223 (Stewart, J., concurring).

70. 582 F.2d 720 (3d Cir.1978).

71. Id. at 740–41 n. 108 (quoting *NLRB v. Winn–Dixie Stores, Inc.*, 361 F.2d 512, 517 (5th Cir.1966).

72. 452 U.S. 666 (1981).

73. 269 N.L.R.B. 891 (1984).

74. 350 F.2d 191 (3d Cir.1965).

75. See, e.g., *Summit Tooling Co.*, 195 N.L.R.B. 479 (1972); *Interstate Tool Co.*, 177 N.L.R.B. 686 (1969); *Transmarine Navigational Corp.*, 152 N.L.R.B. 998 (1965).

76. *Soule Glass and Glazing Co. v. NLRB*, 652 F.2d 1055, 1086 (1st Cir.1981) (quoting *NLRB v.Acme Industrial Products, Inc.*, 439 F.2d 40 (6th Cir.1971)).

77. 376 F.2d 684 (2d Cir.1967).

78. See Kohler, *Distinctions Without Differing Effects: Bargaining in Light of First National Maintenance*, 5 Indus.Rel.L.J. 400 (1983).

79. *Lemon Tree*, 231 N.L.R.B. 1168, 1176 (1977) (citing *P.B. Murtie Motor Transportation, Inc.*, 226 N.L.R.B. 1325 (1976)).

80. *Walter Pape, Inc.*, 205 N.L.R.B. 719, 720 (1973).

81. 209 N.L.R.B. 1006 (1974).

82. *Town & Country Mfg. Co.*, 136 N.L.R.B. 102 (1962).

83. 419 F.2d 1120 (6th Cir.1969).

84. Id. at 1123 (citing *East Bay Union of Machinists, Local 1304 v. NLRB*, 322 F.2d 411, 415 (D.C.Cir.1963), *aff'd sub nom., Fibreboard Paper Products Corp. v. NLRB*, 379 U.S. 203 (1964)).

85. *NLRB v. W.R. Grace Co., Construction Products*, 571 F.2d 279, 282 (5th Cir.1978) (quoting *NLRB v. J.P. Stevens & Co., Inc.*, 538 F.2d 1152, 1162 (5th Cir.1976)).

86. See, e.g., *International Ladies' Garment Workers Union v. NLRB*, 463 F.2d 907, 918 (D.C.Cir.1972) (and cases cited therein).

87. *Lemon Tree*, 231 N.L.R.B. 1168, 1176 (1977) (citing *Stagg Zipper Corp.*, 222 N.L.R.B. 1249 (1976)).

88. *Allied Chemical Workers v. Pittsburgh Plate Glass Co.*, 404 U.S. 157, 164 (1971) (citations omitted).

89. 356 U.S. 342 (1958).

90. 375 F.2d 208 (6th Cir.1967).

91. 412 F.2d 512 (2d Cir.1969).

92. See, e.g., *NLRB v. American Compress Warehouse,* 350 F.2d 365 (5th Cir.1965), *cert. denied,* 382 U.S. 982 (1966); *NLRB v. Tower Hosiery Mills,* 180 F.2d 701 (4th Cir. 1950); *Beyerl Chevrolet, Inc.,* 221 N.L.R.B. 710 (1975).

93. 145 N.L.R.B. 663 (1963).

94. Id. at 664. *Accord, NLRB v. International Hod Carriers,* 384 F.2d 55 (9th Cir. 1967) (union cannot insist that contractor guarantee wages of defaulting subcontractors).

95. *Oil, Chemical & Atomic Workers, Intern. Union v. NLRB,* 486 F.2d 1266 (D.C.Cir. 1973).

96. Id. at 1268 (footnotes omitted). See also *Douds v. Longshoremen's Union,* 241 F.2d 278 (2d Cir.1957) (union's insistence that bargaining cover all Atlantic and Gulf Coast ports and strike in New York to enforce demand held violation of 8(b)(3); *F.W. Woolworth Co.,* 179 N.L.R.B. 748 (1969) (employer's insistence that bargaining sessions with representatives of two different units be held together found violative of 8(a)(5), even though employer was willing to sign separate agreements).

97. *United States Pipe & Foundry Co. v. NLRB,* 298 F.2d 873 (5th Cir.1962) *cert. denied,* 370 U.S. 919 (1962).

98. *AFL–CIO Joint Negotiating Committee for Phelps Dodge v. NLRB,* 470 F.2d 722 (3d Cir.1972).

99. *Utility Workers Union,* 203 N.L.R.B. 230 (1973), *enforced,* 490 F.2d 1383 (6th Cir. 1974).

100. 165 N.L.R.B. 254 (1967), *enforced sub nom., Oil, Chemical and Atomic Workers Int. Union, Local 3–89 v. NLRB,* 405 F.2d 1111 (D.C.Cir.1968).

101. 165 N.L.R.B. at 258.

102. *Oil, Chemical and Atomic Workers Internat'l Union v. NLRB,* 405 F.2d 1111, at 1117 (D.C.Cir.1968).

103. 238 N.L.R.B. 261 (1978).

104. *NLRB v. Reed & Prince Mfg. Co.,* 205 F.2d 131 (1st Cir.1953), *cert. denied,* 346 U.S. 887 (1953).

105. 343 U.S. 395 (1952).

106. *See* note 142 *supra.*

107. 255 F.2d 564 (5th Cir.1958).

108. 442 F.2d 1067 (5th Cir.1971).

109. 219 F.2d 120 (6th Cir.1955).

110. Cf., *McCourt v. California Sports, Inc.,* 600 F.2d 1193 (6th Cir.1979) (no requirement to yield on initial position).

111. 430 F.2d 701 (6th Cir.1970).

112. *Kayser–Roth Hosiery Co.,* 176 N.L.R.B. 999 (1969).

113. 603 F.2d 604 (7th Cir.1979).

114. 465 F.2d 717 (9th Cir.1972).

115. *Case Concrete Co.,* 220 N.L.R.B. 1306 (1975).

116. See *Borg Warner Controls,* 198 N.L.R.B. 726 (1972); *NLRB v. Tomco Communications, Inc.,* 567 F.2d 871 (9th Cir.1978).

117. 148 N.L.R.B. 923 (1964).

118. 140 N.L.R.B. 1103 (1963), *enforced in relevant part,* 331 F.2d 720 (6th Cir.1964).

119. 191 N.L.R.B. 563 (1971), *enforced,* 456 F.2d 201 (8th Cir.1972).

120. *Harowe Servo Controls, Inc.,* 250 N.L.R.B. 958 (1980).

121. *NLRB v. Randle–Eastern Ambulance Service, Inc.,* 584 F.2d 720, 725 (5th Cir. 1978) (citations omitted).

122. 275 F.2d 229 (5th Cir.1960).

123. *New York Post Corp.,* 283 N.L.R.B. No. 60 (1987).

124. *Emeryville Research Center, Shell Dev. Co. v. NLRB,* 441 F.2d 880, 883 (9th Cir. 1971).

125. *Prudential Insurance Co. of America v. NLRB,* 412 F.2d 77, 84 (2d Cir.1969), cert. denied, 396 U.S. 928 (1969).

126. *San Diego Newspaper Guild, Local No. 95 v. NLRB,* 548 F.2d at 323 (1977).

127. *NLRB v. Truitt Mfg. Co.,* 351 U.S. 149, 151 (1956) (quoting *Truitt Mfg. Co.,* 110 N.L.R.B. 856, 856 (1954)). A union is also entitled to information concerning a company's relationship with another firm, the NLRB holds, where it is alleged that the two effectively constitute a single employer, and where the union has demonstrated a reasonable probability that the information will be useful in deciding whether to grieve or to take other action under the collective bargaining contract. *Barnard Engineering Co.,* 282 NLRB No. 86 (1987).

128. See *Ingalls Shipbuilding Corp.,* 143 N.L.R.B. 712, 718 (1963). *Accord Emeryville Research Center, Shell Dev. Co. v. NLRB,* note 194 supra.

129. 131 F.2d 485 (7th Cir.1942).

130. 89 N.L.R.B. 1192 (1950).

131. *Hastings and Sons Publishing Co.,* 102 N.L.R.B. 627 (1953); *Hearst Corp.,* 102 N.L.R.B. 637 (1953); *Post Publishing Co.,* 102 N.L.R.B. 648 (1953).

132. 440 U.S. 301 (1979).

133. *Detroit Edison Co.,* 218 N.L.R.B. 1024 (1975).

134. *NLRB v. Detroit Edison Co.,* 560 F.2d 722 (6th Cir.1977).

135. 218 N.L.R.B. at 1024.

136. 351 U.S. 149 (1956).

137. See *White v. NLRB,* 255 F.2d 564 (5th Cir.1958).

138. 361 U.S. 477 (1960).

139. *Insurance Agents Int. Union,* 119 N.L.R.B. 768 (1957).

140. 380 U.S. 300 (1965).

141. 380 U.S. 278 (1965).

142. See *NLRB v. Great Dane Trailers, Inc.,* 388 U.S. 26 (1967).

143. 351 U.S. 149 (1956).

144. *Rockwell International Corp.,* 260 N.L.R.B. 1345, 1347 (1982).

145. See *Jacobs Mfg. Co.,* 94 N.L.R.B. 1214 (1951), *enforced,* 196 F.2d 680 (2d Cir. 1952).

146. 268 N.L.R.B. 601 (1984).

147. *C & S Industries,* 158 N.L.R.B. 454 at 58 (1966).

148. See e.g., *Tide Water Assoc. Oil Co.,* 85 N.L.R.B. 1096 (1949); *Proctor Mfg. Corp.,* 131 N.L.R.B. 1166 (1961); *Cloverleaf Div. of Adams Dairy Co.,* 147 N.L.R.B. 1410 (1964), *enforcement denied on other grounds,* 350 F.2d 108 (8th Cir.1965); *LeRoy Machine Co.,* 147 N.L.R.B. 1431 (1964); *New York Mirror,* 151 N.L.R.B. 834 (1965).

149. See *Collyer Insulated Wire,* 192 N.L.R.B. 837 (1971).

150. See, *Blue Cross Blue Shield of Michigan,* 286 NLRB No. 50 (1987).

151. See, *United States Utilities Corp.,* 254 NLRB 480 (1981), *Southwest Security Equipment Corp.,* 262 NLRB 665 (1982), and *Chicago Magnesium Castings Co. v. NLRB,* 612 F.2d 1028 (7th Cir.1980).

152. See e.g. *Saveway Stores v. NLRB,* 691 F.2d 953 (10th Cir.1982).

153. See Weyand, Majority Rule in Collective Bargaining, 45 Columbia L.Rev. 556 (1945).

154. See Cox, Rights Under a Labor Agreement, 69 Harv.L.Rev. 601 (1956).

155. 465 U.S. 513 (1984).

156. The new section is 11 U.S.C. § 1113, 98 Stat. 333, 391, which took effect in July 1984.

157. See *In re Wheeling Pittsburgh Steel Corp.,* 50 B.R. 969, 13 B.C.D. 328 (Bkrtcy. W.D.Pa.1985), West, Life After Bildisco: Section 1113 and the Duty to Bargain in Good Faith, 47 Ohio St.Law.J. 66 (1986).

158. An NLRB unfair practice proceeding against an employer is not stayed by bankruptcy proceeding the U.S. Court of Appeals for the 6th Circuit rules. Such a proceeding was not an attempt to enforce a money judgment which would be subject to the stay. See, *NLRB v. Edward Cooper Painting, Inc.,* 804 F.2d 934 (6th Cir.1986).

159. 226 N.L.R.B. 1214 (1976).

160. 170 N.L.R.B. 61 (1968).

161. H.R.Rep. No. 245, 80th Cong., 1st Sess., 19–20 (1947).

162. 29 U.S.C. § 158(d) (1976). See *H.K. Porter Co. v. NLRB,* 397 U.S. 99 (1970).

163. See Getman, The Protection of Economic Pressure by Section 7 of the NLRA, 115 U. of Penn.L.Rev. 1195 (1967) (hereinafter Protection).

164. 304 U.S. 333 (1938).

165. *McKay,* supra.

166. See *Bonnar–Vawter, Inc. v. NLRB,* 289 F.2d 133 (1st Cir.1961).

167. 389 U.S. 375 (1967).

168. 171 N.L.R.B. 1366 (1968) enforced, 414 F.2d 99 (7th Cir.1969), cert denied, 397 U.S. 920 (1970).

169. *Belknap Inc. v. Hale,* 103 S.Ct. 3172 (1983).

170. *NLRB v. Erie Resistor Corp.,* 373 U.S. 221 (1963).

171. 380 U.S. 300 (1965).

172. See generally Gernhardt, Lockouts: An Analysis of Board and Court Cases Since Brown and American Ship, 57 Cornell L.Rev. 211 (1972).

173. *Inter–Collegiate Press,* 199 NLRB 177, aff'd 486 F.2d 837 (8th Cir.1973).

174. Getman, *Protection,* supra, p. 1210–1222.

175. 427 U.S. 132 (1976).

176. *NLRB v. Local 1229, IBEW,* 346 U.S. 464 (1953).

177. See *NLRB v. J.H. Rutter–Rex Mfg. Co.,* 245 F.2d 594 (5th Cir.1957).

178. See *Service Electric Company,* 281 N.L.R.B. 107 (1986).

179. *Pacific Gamble Robinson Co.,* 88 N.L.R.B. 482 (1950).

180. See e.g., *Hawaii Meat Co. v. NLRB,* 321 F.2d 397 (9th Cir.1963). See American *Cyanamid v. NLRB,* 592 F.2d 356 (7th Cir.1979). Holding that permanent subcontracting out of unit work without negotiation converted an economic strike into unfair labor practice strike.

181. See, e.g., *American Ship Bldg. Co. v. NLRB,* 380 U.S. 300 (1965) (lockouts); *NLRB v. MacKay Radio and Telegraph Co.,* 304 U.S. 333 (1938) (permanent replacement of economic strikers); *Philip Carey Mfg. Co.,* 140 N.L.R.B. 1103 (1963), *enforced in part,* 331 F.2d 720 (6th Cir.1964), *cert. denied,* 379 U.S. 888 (1964) (unilateral suspension of insurance benefits).

182. See e.g., *NLRB v. Rubatex Corp.,* 601 F.2d 147 (4th Cir.1979), *cert. denied,* 444 U.S. 928 (1979) (unilateral grant of post strike bonus to union members who worked during a strike but not to members who honored strike, held violative of 8(a)(1) and (5)).

183. See *NLRB v. Crompton–Highland Mills, Inc.,* 337 U.S. 217 (1949).

184. *Burlington Homes, Inc.,* 246 N.L.R.B. 1029 (1979).

185. See *Service Electric Co.,* 281 N.L.R.B. 107 (1986).

186. 321 F.2d 397 (9th Cir.1963).

187. 592 F.2d 356 (1979).

188. See, *Land Air Delivery, Inc.,* 286 N.L.R.B. No. 107 (1987). See also, 240 Bd 400 *Chicago Magnesium Castings Company v. NLRB,* 612 F.2d 1028 (7th Cir.1980).

189. See, e.g., *U.E.W., Local 1113 v. NLRB*, 223 F.2d 338 (D.C.Cir.1955), *cert. denied*, 350 U.S. 981 (1956); *Boeing Airplane Co. v. NLRB*, 174 F.2d 988 (D.C.Cir.1949).

190. See, e.g., *Arundel Corp.*, 210 N.L.R.B. 525 (1974); *United Elastic Corp.*, 84 N.L.R.B. 768 (1949).

191. R. Gorman, Labor Law 438 (1976).

192. 106 N.L.R.B. 1171 (1953).

193. *U.E.W., Local 1113 v. NLRB*, 223 F.2d 338, 341 (D.C.Cir.1955) (footnotes omitted).

194. *Dow Chemical Co. v. NLRB*, 636 F.2d 1352 (3rd Cir.1980).

195. 444 U.S. 212 (1979).

196. 345 U.S. 71 (1953).

197. *Rockaway News Supply Co.*, 95 N.L.R.B. 336 (1951).

198. *NLRB v. Rockaway News Supply Co.*, 197 F.2d 111 (2d Cir.1952).

199. 137 N.L.R.B. 1545 (1962), *modifying*, 130 N.L.R.B. 1208 (1961), *enforced*, 325 F.2d 1011 (D.C.Cir.1963), *cert. denied*, 377 U.S. 905 (1964).

200. See *NLRB v. Alama Express, Inc.*, 430 F.2d 1032 (5th Cir.1970); *Overnite Transportation Co.*, 154 N.L.R.B. 1271 (1965).

201. *NLRB v. Browning Ferris Industries*, 700 F.2d 385 (7th Cir.1986).

202. For a good general discussion tracing the development of the law in this area see *Business Services by Manpower v. NLRB*, 748 F.2d 442 (1986), 121 L.R.R.M. 2835 (1986).

203. 397 U.S. 99 (1970).

204. *Ex–Cell–O Corp.*, 185 N.L.R.B. 107 (1970).

205. See *Auto Prod., Inc.*, 265 N.L.R.B. 331 (1982), see p. 132. In *State Distributing Co.*, 282 NLRB No. 151 (1987), the Board reinstated the collective bargaining agreement negotiated under a previous employer when the new employer unilaterally departed from the wages and benefits of his predecessor's contract. The remedy retroactively reinstates the contract to the time of the takeover and to continue until the parties bargain in good faith to an agreement or impasse. See also, *American Press, Inc.*, 280 NLRB No. 109 (1986), where the Board held that a successor employer cannot avoid his duty to bargain in good faith with the union representing the predecessor's employees by unlawfully refusing to hire seven of these employees.

206. MuCulloch, Past, Present & Future Remedies Under § 8(a)(5) of the NLRB, 19 Labr.L.J. 131 (1968).

207. See *Mastro Plastics Corp. v. NLRB*, 350 U.S. 270 (1956); *NLRB v. Dubo Mfg. Corp.*, 353 F.2d 157 (6th Cir.1965).

208. 236 N.L.R.B. 1160 (1978). In *Brewery Delivery Employees Local 46*, for example, the union had engaged in shop meetings and work stoppages during the term of the collective bargaining agreement "to force the Employer's concession to the unlawful position that the Orange Book [the master agreement which governed parties' rights relationship prior to 1973] was the existing contract." The ALJ (in a decision adopted by the Board) found the union in violation of sections 8(d) and 8(b)(3), and issued a cease-and-desist order.

209. 254 N.L.R.B. 445 (1981).

210. 236 N.L.R.B. 1209 (1978).

211. 226 N.L.R.B. 97 (1976).

212. *Communications Workers of America, Local 1122 v. NLRB*, 562 F.2d 37 (2d Cir. 1977).

213. *NLRB v. System Council T–6, I.B.E.W.*, 599 F.2d 5, 7 n. 7 (1st Cir.1979) (citations omitted).

214. 91 N.L.R.B. 989 (1950).

215. 174 N.L.R.B. 177 (1969).

216. 152 N.L.R.B. 449 (1965).

217. 161 N.L.R.B. 1077 (1966).

218. *NLRB v. Herman Sausage Co.*, 275 F.2d 229 (5th Cir.1960).

Relevant Books, Articles, and Suggested Reading

BOOKS:

Bacharach & Lawler, Bargaining (1981).

Getman & Blackburn, Labor Relations—Law Practice & Policy (1983).

Bok & Dunlop, Labor and the American Community (1970).

Slichter, Healy & Livernash, The Impact of Collective Bargaining on Management (1965).

Rubin & Brown, The Social Psychology of Bargaining and Negotiation (1975).

Walton & McKensie, A Behavioral Theory of Labor Negotiations (1965).

Boyce & Turner, Fair Representation—The NLRB and the Courts (1984).

Attleson, Values and Assumptions in American Labor Law (1983).

Simkin, Mediation and the Dynamics of Collective Bargaining (1971).

ARTICLES:

Schatzki, "Majority Rule, Exclusive Representation and the Interests of Individual Workers: Should Exclusivity be Abolished," 123 Univ.Penn.L.Rev. 897 (1975).

Weiler, "Striking a New Balance: Freedom of Contract and the Prospects for Union Representation," 98 Harvard L.Rev. 351 (1984).

Bartosic & Hartley, "The Employer's Duty to Supply Information to the Union," 58 Cornell L.Rev. 23 (1972).

Schatzki, "The Employer's Unilateral Act—A Per Se Violation Sometimes," 44 Texas L.Rev. 470 (1986).

Harper, "Leveling the Road From *Borg Warner* to *First National Maintenance*—The Scope of Mandatory Bargaining," 68 Virginia L.Rev. 1447 (1982).

Kohler, "Distinctions Without Differing Effects—Bargaining in Light of First National Maintenance," 5 Indus.Rel.L.Journal 400 (1983).

Silverstein, "Union Decisions on Collective Bargaining Goals: A Proposal For Interest Group Participation," 77 Mich.L.Rev. 1485 (1979).

West, "Life After Bildisco—§ 1113 and The Duty to Bargain in Good Faith," 47 Ohio St.L.Jour. 65 (1986).

Cox, "The Duty to Bargain in Good Faith," 71 Harv.L.Rev. 1401 (1958).

Shedlin, "Regulation of Disclosure of Economic and Financial Data," 41 Ohio St.L.Jour. 441 (1980).

Getman, "The Protection of Economic Pressure by Section 7 of the National Labor Relations Act," 115 Univ.Penn.L.Rev. 1195 (1967).

*

Chapter III

THE ENFORCEMENT OF RIGHTS UNDER COLLECTIVE AGREEMENTS

Part I. The Relationship Between Collective Bargaining and Grievance Resolution

A. The Basic Model

1. The Contractual Provisions

A typical collective-bargaining agreement is a complex document, many pages long dealing with a variety of diverse issues. It establishes a detailed wage schedule setting forth rates of pay for different jobs, and step increases based on seniority and provides for overtime pay at specified rates. It contains a job classification system, a clause describing how seniority is to be calculated and how it may be lost, and it provides for promotion on the basis of a compromise between the union's proposal emphasizing seniority and management's desire for unlimited discretion. It lists holidays, sets forth a scheme by which the amount of an employee's vacation may be determined, and establishes priorities in vacation selection. It details the insurance and retirement benefits to which employees are entitled. It contains a clause recognizing certain general managerial prerogatives, and it provides that only unit members may do unit work. It contains a union pledge not to strike during the term of the agreement and a similar management promise not to resort to lockouts. It contains management promises of safe working conditions, no discrimination, and union recognition. It may contain clauses covering career development, substance abuse, child care, and counseling programs. It may deal with the introduction of new technology and contain either limits on, or recognition of, management's rights to subcontract. It will deal with layoffs and plant closings, provide for call-in pay, and set up a maternity leave system. It will contain a clause limiting the employer's right to discharge and discipline by the concept of "just cause," which may or may not be further defined. It may contain a specific absentee program that details how absences are to be calculated and the point at which the employee becomes liable for penalties. It may deal with drug testing and provide for "progressive discipline."

The agreement will also provide a system for the resolution of disputes about its application. Such disputes are inevitable in a unit of any size. The breadth of the agreement, the fact that many of the clauses are complex, that many of the clauses represent compromises

161

between union and management proposals, and that some of the clauses were drafted hastily in the shadow of a strike, means that disputes about their application are bound to arise with some frequency in any unit containing a substantial number of employees.

After World War II, the parties to collective bargaining agreements began increasingly to include provisions for the resolution of these disputes through a grievance system, the final step of which was binding arbitration. The use of such systems spread rapidly and they are included today in the vast majority of collective agreements. Most follow a standard procedure.

When an employee or the union feels that rights under an agreement have been violated, a grievance may be filed. The grievance is a written complaint. It will describe the incident or course of managerial conduct complained of and will specify the terms of the agreement that the union claims were violated. The grievance is initially discussed informally by union stewards and low level supervisors. If not settled, it is dealt with by successively higher levels of management and union officials.

At each stage, management may affirm its original decision, grant the grievance, or offer to settle it through some form of compromise. Under most agreements, the union may withdraw the claims or accept a compromise without obtaining approval from the grievant. If the grievance is not resolved through negotiation, the union has the option of demanding arbitration. Thus, only cases that are not winnowed out by the process of day-to-day negotiation proceed to arbitration.

The agreement typically provides a technique for choosing the arbitrator and declares that his or her decision will be final and binding. Each party pays for its own witnesses and representative. The parties share the arbitrator's fees and the expense of the hearing. The costs in time, money, and dislocation involved in pursuing a grievance to arbitration are such that generally both sides have an incentive to reduce the number of grievances and to settle those that are filed without going to arbitration. The number of grievances can be reduced to the extent that the parties understand the meaning of the contract and try to fulfill their obligations under it. Achievement of these goals in turn can be facilitated by the parties' use of standard language in the contract and by the arbitrator's adhering to decisions in previous cases at the same company or at other companies. It is thus in the interest of both labor and management that a general body of precedent be established to guide them in administering the contract and to provide arbitrators with standards for their future decisions.

2. The Function of the Arbitrator

The role of the arbitrator in the process varies; but in most cases arbitrators function much like judges, holding adjudicatory hearings in which testimony is heard, witnesses are cross-examined, evidence is presented, objections are made, and each side is represented by a professional, who may be a lawyer, a labor relations specialist, or a union business agent. Arbitrators receive written briefs from the parties and explain their awards in written opinions in which they cite opinions of other arbitrators and arbitral doctrine.

This process increases the need for a sophisticated labor relations staff that will study and respond appropriately to arbitration decisions. The fact that arbitration awards will be carefully analyzed by company and union officials influences the arbitrator to write more carefully, which further legalizes the process and makes it more costly.

On the other hand, since part of arbitration's attractiveness stems from the promise of speed, informality, and economy, spokesmen for both labor and management are continually decrying this tendency and frequent efforts are made to reduce the impact or formality by developing inexpensive, expedited procedures that limit the use of lawyers, transcripts, briefs, and written opinions. Thus, at any time the overall system reflects a compromise between a natural tendency towards increased formality and the parties' desire for a quick, simple, and inexpensive system of dispute resolution.

Various techniques have been developed in an effort to accommodate these conflicting goals. One of the most promising is to attempt mediation of the dispute prior to arbitration. Sometimes the mediation effort will be undertaken by the arbitrator prior to hearing the case. After preliminary discussion, the arbitrator, by indirection, may convince one or both of the parties that their case is more doubtful than they realized and thereby persuade them to settle. The difficulty with this approach stems from the mixing of roles.[1] The parties may feel unfairly pushed by the arbitrator and it is not clear whether it is the parties' settlement or the arbitrator's. To avoid the blurring of roles, some parties are now providing for mediation in advance of the hearing by a mediator with no power to impose a settlement. This technique was first utilized systematically in the coal industry in places where the arbitration process was not working well and the relationship of the parties was marred by hostility. Early results suggest that skilled grievance mediation prior to a hearing can lead to settlement of a significant percentage of cases and may also lead the parties to a less confrontational relationship.

3. The Resolution of Disputes in the Absence of Arbitration

Not all collective bargaining agreements provide for arbitration. Those that do not, provide for a variety of other techniques. Some contain the basic grievance process but provide for final disposition of an unresolved dispute by management, some for final resolution by a joint union-management committee, and some contracts specify that if a grievance is not resolved through negotiation, the union has the right to strike over the matter in dispute. Some contracts do not contain a grievance system and, therefore, by implication leave the resolution of disputes concerning the agreement's meaning to the courts under section 301 of the Act. Although the parties are legally entitled to avoid arbitration, as will be discussed below, various legal techniques have been developed with the idea of encouraging its use and discouraging the resort to alternatives.

B. The Impact of a Grievance System on an Ongoing Enterprise

1. Changing Standards

a. INCREASED USE OF SENIORITY

Unions almost invariably favor greater recognition of seniority in promotions and layoffs. From a union's point of view, a policy favoring the use of seniority in these situations has several attractions. First, it helps to establish that it is the agreement and not the employer that is the source of advancement or the protection against layoff. Second, it provides a generally understood and accepted system for avoiding charges of personal favoritism in situations in which the interests of different members of the bargaining unit conflict. Third, and perhaps most significantly, it helps to establish that employees develop personal claims to their jobs and to advancement by virtue of their labor. As already noted, the contract is likely to contain language that constitutes a compromise between the union's desire for promotion and layoff on the basis of seniority and management's desire for discretion. Whatever the final language, management is generally aware in promotion and layoff situations that failure to favor the senior employee will lead to a grievance while his or her selection will not. Management officials desirous of avoiding the costs in time, money, and employee morale that grievances entail will often choose the senior employee even where they think they could prevail in arbitration if they select a junior employee. Moreover, union grievance representatives are likely to push hard for senior employees during the lower stages of the process. Thus, by virtue of the grievance system, seniority is almost certain to play a more significant role in the enterprise than reading the language of the contract would indicate to the inexperienced observer.

b. DISCHARGE AND DISCIPLINE

A high percentage of grievances are filed to protest disciplinary action by the employer. Such grievances are of fundamental importance to both employees and to management, particularly where discharge is involved. One important measure of a union's success is its ability to adequately represent its members in such cases. The importance of just-cause grievances is well understood and arbitrators frequently write long, careful opinions in such cases. An elaborate jurisprudence of "just cause" has developed [2] the basic aspects of which are as follows:

1. The arbitrator evaluates not only the misbehavior of the employee, but also the adequacy of the procedure employed by management in determining his or her fault and deciding on the penalty. This means that employees generally must be given adequate notice of company rules, as well as a chance to explain their behavior, that discipline once invoked cannot be changed, and that it be applied progressively.

2. "Just cause" has been held to imply a requirement of equal treatment, so that if an employer has been willing to tolerate absenteeism from employees generally, it may not, without adequate warning, impose a more severe penalty in a sudden effort to crack down.

3. "Just cause" is limited by its relation to the employment relationship, and employees cannot generally be disciplined for behavior unrelated to their jobs.

Thus to establish a disciplinary system that works effectively, an employer needs to articulate its rules and apply them consistently and progressively. The rules themselves are generally framed, in part at least, with a view to the decisions of previous arbitrators. Thus the grievance system tends to create more equitable but also more formal and legalistic working environments.

2. The Impact of Grievance Systems on Union–Management Relations

The broad sweep of collective-bargaining agreements together with wide-ranging grievance systems means that the union has an institutional interest in almost all aspects of employer-employee relations. This gives management an incentive to develop good working relations with union leadership, whose approach to the filing and processing of grievances can have a great impact on the day-to-day operations of a unionized enterprise.[3] The existence of a grievance procedure provides a union with a relatively inexpensive technique for putting pressure on management. If there are a great number of grievances pending at one time, management personnel will be occupied with grievance resolution and distracted from their other functions. Employees who are to be witnesses will be taken away from their normal tasks to be interviewed or perhaps called in to meetings. If the validity of plant rules is called into question, a decision must be made whether to suspend their operation or risk additional grievances. The involvement of union personnel at the lower levels will not be comparably troublesome to the union since grievance processing is a primary union function.   If a large union and small employer are involved, the union can rely on its national staff and will therefore have much greater resources to throw into the battle.   It is for this reason that when a strong and responsive union represents employees, the existence of grievance machinery is likely to create an incentive for the employer to get along with the union, which often will mean notifying the union in advance of contemplated changes or discipline and on occasion will mean deferring or changing proposed action at the insistence of the union.

When the parties have been negotiating and resolving disputes over a long period of years, a spirit of cooperation may develop in handling grievances.   In such cases, union and management settle into a relationship of reciprocal legitimation in which the benefits flow from the general relationship established, rather than from arbitration itself, which is then rarely necessary.   The grievance machinery can serve as an aid to management because the shop steward or grievance committee will recognize and certify the legitimacy of appropriate instructions.   Management's reliance on the union for this purpose in turn reaffirms the union's key role in the plant.   Some scholars suggest that the grievance machinery serves as an aid to productivity when cooperative relations are established.[4]

3. The Role of the Union

Under the typical collective-bargaining agreement, the union controls both the lower-level bargaining and the presentation of the case in arbitration.[5]   As a result, the successful functioning of the system turns on the expertise, resources, and integrity of the union.   If the grievance committee is not familiar with the contract, it will not encourage the filing of needed grievances, nor will it know which ones should be traded off.   Substantial resources are generally required to pay for arbitration and to hire professional counsel when necessary.   An unresponsive leadership may, through inadvertence or ill will, fail to process meritorious grievances that are important to individuals or groups within the union.   If the union lacks the support of its members, it will be unable to enforce favorable awards and unable to moderate the impact of unfavorable ones at the bargaining table.   Finally, a weak union will not be able to negotiate the standard provisions that provide job protection and ensure the use of seniority.

When labor relations are unsatisfactory, the existence of arbitration may actually exacerbate bad feelings.[6]   In such circumstances the jurisprudence of arbitration encourages management to enforce discipline for all offenses to avoid providing the union with a basis for claiming discriminatory treatment.   The union responds by filing numerous grievances that are regularly denied in the lower steps. The union is forced to go to arbitration frequently, which causes a backlog with concomitant delays in hearing and disposition. The hearing is pervaded with an atmosphere of hostility; it provides the parties with an additional opportunity to berate each other. Conflicts and wildcat strikes are provoked when management takes a disciplinary action or denies a grievance, when arbitration is delayed, or when one of the parties considers an arbitrator's decision unacceptable. All of this makes the grievance machinery a cause of further tension. Of course, such situations cannot be the rule or the parties would reject arbitration. Arbitration is provided for in over 94 percent of collective agreements.[7]

This fact, however, does not provide a total measure of its overall success. To some extent the prevalence of arbitration reflects the lack of acceptable alternatives and the potential usefulness of arbitration in aiding productivity when relations are acceptable. Unions want an external check on management. It would be costly to bring suit each time they believed management violated the agreement, because this would require the constant use of lawyers and courts. Moreover, for various economic, historic, and ideological reasons, unions seek to minimize the use of these institutions. Regular strikes would be tumultuous and costly. The NLRB does not have jurisdiction over most breaches of contract. Of course, if unions were totally dissatisfied with arbitration they might agitate for special courts, but special courts would require a reversal of labor's historic distrust of government involvement and would be unlikely to solve the problems that unions experience with the grievance machinery. In addition, the fact that arbitration offers another technique for exerting bargaining pressure makes it at least as attractive, from a union's perspective, as other means of adjudication. Thus, it is easy to see why arbitration is liked by unions, whether or not it reduces strikes.

From management's perspective, the issue is more doubtful. If arbitration gives the union a new source of pressure, why would management accept it so routinely? The fact that management regularly accepts arbitration does not mean that management always favors it. Provision for union security and limits on discipline, work assignment, and promotion, when lawful, are pervasive in collective agreements not because they are desired by management, but because they are sufficiently important for the union to insist on them as a precondition to agreement. The union will moderate other proposals to achieve such provisions. In addition, for management, strike over contract grievances are far more troublesome. Most other techniques of dispute resolution have substantial drawbacks: court cases may be costly and may involve long delays during which the law of the shop may be confused; agencies or special courts involve government interference or oversight of managerial decision making. Arbitrators partial to employers can be carefully selected to avoid those perceived to have a union bias, and keep their role at least partially controlled. Moreover, if the parties do not pay for the dispute-resolution mechanism, the union may be motivated to pursue many more grievances. Thus, the success of a grievance system is ultimately dependent upon, and inevitably reflects, the collective bargaining relationship that gave rise to it.

Part II.   The Reach of the Judicial Policy Favoring Arbitration

A. The Trilogy

Section 301(a) of the NLRA provides that "suits for violation of contracts between an employer and a labor organization . . . may be brought in any district court of the United States."

The Supreme Court, after some hesitation, held in *Textile Workers Union v. Lincoln Mills of Alabama* [8] that the section announced "a federal policy . . . which placed sanctions behind agreements to arbitrate grievance disputes." Because the policy was derived from a federal statute, it followed that the law to be applied in such suits "is a federal law which the courts must fashion from the policy of our national labor laws."

This opinion was followed three years later by a series of three decisions generally referred to as "the Steelworkers Trilogy" in which the Court articulated more fully the strength and breadth of its support for arbitration. In the first of these decisions, *United Steelworkers of America v. American Mfg. Co.,* [9] the Court rejected a New York doctrine holding that arbitration would not be judicially compelled where the grievance was "a frivolous, patently baseless one." The Court held that arbitration should be ordered regardless of the strength of the claim. The holding was justified by affirming the importance of arbitration and the lack of judicial competence in dealing with such claims:

> "In the context of the plant or industry the grievance may assume proportions of which judges are ignorant . . . arbitration is a stabilizing influence as it serves as a vehicle for handling every and all disputes that arise under the agreement . . . the function of the court is very limited when the parties have agreed to submit all questions of contract interpretation to the arbitrator . . . The processing of even frivolous claims may have therapeutic values of which those who are not a part of plant environment may be quite unaware."

The themes of the value of arbitration and the ignorance of the courts were repeated throughout the three opinions. The Court also justified its conclusion on the grounds that "[t]here is no exception in the no-strike clause and none therefore should be read into the grievance clause since the one is the quid pro quo for the other." This passage is significant in establishing a judicially recognized link between the breadth of these two provisions of the agreement. The passage is predictive of future confusion insofar as the Court undertook what appears to be an empirical assumption concerning the dynamics of the bargaining process without any general factual basis or any investigation into the contractual negotiations that led to the agreement it was construing.

In the second case of the trilogy, *United Steelworkers of America v. Warrior & Gulf Navigation Co.,*[10] the Supreme Court, after once again stressing the special competence of arbitrators, instructed the lower courts to take an extremely broad view of the promise to arbitrate. An "order to arbitrate the particular grievance should not be denied unless it may be said with positive assurance that the arbitration clause is not susceptible to an interpretation that covers the asserted dispute. Doubts should be resolved in favor of coverage." In the third case of the trilogy, *United Steelworkers of America v. Enterprise Wheel & Car Corp.,*[11] the Supreme Court dealt with the enforceability of arbitration awards and instructed the lower courts to grant enforcement routinely whether or not they agreed with the arbitrator. "It is the arbitrator's construction which was bargained for; . . . the courts have no business overruling him because their interpretation of the contract is different from his." The limited nature of the judicial inquiry prior to enforcement was stressed repeatedly. "The refusal of courts to review the merits of an arbitration award is the proper approach to arbitration. . . . A mere ambiguity in the opinion accompanying an award which permits the inference that the arbitrator may have exceeded his authority is not a reason for refusing to enforce the award. Arbitrators have no obligation to the court to give their reasons for an award."

The force of this language was somewhat undercut by the requirement that the arbitrator's award be an interpretation of the contract rather than an interpretation of law or of general public policy. "Nevertheless, an arbitrator is confined to the bargaining agreement—his award is legitimate, so long as it draws its essence from the collective bargaining agreement. When the arbitrator's words manifest an infidelity to this obligation, courts have no choice but to refuse enforcement of the award." The Court did not elaborate on this requirement.

Taken together, the opinions show a clear judicial decision to support the voluntary process of grievance arbitration by putting the force of law behind it. Inevitably, however, the opinions raised questions about application of the policy and about its wisdom.

The most persistent and paradoxical ambiguity that ran throughout the opinions concerns the extent to which the policies favoring arbitration are to be applied regardless of the manifest intent of the parties. For example, how far should the courts stretch the language of the contract to find that something is arbitrable and to what extent should the policy favoring broad interpretation of arbitration clauses, when pursued by judges, be permitted to override the policy favoring arbitral rather than judicial interpretation of the agreement? In enforcing awards, how far should the court's sense of the parties' agreement determine whether the award draws its essence from the agreement? To what extent does the Court's equation of the reach of the arbitration and no-strike clauses depend upon interpretation of the language of the parties?

Beyond these immediate issues, the opinions raised questions about the relationship of the policy favoring arbitration with other policies traditionally recognized in labor relations such as policies dealing with the right to strike and the previously announced central role of the National Labor Relations Board in enunciating national labor policy. Finally, on a more speculative basis, the opinions obliquely raised the question of whether a voluntary system whose attributes were shaped by agreement would be changed or distorted by the efforts of the courts to support it.

B. Enforcement of the Promise to Arbitrate

1. The Complementary Role of Courts and Arbitrators

Questions of arbitrability are rarely addressed to the courts and, when they are, the courts have largely followed the Supreme Court's instruction to construe the promise to arbitrate broadly. For this reason, when one of the parties (almost always the employer) claims that an issue is not arbitrable, that claim is likely to be presented to an arbitrator rather than to the court.

Employers may argue that a grievance should not be heard on the merits, either by claiming that the parties have not agreed in the contract to arbitrate this class of grievances or by arguing that the employee or the union has failed to satisfy one of the procedural requirements or time limits set forth in the contract. The former is sometimes called substantive arbitrability and the latter procedural arbitrability. The statement has frequently been made that substantive arbitrability is for the courts to decide and procedural arbitrability is for arbitrators. In reality, both are usually heard first by arbitrators, whose overwhelming tendency is to decide that matters are arbitrable. Decisions on arbitrability are rarely appealed to the courts and even more rarely reversed when they are. It should be noted that an employer victory based on a procedural failure by the union may turn out to be a temporary one because, as is discussed below, it may lead to a duty of fair representation claim against the union and the subsequent or simultaneous hearing on the merits by the court. For this reason, and because it is widely agreed that the grievance system cannot perform its important role of easing tension and legitimating managerial decisions unless employees feel they've had their day in court, arbitrators and courts are very reluctant to uphold claims based on procedural failure. They will strain interpretation to find either that the requirement was waived by the employer's willingness to proceed under the grievance system or that the error was a harmless one.

2. Arbitrability in the Absence of an Agreement

In *John Wiley and Sons, Inc. v. Livingston*,[12] the Supreme Court reasserted the policy of the trilogy favoring arbitrability despite the merger of the employer with another. In that case, the employer, Interscience Publishers, Inc., which was a party to a collective-bargaining agreement, was absorbed by a larger, non-union employer, John Wiley & Sons, Inc. The sales agreement did not contain a provision making the collective-bargaining agreement binding on the successors of Interscience. Although John Wiley was not a party to the collective-bargaining agreement, the Court found that it was bound by the arbitration provisions. The decision was based on "the central role of arbitration in effectuating national labor policy:"

> "It would derogate from the 'federal policy of settling disputes by arbitration . . .' if a change in the corporate structure or ownership of a business enterprise had the automatic consequence of removing a duty to arbitrate previously established; this is so as much in cases like the present, where the contracting employer disappears into another by merger, as in those in which one owner replaces another but the business entity remains the same."

The Court recognized that it had in this context abandoned traditional contract notions:

> "While the principles of law governing ordinary contracts would not bind to a contract an unconsenting successor to a contracting party, a collective bargaining agreement is not an ordinary contract. . . . Therefore, although the duty to arbitrate, as we have said, supra must be founded on a contract, the impressive policy considerations favoring arbitration are not wholly overborne by the fact that Wiley did not sign the contract being construed."

The holding was a broad one, although the Court recognized that there might be circumstances "in which the lack of any substantial continuity of identity in the business enterprise before and after a change would make a duty to arbitrate something imposed from without, not reasonably to be found in the particular bargaining agreement and the act of the parties involved." In *Nolde Brothers, Inc.*

v. Local No. 358, Bakery & Confectionary Workers Union,[13] the Court held that the duty to arbitrate survived both the closing of the enterprise and the termination of the agreement.

The *Nolde* decision makes clear something that was implicit in *John Wiley*, that the obligation to arbitrate might continue even where the agreement had expired. The Court in *Nolde* stated that so long as the dispute concerned construction of the expired contract, the "presumption favoring arbitrality" continued unless "negated expressly or by clear implication."

In *NLRB v. Burns International Security Services, Inc.,*[14] the Court announced that the obligation to arbitrate in successorship cases existed even though in such cases the agreement itself did not survive the purchase. The Court distinguished the *Wiley* case on the grounds that continuing the agreement was not supported by any national policy comparable to the policy favoring arbitration upon which the *Wiley* decision was based. Indeed the Court pointed out that requiring a party to accept a contract that it did not negotiate was at odds with the policy favoring free collective bargaining.

In *Howard Johnson Co., Inc. v. Detroit Local Joint Exec. Board,*[15] the Court further undercut *Wiley* when it held that Howard Johnson, a successor employer that failed to employ most of the predecessor's employees, was not bound to arbitrate under the former agreement. The Court justified its failure to apply *Wiley* primarily on the grounds that there was not the "continuity of identity in the business enterprise" that occurred when Wiley hired all of the Interscience employees. The Court stated that the continuity of the business enterprise requires "a substantial continuity in the identity of the work force." The Court distinguished a successorship claim resulting from an arms-length transaction between two employers from a successorship claim that was merely a "disguised continuance of the old employer," and it stressed that there are no easy rules to determine when an employer was sufficiently the successor of another to justify the imposition of the rule in *Wiley*. The Court has since endorsed the Board's approach of determining successorship on the basis of the substantial continuity test.[16] The combination of decisions in *Wiley*, *Burns* and *Howard Johnson's* leaves open several significant questions about the availability and scope of arbitration in successorship cases.

a. THE SCOPE OF THE DUTY TO ARBITRATE

The major question raised by *Nolde* and the combination of *Wiley* and *Burns* concerns the necessary relationship between the collective agreement and the facts giving rise to the grievance. It is clear that the duty to arbitrate may exist with respect to a claim that arises after the agreement terminates. *Nolde* itself was such a case. The Court described the dispute—a claim for severance pay—as one that "arises under the contract but which is based on events which occur after its termination." The Court concluded that such claims were arbitrable unless the agreement "expressly excludes [them] from its operations." The issue of whether a particular provision was intended to survive the expiration of the contract was for the arbitrator to decide.

As the Court used the concept of "arises under the agreement," it seemed to refer to the existence of a claim by the union that the agreement applied to the post-agreement facts. In *Nolde* this claim was based partly on the fact that the severance pay accrued to the employees during the terms of the agreement. The Court did not stress that most of the facts on which the claim rested arose during the terms of the agreement. It emphasized instead the union's claim that the contract provision and the grievance system survived the agreement. Such a claim is almost always available to a union in a post-contract situation. So long as the union continues to be representative of the employees under *Burns* or *Fall River*, it can argue that the most recent contract provisions continue to apply because of the prohibition against unilateral change included in the concept of exclusivity. The Board has basically accepted this approach[17] as the basis for a post-contract claim. The only time it would be unavailable to a union that represents employees after termination of an agreement would be either when the agreement itself expressly denied arbitration of post-contract disputes or when the relevant terms were amended by the employer after bargaining over it in good faith to an impasse. The continuity of the grievance system in the presence of an ambiguous arbitration clause may be seen as continuing either because of the strong policy favoring arbitration or as part of the employer's obligation not to make unilateral changes until it has bargained to impasse, or because of some combination of these two. In section 301 actions to compel arbitration, some courts have rejected this approach. They have limited *Nolde* to cases in which the claim was for rights that were violated or that accrued during the term of the agreement.[18]

Courts seeking to limit *Nolde* to such cases can generally find some language in the grievance or arbitration clause limiting its application to "disputes arising under the agreement." Courts that take an expansive view hold that such language does not constitute the express waiver of arbitration required by *Nolde.*

b. THE ARBITRATION PROCESS IN THE ABSENCE OF AGREEMENT

The combination of *Wiley, Burns,* and *Nolde* means that in most successor cases in which the duty to arbitrate continues, the collective agreement which gave rise to it does not. The Court, by separating out the arbitration clause from the contract, inevitably raises questions about the scope of the arbitrator's authority and the standards to be used. Does the arbitrator have the authority to determine that certain obligations that arose under the now-expired agreement are binding on the successor even though the basic agreement is not? If so, does he or she have authority to rule that the successorship clause normally contained in collective agreements applies? And by what standards does an arbitrator, whose authority is typically limited to "interpreting" the agreement, pick and choose among the clauses? If the arbitrator does not apply the agreement, does he or she determine which working standards must remain in force prior to bargaining to impasse under the doctrine of exclusivity? One difficulty in answering any of these questions is that the arbitrators' expertise, experience, and authority are all centered on interpreting the agreement, which is the one task that is apparently unavailable. It would seem inevitable that either the policy of *Wiley* or that of *Burns* must eventually predominate. It is difficult to understand how they may coexist indefinitely.

c. The Enforcement of Successorship Clauses

The decision in *Howard Johnson* made clear that a purchasing employer may avoid arbitration, the agreement and collective bargaining despite the existence of a clause stating that the agreement was to bind not only the parties but their "successors and assigns." Such clauses are to be found in many collective agreements and at one time they were thought to provide for contractual continuity in the event of sale. By now it is well established, however, that a purchaser who is not connected with the seller is not a "successor" nor an "assign" for these purposes, that it is not required to adopt the agreement upon purchase, and that the seller has not violated the agreement by such a sale. This conclusion does not necessarily apply where the original agreement contains stronger language providing for continuity, although it is not clear how much stronger the language must be for the courts to reach a different result. There are cases in which the addition of such language as "it is the intent of the parties that this agreement shall remain in effect for the full term thereof" was held to make the contract binding upon a sale of the business.[19] The trend of the cases, however, is towards the conclusion that unless the successors and assigns clause specifically applies to purchases, a business may be sold without the agreement following the sale. This means that the new purchaser will be free to hire its own work force or to choose among the existing employees without regard to their seniority. The Court in *Howard Johnson* stressed that the "new employers must be free to make substantial changes." The policy behind this approach was the Court's concern that the successors and assigns clause not "inhibit the free transfer of capital."[20] Thus this line of cases, like the line dealing with the duty to bargain over plant closings and sales of the business, began with the Court seeking to protect the interest of the employees affected and ended up with the Court supporting unencumbered management decision-making in the interests of efficiency. The net result is to pose both legal and practical problems for all of the parties involved. The seller generally will want the purchaser to assume the contract both because it feels an obligation to the people it previously employed and because such a course is most likely to insure it against future liability. The seller is rarely in a position to insist, however, if its insistence will imperil the sale. The purchaser faces the problem of deciding how much of the existing operation to continue. If it retains all or most of the existing work force it increases the likelihood that it will be required to recognize the union and possibly to accept the contract. If it seeks to bring in new employees and tries to avoid the union, it loses the benefits of hiring experienced employees and runs a risk that the deal will be enjoined. If it is found to have refused employment to members of the former workforce to avoid unionization, it will be guilty of violating section 8(a)(3) and it will be required to hire the employees and liable for back pay.[21] Since the purchaser has the legal right to avoid being a successor in most situations, the union will have a difficult time in deciding on how hard to fight to get the successor to accept the existing contract. If the union insists it may spoil the sale, perhaps forcing the original employer to go out of business and thereby depriving its members of jobs. Insistance may also motivate the purchaser to refuse to hire the existing employees, something the purchaser might do otherwise. If the union fails to aggressively pursue this issue, it may weaken the protection otherwise provided by its collective agreement and it may subject itself to possible liability under the duty of fair representation. If the union is sued successfully under the duty of fair representation, both it and the employers may ultimately be held liable to the employees who were not hired by the purchaser.

3. Enforcement of the Promise to Arbitrate Matters Covered by the NLRA

Quite soon after the Trilogy, the Supreme Court made clear that the doctrines of preemption and primary jurisdiction do not apply to arbitration. The fact that a grievance includes matters that might constitute a claim under the NLRA does not prevent the promise to arbitrate from being enforceable.[22] In general, the policy of judicially enforcing the promise to arbitrate applies to matters that might also have been dealt with under the NLRA.

C. The Enforcement of Arbitral Awards

The arbitration process works best when both parties feel committed to abiding by an award, except in the most exceptional cases. For the union, this means rejection of the concept of wildcat strikes or other forms of economic pressure to overturn an award prior to negotiating a new agreement; for management, this commitment requires prompt obedience to unfavorable awards and almost never seeking judicial review or requiring the union to do so. Where good relations exist the parties rarely challenge individual awards. The customary response to an award deemed unfair or clearly erroneous in such situations is to obey but to stop using the arbitrator who issued it. When review is sought, the award is generally enforced.

As mentioned above, the Supreme Court in *U.S.W.A. v. Enterprise Wheel & Car Corp.* announced a standard that discouraged serious substantive review of arbitral awards by courts but left an opening should a court feel particularly strongly in any given case that the arbitrator's award was incorrect. The court in such cases need only convince itself that the award did not draw "its essence from the collective bargaining agreement" to justify refusing to enforce the award.

The broad potential reach of the court's power of review under the essence standard set forth in *Enterprise* was first suggested in *Torrington Co. v. Metal Products Workers Local 1645,*[23] in which the arbitrator had ruled on the basis of past practice that the collective agreement provided time off for voting even though the contract did not deal directly with the issue. The court of appeals held that the arbitrator's award exceeded his authority because it did not "stay within the confines of the collective bargaining agreement." The approach taken in *Torrington* permits a court to hold that the award did not draw its essence from the agreement any time the arbitrator's decision involved something more than traditional textual interpretation. Since it is common for arbitrators to look to past practice, arbitration precedent, and common industrial relations practice, as well as legal norms and rules in rendering decisions, the *Torrington* approach, if widely followed, would provide almost plenary review.

The approach taken in *Torrington* seems to be basically inconsistent with the Trilogy, because *Torrington* is calculated to limit arbitrators to textual analysis while the Trilogy applauded arbitrators' ability to look outside the document. "The labor arbitrator's source of law is not confined to the express provisions of the contract, as the industrial common law . . . is equally a part of the collective bargaining agreement. . . . The parties expect that his judgment of a particular grievance will reflect . . . insofar as the . . . agreement permits, such factors as . . . productivity . . . morale . . . his judgment whether tensions will be heightened or diminished." Despite the basic inconsistency, *Torrington* has been widely followed, particularly in the Sixth and Fourth Circuits. A survey undertaken in 1983 of cases involving the enforcement of arbitral decisions since the Trilogy showed that enforcement has been denied in almost one-third of them.[24] This is roughly the same as the percentage of cases in which enforcement is denied to the Board decisions under the traditional substantial evidence standard. The circuits, however, vary greatly in their approach. In the Sixth Circuit, for example, enforcement was denied in 13 of 28 cases, 46.4 percent, while in the Eighth Circuit it was denied only in 3 of 21 cases, 14.3 percent. Curiously, the Second Circuit, in which *Torrington* was decided, was one of the circuits least likely to employ the style of analysis which it exemplified.

An examination of cases in which enforcement was denied reveals that in several circuits the "essence" test has been regularly used to reject awards in which the courts felt that arbitrators did not pay adequate attention to the language of the contract either in interpreting the rights of the parties or in construing their own authority. Thus, in *Sears, Roebuck & Co. v. Teamsters Local 243,*[25] The Sixth Circuit held that the arbitrator could not substitute a cost-benefit balancing test to determine the reasonableness of subcontracting in place of the explicit treatment of the subject in the collective-bargaining agreement. In *City Electric, Inc. v. Local 77, Intern. Brotherhood of Elec. Workers,*[26] the Court held that an arbitrator could not direct the parties to bargain about travel allowances, a topic not explicitly covered by the collective-bargaining agreement.

Awards also have been rejected because the remedy ordered was neither explicitly provided for by the agreement nor logically related to the provision breached. Two Fourth Circuit decisions hold that any award not justifiable by one of these standards is "punitive" and therefore beyond the arbitrators' contractual power.[27] Courts also have routinely declined to enforce arbitration awards in which significant legal concepts have been misapplied or improperly ignored.[28] The growing applicability of legal standards in arbitration cases thus inevitably invites a more rigorous review of the decisions.

The Supreme Court has recently restated the trilogy policy favoring minimal judicial review of arbitral opinions. In *Paperworkers v. Misco, Inc.,*[29] it reversed an opinion by the Fourth Circuit refusing to enforce an arbitral award on the grounds that it contravened public policy. The award in question had ordered the company to reinstate an employee who had been found in possession of marijuana. In rejecting the circuit court's decision, the Supreme Court stated "as long as the arbitrator is even arguably construing or applying the contract . . . that a court is convinced he committed serious error does not suffice to overturn his decision." While the Court's language clearly seemed to contemplate a generous construction of the "essence" standard, it is not clear that the courts of appeals which have taken a different view will feel compelled to change their approach. The majority opinion by Justice White also stated that an opinion to be enforceable under the essence standard "cannot simply reflect the arbitrator's own notions of industrial justice." It would not be surprising for this language to take on a life of its own and be regularly quoted by those courts desirous of imposing a stricter standard of review than that suggested by the opinion in the Paperworkers case.[30]

The Supreme Court in *Enterprise* stressed that arbitrators are not required to justify their awards in order to get them enforced, and thus far there has been little authority directly requiring justification. Nevertheless, one might anticipate, as an adjunct of the "essence" test, the development of a requirement that the arbitrator specify enough to demonstrate that the source of the award is the contract.

There are far few, if any, cases rejecting awards on the basis of previous arbitral decisions. Some cases have suggested that collateral estoppel might apply when the precise issues have been decided between the parties, but the courts have thus far shown no inclination to insist that a particular arbitrator's opinion be consistent with that of other arbitrators. Nevertheless, it seems possible that courts will eventually use arbitral precedent to decide what is within the "essence" of a collective-bargaining agreement. In general the cases show a slow but steady movement toward greater judicial review in a direction likely to discourage the innovative aspects of arbitration and to make it more like traditional court adjudication.

Part III.   Arbitration and the Discouragement of Strikes

A. The Basic Policy

The policy favoring arbitration has, as a judicially developed corollary, the effort to discourage strikes over issues that are arbitrable. The Supreme Court has drawn this connection both in construing and in enforcing collective agreements. Thus, in *Local 174, Teamsters v. Lucas Flour Co.*,[31] the Court held that a clause in a collective agreement providing for the settlement of disputes through arbitration should, as a matter of federal law, be construed as a promise by the union not to strike over issues subject to arbitration, even where the contract did not contain a no-strike clause. The Court claimed that "to hold otherwise would obviously do violence to accepted principles of traditional contract law," but it did not explain which principles. The Court rested its holding primarily on the grounds that "a contrary view would be completely at odds with the basic policy of national labor legislation to promote the arbitral process as a substitute for economic warfare."

In terms of traditional contract analysis, the decision is hardly persuasive, for in the context of labor negotiations the omission of a no-strike clause is likely to represent a specific refusal by the union to enter into such an undertaking. It could well be the case that management proposed such a clause and attempted in various ways to convince the union to accept its inclusion in the contract. A union as powerful as the Teamsters could be in a position to refuse and still obtain an agreement. This point was powerfully noted by Justice Black in dissent:

> "It is difficult to believe that the desire of employers to get such a promise and the desire of the union to avoid giving it are matters which are not constantly in the minds of those who negotiate these contracts. In such a setting to hold—on the basis of no evidence whatever—that a union, without knowing it, impliedly surrendered the right to strike by virtue of 'traditional contract law' or anything else is to me just fiction."

The *Lucas Flour* decision demonstrates the Court's willingness to use an essentially intention-defeating construction of agreements in order to pursue the policy of encouraging the use of arbitration in place of strikes for the settlement of disputes about the interpretation of agreements.

In *Boys Markets, Inc. v. Retail Clerk's Union, Local 770*,[32] the Court utilized this policy to reverse its earlier holding and create an exception to the Norris-LaGuardia Act's explicit language forbidding the issuance of injunctions in labor disputes. The Court had previously held in *Sinclair Refining Co. v. Atkinson*[33] that "the anti-injunction provisions of the Norris–LaGuardia Act preclude a federal district court from enjoining a strike in breach of a no-strike obligation under a collective bargaining agreement. . . .." In the *Boys Markets* decision, the Court overruled *Sinclair* for those cases in which a strike is sought to be enjoined "because it is over a grievance which both parties are contractually bound to arbitrate." The Court justified its conclusion in terms of the "devastating implications" of a contrary result on the policies first enunciated in the Steelworkers Trilogy.

> "As we have previously indicated, a no-strike obligation, express or implied, is the quid pro quo for an undertaking by the employer to submit grievance disputes to the process of arbitration. . . . Any incentive for employers to enter into such an arrangement is necessarily dissipated if the principal and most expeditious method by which the no-strike obligation can be enforced is eliminated."[34]

Once again, the Court seemed to be basing its decision on a highly questionable assumption. It is possible that employers may not agree to use arbitration in order to enforce the no-strike clause, but may agree to use arbitration to resolve grievances and thereby make use of the no-strike clause unnecessary. The prospect of a strike might encourage their reliance on arbitration rather than making it worthless.

The *Boys Markets* decision represents a curious compromise solution to the issue of the specific enforceability of no-strike clauses. The Court had been sharply divided when it faced this issue directly in

Sinclair. The majority concluded that Norris-LaGuardia prevented the grant of injunctions against such strikes because of the breadth of its language, the general policy of limiting judicial intervention in labor disputes, and the fact that Congress despite repeated efforts had failed to enact an amendment to Norris-LaGuardia for no-strike clauses. The dissent argued that the specific enforcement of promises voluntarily entered into was a far cry from the abuses at which Norris-LaGuardia was aimed. They pointed out that the labor injunction was a threat to unions when it was used to thwart organization or prevent strikes based on judicially declared policies. When a no-strike clause is enforced, it is used in support of the legislatively declared policy of free collective bargaining. It is curious that the Court should reject the strong arguments in favor of injunctions in support of collective bargaining but to accept similar arguments based upon the policy favoring labor arbitration, which is largely derived from and is inevitably related to the concept of free collective bargaining. The argument would have greater weight had the union simply been held to its contractual commitments on the grounds that it had freely bargained away its right to strike. The confusion that this compromise reflects is suggested by *Buffalo Forge Co. v. United Steelworkers of America.*[35] In that case, the Court refused to extend the use of injunctions to violations of no-strike clauses where the matter over which the union was striking was not "subject to the arbitration provisions of the contract." The case involved a sympathy strike by a sister local, a matter not covered by the agreement. The decision, together with the *Boys Markets* case, leads to the paradoxical result that a union has greater ability to strike over a matter not of primary concern to its members than it does when the issue directly affects them.

B. The Courts and *Boys Markets* Injunctions

1. The Conflict Between Policy and Results

The system of legal rules developed by the Supreme Court in support of arbitration is avowedly based on the desirability of having arbitrators, not courts, construe collective-bargaining agreements. In fact, however, the combination of *Boys Markets* and *Buffalo Forge* rules compel the courts to play a significant role in contract interpretation and gives them the first and last word about the rights of the parties. In deciding whether to grant an injunction under *Boys Markets,* the court must construe the agreement to see whether it provides for arbitration of the issue that caused the strike, must consider the no-strike clause to determine whether it was violated, and must otherwise evaluate the relationship of the parties to decide whether to issue an injunction.

2. The Breadth of the Promise to Arbitrate

In *Gateway Coal*,[36] the Court announced that the policy declared in *Warrior & Gulf* favoring the broadest possible construction of the promise to arbitrate applied in *Boys Markets* cases as well as it does in cases in which the union is seeking to compel arbitration where a no-strike clause exists. This conclusion seemed inevitable given the fact that in both *Boys Markets* and *Buffalo Forge* the Court tied the grant of injunctions solely to the policy of encouraging arbitration. Nevertheless, the ensuing cases suggest a somewhat greater hesitation by the courts to find matters arbitrable for *Boys Markets* purposes than for purposes of ordering one of the parties to proceed the arbitration.

3. Construction of the No–Strike Clause

As noted above, the *Lucas Flour* case established a strong presumption favoring the implication of a no-strike clause coextensive in its reach with the arbitration clause even when such a clause would not be implied on the basis of traditional contractual techniques of construction. In *Gateway Coal*, the Court affirmed the appropriateness of implying a no-strike clause as a prelude to the issuance of an injunction in the absence of any basis other than the existence of an arbitration clause. The *Lucas Flour–Gateway Coal* approach does not amount to the automatic implication of a no-strike promise to match the reach of the no-strike clause. If the contract specifically grants a right to strike over matters subject to the grievance system, the courts will honor the provision.[37] In addition, courts have occasionally held, following *Mastro Plastics*,[38] that a no-strike clause did not apply to employer conduct that constituted a serious unfair labor practice.[39]

4. Other Preconditions to the Issuance of an Injunction

The courts routinely order the employer to arbitrate promptly the issue in dispute as a condition of a *Boys Markets* injunction. Where, for some reason, a stay or delay in the order to arbitrate is called for, the courts generally will not grant an immediate injunction. Some courts insist that there be an existing breach of the no-strike clause before they will issue an injunction. Other courts have been willing to grant injunctions against future strikes where past violations of no-strike clauses have been demonstrated.[40] The grounds upon which such injunctions will be issued vary from circuit to circuit. The grant of an injunction absent a strike seems to stretch the reach of the *Boys Markets* decision needlessly, particularly since the Supreme Court in *Boys Markets* was careful to point out that its decision marked only a limited exception to the policy of the Norris–LaGuardia Act.

The Court in *Boys Markets* stressed that an injunction should not issue automatically wherever a union breaches a no-strike clause over an arbitral issue. It instructed the lower courts that they must still evaluate traditional equitable considerations. Although courts regularly allude to equitable considerations, they have only rarely refused to grant an injunction on such grounds. On some occasions, however, injunctions have been refused on grounds such as (a) that the union stood to be harmed more by the grant than the employer stood to be harmed by the denial; [41] (b) that the employer's case under the contract was too weak to justify an injunction.[42]

5. Injunctions to Preserve the Status Quo

The most confusing and potentially far-reaching issue that has emerged in the aftermath of *Boys Markets* is whether and upon what grounds the court should issue injunctions against employer action in order to preserve the status quo pending arbitration. Some lower court judgments reflect the conclusion that an injunction against employer action is frequently necessary to preserve the union's stake in an upcoming arbitration. They have viewed the injunction against the employer as the reasonable counterpart of the strike injunction legitimated by *Boys Markets*. Injunctions have thus been issued to prevent employers from completing actions that allegedly violate the agreement that would be difficult to undo and that would be likely to have a major impact on the employees such as closing down a part of the enterprise, moving, selling to non-union purchaser, or subcontracting.[43] Two inter-related issues are posed by such cases: (a) questions about whether injunctions may be issued under the umbrella of the *Boys Markets* decision as an adjunct of the policy favoring arbitration, thereby evading the procedural obstacles of the Norris–LaGuardia Act; and (b) questions about the substantive issues, the contractual language that is required to support a preliminary injunction based on the conclusion that an employer has limited his right to take action.

The courts of appeals are in disagreement concerning the propriety of issuing injunctions against the employers in "labor disputes" without consideration of Norris–LaGuardia. Some courts have held that such injunctions are appropriate by virtue of the underlying rationale of *Boys Markets,* which is to make the promise to arbitrate meaningful so that unions will consider arbitration as a viable substitute for the strike. They urge that unless unions receive judicial support for their undertaking to arbitrate, they will view the courts and the process as unfair and will be unwilling to give up the right to strike in exchange for a one-sided process, which permits injunctions only against them.[44]

Other opinions have rejected the approach, pointing out that the employer almost never has made a promise not to take unilateral action prior to arbitration comparable to the union's promise not to strike and the *Boys Markets* case must be understood as underlining the particular importance of the no-strike promise that is typically the only one made by the union and the quid pro quo for the entire system of arbitration.[45]

There is also division about the extent to which an agreement may be construed to prohibit major entrepreneurial action neither directly prohibited nor directly permitted by the agreement. The implication of such a limit is inconsistent with the Court's language in *First National Maintenance*,[46] stressing the need for uninhibited decision-making with respect to investment policy and refusing to place limits on the use of such power as an adjunct to the collective-bargaining process. Nevertheless, the issues are separable because the employer may bargain away the power granted by *First National Maintenance*. At one time the Board and some courts implied a promise by the employer not to take drastic action, such as moving, in order to obtain lower wage ratios as a necessary implication of the collective-bargaining agreement. Thus, in *Milwaukee Spring Division of Illinois Coil.*,[47] the Board held that an employer, which moved its operations during the term of an agreement in order to obtain lower labor cost, was guilty of an improper "midterm modification" of the agreement, thereby violating section 8(a)(5). A similar conclusion was reached by the Ninth Circuit, upholding the Board in *Los Angeles Marine Hardware Co. v. NLRB*.[48]

However, the newly established Reagan Board granted a rehearing in the *Milwaukee Spring*[49] case and rejected the earlier Board's implications of a promise not to relocate. In the course of this opinion, the Board overruled its earlier precedent limiting management's ability to take action outside the contract which had the effect of reducing the contract's value to the union.

It is unlikely that the current Board will deal with the issue of implied limits on employer action. It is more likely that this issue will be deferred to arbitration under the *Collyer* doctrine discussed below. Arbitrators who have dealt with the question of implied limits have resolved it in a variety of ways. Some have held it to be an implied condition of the contract that no major action will be undertaken to make its provisions meaningless. Other arbitrators have held that management may continue to make basic decisions as long as it acts in good faith. The concept of good faith, like the concept of discrimination, has been variously defined in such cases. Some arbitrators hold that a decision to move or subcontract based on lower labor costs is not made in good faith; others hold that bad faith requires a vindictive attitude towards the union not based on economic consideration. For the most part, the trend of all decisions by Board, courts, and arbitrators is to permit managerial decisions not clearly restricted by the contract.

Part IV. The Relationship Between the Union and the Individual Grievant in Arbitration

A. The Duty of Fair Representation

1. The Role of the Courts

In *Vaca v. Sipes*,[50] the Supreme Court held that a union could negotiate a grievance system under which it has the right to settle the grievant's claim prior to arbitration. The Court concluded that such power in the union would often be necessary for the successful operation of the system.

> ". . . Through this settlement process, frivolous grievances are ended prior to the most costly and time-consuming step in the grievance procedures. Moreover, both sides are assured that similar complaints will be treated consistently, and major problem areas in the interpretation of the collective bargaining contract can be isolated and perhaps resolved. And finally, the settlement process furthers the interest of the union as statutory agent and as coauthor of the bargaining agreement in representing the employees in the enforcement of that agreement."[51]

The Court rejected the argument that an employee should be able to control his or her own grievance on the grounds that such a conclusion would undermine the effectiveness of the grievance process by "destroying the employer's confidence in the union's authority and returning the individual grievant to the vagaries of independent and unsystematic negotiation."

The Court felt that an individual-rights-based approach would prove too costly:

> "Moreover, under such a rule, a significantly greater number of grievances would proceed to arbitration. This would greatly increase the cost of the grievance machinery and could so overburden the arbitration process as to prevent it from functioning successfully. . . . It can well be doubted whether the parties to collective bargaining agreements would long continue to provide for detailed grievance and arbitration procedures of the kind encouraged by L.M.R.A. § 203(d), supra, if their power to settle the majority of grievances short of the costlier and more time-consuming steps was limited by a rule permitting the grievant unilaterally to invoke arbitration. Nor do we see substantial danger to the interests of the individual employee if his statutory agent is given the contractual power honestly and in good faith to settle grievances short of arbitration. . . ."

The Court seemed willing to subordinate the individual's claim to the group's interest. In order to protect employees against abuse of the union's power in this regard, the Court held that the employee could bring suit against the union if the union breached its duty of fair representation and could join the employer in the suit. In such a suit, an employee who prevails against the union is entitled to a judgment on the merits of his or her claim against the employer.

The conclusion that the duty of fair representation could be enforced through a suit under section 301 was not an obvious one. Such actions are not provided for explicitly by the language of the section because they are not literally "suits for violation of contracts between an employer and a labor organization." Moreover, since a breach of the duty of fair representation had been held to constitute an unfair labor practice under existing precedent, a strong argument existed that the sole remedy for violation was in a charge brought before the Board. The Court in *Vaca* rejected this argument essentially on the grounds that the Board, which would not have jurisdiction over the employer, could not provide a remedy for the underlying grievance if the employee's claim proved meritorious.

The Court in *Vaca* specifically rejected the argument that the remedy should be limited "to a decree compelling the employer and the union to arbitrate the underlying grievance." It concluded that the arbitral remedy might not be adequate when the union was partly liable and that in other cases "the arbitrable issues may be substantially resolved in the course of trying the fair representation controversy."

The opinion in *Vaca* stressed promotion of the grievance process as the law's chief priority even when that means the possible diminution of individual claims. However, by providing for a judicial remedy for contract breaches that accompany the breach of the duty of fair representation rather than returning the parties to the arbitration process, the Court undercut its own reasoning. In such a case, the arbitrator's opinion that is provided for in the agreement, and that the Court enthusiastically praised in the Steelworker's Trilogy, agreement is replaced by a judicial decision.

In *Hines v. Anchor Motor Freight, Inc.,*[52] the Court also held that a breach of the duty of fair representation by the union could deprive the employer of the bargained for finality of the arbitrator's award. In that case, the Court permitted the employee to bring a section 301 suit against both the union and the employer even though an arbitrator acting in good faith had already rejected the grievance. The Court specifically concluded that "the union's breach of duty relieves the employee of an express or implied requirement that disputes be settled through contractual grievance procedures if it seriously undermines the integrity of the arbitral process the union's breach also removes the bar of the finality provisions of the agreement."

Thus, despite the Court's praise for arbitration and voluntary settlement, *Vaca* and *Hines* together significantly lessen the authority of arbitration and substantially increase the role of the judiciary in determining the meaning of collective agreements.

2. The Concept of Fair Representation

The Court in *Vaca* did not define the duty of fair representation except in general terms:

> "A breach of the statutory duty of fair representation occurs only when a union's conduct toward a member of the collective bargaining unit is arbitrary, discriminatory, or in bad faith. . . .
> Though we accept the proposition that a union may not arbitrarily ignore a meritorious grievance or process it in perfunctory fashion . . . a breach of the duty of fair representation is not established merely by proof that the underlying grievance was meritorious." [53]

Much of the Court's discussion in the *Vaca* decision focused on the intent of those who acted for the union. The language in that part of the opinion suggests that a breach of the duty of fair representation requires improper motivation. However, by using such terms as "arbitrary" and "perfunctory" in describing conduct that constitutes a breach of the duty of fair representation, the Court by implication suggested that a breach might occur if the union was motivated by indifference or even incompetence rather than malevolence. This confusion has not been resolved in later opinions. The Court seemed to adopt a more intent-oriented definition in *Amalgamated Association of Street Employees v. Lockridge*.[54] Justice Harlan, writing for the Court, stated that a breach of the duty requires conduct that is "intentional, severe, and unrelated to legitimate union objectives. . . ." In other cases, however, the Court has suggested a more expansive definition of the duty. In *Clayton v. International Union, United Auto. Workers*,[55] the Court stressed that an internal union remedy for cases involving "fraud, discrimination, or collusion with management," was narrower than "the arbitrary, discriminatory, or in bad faith standard for breach of the duty of fair representation that we developed in *Vaca v. Sipes*." The Court's discussion, while not explicit, seemed to contemplate a significant non-intent-oriented reach for the term "arbitrary."[56]

The issue of the state of mind necessary for a breach of the duty of fair representation has been dealt with repeatedly by the courts of appeals which have not been uniform in result. There is inconsistency between and within the circuits. Much seems to turn on how the courts conceptualize a grievance and the union's role in the system.[57]

There are two basic approaches: a process model and an individual rights model. Those who adopt the process model treat the grievance system as an aspect of collective bargaining and the union's role in it as quasi-legislative, involving the settling of terms and conditions of employment for the employees generally through the grievance system. Such courts accord a union considerable leeway in grievance handling and take a restrictive view of the duty of fair representation. Courts that adopt the "individual rights" model apply the duty of fair representation more stringently. They are apt to find a violation whenever there are any acts by the union that lead to loss of contractual rights without adequate justification.

There is much to be said for both approaches. The process orientation gives union officials more leeway. Limiting the duty of fair representation to cases in which a union intentionally acts contrary to the interests of employees for improper reasons minimizes judicial involvement with grievance processing. When courts evaluate the behavior of the union officials in grievances their conclusions are likely to be uninformed. Most courts do not understand either the tactical considerations that union officials must take into account or the administrative, political, and economic pressures that limit what they can achieve. It is difficult for courts to evaluate whether union officials have behaved properly without incorporating into their evaluation, standards more appropriate to lawyers than to union stewards. Courts sometimes lose sight of the fact that unions are and should be associations of workers, not of lawyers. When courts actively monitor the grievance process, they inevitably change it. Unions become concerned with preventing liability, which means fewer compromises and a more formal, legalistic grievance structure. Moreover, an approach that places a heavy burden upon the union inevitably penalizes the employer. To the extent the duty has been breached in handling a grievance, the finality of the result becomes undependable. Both arbitration awards and grievance settlements may be overturned. Employers thereby lose one reason for committing to a broad arbitration scheme and may have less interest in compromise with unions, that do not have the ability to assure them that a compromise deal will stand up. Indeed, the concerns with the well-being of the grievance process which led the court in *Vaca* to reject direct control by the grievant of the claim mitigate against too sweeping an application of the duty of fair representation.

Some courts, particularly the Seventh Circuit Court of Appeals, have sought to limit the application of the duty of fair representation to those cases in which a union "deliberately and unjustifiably refuses to represent the worker" or to cases in which the union's behavior "is so close to intentional wrongdoing that the law treats it as the same thing." [58]

But despite the powerful reasons for limiting the reach of the duty to cases of intentional wrongdoing, the majority of courts of appeals have not done so. There are several reasons why an intent standard has proved so difficult to maintain. First, the moral and psychological line between intentional wrongdoing and indifference is difficult to establish as a matter of proof in particular cases, and, when made, the distinction will often not refer to a psychological difference worthy of legal recognition. Assume that a longtime union member with much company seniority is discharged for absenteeism. The grievance is handled through the arbitration stage by a union official, who fails to contact the grievant's physician to find out whether the absences were excusable under the company's absence program. The union official, if not hostile to the employee, obviously failed to recognize his responsibility to protect him or her. In such a case, most courts would be little inclined to base a decision against the employee on the ground that the union's behavior was based on lack of concern rather than active hostility. Even the Seventh Circuit in such a case might conclude that constituted "wrongdoing" that the law treats the union steward's behavior as "intentional wrongdoing." Once the courts find the duty breached by culpable indifference, it becomes almost impossible to distinguish such cases from cases of obvious negligence. In most cases involving failure to take obvious actions in the employee's interest, the fact finder will be confused as to the union officials' motivation and will be reluctant to exculpate the union because personal hostility or invidious discrimination has not been shown. The easiest way to avoid such a result is to conclude that breach of the duty does not turn on such niceties of motivation. The courts' impulse to be protective of grievants in such instances is inevitable. Many duty of fair representation grievants are sympathetic claimants—longtime employees, women, minority group members, or union activists who have lost their jobs. The sense that the employee has been the victim of behavior amounting to collusion between the union and the company, whether conscious or not, is often present in such cases. In addition, duty-of-fair-representation cases present an evidentiary paradox. Unions that are interested in helping an employee to win a lost or compromised grievance may purposely do a poor job of defending their own role. Unions that ardently defend themselves may thereby suggest themselves to be suspiciously contrary to the employee's well-being. This adds to the uncertainty which fact finders may feel in characterizing motive—an uncertainty that has probably expedited the trend towards a more objective standard.

Most courts of appeals have moved gradually towards an individual rights model of the duty of fair representation.[59] In the first few years after the opinion in *Vaca*, they generally insisted upon a showing of bad faith or hostile intent as a prerequisite to a finding that the duty of fair representation was violated. Gradually, however, they began to find violations in cases in which the union's failure to satisfactorily represent the grievant could be characterized as "outrageous," but in which there was no direct proof of a hostility towards the grievant. The next step was to insist that the union have a legitimate reason for compromising grievances and to establish minimum standards of competence for union grievance handling. This development has predictably taken place through expansion of the concept of "arbitrary" behavior. In general, the cases developing the duty have dealt with one or more of the following questions:

1. Does a union act in an arbitrary fashion when it mishandles a grievance through negligence or incompetence?

2. To what extent must the union act in a judicial role when a grievance involves competing interests within the union?

3. May a union be found guilty of a violation if it bargains away a meritorious grievance on behalf of some other interest deemed by the union leaders as more worthy?

3. Union Competence and the Duty of Fair Representation

The Court in *Vaca* emphasized the importance of permitting the union considerable discretion in the handling of grievances, and it suggested that a union acting in good faith could settle or refuse to pursue a grievance without violating the duty. Nevertheless, as suggested earlier the courts have gradually begun to develop a requirement of minimum competence for unions in processing grievances. This means that union action foreclosing a grievance must meet some standard of rationality. An obligation seems to include at least three major components:

1. a duty to investigate the grievant's claim and the case against him before deciding to withdraw it; [60]

2. a duty not to ignore the time limits [61] and procedural requirements of the grievance system;

3. a duty to make a reasonable effort to present the grievant's case to management effectively.[62]

The first two requirements are matters that may be satisfied easily by a union without regard to the professional training of its representatives. It is not too much to expect that representatives of a union that negotiates time limits should pay attention to them, and at least one court of appeals has been willing to find a violation in such cases of "ministerial" error on the basis of simple negligence.[63] Similarly, as long as the courts do not judge the reasonableness of a union's decision not to go forward, it is fair enough that it be required to demonstrate or at least articulate a reason other than its hostility to the employee. Judgments concerning the quality of representation, however, contain the greatest potential for unfairness. At the very outset, it is troubling to make union liability turn on how well the union performs its part in a process that almost certainly would not exist except for its efforts, vindicating rights that also would not exist except for its efforts. Beyond that, such issues leave the greatest room for differences of judgment and contain the greatest potential for confusing the standards to be applied. As the Court of Appeals for the Sixth Circuit noted, "We must remind ourselves that union representatives handling these sorts of matters are not (or need not be) lawyers, and a case claiming a breach of the duty of fair representation is not the same as a legal malpractice case." [64]

Inevitably the attempt to strike a balance that protects the employee but that does not impose unrealistic standards for the union has proved to be very difficult. For example, how much and how competent an investigation may be fairly required of a union in deciding whether to go forward with a grievance? All courts agree that a thorough investigation is not required but, on the other hand, most courts now demand some effort to find out what happened or whether the grievant has a valid claim. Key witnesses must be interviewed unless the expense is likely to be prohibitive, and clearly relevant documents should be examined. These are steps that do not turn on professional competence. It is less clear whether the union has any obligation to investigate legal or arbitrable precedents so as to evaluate the strength of the grievant's case under the contract. If such an obligation exists, it is a fairly mild one and limited to discharges or grievances of considerable seriousness. For several reasons, the cases show a gradual increase in the union's obligation. There is a natural tendency to analyze the cases from the perspective of the grievant, whose important personal interests are affected by the union's level of competence. Has the union taken those steps that the grievant might reasonably expect? If the answer is no, the courts are likely to find a violation. Indeed, in many of the cases the courts seem to read implications of hostility into the union's failure to take steps thought obvious by them.[65]

Nevertheless, it is difficult to define reasonable expectation in grievance handling. The cases differ widely in terms of the underlying facts, the relevant contracts, the resources, staff, and professional experience of the union. The type of behavior that might reasonably be expected of a particular union responding to specific factual circumstances under a particular contract can only be related generally in terms of a vague conclusionary standard to what might be reasonably required of another union in a different situation. As a result of these factors, the standards are vague, vary greatly in their application, are often unrealistic and leave unions with little guidance. The result is that most unions, to play it safe, take questionable grievances to arbitration. This results in the processing of meritless cases and taints the union with a losing arbitration record. The failure to clearly define a standard, however, leaves the union with no alternative. It is a safer course to spend money on a meritless grievance than to spend money defending duty of fair representation claims.

4. The Union as Adjudicator of Competing Interests

There are, as already noted, several types of cases in which a grievant may be opposing another employee.

1. The question may be which of two employees is entitled to a job under a contract clause providing for promotion on the basis of a mixture of ability, past performance, and seniority. Such cases typically arise when the junior employee is awarded a job by the employer and the senior employee files a grievance.

2. Who is vulnerable to layoffs? Does the senior employee have the right to "bump" lower-rated employees in case of a layoff?

3. How is seniority to be computed on the merger of two facilities with separate seniority rosters represented by the same union? Typically the issue arises when an older facility with a great number of senior employees is merged into a newer unit in which most of the employees have less seniority. In such cases, the older employees are seeking to have the seniority lists merged (dovetailed) while the employees of the remaining facility want to have the older employees treated as newcomers and added to the end of their seniority roster (endtailing).

Such grievances obviously place the union in very difficult and delicate situations. Many unions have responded by developing a firm rule favoring seniority whenever there is a conflict between senior and junior employees in a single unit, and insisting upon endtailing in cases of merger. Neither the courts nor the Board have generally overruled the union's judgment in such cases, but they have attempted to oversee the procedures followed and have, on occasion, held that the union violated its duty of fair representation if it did not give the employees whose interest it opposed an opportunity to present their evidence to the appropriate union officials. Thus, the Eighth Circuit in *Smith v. Hussmann Refrigerator Co.,*[66] concluded that the union breached its duty of fair representation by failing to give the junior employees an opportunity for a hearing before supporting the grievance of the senior employees on a promotion issue. This opinion reflects a profound misunderstanding of the legitimate institutional concerns of union officials involved in grievance handling. Their need is for a principled basis on which to take a position, understood even by the employees they oppose. Commitment to seniority is such a principle. Employees generally recognize that the union has such a commitment and that each employee who works long enough will ultimately come to benefit from it. An adjudicatory model, under which the union regularly reconsidered its position, would inevitably be more divisive for the union because it suggests a discretionary judgment based on a preference for one individual over another. The union's role in championing seniority in the grievance is almost certainly no more than a continuation of the position it took at negotiations where the employer sought to limit the seniority on the basis of job qualifications and training and the union sought to give greater weight to seniority. Thus, the employer seeking to promote a junior employee and the union protesting his action through a grievance represents a classic example of the parties using arbitration as a continuation of the collective-bargaining process.

Many of the duty-of-fair-representation cases involving competing employee interests reject the collective bargaining approach to grievance handling in favor of an individual rights-based analysis. Both the Board and the courts frequently insist that the union make a quasi-judicial determination of such issues and not rely on the political process. In *Teamsters (Rhodes and Jamieson Ltd.)* and *Marilyn Holman,*[67] an employee faced with the elimination of his job position, requested that the union seek another job for him. Instead, the union put the issue of bumping rights to a vote of its membership during a series of layoffs by the employer. The issue concerned not just this employee, but four different classifications of employees. The union members, whose interests might have been adversely affected by a decision favorable to the employee, voted against supporting bumping rights, and the employee could not be reassigned.

The Board held that the union violated its duty of fair representation under section 8(b)(1)(A). The Board concluded that under the contract, the employee was entitled to reassignment and that the union abdicated its responsibilities by putting the issue to a vote. The Board felt that the union's interpretation of the contract was not reasonable and that the union had breached its duty of "fair and impartial" treatment. Bad faith and hostile discrimination were specifically rejected as necessary to a finding of a violation as the Board opinion stated: "Implicit in *Miranda Fuel* is the idea that a union breaches its fiduciary duty when it deprives some employees of their clear contractual rights because a majority of its members want it to."[68]

Both the Board and the courts have sometimes required that the union proceed in a quasi-judicial mode in dealing with the question of endtailing or dovetailing for mergers. In *Barton Brands, Ltd.,*[69] one company acquired another in a merger. The seniority rosters were consolidated via endtailing the employees of the acquired company after a union-wide vote. Later, the vice president of the union, in an election campaign, bragged that he was instrumental in getting the rosters endtailed. The Board held, and the Court agreed,[70] that the union violated its duty to the employees of the acquired company because it advocated endtailing for political purposes. The union officials were held as a result not to have acted in good faith. There have been several similar court opinions.

These opinions make sense so long as they are conceptualized in terms of a union obligation to vindicate employee rights, a concept that inevitably places on the union the judicial obligation of determining the extent of those rights before acting. If one sees the grievance system as an extension of the bargaining process, however, the conclusion is less obvious. The union's primary goal in bargaining should be to effectuate the will of its membership. This will mean favoring some interests over others, and pursuing some claims and abandoning others in accordance with that expression. Unions in collective bargaining should be able to base their judgments on majority choice so long as they do not thereby express an illegitimate preference favoring one group over another because of racial, ethnic, or gender-based considerations. Permitting unions leeway to act in this manner is in accordance with the national policy favoring democracy.[71] The policy should be subject to limitation where clear contractual language favors a claim that is contrary to majority sentiment. When, however, legitimate basis for disagreement exists, unions are not doing anything invidious by basing their actions on the will of their membership as currently divined.

5. Settling a Grievance for Reasons Unrelated to the Merits

It is possible that a union will want to settle a grievance short of arbitration for any number of reasons. It may want to sacrifice all or part of one claim in order to get a more favorable settlement in another, in order to protect its treasury, to appease the employer, or even to wait for a more favorable case for an important issue of contract interpretation. The courts have shown considerable confusion about the propriety of the union acting in this fashion. In general, the courts have been willing to permit settlement in the institutional interests of the union in a wide variety of circumstances, if the union officials were not motivated by hostility toward the grievant and their judgment about the desirability of a settlement seemed reasonable. The Supreme Court's decision in *Vaca* seemed to look with favor on the settlement process if this standard was met. Nevertheless, as the courts have gradually moved towards an individual-rights approach to grievances, they have began to find violations of the duty of fair representation when a union trades away a grievance without being able to justify its action in terms of a reciprocal management commitment on a case legitimately considered stronger.[72] One may expect judicial scrutiny of the "horse trading" of grievances to increase.

B. Procedural Requirements

1. Exhaustion

It is well settled that before an employee may bring an action for breach of the duty of fair representation under section 301, he or she must first exhaust whatever reasonable procedures are provided for under the collective agreement. The courts have had a difficult time, however, in dealing with the question of whether an employee must first exhaust internal union procedures. In *Clayton v. International Union, United Auto. Workers,*[73] the Court held that "where an internal union appeals procedure cannot result in reactivation of the employee's grievance or an award of the complete relief sought in his section 301 suit, exhaustion will not be required with respect to either the suit against the employer or the suit against the union." The Court gave short shrift to the argument that an exhaustion requirement would permit unions to regulate their internal affairs "without undue judicial interference." It found this policy inapplicable because it is "strictly limited to disputes arising over *internal* union matters such as those involving the interpretation and application of a union constitution."

The Court did not explain why the policy did not apply to the question of how the union should proceed in handling a grievance nor why this was not an appropriately internal affair. It recognized that exhaustion in such circumstances was supported by another significant aspect of federal policy, the encouragement of "private rather than judicial resolution of disputes." However, the Court refused to apply that policy "lest employees with meritorious section 301 claims be forced to exhaust themselves and their resources.

Because the situation in which an internal union remedy could provide the relief sought in section 301 suits is difficult if not impossible to imagine, the *Clayton* decision is tantamount to a total rejection of internal exhaustion prior to bringing a suit based on breach of the duty of fair representation.

2. The Allocation of Damages

The Court in *Vaca* made clear that in general, where the issue arose because the employer breached the collective agreement, the employer should be primarily liable for the remedy.

> "Though the union has violated a statutory duty in failing to press the grievance, it is the employer's unrelated breach of contract which triggered the controversy and which caused this portion of the employee's damages. The employee should have no difficulty recovering these damages from the employer, who cannot, as we have explained, hide behind the union's wrongful failure to act; in fact, the employer may be (and probably should be) joined as a defendant in the fair representation suit. . . . It could be a real hardship on the union to pay these damages, even if the union were given a right of indemnification against the employer. With the employee assured of direct recovery from the employer, we see no merit in requiring the union to pay the employer's share of the damages."

The *Vaca* opinion suggested that the damages for breach of the employee's rights under the collective agreement were essentially the responsibility of the employer who breached the contract. "[D]amages attributable solely to the employer's breach of contract should not be charged to the union." [74]   Where an employee proved that a discharge was a violation, most courts in the aftermath of *Vaca* limited unions to incidental damages and charged the employer for back pay.   In *Bowen v. U.S. Postal Service,* [75] however, the Supreme Court rejected this approach and instead insisted that in applying the duty of fair representation:

> "[I]t would indeed be unjust to prevent the employee from recovering in such a situation.   It would be equally unjust to require the employer to bear the increase in the damages caused by the union's wrongful conduct.   It is true that the employer discharged the employee wrongfully and remains liable for the employee's backpay.   See *Vaca,* supra, at 197.   The union's breach of its duty of fair representation, however, caused the grievance procedure to malfunction resulting in an increase in the employee's damages.   Even though both the employer and the union have caused the damage suffered by the employee, the union is responsible for the increase in damages and, as between the two wrongdoers, should bear its portion of the damages."

It is too early to tell what the results of this decision will be. Unions may be able to avoid liability by internal review systems seeking to reopen lost cases and contractual disclaimer, but none of this is yet clear.   In those cases in which unions are not able to divest themselves of liability, the practical consequences may be great, particularly because some courts have held that in cases of gross violation unions might be liable for mental distress.   In such cases, the liability for back pay might be enough to substantially affect the treasury of small unions or impoverish others.   This potential liability will inevitably force unions to treat grievances with an eye to liability, thereby discouraging the type of settlements that the court in *Vaca* sought to encourage.   The reach of potential liability for action undertaken in good faith may also deter courts from applying the duty of fair representation quite as easily as they have to date.

Part V.   The Role of Arbitration in Enforcing Statutory Rights

A.   The Problem of Competence

Arbitration, because of its mix of adjudicatory and bargaining elements, is a good way to resolve questions of contract interpretation left ambiguous as a result of collective bargaining.   It is the parties' process and it works because arbitrators are motivated, instructed, and aided to focus on the parties' goals and relations. Because of its private nature, arbitration can function without lawyers and in a variety of modes, often stressing informality, speed, compromise, and understanding of industrial relations rather than law.

Arbitration may or may not be suited to deal with legal issues. Where both sides are represented by attorneys, the arbitrator is a labor law expert, the case is carefully tried, the legal issues are briefed, a transcript is made, and the parties file briefs, the process can deal as effectively with questions of law as most courts. However, the combination of these elements is the exception rather than the rule, and there are various reasons why the parties may be unwilling or unable to provide them in a case in which a legal issue is posed.

1. The elements necessary to make the process well equipped to deal with legal issues are costly.

2. The parties may not be aware in advance of the bearing of the legal issue.

3. The issue may be seen as peripheral.

4. The parties may have a permanent arbitrator or a panel of arbitrators who are not labor law experts or even lawyers.

5. There is limited appeal from an erroneous statutory construction or interpretation.

Very often one or another of the parties is unaware of, or ill prepared to try, the legal issues. When this happens, even if the arbitrator is an expert, it will be difficult for her to deal adequately with the legal issue. This difficulty will, of course, be exacerbated when the arbitrator is not familiar with the issue posed, when there is no transcript, when briefs are not filed, or when the arbitrator is under time pressure. Thus the arbitral process generally is poorly equipped to deal with legal issues and it makes sense for arbitrators to try and decide grievances without reference to external law. Sometimes this is impossible because the contract specifically incorporates external law and commands the arbitrator to apply it. Much more frequently, however, legal issues arise indirectly. In cases in which the arbitrator could resolve the questions without reference to external law, the issue of whether to consider legal precedents is always difficult. To address the law inevitably increases expense, formality, and delay. The risk of mistake is significant and the difficulties of correcting mistakes formidable given the limited review that courts and agencies typically impose on arbitral decisions. On the other hand, if the arbitrator ignores the law, the result may be *de novo* legal procedures that are time consuming and expensive. Ignoring the law also creates the possibility that disputes will be resolved in ways inconsistent with the legal rights of the parties through a process sanctioned by law. It is because of the unsatisfactory nature of the choices that critics have concluded that arbitration as a process works best when it is purely contractual. Nevertheless, as the amount of regulation of the work-place grows, it is inevitable that the legalization of arbitration will continue.

Currently, difficult legal questions arise in a variety of situations in arbitration. The most common involves complementary general policies when external law and the contract use similar language, a situation that is typical in such areas as health and safety, employment discrimination, and union recognition. Most contracts will require safe working conditions, and will contain a pledge against discrimination and one promising to recognize the union as the sole representative of the employees. Each of these provisions duplicates to some extent statutory coverage framed in similar language, the construction of which has led to the establishment of a comprehensive and technical body of law. When the parties negotiated the contract language, it is doubtful that they knew of or intended to agree to the specific statutory interpretations or that they intended their contract to be governed by legal rulings. On the other hand, the contractual language is typically quite general and must be given meaning by outside sources, and the law is one logical source. Thus it makes sense to consider the law in such situations but not necessarily to be bound by it. To consider the law without addressing it fully, however, is apt to be misleading because of the high level of complexity in each of these areas. Because of the difficulty of discovering the law and because of the belief that legal and contractual standards should not necessarily be the same, many arbitrators pay little attention to the law even when it is brought to their attention by the parties (something that is itself rarely done). Thus the use and acceptance of law by arbitrators in these areas differs, but in general the law is looked to much less frequently by arbitrators than it might be by courts were they to play a major role in interpreting agreements.

Sometimes general contractual standards are thought to incorporate specific legal concepts. Thus the concept of just cause, it is generally agreed, has to be defined to exclude conduct within the statutory category of protected activity. Sometimes the action for which the employee has been disciplined grows out of union organizing activity or efforts to protest wages or working conditions, which are the core concepts of section 7 of the NLRA. Arbitrators uniformly recognize that basic union activity does not constitute cause for discharge and most arbitrators are willing to consider the Board's interpretation of section 7 in construing the concept of just cause if it is raised by the union. Where the matter is not raised by the union, arbitrators vary. Some will independently address the relationship, but most ignore the section 7 issue and limit themselves to analysis of arbitral precedent. Even when the matter is raised by the union, arbitrators vary in the extent to which they will be bound by Board precedent concerning the limits of section 7; for example, in dealing with refusals to cross picket lines, some arbitrators have concluded that good cause exists even where the Board would hold the activity protected.

The most troublesome area arises when the policies of the contract and the approach of the law are different or opposed, as was the case when Title VII was thought to outlaw the application of seniority to minority and women employees in most situations. The unsatisfactory nature of arbitration as a forum in which to vindicate complex or questionable legal standards is most evident in such situations. For a long time, the issue of the disparate impact of seniority on minorities went unnoticed. Then arbitrators responded by a simplistic application of a proviso excluding bona fide seniority plans from the reach of Title VII of the Civil Rights Act. Then arbitrators began to apply concepts of disparate impact following a series of court rulings. However, arbitrators rarely applied these concepts in as sophisticated a way as the courts did. Finally, the Supreme Court rejected the argument that Title VII was violated by seniority schemes not motivated by a desire to discriminate,[76] inevitably casting doubt upon a whole series of rendered awards. It was not until the law became clear that arbitrators were able to deal with it successfully.

The question of whether an arbitrator should, in the case of conflict, follow the law or the contract has provided a focus for analyzing the peculiar nature of arbitration as a private process that serves public purposes. It has been the subject of extensive, sometimes heated debate, among arbitrators. The debate was begun by two distinguished arbitrator-scholars, Bernard Meltzer and Robert Howlett.[77] Meltzer took the position that arbitrators should follow the contract and ignore the law; Meltzer argued that the process is not well equipped to deal with such issues. Howlett took the contrary position that the law must be seen as an overriding element of every collective agreement. He pointed to the importance of arbitration in the labor relations system and the importance of legal rights for employees. Both sides were well presented, but most arbitrators favored Meltzer's position, which was probably inevitable given the fact that the touchstone of the arbitration process is the desire of the parties. Since then, an intermediate position advanced by Robert Mittenthal and Michael Sovern [78] has seemed to gather momentum. They argue that an arbitrator should ignore a legal rule requiring something that the contract forbids, but should honor a statutory provision forbidding something that the contract requires, on the grounds that it is worse to order something illegal than to require some other agency to compel mandated action. There have been many other commentators who have entered the debate favoring one of the stated positions or advancing a variation of their own. In practice, however, the issue almost never seems to arise. It is rare for an arbitrator to be squarely faced with a conflict between the contract and the law. If an arbitrator believes that the contract is ambiguous and the law clear, he can interpret the contract to harmonize with the law, an approach agreed to by both sides in the Meltzer–Howlett debate. If the contract is clear and the law confused, the overwhelming majority of arbitrators will construe the contract and ignore the law, with perhaps some language acknowledging the problems of arbitration in resolving legal questions. It is only when both are clear and point in different directions that the problem posed by Meltzer and Howlett arises. Because most collective agreements are negotiated professionally with lawyers playing a key role in drafting, such situations are rare. Moreover, lawyers are generally available for advice in the early stages of the grievance process, and can settle a case in which such a conflict arises. Thus the question of direct contradiction has been of greater interest to scholars than practical importance to the process.

B. The Problem of Overlap

As already noted, a grievance may arise out of facts that would also constitute an unfair labor practice. The two areas in which this is most likely to occur are unilateral employer actions and discipline. When an employer takes action during the term of an agreement—by changing wages, hours, or working conditions, for example, or by subcontracting or introducing new machinery—the union may file a grievance alleging that such action is forbidden by the contract. It also may file a charge claiming that the employer's conduct constitutes modification of the contract under section 8(d) or unilateral action without bargaining and therefore violates section 8(a)(5). Similarly, when an employee is discharged, the union might file a grievance claiming that the conduct on which the discharge was based does not constitute just cause for discharge or else it may file a charge with the Board alleging that the conduct in question is protected activity and the discharge constitutes a violation of the NLRA. The question of how to handle such cases is a difficult one, implicating important, contradictory national policies. There is much authority supporting the position that the statutory rights created by the NLRA require, for their elaboration and vindication, the opportunity to be heard by the Board. On the other hand, there is the strong national policy encouraging voluntary settlement through arbitration. These differing theoretical positions have significant practical implications in shaping the extent to which the Board will exercise its statutory jurisdiction.

From the perspective of the union, which is almost always the moving party in a contractual grievance, each forum has its advantages and disadvantages. The advantages of arbitration include speed, informality, and greater control over the process by virtue of the union's role in presenting the grievance and selecting the arbitrator. The concept of just cause is also broader in its impact on the disciplinary process than the concept of protected activity. It includes an investigation into the propriety of the employer's behavior, while protected activity concerns only the employee's behavior. Similarly, with regard to unilateral employer action, there are advantages to arbitration because (a) the concept of modification requires something more fundamental than a mere breach; and (b) a finding of contract breach is preferable to a finding that section 8(a)(5) has been violated because of failure to negotiate. The remedy is more permanent, usually involving an order to retract the action, which can only be legitimated by subsequent agreement, while in the case of unilateral action the employer is required only to bargain to impasse. On the other hand, there are several reasons why a union may prefer Board adjudication. The Board provides counsel and a hearing officer without cost if its investigation indicates that the charge is meritorious. By contrast, in arbitration these expenses are borne by the parties. In arbitration, the employee who files a grievance is largely at the mercy of the union, which negotiates possible settlement, chooses the arbitrator, and presents the case. Because of the union's central role, there is a danger that arbitrators will not have presented, or will overlook, the rights of employees when they conflict with the interests of the union. When a charge is filed with the NLRB, however, the Board itself controls the investigation and handling of the case, thereby preventing the union from defeating the employee's claim. Thus, unions and individual grievants would prefer a system in which overlapping claims might be advanced in both forums. If concurrent jurisdiction is not available, the union would prefer to choose in each case in which forum to initiate its complaint. From the employer's perspective, the most desirable outcome is to have only one single hearing in each case, in most cases before an arbitrator.

C. The Labor Board's Accommodation to Arbitration

1. Deference to Arbitral Awards

In *Spielberg Manufacturing Co.,*[79] the Board announced that it would defer to already rendered arbitral decisions if three conditions are met: (a) the proceedings appear to have been fair and regular; (b) all parties have agreed to be bound; (c) the arbitrator's decision is not "clearly repugnant" to the policies of the NLRA. In *Raytheon Co.,*[80] it added a fourth requirement: that the arbitrator has ruled on the NLRA issue.

As might be expected from their generality and lack of precision, the application of *Spielberg* standards has been somewhat erratic, and the Board has swung back and forth between rare and excessive deferral.

a. Repugnancy

The concept of repugnancy to the policies of the Act has been especially productive of confusion. At times the standard was met almost whenever the Board concluded that it would have decided the case differently from the way it was decided by the arbitrator. In its 1984 *Olin Corp.* decision,[81] however, the Board redefined the concept of repugnancy so as to make such a finding much less likely. It stated that an arbitrator's award does not have to be totally consistent with Board precedent, and that deferral is to be granted unless the award is "palpably wrong," which only occurs when the award is "not susceptible to an interpretation consistent with the Act."

b. Fair Procedures

In general, fair procedures mean that the panel be neutral (selected by means agreed to by the parties), that there be an opportunity for both sides to present and refute evidence, and that there be a reasoned award. The Board has been particularly concerned in disciplinary cases that the interest of the grievant be represented. It has not simply assumed that the union has done so. The Board has been attentive to claims that the union was indifferent or hostile to the employee's interests, except when the employee has been represented by independent counsel. Indeed, recent cases have suggested that the requirement of fair and regular proceedings is best conceived as an adjunct of the duty of fair representation: a standard for evaluating the honesty and efficacy of the union's handling of the grievance.

Typical of Board decisions rejecting deferral when fair representation issues are involved is *Consolidated Freightways Corp.*[82] In that case, the discharged union steward was running for the position of business agent on a ticket opposing incumbent union leadership and the current business agent represented him in the arbitration proceedings. The Board refused deferral.

c. The Requirement That the Arbitrator Pass on the NLRA Question

The Board has had a difficult time in determining when the requirement is met. If the arbitrator specifically deals with or defers the NLRA questions, the Board's task is fairly simple, but the arbitrator may not mention to the NLRA at all and yet by implication pass on the claim. In deciding some grievances, the related NLRA issue is necessarily dealt with through factual determinations and contractual analysis of the type that arbitrators routinely undertake. For example, a finding that the employer, by contract, was given the power to subcontract, automatically establishes that it did not violate section 8(a)(5) by doing so. Other questions are less clearly resolved in this way.   A determination that two employees who refused an order were fired for "insubordination" does not address the question of whether they were engaged in protected activity under section 7 of the Act. Even if the arbitrator states in her opinion that the discharge was not for protected activity, it might be unclear whether she was applying the same standard as the Board.   If an arbitrator states that an employee was fired for lateness, he is indirectly ruling on the question of whether the stated reason is a subterfuge for union activity, but he may or may not have addressed the question specifically in deciding the case directly.   In all of these situations, the degree to which the arbitrator is competent to deal with the statutory question varies with the issue and the particular arbitrator's background and experience.

Although the Board's standard for deferral speaks in terms of the requirement that the arbitrator has passed on the legal issue, the cases show that the Board is likely to find this requirement has been met where the statutory issue is of the type necessarily decided through factual determination or traditional contract interpretation.   In discharge cases, if there is any ambiguity, the Board is more likely to hold that the subterfuge issue has not been dealt with.   Indeed, over the years some Board members have refused to defer in discrimination cases in which the arbitrator has not specifically addressed the subterfuge claim.

In the *Olin* case the current Board decided that if the contractual issue (a) is "factually parallel" to the unfair labor practice issue, and (b) the arbitrator was presented generally with the facts relevant to resolving the unfair labor practice, it will presume that the statutory issue has been adequately considered by the arbitrator.   Further, the burden of proof is now on any party requesting the Board not to defer to the arbitrator.   This conclusion together with the Board's "palpably wrong" standard on repugnancy was obviously intended to make it extremely difficult for either party to successfully challenge an arbitrator's decision.

d. APPLICATION OF SPIELBERG DOCTRINE TO THE REPRESENTATION AREA

In *Raley's Inc.,*[83] The Board announced that deferral according to the *Spielberg* criteria extended to representation cases.   In that case, the Board honored an arbitration award holding that janitors and bottle sorters were covered by the contract between the employer and the union intervening in the Board proceeding and therefore barred the election sought by the petitioning union.   The Board found the award sufficient under *Spielberg* even though the petitioning union was not a party to the arbitration because the Board found that the employer had adequately represented the union's position.

The Board retreated from this position in *Westinghouse Electric Corp.*,[84] which established a strict standard for non-repugnance in such cases:

"[T]he ultimate issue of representation could not be decided by the Arbitrator on the basis of his interpreting the contract under which he was authorized to act, but could only be resolved by utilization of Board criteria for making unit determinations. In such cases the arbitrator's award must clearly reflect the use of and be consonant with Board standards."

Since then, even when the arbitrator took into consideration Board standards as to unit-determination, the Board has generally refused to defer. The Board was also likely to find the representation of third party interests at arbitration proceedings inadequate. The Board in *Marion Power Shovel* [85] abandoned the approach taken in *Raley's*, emphasizing the lack of expertise of the arbitrator in interpreting statutory policy:

"This dispute thus presents issues of whether a question of representation is present and what is the appropriate unit. . . . We do not believe the Board should defer consideration of these issues to the parties' contract arbitration procedure. The determination of questions of representation, accretion, and appropriate unit do not depend upon contract interpretation but involve the application of statutory policy, standards and criteria. These are matters of decision for the Board rather than an arbitrator."

This position is both sensible and responsive to the criticisms of excessive deferral made by the courts in several recent cases. Whether the Board will continue to acknowledge its own wisdom is problematic given the Board's tendency to swing back and forth in this area.

2. Deferral to the Arbitral Process Prior to Award

In *Dubo Mfg. Co.*,[86] the Board instructed the General Counsel that it might be appropriate to refuse to issue a complaint when the subject matter was being litigated in an ongoing arbitration process. This approach was made discretionary. Judgments were to be made in each case about whether this was a matter peculiarly appropriate for Board decision. *Dubo* was superseded by *Collyer Insulated Wire*,[87] in which the NLRB announced a policy of systematic refusal to proceed with cases that could be the subject of a grievance under an existing system culminating in binding arbitration. In cases coming within the *Collyer* doctrine, the Board does not hold a hearing, but it retains jurisdiction to evaluate the arbitrator's decision in accordance with the *Speilberg* standards discussed above.

The *Collyer* doctrine originally covered cases alleging discrimination against individuals as well as cases stemming from unilateral employer action. In cases arising from claims of individual discrimination, however, the Board developed the practice of refusing to defer when there was significant reason to suppose that the interests of the individual and the union that would represent him in processing a grievance were sufficiently diverse that the union might be expected not to handle the grievance adequately.

The *Collyer* approach was controversial within the Board from the first. Originally two members of the Board considered it a shameful abdication of Board responsibility. Two members supported it strongly and sought to apply it broadly and one member went along, despite misgivings.[88] Scholarly response to the doctrine was both voluminous and conflicting. Some saw it as an act of creative administration, calculated to protect the Board's resources and remove it from contract enforcement—an area in which it did not belong.[89] Others saw it as a blow to unions' statutory interests and to individual rights.[90] In general, commentators were more favorable to its application in refusal-to-bargain cases than cases alleging discriminatory discharge or discipline. They argued that the possibility of union-employee conflict seemed greatest in disciplinary cases and they pointed out that the statutory right of the employee involved in such cases did not arise from the agreement.[91]

About five years after the *Collyer* decision, the Board once again addressed the deferral issue in two cases that revealed that the conflict of views had not substantially changed in either direction. In *Ray Robinson Chevrolet,*[92] the Board narrowly reaffirmed *Collyer* in refusal-to-bargain cases, and in *General American Transportation Corp.,*[93] the Board, in three separate strongly worded opinions, announced that it would no longer defer in discrimination cases. This approach of limited deferral developed by the Carter Board, however, was quickly rejected by the Reagan Board.

In *United Technologies,*[94] a companion case to *Olin,* the Reagan Board overruled *General American Transportation Corp.* The employer in that case allegedly violated section 8(a)(1) by threatening an employee with disciplinary action if she took a grievance to the second step. The administrative law judge rejected the employee's request for Board deferral, relying on *General American Transportation.* The Board majority, after expounding at length on the importance of the grievance-arbitration process, held that even in cases involving the claim of retaliation for the exercise of statutory rights, it would defer to arbitration. Member Zimmerman issued a strong dissent. The opinions in *United Technologies* replicated the original debate in *Collyer,* with the addition of intervening authority and generalizations about the experience under *Collyer.*

The Board majority, without any factual basis and ignoring the many criticisms, announced that "the experience under *Collyer* was extremely positive." [95] It reasserted the conclusion that deferral was implicitly included in collective agreements providing for arbitration. "In our view, the statutory purpose . . . is ill-served by permitting the parties to ignore their agreement and to petition this Board in the first instance. . . ." This conclusion does not reflect the realities of collective bargaining. Parties who agree to a broad clause do not thereby undertake to bypass the Board in cases of overlapping claims. The Board majority in *United Technologies* relied on the *Spielberg* doctrine for the claim that statutory rights would continue to be protected—a remarkable position to take simultaneously with the issuance of the *Olin* decision.

United Technologies was decided during the period of the Dotson Board's greatest activism in reversing previous policies. Since then the Board's approach has moderated somewhat in most areas, and this has reflected itself among other things in greater exercise of caution in deferral.[96] The case that best reflects this increased caution is *U.S. Postal Service*. In that case it was alleged that the employer violated section 8(a)(3) and section 8(a)(4) by discharging a union steward who filed unfair labor practices against it. The union also claimed that the employer violated section 8(a)(5) by denying its request for the names of its officers and stewards who had applied for supervisory positions. The Board concluded that the statutory interests involved militated against deferral. It stated that "deferral is inappropriate where the union has sought information that is relevant to the performance of its statutory function". The attitude expressed in this statement, if generally adopted, would make deferral unavailable in a variety of cases in which important statutory interests are involved.

One reason why developing a consensus about the *Collyer* doctrine has been so difficult is that its proponents have sought to justify it on the basis of several somewhat inconsistent rationales that have different implications about the way it should be administered.

The original decision in *Collyer* rested in significant part on arbitrators' "special skill and experience in deciding matters arising under established bargaining relationships." [97] The conclusion that arbitrators possess such special ability is stated without explanation and it seems to be one of the great largely unexamined assumptions of labor law. A careful examination of the elements of such decision making—(a) accurate factual determination, (b) understanding the impact of decisions on industrial violations, (c) consistency in interpreting language, and (d) conformity with national labor law policies—suggest that the Board is better equipped with respect to items (a), (c), and (d) by virtue of its more elaborate processes and more limited precedent, and that item (b) would largely depend upon the background of the decision makers, which in general is fairly similar for the two groups. This rationale does not seem to apply with obviously greater force to either section 8(a)(3) or (5) cases.

Deferral has also been justified in terms of:

1. the advantages of arbitration as a process, its speed, formality and a flexibility;

2. the desire to encourage voluntary settlements;

3. the conservation of Board resources; and

4. the notion that arbitration is best understood as a part of the collective-bargaining process.

None of the other reasons point as clearly to a distinction between duty to bargain and employer retaliation cases as does the argument that arbitration is an integral part of the collective-bargaining process. Arbitration is often either consciously or unconsciously used to complete items left unfinished in the basic contract negotiations. It is structured in such a way that the arbitrator's decisions are most likely to reflect what the parties would have decided if they had themselves achieved agreement on the item in question.

Given the intimate connection between arbitration and negotiation, it is somewhat fictional to conclude in cases involving unilateral action that an employer willing to arbitrate is unwilling to bargain. Section 8(a)(5) was not really intended for the policing of collective agreements. Its goal is to protect the central role of the union as the representative of the employees, something that is well achieved through arbitration.

This is a powerful rationale for deferral in section 8(a)(5) cases, but it points to the danger of applying *Collyer* in cases that involve the right to be free of retaliation, an interest not subject to the bargaining process.

During the period when *Collyer* opponents constituted a majority of the Board, two additional techniques for limiting its application were developed. The Board in some cases took a very strict view of the concept of voluntary agreement to arbitrate that undergirds the *Collyer* doctrine and held that when the issue of arbitrability is contested, it will not defer.[98] Secondly, the Board in a few cases took an expansive approach to the concept of individual rights and protected activity, sometimes concluding that the enforcement of any rights under a contract is protected activity and hence not subject to deferral. Another technique for limiting deferral was contained in the suggestion of the D.C. Circuit Court of Appeals that the Board consider whether requiring arbitration will place an undue financial burden on either party.[99] This approach, if followed, would inevitably lead to a substantial reduction of the number of cases subject to deferral, particularly where small, independent unions are involved.

D. The Role of the Courts in Adjusting the Relationship Between Arbitrators and Other Forums

1. Enforcement of the Promise to Arbitrate Matters Covered by the NLRA

In *Smith v. Evening News Ass'n,*[100] the Supreme Court held that the possibility that a matter might be dealt with under the NLRA does not prevent the promise to arbitrate concerning it from being enforceable. The major question in this area remaining after the *Smith* case was whether there are some cases so peculiarly appropriate for the Board that a court might decline to enforce the promise to arbitrate a grievance. In *Carey v. Westinghouse Electric Corp.,*[101] the Supreme Court went a long way toward rejecting the concept of primary Board jurisdiction in any matter contractually subject to arbitration under the standards announced in the Trilogy. The case involved a grievance by the IUE claiming that certain employees represented by another union were in fact engaged in production and maintenance work. By Board certification and contract, the IUE was recognized as the representative of production and maintenance workers. It was not clear whether the IUE was claiming that it was entitled to represent the people currently doing the work as part of its unit or whether it sought to have this work reassigned to the people it currently represented. The Supreme Court said that regardless of the nature of the claim, the matter was appropriate for arbitration if the matter represented a claim to the work. The Court pointed out that the NLRA did not provide a mechanism for handling such a dispute prior to a strike, which would invoke the complex procedures of section 10(k).

Even if the case involved the right to represent particular employees, something that might be deemed peculiarly within the expertise of the Board, the Court felt that the policy of encouraging settlement through arbitration applied.

> "However the dispute be considered—whether one involving work assignment or one concerning representation—we see no barrier to use of the arbitration procedure. If it is a work assignment dispute, arbitration conveniently fills a gap and avoids the necessity of a strike to bring the matter to the Board. If it is a representation matter, resort to arbitration may have a pervasive, curative effect even though one union is not a party.

> "By allowing the dispute to go to arbitration its fragmentation is avoided to a substantial extent; and those conciliatory measures which Congress deemed vital to 'industrial peace' (*Textile Workers v. Lincoln Mills,* supra, [353 U.S. at] 455 [77 S.Ct. 917]) and which may be dispositive of the entire dispute, are encouraged. The superior authority of the Board may be invoked at any time. Meanwhile the therapy of arbitration is brought to bear in a complicated and troubled area."

The decision in *Carey* established that the policy of encouraging resort to arbitration applied with continuing vitality to matters governed by the NLRA.   It did not purport to establish a flat rule that arbitration is never to be rejected because of possible conflict with the Board. Lower federal courts have sometimes refused to order a matter arbitrated when they believed that the issue has been or was in the process of being resolved through the Board, since its decision would supercede any arbitration award anyway.   There have been almost no cases where the courts have refused to order arbitration based on the subject matter of the dispute.

E.   The Role of the Courts in Adjusting the Relationship Between Arbitrators and the Board

1.   *Spielberg*

The *Spielberg* doctrine itself has been accepted by the courts, but they have acted as a counterweight to Board policies, either extending or rejecting deferral.   In particular, the question of arbitral competence has been a continuing concern of the courts in reviewing Board decisions under *Spielberg.*

In *Distillery Workers v. NLRB,*[102] the Second Circuit was more hospitable to deferral than the Board.   The issues were whether the company violated the contract or its duty to bargain prior to taking unilateral action when it instituted new collection procedures for its salesmen.   The arbitrator found that the agreement did not cover collection procedures so that there was no violation of the language of the contract.   He also found that the new procedures did not change past practice.   The Board refused to defer to the award because the contract did not address the collection procedure issues and precluded consideration of past practices relating to them.

The Second Circuit reversed the Board because the arbitrator "plainly did consider past practice."   The Court reasoned that even though the arbitrator did not specifically deal with the claim that the company had refused to bargain over a unilateral change in working conditions, he did decide that the new procedures did not impose a change in rules, which determination was both within his area of competence and determinative of the NLRA issue.   "This determination . . . was necessarily dispositive of the statutory issue: if no change in working conditions was imposed, no duty to bargain arose, and no unfair labor practice could have been committed."   The Court found that the contractual and statutory issues were "congruent," and ordered the Board to follow its own rules and defer to the award.[103]

On the other hand, courts have insisted that the arbitrator's competence to decide factual and contract issues does not extend to technical legal issues.   In *Stephenson v. NLRB,*[104] the Court stated:

"[T]he Board should not defer when the issue presented involves primarily a statutory rather than a contractual or factual issue." [105]

The District of Columbia Circuit Court has also said that deferral is only proper when the arbitrator confines the inquiry to issues within his or her competence. In *Banyard v. NLRB,*[106] an employee was fired for refusing to drive a truck he claimed was unsafe. The Court held that the contractual issue of whether his refusal to drive was justified was not congruent with the statutory issue of whether that refusal was a protected protest of unsafe conditions under federal law. The Court explained that there was a possibility that different standards would apply to the employee's refusal and that different facts would need to be considered. Under the statutory issue, the Board would apply an objective standard of whether a reasonable man would have considered the conditions unsafe. The court was unable to ascertain the arbitrator's standard from his opinion and rejected the Board's attempt to defer.

Given the courts' traditional concern with deferral in cases of serious statutory violation, it is not surprising that the *Olin* decision has met with judicial disapproval in several cases. The Ninth Circuit, in *Garcia v. NLRB,*[107] overturned the Board's decision to defer in a case in which an employee had been disciplined for refusing to violate a state law. The court concluded that the arbitrator's award was "palpably wrong" because it violated public policy. In *Darr v. NLRB,*[108] a decision by the D.C. Circuit, an employee was discharged for circulating a petition protesting some discharges and changes in the company break schedule. The arbitrator specifically found that the discharge was both a violation of the contract and of the NLRA. He also noted that the remedies under each approach would be different. He specifically declined to enforce the NLRA and ordered the lesser contract-based remedy of reinstatement without back pay. The Board's administrative law judge found the arbitral award clearly repugnant to the Act and therefore refused to defer. The Board, however, found that "the judge had substituted his judgment for that of the arbitrator's contrary to the principles of deference mandated by *Olin Corp.*"[109] The Board noted that the arbitrator had found the respondent partly at fault. "It is the essential nature of the arbitration process to balance the competing claims of the parties by adjusting the equities involved to reach a harmonious result. . . . That is what the parties have agreed upon. . . ."[110] The Board, therefore, accepted the award.

The court of appeals reversed and remanded the case to the Board after expressing considerable unhappiness with the Board's lack of theoretical consistency and its cavalier disregard of employee's statutory rights.

"We cannot clearly discern from the Board's decision in this case why it deferred to the arbitrator's award: its decision appears based on an admixture of theories. The Board's comment that the arbitrator's balancing of equities 'is what the parties have agreed upon' seems to partake of the . . . theory that the parties agreed to a contractual standard governing discipline that is different—providing in some cases less protection and in some cases greater—than that afforded by the NLRA. But the Board does not explicitly set forth a waiver theory or even consider whether a union can legitimately waive an individual employee's rights under Section 8(a)(1) and (3) of the Act. . . .

"If instead the Board's decision was based on a theory of deferral predicated on the premise that Darr's NLRA rights were litigated before the arbitrator, the Board must explain how the statutory claim merged into the contract claim when the arbitrator himself treated the NLRA cause of action as outside his jurisdiction. . . .

"We have profound doubts that the Board may defer to an arbitrator's award merely because the award is roughly analogous to that which the Board would grant—a sort of 'Kentucky Windage' approach. . . ." [111]

The court's frustration is evident and understandable, its opinion thought out and well crafted. It is questionable whether the Board will be able on remand to articulate a theory of deferral that the Court would find satisfactory.

In *Taylor v. NLRB*,[112] the Eleventh Circuit Court of Appeals specifically rejected the *Olin* doctrine as a failure. The court criticized the Board's approach for being inadequate to protect employees' rights, for giving away too much of the Board's responsibility, for ignoring the practical realities of the arbitration process whereby individual rights might be traded away to advance collective interest, and for overlooking instances where statutory and contract issues may be factually parallel but involve distinct elements of proof and questions of factual relevance. This opinion is the only one in which a court has specifically rejected the *Olin* doctrine so far. However, the doctrine's inconsistency with the language of the statute, with traditional views of the Board's role, and with developing judicial awareness of the weaknesses of arbitration as a technique for resolving statutory rights is likely to mean that *Olin* will continue to have rough sledding in the courts.

2. *Collyer*

The Board's right to defer to arbitrators had been affirmed by numerous courts of appeals' decisions and by dicta by the Supreme Court. However, the courts of appeals have expressed concern about the dangers of *Collyer* and they have on occasion denied the Board's right to defer when there was reason to believe that individual statutory interests would not be adequately represented at the arbitration hearing. Moreover, while the Supreme Court has referred favorably to the *Collyer* doctrine in dictum, it has rejected the concept of deferral to arbitration both with respect to Title VII in *Alexander v. Gardner–Denver Co.*[113] and with respect to the Fair Labor Standards Act in *Barrentine v. Arkansas–Best Freight Systems, Inc.*[114] In both cases the Court concluded that neither the promise to arbitrate nor an actual award precluded resort to the statutory remedy. In *Alexander v. Gardner–Denver,* dealing with the relationship between arbitration and Title VII rights, the Court seemed to reject much of the reasoning that has been used to support the *Collyer* doctrine. The doctrine rests in large part upon the Board's desire to conform with the national policy of encouraging the use of arbitration to settle labor disputes. The *Gardner–Denver* opinion makes clear, however, that this policy does not extend so far as a preference for arbitration in place of a statutorily created forum. As the Court stated:

> "The distinctly separate nature of these contractual and statutory rights is not vitiated merely because both were violated as a result of the same factual occurrence. And certainly no inconsistency results from permitting both rights to be enforced in their respectively appropriate forums."[115]

Moreover, the Court in *Gardner–Denver* recognized that arbitration is a poor forum for vindication of statutory rights. The Court wrote:

> "Arbitral procedures, while well suited to the resolution of contractual disputes, make arbitration a comparatively inappropriate forum for the final resolution of rights created by Title VII. This conclusion rests first on the special role of the arbitrator, whose task is to effectuate the intent of the parties rather than the requirements of enacted legislation. Where the collective-bargaining agreement conflicts with Title VII, the arbitration must follow the agreement. To be sure, the tension between contractual and statutory objectives may be mitigated where a collective-bargaining agreement contains provisions facially similar to those of Title VII. But other facts may still render arbitral processes comparatively inferior to judicial processes in the protection of Title VII rights. Among these is the fact that the specialized competence of arbitrators pertains primarily to the law of the shop, not the law of the land."[116]

The Court also pointed out that the fact-finding process in arbitration "usually is not equivalent to judicial fact-finding,"[117] and summarily rejected the argument that the promise to arbitrate constitutes a waiver of the right to pursue the statutory remedy. The Court stated, "[b]oth rights have legally independent origins and are equally available to the aggrieved employee." [118] Indeed, the Court suggests that the union could not properly waive the statutory forum on behalf of the employee even if it chose to do so. The Court also refused to adopt a rule requiring federal courts to defer to already issued arbitration awards in certain defined circumstances. The result of such a rule would be:

> "to deprive the petitioner of his statutory right to attempt to establish his claim in a federal court. . . .
>
> "Furthermore, we have long recognized that 'the choice of forums inevitably affects the scope of the substantive right to be vindicated.'" [119]

The reasoning in *Gardner–Denver* is applicable to claims arising under the NLRA. The distinction drawn by the Court between statutorily created rights and forums and contractually created rights and forums is identical in the two situations. The procedural weaknesses in arbitration are the same under the NLRA as under Title VII, as are the limits on the arbitrator's jurisdiction and competence. In fact, the authority cited by the Court for the limited nature of the arbitrator's authority includes articles addressed mainly to the arbitrator's role in enforcing rights under the NLRA. Thus, except for duty-to-bargain cases, there is no more reason to imply a waiver of the statutory forum in NLRA cases than in those arising under Title VII. The opinion itself recognizes the basic similarity of the two situations:

> "The resulting scheme is somewhat analogous to the procedure under the National Labor Relations Act, as amended, where disputed transactions may implicate both contractual and statutory rights." [120]

At one time it was thought that the *Gardner–Denver* opinion represented a special rule limited to allegations of racial discrimination. However, in *Barrentine.* the Court applied the reasoning to statutory rights under the Fair Labor Standards Act (FLSA). It held that a group of truck drivers could bring an action under that statute despite their claim being rejected under the grievance system.

Although it paid homage to the Trilogy and the policy of promoting arbitration, the Court drew a firm distinction between statutory and contractual rights:

> "Not all disputes between an employee and his employer are suited for binding resolution in accordance with the procedures established by collective bargaining. While courts should defer to an arbitral decision where the employee's claim is based on rights arising out of the collective bargaining agreement, different considerations apply where the employee's claim is based on rights arising out of a statute designed to provide minimum substantive guarantees to individual workers." [121]

As it did in *Gardner–Denver*, the Court in *Barrentine* emphasized the limits of the arbitrator's role. It referred to difficulties in construing FLSA, and concluded that whereas "an arbitrator may be competent to resolve many preliminary factual questions, such as whether the employee 'punched in' when he said he did, he may lack the competence to decide the ultimate legal issue. . . ." [122] It also observed that "[b]ecause the arbitrator is required to effectuate the intent of the parties, rather than to enforce the statute, he may issue a ruling that is inimical to the public policies underlying the FLSA. . . ." [123] In *Marshall v. N.L. Industries, Inc.,*[124] the Seventh Circuit applied *Gardner–Denver* to permit an action under the Occupational Health and Safety Act after a grievance dealing with the same subject.

> "Like Title VII, this legislation was passed to mobilize the resources of the federal government in an effort to eradicate a specific group of problems confronting workers nationwide. . . . Enacted after the Supreme Court developed its policies encouraging deference to arbitration in a pure collective bargaining context, the OSHA legislation was intended to create a separate and general right of broad social importance existing beyond the parameters of an individual labor agreement and susceptible of full vindication only in a judicial forum." [125]

The reasoning of these cases is persuasive and broadly applicable. Together they announce a federal policy favoring the vindication of statutory rights through public forums rather than through arbitration. This policy should be applied to rights under the NLRA that do not turn on construction of the agreement but rather on articulating and effectuating the policies of the statute. It must be recognized that the role of the courts in enforcing labor statutes is less significant than the role assigned to the Board in enforcing rights under the NLRA. The courts initially approved the *Collyer* doctrine, but they also approved the split approach of *GATC* and *Roy Robinson Chevrolet* differentiating between duty-to-bargain and retaliation cases. The Court's reference to *Olin* and *United Technologies* has ranged between cautious and hostile. Such an approach seems entirely consistent with, if not required by, *Alexander v. Gardner–Denver* and *Barrentine*.

Part VI. Labor Arbitration and the Demise of Employment at Will

The jurisprudence of just cause changed the nature of the employment relationship in unionized enterprises giving employees significant job security and motivating employers to articulate standards and refine their processes for dealing with infractions and absenteeism. One inevitable result was agitation for the judicial development of greater job security in the non-union sector. The early proponents of judicial change specifically based their proposals on the experience under collective agreements. This agitation has had significant success in state courts in recent years. The old doctrine of employment at will—the notion that an employee could be discharged for any reason or no reason—has given way before a variety of judicially imposed limitations. In a significant number of jurisdictions, courts now read into the employment contract a promise not to discharge or impose significant discipline except for cause.[126] A great many decisions applying this doctrine have recently been issued and in a number of cases substantial monetary awards have been made to improperly discharged employees.[127] This has seemed to provide desirable social change in the development of parallel union and judicial protection for job rights. It is instructive, however, to note the differences between protections afforded by collective bargaining and protection afforded through the courts.

If an employer in a nonunionized context is to continue to be free to set the terms of employment, much of the protection afforded by the just cause standard under collective bargaining can be offset by individual agreements. Employers are beginning to respond to the new changes by amending handbooks and making the original employment undertaking more clearly qualified.[128] In the unionized context, the employer may not deal with individual employees, and therefore he may not utilize any advantage in bargaining power over individuals to undercut the protections of the collective-bargaining agreement. One of the interesting points about union-management relations is that protections are afforded even though the parties are permitted enormous leeway in setting their own terms and conditions.

An individual employee without union protection would be vulnerable to harassment to force him to resign, even after a successful law suit. The employee could not relitigate every instance of harassment. As Professor Summers, a strong proponent of the extension of just cause, has noted, "unfamiliarity with legal procedures and reluctance to become involved in them" will deter most employees from litigating when the loss is not substantial.[129] The problems of retaliation cannot adequately be dealt with by continuous resort to the legal process. The NLRB's provision of legal protection against retaliation includes an experienced administrative apparatus, yet research indicates that most discriminatorily discharged employees either do not, in fact, return to their jobs, or if they do, are soon forced to leave.[130] Fear of retaliation and harassment are the main reasons for leaving. Although the Board's procedures are excellent and its formal remedial power great, it is unable to prevent harassment or discrimination.

Arbitration awards favorable to employees under collective agreements are routinely obeyed and are rarely undercut. The collective-bargaining agreement provides protection against the use of discretion as a form of reprisal. For example, if the arbitrator orders an employee's reinstatement, management cannot provide him with inferior wages or working conditions without violating the seniority clause or his job description. Moreover, reprisal would make the union more intransigent in settling grievances and would lead to the filing of new ones. The employer who sought to undercut the agreement might also be faced with protest strikes.

Moreover, when a union is on the scene and representation is provided for, it is the employer who is likely to be put at a disadvantage by a multiplying number of grievances. Since it is important to a union to maintain the integrity of grievance procedures, any inclination of the employer to retaliate against the employee must be balanced against the desirability of maintaining or developing good relations with the union.

Thus, collective bargaining provides protection and representation for employees that makes the contractual right not to be disciplined except for just cause a meaningful one. In the non-union sector, as a practical matter, the right is likely to be invoked where there is enough money involved to make it worthwhile to bring a lawsuit. In fact, the cases suggest that the legally developed rules against unjust discharge provide a remedy primarily for corporate executives, professionals, and well-paid employees fired under egregious circumstances.[131]

FOOTNOTES

1. The parties may be reluctant to reveal a willingness to compromise before someone who may later be asked to rule on the merits should mediation fail.

2. See Abrams J. Nolan, Toward a Theory of "Just Cause" in Employee Discipline Cases, 85 Duke L.J., 594 (1985).

3. See Getman, Labor Arbitration and Dispute Resolution, 88 Yale L.J. 916 (1979); Feller, A General Theory of the Collective Bargaining Agreement, 61 Calif.L.Rev. 663 (1973).

4. See, e.g., D. Bok & J. Dunlop, Labor and the American Community 266 (1970) (grievance procedures can improve morale; "net effect of collective bargaining is to increase productivity"); L. Sayles & G. Strauss, supra note 11, at 22 (grievance procedure not just "a purely negative method of appeal *against* management," but "a continuous process of problem solving"); cf. Brown & Medoff, Trade Unions in the Production Process, 86 J.Political Econ. 355 (1978) (econometric data show positive impact of unionization on productivity).

5. See F. Elkouri & E. Elkouri, supra note 11, at 125–29; L. Sayles & G. Strauss, supra note 11, at 27–33.

6. One of the authors (Getman) was a permanent umpire in an institution in which relations had so deteriorated that the union filed a grievance about management's refusal to compromise grievances.

7. U.S. Bureau of Labor Statistics Dep't of Labor, Bull. No. 1425-6, Arbitration Procedures (1966).

8. 353 U.S. 448, 40 L.R.R.M. 2113 (1957).

9. 363 U.S. 564, 46 L.R.R.M. 2414 (1960).

10. 363 U.S. 574, 46 L.R.R.M. 2416 (1960).

11. 363 U.S. 593, 46 L.R.R.M. 2423 (1960).

12. 376 U.S. 543, 55 L.R.R.M. 2769 (1964).

13. 430 U.S. 243, 94 L.R.R.M. 2753 (1977).

14. 406 U.S. 272, 80 L.R.R.M. 2225 (1972).

15. 417 U.S. 249, 86 L.R.R.M. 2449 (1974).

16. See Chapter One (pages ___-___.)

17. *American Sink Top & Cabinet Co.,* 242 N.L.R.B. 408 (1979).

18. See Leonard, Post Contractual Arbitrality After Nolde Brothers, 28 NYLS Law Rev. 257 (1983).

19. See *National Tea Company* (Teple 1973).

20. 417 U.S. at 255, 86 L.R.R.M. at 2451. In *Howard Johnson,* the clause specifically applied to purchasers but was not binding. The Court indicated that the seller would be liable for breach of the agreement. Presumably, the union could seek damages. The Union could seek to enjoin a sale where the employer selling had not required the buyer to assume the contract. See, e.g., *Howard Johnson,* footnote 3, *ILGWU v. Bali Co.,* 649 F.Supp. 1083, 123 L.R.R.M. 3210 (D.C.P.R.1986) (injunction against plant removal pending arbitration).

21. *American Press v. NLRB,* 126 L.R.R.M. 3131 (1987).

22. *Smith v. Evening News Ass'n,* 371 U.S. 195, 51 L.R.R.M. 2646 (1962).

23. 362 F.2d 677, 62 L.R.R.M. 2495 (2d Cir.1966).

24. Simon, Judicial Review of Labor Arbitration: Under What Conditions Will a Grievance Arbitration Award be Overturned by the U.S. Courts of Appeals 1980–1983. Supervised Analytic Writing Paper, Yale Law School 1983. On file with author.

25. 683 F.2d 154, 110 L.R.R.M. 3175 (6th Cir.1982), *cert. denied,* 460 U.S. 1023, 12 L.R.R.M. 2896 (1983).

26. 517 F.2d 616, 89 L.R.R.M. 2535 (9th Cir.1975), *cert. denied,* 423 U.S. 894, 90 L.R. R.M. 2614 (1975).

27. *Textile Workers Union v. American Threac Co.,* 291 F.2d 894 (4th Cir.1961); *Monongahela Power Co. v. Local 2332, IBEW,* 566 F.2d 1196 (4th Cir.1976).

28. See, e.g., *W.R. Grace and Co. v. Local Union 759, Intern. Union of United Rubber Workers,* 461 U.S. 757, 766, 113 L.R.R.M. 2641 (1983); *International Union, UAW v. Keystone Consolidated Industries, Inc.,* 728 F.2d 1400, 121 L.R.R.M. 2702 (7th Cir.1986) (Awards violative of public policy cannot be enforced).

29. 126 L.R.R.M. 3113 (1987).

30. The Court did not really set forth standards concerning the principal question of "when courts may set aside arbitration awards as contravening public policy."

31. 369 U.S. 95, 49 L.R.R.M. 2717 (1962).

32. 398 U.S. 235, 74 L.R.R.M. 2257 (1970).

33. 370 U.S. 195, 50 L.R.R.M. 2420 (1962).

34. 398 U.S. at 247–48.

35. 428 U.S. 397, 92 L.R.R.M. 3032 (1976).

36. *Gateway Coal Co. v. United Mine Workers,* 414 U.S. 368, 85 L.R.R.M. 2049 (1974).

37. See, e.g., *Waller Bros. Stone Co. v. United Steelworkers, District 23,* 620 F.2d 132, 104 L.R.R.M. 2168 (6th Cir.1980).

38. *Mastro Plastics Corp. v. NLRB,* 350 U.S. 270, 37 L.R.R.M. 2587 (1956).

39. See *NLRB v. Laborer's, Local No. 721,* 649 F.2d 33, 107 L.R.R.M. 2406 (1st Cir. 1981) (unfair labor practice must "threaten the integrity of the collective bargaining relationship" to fall under this doctrine).

40. See, e.g., *United Parcel Service (N.Y.), Inc. v. Teamsters, Local 804,* 698 F.2d 100, 112 L.R.R.M. 2648 (2d Cir.1983).

41. See, e.g., *Anheuser–Busch, Inc. v. Teamsters Local No. 633,* 511 F.2d 1097, 88 L.R.R.M. 2785 (1st Cir.1975), *cert. denied,* 423 U.S. 875, 90 L.R.R.M. 2744 (1975).

42. See, e.g., *Dresser Industries v. United Steelworkers of America, Local 4601,* 110 L.R.R.M. 261 (W.D.N.Y.1981).

43. See, e.g., *Lever Bros. Co. v. International Chemical Workers,* 554 F.2d 115, 95 L.R.R.M. 2438 (4th Cir.1976).

44. *Amalgamated Transit Union, Div. 1384 v. Greyhound Lines, Inc.,* 529 F.2d 1073 (9th Cir.1976).

45. *Amalgamated Transit Union, Division 1384 v. Greyhound Lines, Inc.,* 550 F.2d 1237 (9th Cir.1977).

46. *First National Maintenance Corp. v. NLRB,* 452 U.S. 666, 107 L.R.R.M. 2705 (1981).

47. 265 N.L.R.B. 206 (1982).

48. 602 F.2d 1302, 102 L.R.R.M. 2498 (9th Cir.1979).

49. 268 N.L.R.B. 601 (1984).

50. 386 U.S. 171, 64 L.R.R.M. 2369 (1967).

51. 386 U.S. at 191–92, 64 L.R.R.M. at 2377 (footnote omitted).

52. 424 U.S. 554, 91 L.R.R.M. 2481 (1976).

53. 386 U.S. at 190–91 at 2376–78.

54. 403 U.S. 274 (1971).

55. 451 U.S. 679 (1981).

56. An approach which has been followed by most courts of appeals.

57. See, Malin, Individual Rights Within the Union (BNA 1987) Chapter 8.

58. *Graf v. Elgin, Joliet and Eastern Ry. Co.,* 697 F.2d 771, 112 L.R.R.M. 2462 (1983).

59. See Malin, supra, n. 57; Summers, the Individual Employee's Rights Under The Collective Agreement; What Constitutes Fair Representation, 126 U. of Penn.L.Rev. 251 (1977).

60. *De Arroyo v. Sindicato De Trabajadores Packinghouse,* 425 F.2d 281, 74 L.R.R.M. 2028 (1st Cir.1970), cert. denied, 400 U.S. 877 (1970).

61. *Ruzicka v. General Motors Corp.,* 707 F.2d 259, 113 L.R.R.M. 2562 (6th Cir.1983), cert. denied, 464 U.S. 982 (1983).

62. *Taylor v. Belger Cartage Service, Inc.,* 762 F.2d 665, 119 L.R.R.M. 2430 (8th Cir. 1985).

63. *Galindo v. Stoody Co.,* 793 F.2d 1502 (9th Cir.1986).

64. *Stevens v. Teamsters, Local 600,* 794 F.2d 376, 122 L.R.R.M. 3040, 3041 (8th Cir. 1986).

65. *Thompson v. International Ass'n of Machinists,* 258 F.Supp. 235 (E.D.Va.1966).

66. 619 F.2d 1229 (8th Cir.1980).

67. 217 N.L.R.B. 616 (1975).

68. 217 N.L.R.B., at 619.

69. 213 N.L.R.B., 640.

70. *Barton Brands, Ltd. v. NLRB,* 529 F.2d 793, 91 L.R.R.M. 2241 (7th Cir.1976).

71. See Freed, Polesby & Spitzer, Unions, Fairness, and the Conundrums of Collective Choice, 56 S.Cal.L.Rev. 461 (1983).

72. *Gregg v. Teamsters, Local 150,* 699 F.2d 1015 (9th Cir.1983).

73. 451 U.S. 679, 107 L.R.R.M. 2385 (1981).

74. 386 U.S. at 197, 64 L.R.R.M. at 2379–2380.

75. 459 U.S. 212, 112 L.R.R.M. 2281 (1983).

76. *International Brotherhood of Teamsters v. United States,* 431 U.S. 324 (1977).

77. Meltzer, Ruminations About Ideology, Law and Labor Arbitration, In The Arbitrator, the NLRB and the Courts; Howlett, The Arbitrator, the NLRB and the Courts, Proceeding of the 20th Annual Meeting, National Academy of Arbitrators, 1967.

78. The writings are summarized in Feller, The Coming End of Arbitrators Golden Age Proceedings, National Academy of Arbitrators, 20th Annual Meeting 97 (1976).

79. 112 N.L.R.B. 1080 (1955).

80. 140 N.L.R.B. 883, set aside on other grounds, 326 F.2d 471, 55 L.R.R.M. 2101 (1st Cir.1964).

81. 268 N.L.R.B. 573 (1984).

82. 257 N.L.R.B. 177 (1981); 108 L.R.R.M. 1165.

83. 143 N.L.R.B. 256 (1963).

84. 162 N.L.R.B. 768 (1967).

85. 230 N.L.R.B. 576 (1977).

86. 142 N.L.R.B. 431 (1963).

87. 192 N.L.R.B. 837 (1971).

88. Then Chairman Miller and member Kennedy favored broad application; members Fanning and Jenkins dissented and Brown concurred.

89. See, e.g., 85 Zimmer, Wired For Collyer, 48 Ind.L.J. 141 (1973).

90. See, e.g., 86, Getman, Collyer Insulated Wire: A Case of Misplaced Modesty, 49 Ind.L.J. 57 (1973).

91. See Schatzki, Resolution of Contract Disputes Under § 8(a)(5), 50 Texas L.Rev. 225 (1972); Rejoinder 49 Ind.L.J. 76 (1973).

92. 228 N.L.R.B. 828 (1977).

93. 228 N.L.R.B. 808 (1977).

94. 268 N.L.R.B. 557 (1984).

95. *United States Postal Services*, 282 N.L.R.B. 102; 125 L.R.R.M. 111 (1987). See also *Litton Systems*, 125 L.R.R.M. 1081 (1987).

97. 192 N.L.R.B. 839.

98. *National Rejectors Industries*, 234 N.L.R.B. 251 (1978).

99. *Local Union 2188, IBEW v. NLRB*, 494 F.2d 1087 (D.C.Cir.1974).

100. 371 U.S. 195, 51 L.R.R.M. 2646 (1962).

101. 375 U.S. 261, 55 L.R.R.M. 2042 (1964).

102. 664 F.2d 318, 107 L.R.R.M. 3137 (2d Cir.1981).

103. 664 F.2d at 325, 107 L.R.R.M. at 3142.

104. 550 F.2d 535, 94 L.R.R.M. 3224 (9th Cir.1977).

105. 550 F.2d at 537, 94 L.R.R.M. at 3225.

106. 505 F.2d 342, 87 L.R.R.M. 2001 (D.C.Cir.1974).

107. 785 F.2d 807, 121 L.R.R.M. 3349 (9th Cir.1986).

108. 801 F.2d 1404, 123 L.R.R.M. 2548 (D.C.Cir.1986).

109. 801 F.2d at 1406–07, 123 L.R.R.M. at 2550 (1986).

110. Quoted in 801 F.2d at 1407, 123 L.R.R.M. at 2550 (1986).

111. 801 F.2d at 1408–09, 123 L.R.R.M. at 2551, 2552 (1986).

112. 786 F.2d 1516, 122 L.R.R.M. 2084 (11th Cir.1986).

113. 415 U.S. 36, 7 FEP 81 (1974).

114. 450 U.S. 728, 24 WH 1284 (1981).

115. 415 U.S. at 50, 7 FEP at 86.

116. 415 U.S. at 56–57, 7 FEP at 89.

117. 415 U.S. at 57, 7 FEP at 89.

118. 415 U.S. at 52, 7 FEP at 87.

119. 415 U.S. at 56, 7 FEP at 88 (quoting *U.S. Bulk Carriers v. Arguelles*, 400 U.S. 351, 359–60, 76 L.R.R.M. 2161, 2164 (1971) (Harlan, J., concurring).

120. 415 U.S. at 50, 7 FEP at 86 (footnote omitted).

121. 450 U.S. at 737, 24 WH at 1287.

122. 450 U.S. at 743, 24 WH at 1290.

123. 450 U.S. at 744, 24 WH at 1290.

124. 618 F.2d 1220 (7th Cir.1980).

125. 618 F.2d at 1222.

126. See, e.g., *Newfield v. Insurance Co. of the West,* 156 Cal.App.3d 440, 203 Cal. Rptr. 9 (1984).

127. See, e.g., *Wolk v. Saks Fifth Avenue, Inc.,* 728 F.2d 221 (3d Cir.1984).

128. Sears, Roebuck & Co. issued a nationwide disclaimer on its employment application. It has been found to create an employment at will. *Reid v. Sears, Roebuck & Co., Inc.,* 588 F.Supp. 558 (E.D.Mich.1984).

129. Summers, Individual Protection Against Unjust Dismissal: Time for a Statute, 62 Va.L.Rev. 481 (1976).

130. Attleson, et al., Collective Bargaining in Private Employment, Unit 1, p. 333, 1984.

131. The resort to lawsuits for damages for wrongful discharge is growing even among employees covered by collective bargaining agreements. This is probably so because the damages can include pain and emotional suffering whereas arbitrators can only award backpay and reinstatement.

Relevant Books, Articles, and Suggested Reading

BOOKS:

Zach (ed.), Arbitration in Practice (1984).

Elkouri & Elkouri, How Arbitration Works (1973).

American Audubon Society, The Future of Labor Arbitration (1976).

Fleming, The Labor Arbitration Process (1965).

Kuhn, Bargaining in Grievance Settlement (1961).

McKelvey (ed.), The Duty of Fair Representation (1977).

Slichter, Healy & Livernash, The Impact of Collective Bargaining on Management (1960).

ARTICLES:

Epstein, "In Defense of the Contract at Will," 51 U.Chicago Law Rev. 947 (1984).

Proceedings of the National Academy of Arbitrators Vols. 1–41 (Each volume contains valuable articles about the law and practice of arbitration).

Goldberg, "The Mediation of Grievances Under a Collective Bargaining Contract: An Alternative to Arbitration," 77 Northwestern Univ.L.Rev. 270 (1982).

Summers, "Collective Agreements and the Law of Contracts," 78 Yale L.J. 525 (1909).

Feller, "A General Theory of the Collective Bargaining Agreement," 61 Calif.L.Rev. 663 (1973).

Getman, "Labor Arbitration and Dispute Resolution," 88 Yale L.J. 916 (1979).

Summers, "Individual Protection Against Unjust Dismissal: Time For a Statute," 62 Virginia L.Rev. 486 (1976).

Summers, "The Individual Employee's Rights Under the Collective Agreement: What Constitutes Fair Representation," 126 U. of Penn.L.Rev. 251 (1977).

Cantor, "Strikes Over Non–Arbitrable Labor Disputes," 23 Boston College L.Rev. (1982).

Summers, "The Rights of Individual Workers," Fordham L.Rev. 1082 (1984).

Nolan & Abrams, "American Labor Arbitration: The Early Years," 35 Univ. of Florida L.Rev. 373 (1983).

Nolan & Abrams, "American Labor Arbitration: The Maturing Years," 35 Univ. of Florida L.Rev. 557 (1983).

VanderVelde, "A Fair Process Model for the Union's Duty of Fair Representation," 67 Minn.L.Rev. 1079 (1983).

Harper, "Union Waiver of Employee Rights Under the NLRB, Part II, A Fresh Approach to Board Deferral to Arbitration," Indus. Rel.L.J. 680 (1981).

Meltzer, "Labor Arbitration and Overlapping and Conflicting Remedies to Employment Discrimination," 39 Univ. of Chicago L.Rev. 30 (1971).

Goetz, "Arbitration After Termination of A Collective Bargaining Agreement," 63 Virginia L.Rev. 693 (1977).

Peck, "A Proposal to _____ NLRB Deferral to the Arbitration Process," 60 West L.Rev. 355 (1985).

Schatzki, "NLRB Resolution of Contract Disputes Under Section 8(a)(5)," 50 Texas L.Rev. 225 (1972).

Leonard, "Post Contractual Arbitrability After Nolde Brothers: A Problem of Conceptual Clarity," 28 New York School L.Rev. 257 (1983).

Getman, "Collyer Insulated Wire: A Case of Misplaced Modesty," 49 Ind.L.J. 57 (1973).

Chapter IV

UNION ECONOMIC PRESSURE: STRIKES, PICKETING, AND BOYCOTTS

Part I. Basic Concepts—Historical Development

From the Colonial period until the passage of the Wagner Act in 1935, labor law was primarily developed by state courts applying common law concepts with little statutory guidance. During the early years of the Republic there was almost no direct precedent dealing with the legal status of strikes. Because such activity was unusual and threatening to many, it was initially dealt with under the criminal law doctrine of conspiracy. Conspiracy is a crime whose boundaries are quite vague, but that is often used to deal with unpopular or threatening political movements. The basic concept is that combinations of persons to achieve an improper goal pose a special threat to the society. In order for a combination of persons to constitute a conspiracy, it is not necessary that their purpose be criminal or even unlawful when pursued by an individual. A combination to achieve a goal contrary to public policy might suffice. Because unions are by definition combinations, and because their long range goals and immediate objectives can both be characterized as contrary to public policy, the very existence of unions and most union activity was vulnerable under this doctrine.

Efforts to use economic pressure in support of union organizing were particularly vulnerable under the doctrine of conspiracy because such pressure was aimed at forcing an employer to do something he would not do voluntarily. In addition, it had the inevitable consequence of injuring employees who chose not to join. The first recorded indictment in this regard was the famous Philadelphia Cordwainers' case.[1] In that case, the Recorder instructed the jury that "a combination of workmen to raise their wages may be considered from a two-fold point of view; one is to benefit themselves, the other to injure those who do not join their society. The rule of law condemns both." Although this case indicated that any union activity was criminal, the criminal conspiracy doctrine was not as widely applied as the language of the case would suggest. The bringing of charges against combinations of working people was often politically unpopular, and there was always a body of professional opinion that opposed the employment of the criminal conspiracy doctrine in this way. Most of the indictments involved efforts to use economic pressure in support of organizing or in support of what is today considered a secondary boycott.[2]

The criminal conspiracy doctrine as applied to labor unions was largely abandoned by the courts after the 1842 decision of Justice Shaw of the Supreme Judicial Court of Massachusetts in *Commonwealth v. Hunt.*[3] Justice Shaw insisted that the combination of workers to improve their economic situation was not automatically illegal as long as they sought lawful goals through legitimate means.

According to Justice Shaw:

> "Stripped, then, of these introductory recitals and alleged injurious consequences, and of the qualifying epithets attached to the facts, the averment is this: that the defendants and others formed themselves into a society, and agreed not to work for any person, who should employ any journeyman or other person, not a member of such society, after notice given him to discharge such workman. . . . Nor can we perceive that the objects of this association, whatever they may have been, were to be attained by criminal means. The means which they proposed to employ, as averred in this count, and which, as we are now to presume, were established by the proof, were, that they would not work for a person, who, after due notice, should employ a journeyman not a member of their society. Supposing the object of the association to be laudable and lawful, or at least not unlawful, are these means criminal? The case supposes that these persons are not bound by contract, but free to work for whom they please, or not to work, if they so prefer. In this state of things, we cannot perceive that it is criminal for men to agree together to exercise their own acknowledged rights, in such a manner as best to subserve their own interests."[4]

Although *Commonwealth v. Hunt* marked the end of the criminal conspiracy doctrine, it left open the question of which union means and which goals might be deemed unlawful. In particular, it left open the question of the circumstances under which strikes and picketing might be considered improper under tort doctrine.

As late as 1896, in *Vegelahn v. Guntner*[5] the Massachusetts Supreme Judicial Court granted an injunction against peaceful picketing at the premises of a struck employer with whom the union had a dispute about wages. It granted the injunction on the grounds that the picketing interfered with the employer's relationship with employees who did not support the strike. The court held that:

> "An employer has a right to engage all persons who are willing to work for him, at such prices as may be mutually agreed upon, and persons employed or seeking employment have a corresponding right to enter into or remain in the employment of any person or corporation willing to employ them. . . . No one can lawfully interfere by force or intimidation to prevent employers or persons employed or wishing to be employed from the exercise of these

rights. . . . Intimidation is not limited to threats of violence or of physical injury to person or property. It has a broader signification and there also may be a moral intimidation which is illegal." [6]

To remedy the union's misconduct, the court approved an injunction ordering the union to refrain from any action "organized for the purpose of annoying, hindering, interfering with, or preventing any person or persons who now are or may hereafter be in the employment of the plaintiff, or desirous of entering it, or from continuing therein." [7]   The opinion was subject to a strong dissent by Justice Holmes who argued that the infliction of harm upon the plaintiffs was justified by public policy in favor of "free competition." [8]

Most state courts eventually came to accept the legitimacy of picketing at the premises of a struck employer in furtherance of a dispute over wages or working conditions. Nevertheless, the reasoning employed and result reached in *Commonwealth v. Hunt* is typical, in three important respects, of the decisions in subsequent cases limiting the right to strike. First, it focused much of its analysis on the rights of employees who did not support the union and on their relationship with the employer. Second, it found the very fact of picketing, even though peaceful, to be a form of intimidation. Finally, it sought to remedy the problem by issuing a broad injunction against further picketing.

Injunctions against strikes were a powerful employer weapon for several reasons. They could be obtained very quickly, generally before the picketing caused much harm. In fact, a single judge who agreed with the employer's position might issue an injunction even before a formal hearing could be held. Oftentimes judges would issue a temporary restraining order simply on the application of the employer. While the legitimacy of the injunction thus issued could be tested on appeal, that involved a time consuming and expensive process. Further, injunctions were written in legal language (often by the employer's lawyer) but directed to employees who thereafter acted at peril of being found in contempt for violating its terms. The penalties for contempt included fines against the union and imprisonment for its members.[9]

Justice Holmes's dissent in *Vegelahn v. Guntner* proved to be persuasive in part. Eventually, most courts were willing to accept the legitimacy of strikes for higher wages or improved working conditions and were equally tolerant of peaceful picketing at the premises of the employer being struck. The concept of free competition, however, was much less persuasive with respect to strikes for the purpose of achieving recognition. Because such strikes were aimed, in part, at those employees who did not join the union, they were treated by the courts not as economic disputes between capital and labor, but as disputes "between laborers all of the same craft, and each having the same right as any of the others to pursue his calling."[10]   Similarly, secondary employers were perceived as neutrals rather than as parties to the economic competition that gave rise to the primary dispute. Employers also were able to improve their chances for injunctions against union organizing activity or strikes by getting their employees to sign agreements pledging not to join a union during the period of their employment.   In *Hitchman Coal & Coke Co. v. Mitchell,*[11] the United States Supreme Court upheld the grant of an injunction against a strike on the grounds that it was aimed at convincing employees to violate their contractual promises.   Thereafter, such contracts were often the basis for the grant of an injunction against strikes for organizations purposes.

The Sherman Anti-trust Act[12] added another legal basis for the granting of injunctions against strikes for organizational purposes, secondary boycotts, and strikes that might have a major effect on the economy.   In *Loewe v. Lawlor,*[13] the Supreme Court held that unions were not exempted from the Act's provisions and that a campaign by unions, through boycotts, to force non-union hat manufacturers to sign up could be attacked under the Act as an unreasonable restraint of trade.

The legal limits on strike activity developed by the courts during the later part of the 19th century and the early part of the 20th century led to considerable political agitation by unions and their supporters.   The Clayton Act,[14] passed in 1914 to amend the Sherman Act, contained two provisions that were generally thought to eliminate the use of injunctions against union activity under the antitrust laws. The major provision, section 20, prohibited the granting of an injunction prohibiting strikes or boycotts in any "case between an employer and employees . . . involving or growing out of a dispute concerning terms or conditions of employment."   In *Duplex Printing Press Co. v. Deering,*[15] the Supreme Court held that this language applied only to strikes and picketing by employees against their own employer concerning their own terms and conditions of employment.   This constriction, which permitted the courts to grant injunctions in cases of secondary economic pressure and in cases of stranger picketing for purposes of organization, was deemed necessary on the grounds that the provision "imposes an exceptional and extraordinary restriction upon the equity powers of the courts of the United States and upon the general operation of the anti-trust laws, a restriction in the nature of a special privilege or immunity to a particular class, with corresponding detriment to the general public."[16]   The quoted language is just one of many judicial statements expressing the idea that to permit economic pressure outside the confines of a classical economic strike would be dangerous to the well-being of society.

Even where primary strike activity took place, injunctions by state courts might be issued on the grounds that the activities engaged in involved acts of violence or threats of violence. As already noted, many courts were prepared to find the threat of violence quite easily in a strike situation because many viewed the picket line as inherently coercive. Moreover, when acts of violence took place on the picket line, many courts were disposed to find the union responsible and to use that as the basis for an injunction. Thus despite labor's apparent political victory in the passage of the Clayton Act, courts continued to issue injunctions in many different types of labor disputes.

Inevitably, unions came to see the courts as their enemy and lobbied for legislation directly limiting the power of the courts to issue injunctions in labor disputes. The unions were aided by growing criticism of the labor injunction by scholars, lawyers, and judges. Probably the most influential criticism came from Frankfurter and Green in their book *The Labor Injunction,* which detailed the historical abuses connected with the issuance of labor injunctions.[17] In 1932, Congress passed the Norris–LaGuardia Act,[18] which severely limited the rights of federal courts to issue injunctions in labor disputes. The Act declared that no federal court had jurisdiction to issue an injunction in a case arising from a "labor dispute" except in conformity with its provisions. With the Supreme Court's opinion in *Duplex Printing* in mind, the term "labor dispute" was broadly defined to include "any controversy concerning terms or conditions of employment or concerning the association or representation of persons . . . whether or not the disputants stand in the proximate relation of employer and employee." Once a labor dispute was found, the courts were forbidden to issue any injunction that forbade either the refusal to work or peaceful picketing. Injunctions could be issued to prevent threats or violence, but only after a hearing and after detailed findings to show that such an injunction was needed. The Act also outlawed "yellow dog" contracts—pledges extracted from employees not to join unions.

In *United States v. Hutcheson,*[19] the Supreme Court held that because of the policy reflected in the Norris–LaGuardia Act against federal interference with peaceful strikes and picketing, strikes and boycotts in support of a jurisdictional claim did not violate the Sherman Act. The Court thereby specifically overruled *Duplex Printing v. Deering.*

Despite the breadth of its language, which the courts generally respected, the Norris–LaGuardia Act was limited because it did not apply to state courts and because it did not purport to change the substantive law governing the legality of strikes and boycotts. As a result, state courts were still free to issue injunctions based on the means-end approach. In some states, the Norris–LaGuardia Act was supplemented by similar legislation and in other states the courts began to approach strikes and picketing more sympathetically. Nevertheless, many forms of economic pressure, in particular organizational strikes, and boycotts in support of strikes, remained of questionable legal status in most states and were subject to injunctions. In 1935, with the passage of the Wagner Act,[20] union economic pressure was given legal protection and largely removed from state jurisdiction under the doctrine of federal preemption. The Wagner Act contained no union unfair labor practices and it specifically protected the right to strike and engage in other "concerted activity for purposes of . . . collective bargaining and . . . mutual aid and protection." The period after passage of the Wagner Act was the point in time during which strikes and other forms of economic pressure were given their greatest legal protection. The federal courts were prohibited from issuing injunctions by virtue of Norris–LaGuardia and by virtue of the substantive rights recognized by the statute. Their jurisdiction was further limited by the statutory scheme, which granted primary jurisdiction in almost all labor disputes to the National Labor Relations Board. Under the Act, employers were forbidden from making participation in strikes and other economic pressure a basis for discipline of employees. A specific labor exemption to the antitrust laws was recognized. State law was largely preempted with respect to matters covered by the National Labor Relations Act, and the Act's jurisdiction was broadly stated and construed to apply to virtually all private employers other than those in agriculture. Some limited state jurisdiction remained, but even that had to be exercised in a manner consistent with the federal scheme. During this period, for the only time in American labor law, not only was there a legal right to engage in primary strikes over wages and working conditions, but strikes for purposes of organizing, obtaining recognition, claiming work, or aiding other unions were also protected against either employer or judicial action.

This happy period from the union perspective came to an end with the passage in 1947 of the Taft–Hartley Act.[21] The development of the law thereafter may be seen as a continual process of limiting the right to strike and expanding the use of the labor injunction. Section 8(b)(4) of the Taft–Hartley Act sought to outlaw secondary strikes, using very broad language that had the potential to severely limit the protection previously afforded to traditional primary strikes. Section 8(b)(4) also prohibited some forms of recognitional and jurisdictional strikes. In addition, sections 8(b)(1)(A) and 8(b)(2) made general union interference with employee rights unlawful. With the new language, the public policy of the law with respect to strikes and picketing, which had been fairly clear under the Wagner Act, became once again contradictory and vague. This meant that the law's effect would turn significantly upon the way in which the general and confusing language of the statute was interpreted by the NLRB and the courts. While certain provisions broadly protected the use of economic pressure, others broadly outlawed it. There were specifically defined union unfair labor practices and general language against "restraining or coercing employees in the exercise of their rights under section 7." Thus, the possibility existed for reinstating or even extending much of the old precedent prohibiting certain types of strikes. However, the language previously used to protect the use of economic pressure remained in the statute. With passage of the Landrum–Griffin Amendments in 1959, the statute was made even more complex and even more inconsistent with its original approach to economic pressure.[22] These amendments prohibited strikes for organization or recognition and further limited the right of unions to seek support from each other. As a result of these changes, confusion and technical distinctions were inevitable, and the role of lawyers in labor relations became more and more prominent.

Part II. The Constitutional Status of Strikes and Picketing

A. Introduction

Successful strikes require two types of behavior: refusals and inducements. The essential refusal, of course, is refusal by employees to work for the struck employer until the union's demands are met. A typical strike, however, may also involve refusals by other employees to pick up from, deliver to, or otherwise deal with the struck employer and refusals by customers to patronize the struck employer. In addition, in order to avoid disruptions, other employers may refuse to purchase from or hire the struck employer.

The inducements, on the other hand, are acts by the union and its supporters seeking to convince people who would otherwise deal with the employer to refuse to do so. Inducements take the form of speeches, notices, strike votes, letters, handbills, and picket lines, which are the techniques by which the request to refuse is made most powerfully and personally.

Constitutional debate has dealt with both the refusals and the inducements, particularly with the status of picketing. Unions and their supporters have argued that neither the federal government nor the states may prohibit either the refusals to deal with the struck employer or peaceful efforts to induce such behavior. In the context of labor relations, this argument has been regularly rejected. The Supreme Court has recognized broad regulatory power by the federal government and by the states over both of these areas. The reasons why the Court has recognized greater governmental power to regulate such conduct in the area of labor relations than elsewhere has never been adequately explained by the Court, and the reasons are far from obvious.

B. The Constitutional Status of Inducements

1. Picketing

The extent to which the constitution protects peaceful picketing has been the subject of considerable litigation. The broadest recognition of a constitutional right to picket came in the early case of *Thornhill v. Alabama*,[23] in which the Court struck down an Alabama statute that forbade "Loitering or Picketing" "without just cause . . . about the premises or place of business (of anyone) engaged in lawful business for the purposes of hindering, delaying or interfering . . ."[24] The Court made clear that it considered peaceful picketing a legitimate technique by which unions could publicize their positions. It announced that "in the circumstances of our times, the dissemination of information concerning the facts of a labor dispute must be regarded as within that area of free discussion that is guaranteed by the Constitution."[25] Shortly thereafter, however, the Court narrowed the scope of this holding in a series of cases which held that picketing, even though peaceful, might be prohibited when its purpose was in violation of a legitimate state policy. The policies that the Court acknowledged in this regard were state policies aimed at preventing the spread of industrial disputes to neutral employers and policies aimed at preventing unions from picketing to obtain recognition from employers whose employees did not wish to be represented. In each case, the Court based its conclusion in part on the grounds "that picketing, even though 'peaceful,' involved more than just communication of ideas."[26]

The classic formulation of this concept was contained in Justice Douglas's concurring opinion in *Bakery and Pastry Drivers Local 802 v. Wohl*,[27] in which he stated that "Picketing by an organized group is more than free speech since it involves patrol of a particular locality and since the very presence of a picket line may induce action of one kind or another quite irrespective of the nature of the ideas which are being disseminated." The meaning of this passage, which has been repeatedly quoted with approval in Supreme Court decisions, is far from clear. It seems to rest on two questionable conclusions that are joined together somewhat uneasily. The first conclusion is that a picket line is inevitably intimidating. This is suggested particularly by the word "patrol," which has a military connotation. Patrols are generally maintained in the military to repulse by force, if necessary, enemy incursions into an occupied area. This interpretation is reinforced by the words beginning "may induce action," because the source of the action is not specified. The second notion is that labor picketing is an appeal not to reason but to one's obligations as a union member or supporter.

The difficulty with the analysis based on the equation of picketing and intimidation is that both the factual setting in which picketing takes place and the belligerence of the pickets varies greatly from situation to situation. A single person standing silently with a sign has been held to be picketing. There is little basis for believing that passersby feel threatened by such behavior; nonetheless, the analysis of the Court for these purposes treats all peaceful picketing alike. Nor has the Court ever specifically endorsed this questionable factual assumption.

The difficulties with the second, automatic-response rationale are equally significant. To the extent that this rationale suggests that emotional appeals to class loyalty, political beliefs, or group identification are entitled to lesser protection than more cerebral appeals, it is contradicted by considerable First Amendment authority denying that speech may be banned based on its content, subject matter, or emotional nature. A more sophisticated version of this argument is that union members feel bound to respond to picket lines, not because they share the views of the pickets, but because they fear union retaliation should they ignore a picket line. This argument is bolstered by the fact that many union constitutions specifically require honoring picket lines and that under the Act employees may become union members not because they share the union's philosophy but because they are required to by a union security agreement or because they are influenced by the power that adheres to union incumbency. If this is the concern that legitimates regulation of picketing, it would suggest a constitutional difference between picketing directed to employees and picketing directed to non union employees, customers and other members of the general public.

At one time, the Court seemed to recognize a distinction based upon the status of those to whom the picketing was directed. In *NLRB v. Fruit and Vegetable Packers, Local 760*,[28] the Supreme Court strained the language of the statute in order to permit product picketing directed to customers of a secondary employer. The Court made clear that similar picketing directed to secondary employees would have violated the Act. Its opinion seemed to rest in part on the "concern that a broad ban against peaceful picketing might collide with the guarantees of the First Amendment."[29]

In a subsequent case, *NLRB v. Retail Store Employees Union, Local 1001 (Safeco)*,[30] the Court rejected the conclusion that picketing directed to consumers is entitled to special constitutional protection. The Court held that section 8(b)(4) of the Act prohibited picketing directed to consumers asking them to boycott the product of the primary employer when that picketing "is reasonably calculated to induce customers not to patronize the neutral parties at all."[31] The Court's plurality opinion treated the First Amendment issue as insignificant, merely noting that "such picketing spreads labor discord by coercing neutral parties to join the fray."[32]

Two Justices, Blackmun and Stevens, joined the opinion but specifically disassociated themselves from the Court's perfunctory treatment of the constitutional issue. Justice Blackmun's concurrence rested on the conclusion that Congress had, in the secondary boycott provision of the NLRA, struck a "delicate balance between union freedom of expression and the ability of neutral employers, employees and consumers to be free from coerced participation in industrial strife." [33] This language reflects an emerging theme in first amendment analysis in labor cases, namely that restriction on speech becomes justified by virtue of being part of a system of complex regulation that inhibits both sides and from which unions derive considerable benefit. Justice Steven's concurrence, which specifically rested on the special nature of labor picketing, quoted with approval the famous Douglas language in *Wohl.*

The *Safeco* case holds that consumer picketing in labor cases is not entitled to constitutional protection, even when totally peaceful and directed to the struck product rather than the secondary enterprise. The constitutional basis for the Court's conclusion, however, is unclear. The decision seems to rest in part on the special quality of picketing and in part on the fact that inducements to boycott those characterized by the Court as neutrals are subject to governmental regulation.

The Court has indicated that first amendment protection is less applicable for labor picketing than for picketing for other social movements that the Court considers as "political." The distinction was drawn by the Court in *NAACP v. Claiborne Hardware Co.,*[34] in which it held that activity (including picketing) that could have been held to be illegal secondary boycott activity in the labor context was constitutionally protected when undertaken by the NAACP for the purposes of achieving racial equality in employment. Although the Court relied in part on *Thornhill* for the conclusion that picketing was a form of speech, it distinguished the cases upholding regulation of labor picketing on the grounds that such cases involved "economic regulation" and did not involve the type of political speech that rests on "the highest rung of first amendment values." [35] The distinction between political and labor speech seems rather astonishing given the long-time political debate over the value and need for unionism and the political focus of many unions.

That part of the Court's opinion distinguishing between labor and political speech has been widely criticized by commentators who have pointed out that the rules governing application of the first amendment to labor cases remain vague and contradictory.[36] This confusion has been illustrated and compounded most recently by the Court's opinion in *Edward J. DeBartolo v. Florida Gulf Coast Building and Construction Trades Council.*[37] The Court in that case held that peaceful union handbilling aimed at consumers, which was not within the protection of a special exculpatory proviso to § 8(b)(4),[38] was nevertheless outside the statutory language, "threaten, coerce, and restrain," of § 8(b)(4)(ii), and therefore lawful. The result was clearly based on the Court's conclusion that a contrary construction would violate the Constitution. "The courts will . . . not lightly assume that Congress intended to infringe constitutionally protected liberties." The opinion by Justice White distinguished its earlier decision in the *Safeco* case on the grounds that "picketing is qualitatively different from other modes of communications," citing with approval Justice Steven's special concurrence in *Safeco.*

The Court thus seemed to abandon the *Safeco* majority rationale which was based on the general authority of Congress to prevent the spread of industrial disputes to neutral parties. Since the Court now seems to rest its constitutional analysis on the distinction between picketing and other forms of communication, it seems inevitable that it will have to elaborate more explicitly the circumstances under which peaceful picketing might be described as coercive. It cannot remain the law that one stationary person standing with a sign is engaging in conduct which is constitutionally regulatable while several people delivering the same message through handbills are protected by the first amendment.

The distinction between picketing and handbilling in labor cases makes even less sense in light of the Court's willingness in *Claiborne* to extend the mantle of constitutional protection to far more vigorous picketing which it described as "political." Nor is it clear after *DeBartolo* that peaceful labor picketing is to be treated as commercial rather than political speech, although that was the implication of the courts discussion in *Claiborne.* In a passage certain to require subsequent explication, the Court in *DeBartolo* stated:

> "We do not suggest that communications by labor unions are never of the commercial speech variety and thereby entitled to a lesser degree of Constitutional protection. The handbills involved here, however, do not appear to be typical commercial speech . . . for they pressed the benefits of unionism to the community and the dangers of inadequate wages to the economy and the standard of living of the populace."

The discussion suggests that union communications which address general issues of the role are political speech. It would be a relatively simple task for unions to make this an element of all picket signs. If the Court adopts this approach to identifying political speech, it should expand the protection of peaceful picketing by unions. At the very least, the Court will be forced to readdress the issue in a more systematic fashion.

2. Appeals Made Away From the Premises of the Secondary Employer

Appeals by union officers to their own members to refuse to handle goods of another employer clearly fall within the prohibition of the Act and have been held not protected by the First Amendment. Thus, the Court summarily denied First Amendment protection to an appeal by the head of the Longshoreman's union who had instructed union members to refuse to unload Soviet vessels.[42] The Court summarily categorized the union's conduct as "designed not to communicate but to coerce."[43] Although the Court's language in the Longshoreman's case apparently referred directly to the refusal, the communication by the union president to his members was specifically found to violate the Act. The Court partly explained its conclusion on the grounds that "a national labor union has chosen to marshall against neutral parties the considerable powers denied by its locals and itself under the Federal labor laws."[44] Although this language might suggest greater ability by a non-incumbent union to such a secondary boycott by its members, there is little else in the decided cases to support such a distinction, and it is unlikely that the courts would, in fact, accept it.

The Supreme Court has not ruled directly on handbills directed to secondary employees by employees who are not members of the same union. Now that the Court has held that customer appeals are constitutionally protected, it will eventually be required to consider the issue. The current Court, which has stressed the policy against the spread of disputes over the rights of expression in cases of secondary boycott, would likely hold such appeals unprotected by the Constitution. Although the closest relevant authority seems to point in different directions.

C. Constitutional Protection of Refusal

1. Refusals by Customers

In the *Claiborne*[45] case, the Supreme Court held that politically motivated consumer boycotts are constitutionally protected. It is not clear whether a boycott by customers on behalf of a labor union would be entitled to similar protection, though such a boycott seems analytically identical to the boycott held constitutionally protected in *Claiborne*. In each case, customers are making economic choices to influence the hiring and labor policies of a company in support of a group thought to be economically disadvantaged. Nonetheless, as noted above, the Court has distinguished labor boycott activity from political boycott activity, and the standard by which boycotts are to be judged is an extremely vague one. "A government regulation is sufficiently justified . . . if it furthers an important . . . governmental interest . . . . is unrelated to the suppression of free expression and if the incidental restriction on alleged First Amendment freedom is no greater than is essential to the furtherance of that interest." [46] Whether the Court would hold that regulation of customer boycotts is "related to the suppression of free expression" seems highly problematic.

2. Refusals by Employees

Refusals by employees to work on goods of another employer that are somehow attributable to the union constitute a violation of section 8(b)(4)(i)(B) of the Act. In the *Longshoreman's* case, the Court denied such conduct constitutional protection. It is not totally clear why the Court reached this result. It is not clear, for example, why an employee does not have a constitutional right to refuse to work unless certain conditions are met, and why a group cannot join together in such a refusal. The answer is not simply based on contract principles. In neither the *Longshoreman's* case, nor in any of the other cases applying section 8(b)(4) to refusals, did the Court place its analysis on this ground. Moreover, if the limitations were based on the contract, that would merely push the constitutional issue back to section 8(e), which *forbids* agreements whereby employers agree to permit employees to refuse to handle work on goods supplied by another employer. A full constitutional exploration of this issue is beyond the scope of this work. It is enough for our purposes to suggest that the Court has never really considered the constitutional status of refusals to work and that this failure has made it difficult to analyze the constitutional status of related actions such as appeals to employees through handbills or speech.

Part III. The Regulation of Picketing In Support of Organizing

A. Introduction

There is no more complex issue and none that has been litigated under more different theories than the right of unions to use strikes and picketing in support of organizing efforts. As noted above, its legality has been tested under both criminal and civil common law, under the Sherman and Clayton Acts, under the First Amendment and various state constitutions, and under various provisions of the NLRA. The amount of legal literature dealing with various aspects of this issue is enormous. One of the reasons why the issue has been so pervasive is that it arises in myriad factual contexts, each posing different questions of fairness and legality.

A union that has organized a majority or a substantial minority of an employer's employees may resort to a strike after it has been denied recognition, in effect relying on the absence of union supporters from their job as a way of demonstrating the union's power. Such strikes were common before the law provided a technique by which a union might prove its majority in an election. In fact, they still occur in situations in which the union feels that the employer is vulnerable to economic pressure and where the union feels that it might well lose an NLRB-conducted election after an employer campaign. A union that does not have substantial support within the workforce or that feels that a simple primary strike for recognition would fail may attempt to obtain recognition by disrupting the targeted employer's relations with customers and other businesses. This may be done through activities at the targeted employer's premises in the form of appeals to customers or to employees making pickups or deliveries to refrain from dealing with the employer. Additionally, the union may establish picket lines where the targeted employer's products are sold or at the premises of other employers with which the employer does business.

In situations in which the union does not have substantial support within the work force, its economic pressure may be directed at the employees of the targeted employer by demonstrating that failure to join up will be harmful to them economically. In most situations, the goals of pressuring the employer to recognize the union and of pressuring the employees to join up coexist as part of a single strategy. The legitimacy of these tactics may well depend upon the way in which they are characterized. Thus, for example, consumer boycotts directed against employers with whom the targeted employer deals may be seen as legitimate efforts by labor to appeal to those who share its values to exercise their rights in a manner consistent with their beliefs. On the other hand, consumer boycotts may be viewed as unfair efforts to bring pressure on neutral employers in furtherance of a dispute to which they are not a party. Likewise, picketing by an outside union at the premises of a targeted employer may be seen as an effort to sway the choice of the employees or, in the alternative, as an effort to coerce the employees' choice. It is not surprising that the law has varied over time as the attraction of organized labor to the Board and courts has varied.

B. Application of the National Labor Relations Act to Recognitional Picketing

1. The Relevant Statutory Provisions

a. THE TAFT–HARTLEY APPROACH

In 1947, section 8(b)(4)(C) of the Taft–Hartley amendments specifically outlawed union picketing for recognition where the employer was already obligated to bargain with another union certified by the NLRB.[47] That provision was enacted together with section 8(b)(4)(D), which bars a union from using economic pressure to secure the assignment of work to its members from another group of employees in furtherance of a jurisdictional claim. Neither of these provisions, however, met the problem presented by picketing for recognition where there was no union recognized or where an incumbent union had been recognized, but not certified, by the NLRB. An employer faced with picketing for recognition in such circumstances had no avenue of relief.[48] Moreover, these sections were limited to picketing for recognition, which permitted unions to argue that their picketing was directed to employees rather than to the employer. Because it is often very difficult to distinguish recognitional from organizational purposes in picketing, the application of these sections was generally doubtful in particular cases.

b. THE LANDRUM–GRIFFIN AMENDMENTS

The 1959 Landrum–Griffin amendments to the NLRA were preceded by well-publicized hearings. These hearings included abundant testimony of Teamster union corruption and also considerable testimony about the use by the Teamsters of picketing and threats to picket as an organizational technique. The technique, referred to as "blackmail picketing" by opponents and as "top down organizing" by union officials, was simple. A union would request recognition from an employer under threat of establishing a picket line if recognition was refused. Such a picket line, ostensibly aimed at the employees sought to be organized, would have significant impact upon the employer because of the refusal of customer's employees to cross the picket line in order to make pickups and deliveries. The employer would either resist and suffer the effects of unlimited picketing or simply sign an agreement recognizing the union and requiring its employees to join up. Because the drivers who make the bulk of pickups and deliveries are frequently members of the Teamsters, the technique is especially effective when used by them and was a major facet of Teamster organizing. Thus, many in Congress came to identify organizational picketing with the Teamsters, corruption, and indifference to employee rights. On the other hand, organizational picketing has a long history of use by reputable unions under different circumstances in response to employer threats and intransigence. This led to a heated debate in Congress between those who wanted to outlaw all use of strikes and picketing in support of organizing and those who wanted only a limited intrusion on what they considered a legitimate aspect of the right to strike. The result was a statutory scheme (set forth in section 8(b)(7) of the Act) that represents an uneasy compromise between the competing points of view.[49] The section is notable both for the breadth of its application and for its exceptions and ambiguities. Section 8(b)(7) outlaws picketing or threats of picketing for either organizational or recognitional purposes in three situations:

1. Where another union was lawfully recognized—section 8(b)(7)(A);

2. Where a valid NLRB election had been held in the past twelve months—section 8(b)(7)(B); or

3. Where there was no outstanding recognition and no election within the past twelve months. Under such circumstances, a union could picket for a reasonable period not to exceed thirty days without filing a petition for election—section 8(b)(7)(C).

The most significant of these provisions was 8(b)(7)(C), which dealt with recognition or organizational picketing generally, and which is the aspect of the section most marked by compromise and confusion.

Violations of section 8(b)(7) were added to those unfair labor practices listed in section 10(*l*), mandating that the General Counsel seek injunctive relief in federal court if, after the filing of the charge, the General Counsel found reasonable cause to believe violations of any of these sections had occurred. The statutory scheme is to provide speedy relief from the picketing in advance of the Board's determination on the merits of the charge and then to submit the representation issue to the election process.[50]

2. The Statutory Scheme

a. THE ILLEGAL MEANS: "TO PICKET OR TO BE PICKETED, OR THREATEN TO PICKET . . ."

The Act does not define picketing, and the term is used for the first time in the 8(b)(7) legislation. Presumably, Congress had a generalized notion of picketing as the traditional patrolling by a group of employees holding picket signs near the employer's place of business.[51] The Board, however, has interpreted "picketing" liberally, focusing on some type of union activity near the entrances to the employer's business and the results of such activity. Thus, a union that commenced handbilling after having been enjoined from organizational picketing following a decertification election was held to be "picketing" in violation of 8(b)(7)(B).[52] The Board stated that:

"The important feature of picketing appears to be the posting by a labor organization or by strikers of individuals at the approach to a public place of business to accomplish a purpose which advances the cause of the union such as keeping customers away from business.[53]

The posting of individuals—the pickets—need not be continuous so long as their presence is noticeable. Thus where pickets placed their placards in a snow bank at the plant entrance and watched from their cars, emerging only to confront approaching truckers, the Board found picketing because the employees and truckdrivers understood the signs to be picket signs.[54]   The Second Circuit, in affirming the Board's decision, suggested the basic elements of picketing were (a) the posting of signs and (b) personal confrontations.[55]   In most cases, the carrying of a sign is a basic touchstone of picketing.

The statutory language includes threats of picketing as well as actual picketing, and the Board and courts treat a threat to picket the same as actual picketing.   The reasoning behind this position is that "Congress' purpose . . . was to prevent a labor organization from coercing an employer into recognizing it as the collective bargaining representative without regard to employee preference and Congress recognized both picketing and the threats to picket as the evils to be proscribed.[56]

b.   The Illegal Purpose: Picketing for the Object of Recognition or Organization

Section 8(b)(7) proscribes picketing only where an object is recognition, bargaining, or organization.   Picketing for any other object is not limited by the section.   The determination of the "true" object of the picketing is often extremely difficult to make because the immediate objective of the union may be limited, while its ultimate objective remains to achieve recognition.   The Board has stated: "We might well concede that in the long view all union activity including strikes and picketing has the ultimate economic objective of organization and bargaining.   But we deal not with abstract ideology.   Congress itself has drawn a sharp distinction between recognition and organization picketing and other types of picketing."[57]   Although the picketing could have more than one objective, a violation occurs if one of the objects is immediate recognition or organization.

(1) *"Area Standards Picketing"*

(a) *The General Concept*

"Area standards" picketing is picketing that publicizes the fact that an employer does not meet the area standards achieved by the picketing union in its contracts with other employers.   When the Board first considered area standards picketing, it reasoned that picketing over matters typically dealt with through collective bargaining was implicitly picketing for recognition.[58]   After a change in membership, the Board reversed itself and decided that "a union may legitimately be concerned that a particular employer is undermining area standards of employment by maintaining lower standards.   It may be willing to forego recognition and bargaining provided subnormal working conditions are eliminated from area considerations."[59]   The Board has thereby created the possibility of an effective alternative to recognitional picketing outlawed by the section.

The determination of the union's immediate or primary objective in area standards picketing is made on the basis of its factual context. Any union action signaling that the picket line will be removed on the grant of recognition will be enough to deny the claim that its object is to protect area standards. Employers frequently receive such statements from unsophisticated union officials. In addition, signs or handbills with a message that reveals a recognitional objective will be determinative, even where the union has disclaimed such an objective and limited the effect of the picketing. Area standards picketing is regarded by the Board as intended to reach the public and inform them of the employer's failure to meet area standards. Therefore, where the picketing seems primarily aimed at interfering with the delivery of goods and services to the employer rather than informing the public, that may be considered in determining whether the real purpose of the picketing was recognitional.[60] The sincerity of the union's claimed objective may be tested by its treatment of other substandard employers and by evidence of its knowledge and concern with the picketed employer's pay scale.[61]

(b) *Changed Objective*

The problems of determining whether the purported area standards picketing is a subterfuge arises in any case in which the union starts out clearly picketing for recognition or organization and then claims to have changed its purpose to area standards. This often arises in situations where recognitional picketing has been enjoined or after an election has been held where the union fails to achieve a majority. In these situations, the previous union activity seems almost inevitably relevant to the union's present intent. Yet the Board is reluctant to presume the continuation of an illegal objective. While not treating the past recognitional activity as a presumption of illegal purposes, the Board does regard it as a fact to be considered.[62] The determination in these circumstances turns on what objective steps the union has taken to demonstrate that it has, in fact, changed its purpose. Failure to notify the employer that the union does not seek representation will generally lead to the finding of a violation. It is not enough that the union makes its disclaimers to the Board if it fails to notify the employer.[63]

While failure to disclaim will result in a determination that the union has not really changed its objective, sending a disclaimer will be considered as only one factor in judging the union's objective. The Board also considers as significant whether there has been a hiatus period between the recognitional picketing and the purported area standards picketing.[64]

(2) Picketing for Grievances or Unfair Labor Practices

There are times when the union may allege the correction of grievances or unfair labor practices as the reason for the picketing. In these situations, the Board has weighed the nature of the claimed objectives to determine if they are the real basis for the picketing rather than an excuse for recognition picketing. Picketing for the reinstatement of discharged employees does not indicate a recognition purpose where the employer could resolve the matter by reinstating the employee without negotiating with the union.[65] Where a union demanded that the employer hire all its members who were employed by the firm's former subcontractor, however, the Board concluded that union recognition was a certain consequence of granting the union's request, and the picketing was held to be improper.[66]

c. SECTION 8(b)(7)(A): PICKETING WHERE ANOTHER UNION IS LAWFULLY RECOGNIZED

Picketing for recognition or organization is proscribed "where the employer has lawfully recognized in accordance with the Act any other labor organization and a question concerning representation may not appropriately be raised under 9(c) of this Act."

In 1959, with the enactment of section 8(b)(4)(C), Congress made recognition picketing illegal where the employer had recognized a union following an NLRB election and Board certification. By passage of Section 8(b)(7)(A), it sought to extend that protection to employers who had recognized a union without an election, presumably by a card count or other demonstration of the union's majority status. In such cases, a rival union can defend its picketing on the grounds of the illegality of the original recognition, by claiming that the recognized union did not enjoy majority status and was therefore illegally assisted. The Board has held that the issue of the lawfulness of the incumbent union's recognition, however, can be raised only within six months of the initial recognition. This is because a charge of illegal assistance could not be raised after that period under section 10(b) of the Act.[67] Similarly, the incumbent's status may not be challenged if a question of representation could not be raised because of the application of the Board's contract bar rules described in Chapter One.

Where the recognized union remains a minority and the challenge to this minority status is timely, the Board will find no violation of 8(b)(7)(A). On the other hand, where no lawful recognition has taken place the Board will treat the picketing as recognition picketing under section 8(b)(7)(C).[68]

d. Section 8(b)(7)(B): Picketing Within Twelve Months of a Valid Election

Section 8(b)(7)(B) bans picketing for recognition "where within the preceding twelve months a valid election has been conducted." This reflects the view that where the employees have made known their views concerning representation, both the employer and the employees are entitled to a respite from the harassment of recognition or organization picketing for a substantial period. In calculating the appropriate time period under this subsection, the Board holds that the certification date rather than the date of balloting is significant because the balloting is only a step in the determination of a "valid election." In the event of picketing after the certification, the twelve-month period runs from the date the picketing ceases, either voluntarily or involuntarily. This is based on the congressional intent to provide a full year of relief from such picketing for the employees and the employer. To rule otherwise would reduce the period.[69] Moreover, because under section 9(c)(3) the Board is precluded from holding an election in the same unit for twelve months after an election, the provision preserves the integrity of the election process. Section 8(b)(7)(B) interrelates with section 8(b)(7)(C)'s provision for an expedited election. A union picketing a non-union employer for recognition may be subject to an expedited election if the employer files an 8(b)(7) charge and a representation petition.[70] In the event the union fails to win a majority in the election, 8(b)(7)(B) applies to bar any subsequent recognition picketing.

In order to invoke the bar, the election has to be "valid" according to the statutory language. In evaluating this issue, the Board has allowed the picketing union, in defense of the charges, to go beyond the usual issues concerning the validity of an election, i.e., the conduct surrounding the election and the reliability of the results. The union may litigate whether the nature of its original picketing would have violated section 8(b)(7)(C) had it gone beyond thirty days and, therefore, whether an expedited election should have been ordered.[71] Thus, where a union established that its initial picketing was valid picketing under the proviso to section 8(b)(7)(C), the Board ruled that an expedited election should not have been held and was not "valid." The union's continued picketing was, therefore, not in violation of section 8(b)(7)(B).[72]

e. Section 8(b)(7)(C): Picketing for Recognition or Organization

By far the most significant section of 8(b)(7) is its limitation on peaceful picketing of non-union employers. Prior to the 1959 amendments, picketing under such circumstances was considered a legitimate tool of unions and was held to be permissible under the Act. The section permits the picketing for a limited period and then contemplates quickly resolving through an election the recognition issue raised by the picketing.   If no election is held, the Act provides for the Regional Director to seek an injunction to end the picketing after thirty days.   Presumably, an employer faced with recognition picketing by a minority union would be able to resist the pressure to recognize it because the picketing will have a foreseeable end.   Moreover, the employer does not have to wait for the period to end.   It can file a charge and petition for an expedited election that will express the employees' will.   Once the election is held, if the employees vote against representation, the union's continued picketing would violate section 8(b)(7)(B).

(1) Picketing for a Reasonable Period

The determination of what is a reasonable period of time for picketing is left largely to the Board's discretion.   In *NLRB v. Sapulpa Typographical Union No. 619*,[73] the Tenth Circuit stated that "the statute does not provide specific standards for measurement of a 'reasonable period,' but delegates to the Board authority to make that determination in light of the facts presented in each case."   In *Sapulpa,* the union had argued that the statute presented no clear standards for assessing reasonableness and was therefore unconstitutionally vague.   In rejecting that argument, the court quoted from *NLRB v. Local 239, International Brotherhood of Teamsters* [74]:

> "The statute plainly contemplates thirty days as the outer limit, with power in the Board, subject to review by the courts, to fix shorter periods as 'reasonable' ones according to particular fact situations . . . ..   And as so construed, the constitutionality of this clause stands unimpaired."

The Board's current interpretation of a "reasonable period" was stated by the Associate General Counsel in a memorandum: "Absent some special characteristic of the picketing (e.g., violence) or some special nature of the enterprise (e.g., deals in perishables), the Union is entitled to 30 days to place picketing pressure on the Employer." [75]

The Board's approach to reasonableness is tied to the availability of the election for resolving the representation issue raised by the picketing.   Therefore, the picketing period will be deemed "unreasonable" in less than thirty days where there is no possibility of holding an election.   Where the union engages in violence at the picket line, or mass picketing, or other unfair labor practices that would prevent the holding of an election, the picketing would be deemed to be for an unreasonable period and enjoined.[76]   This would hold even where the union attempts to cure the violation by filing a petition for an election.   Under this reasoning, because the union has, by its acts, foreclosed the possibility of a fair and free election to resolve the issue of representation, it cannot be allowed to continue picketing and thereby benefit from its own wrongdoing.

A union may not trigger the expedited election procedure by picketing and filing for an election. To permit an expedited election under such circumstances would encourage recognition picketing as a union device for obtaining a speedy election.[77]

(2) The Impact of Employer Unfair Labor Practices

Under the statute, the filing of a meritorious section 8(a)(2) charge may be a defense to a section 8(b)(7) violation. Such charges will prevent the Regional Director from seeking an injunction in section 8(b)(7) cases. Because this is the only specific unfair labor practice defense, it has been argued that no other claim of unfair labor practice should prevent the Regional Director from seeking an injunction. The first time the issue was considered by the Board in the *Blinne* case, it took this view.[78] Bolstering the statutory construction was the legislative history surrounding the provision. Congress had rejected a proposal to have any employer unfair labor practices constitute a defense to a charge of 8(b)(7). Upon a change in Board personnel, however, the *Blinne* decision was recalled and reconsidered.[79] The Board reasoned that the statutory scheme for enjoining organization picketing centered on the availability of an election to resolve these disputes. The long-standing policy of the Board prior to the enactment of section 8(b)(7) was that employer unfair labor practices would prevent an election from being held. The Board reasoned that Congress could not have meant to force a union to an election in those circumstances. However, it also feared that to allow the picketing union to obtain a delay simply by filing charges would encourage the filing of charges as a dilatory tactic. As a result, the Board concluded that a union could prevent an injunction by filing both a timely petition and unfair labor practice charges. The Board would not act upon the petition while investigating the charges. If the charges were dismissed, the petition would be processed and the election could go forward. If the charges were found meritorious, the union would be able to continue picketing until the unfair labor practice was corrected and an election could be held. If the union did not petition for an election, the Board would find it in violation of section 8(b)(7) despite the filing of charges. The Board excepted meritorious charges of section 8(a)(5). It held that an election petition need not be filed together with such a charge, on the grounds that a claim of refusal to recognize or bargain implicitly assumes the union's majority status and is inconsistent with an election petition.

The Board's reasoning seems overly technical and conceptual, but the scheme it adopted is easily accommodated to and does little violence to any of the Act's important principles.

(3) The Informational Picketing Proviso

In addition to allowing unions a limited "reasonable period" for traditional organizing picketing, section 8(b)(7)(C) contains a proviso that permits an unlimited period of picketing "for the purpose of truthfully advising the public (including consumers) that an employer does not employ members of, or have a contract with, a labor organization. . . ." [80] Where this standard is met, the picketing does not violate section 8(b)(7) unless it induces an individual in the course of his employment "not to pick up, deliver or transport any goods or not to perform any services."

This section once again reflects the strange notion, evidently generated by constitutional considerations, that it is legitimate for a union to appeal to the general public to support a picketing union's organizing efforts, but improper to appeal to other workers. The statutory approach thus set out is complex and difficult to apply consistently.

As indicated, the proviso to section 8(b)(7)(C) allows picketing where the purpose is to truthfully advise the public that the employer does not employ union members or have a contract with the union. The Board has held that including the language of the proviso on a picket sign is evidence of a recognitional object but privileged if within the terms of the proviso. It took the Board two panels to agree on this view. In *Crown Cafeteria*,[81] the first panel found that proviso picketing must have a purely informational objective. The then newly appointed Kennedy Board reconsidered *Crown* and determined that in order for the proviso to be meaningful, there must be a recognitional objective from which the proviso is an exception.[82] The courts have accepted this latter conclusion so long as the picketing is aimed strictly at consumers. Thus, the Second Circuit has stated that the proviso "gives the union freedom to appeal to the unorganized public for spontaneous popular pressure upon an employer; it is intended, however, to exclude the invocation of pressure by organized labor groups or members of union, as such." [83]

Under the Board's current approach, the object of the union's picketing is to be examined. If the union is seeking a response from the public, its picketing is within the proviso unless it effects deliveries. If the union is seeking a response from organized labor, its picketing is not privileged regardless of its effect.[84] Picketing that is located at nonpublic employee or delivery entrances, therefore, automatically violates the conditions of the proviso and forfeits its exempt status. Further, to come within the proviso, the picketing must address the public. Picketing with signs that say "On Strike" does not meet this condition because of its historic appeal to other union employees.[85]

The Board has adopted a distinction between picketing appealing to the public and so-called "signal" picketing, which is ostensibly directed to the public but is actually signaling other union employees to observe its picket line.[86] While this distinction is hard to define, the bottom line measure—its effects—are easy to observe. If such signals are being given, they will reveal themselves in the refusal to make deliveries or perform services and thereby take the picketing out of the exception. Further, the publicity must be truthful. If the information makes false claims, e.g., inaccurate information claiming substandard conditions, the picketing will be violative of the Act.[87]

(4) Effects of the Picketing on Deliveries and Services

Refusals to make pickups or deliveries may cause picketing to fall outside the protection of the proviso.[88] However, the Board holds that the impact must be significant. Isolated incidents of refusals to pick up or deliver will not be enough to disqualify the picketing. In addition, the picketing must have a "significant actual impact" on the employer's business. The Board's construction reflects its concerns that misguided refusals not convert clearly informational picketing into an unfair labor practice.

In *Barker Bros.,*[89] the principal case establishing this approach, the union had taken affirmative measures to see that no refusals by delivery men or suppliers would occur. Picketing was confined to public entrances and took place only during hours when the stores were open to the public. Nevertheless, there had been two work delays, three deliveries turned away, and several delays during the twelve weeks that twelve stores were picketed. The Board found that the incidents did not have a substantial impact on the business and that the picketing came within the proviso.

Inevitably, the Board's application of the "substantial impact" standard has been inconsistent. Thus an employer that had to modify its way of receiving supplies was deemed to have suffered a substantial impact, while another was not where the Board felt that the alteration was a matter of convenience and not necessitated by the picketing. The Board's decision in *Barker Bros.* to read a substantial impact standard into the exception to the informational picketing proviso can conflict with its general emphasis on the union's purpose. Focusing on the impact on the employer's operations makes the legality of the union's activity turn not on the quality of the union's acts, but on the operational vulnerability of the employer.

Finally, it should be noted that if the picketing is not for a proscribed object, e.g., area standards picketing, it would not be subject to the conditions of the proviso because it would be outside of section 8(b)(7) entirely. Even if deliveries were interrupted, such picketing could continue beyond thirty days and would not trigger the expedited election procedures.

C. Conclusion

It is difficult to tell what significance section 8(b)(7) has had. It is sufficiently technical to have provided a large body of case law concerning its application. Nonetheless, its very technicality, particularly over the issue of objectives, has meant that the threat to picket could not lightly be ignored by vulnerable employers. In any case, for a variety of prudent economic and tactical reasons quite apart from is legality, most unions have not used picketing for organizational purposes. Thus, while there has probably been a decrease in organizational picketing since the passage of section 8(b)(7), it is not clear that there is a causal relation between those phenomena. It seems likely that declines in union finances, membership, and militancy have combined to make the tactic more expensive and less effective.

Part IV. Secondary Boycott Provisions

A. The Statutory Scheme

In 1947, most secondary boycotts were made unfair labor practices by section 8(b)(4) of the Taft–Hartley Act. The core concept was that it was unfair for a union that had a dispute with employer A to attempt to cause a strike at the premises of employer B in order to cause B to stop doing business with A.[90]

The legislative history of the provisions indicate that Congress was originally concerned with secondary pressures used to force recognition on small businesses where the union had not been chosen by the employees or where another union had been certified as the bargaining agent. Congress also cited instances where unions had engaged in product boycotts, refusing to handle or work on goods unless manufactured by employers with contracts with that union. Congress overwhelmingly opposed the use of secondary pressure in both these situations. Some felt, however, that secondary activity was justified when used in support of demands for higher wages or other terms and conditions of employment. They agreed with then President Truman's declaration that some secondary boycotts were justifiable and that "the structure of an industry sometimes requires unions, as a means of self-preservation, to extend the conflict beyond a particular employer."[91] This varying attitude was rejected and no effort to define an acceptable secondary boycott was made.

The lack of differentiation contained in the statute was explained by Senator Taft as follows:

"It has been set forth that there are good secondary boycotts and bad secondary boycotts. Our committee heard evidence for weeks and never succeeded in having anyone tell us any difference between different kinds of secondary boycotts. So we have to broaden the provision dealing with secondary boycotts as to make them an unfair labor practice." [92]

The language of the provision, however, does not speak in terms of secondary boycott, nor is it restricted to union activity for specific purposes. The statutory language makes it an unfair labor practice for a labor organization to "engage in or induce" an employee to "engage in a strike or a refusal in the course of his employment to use . . . or otherwise handle or work on any goods . . . or to perform any services"—the unlawful means—"where . . . an objective thereof is . . . forcing or requiring any person to cease using . . . or otherwise dealing in the products of any other producer or . . . to cease doing business with any other person. . . ."—the unlawful objectives.

The language of the section has led to results that are inconsistent with the original concerns. The breadth of this language is sufficient to permit its application to almost any strike where the union seeks to prevent pickups and deliveries. Nonetheless, the courts have interpreted it in light of the stated objective of outlawing secondary activity.

Although section 8(b)(4) has been described as protecting neutral employers, the statutory machinery may be activated by the primary employer. Thus in situations where neutral employers are unwilling to complain about potentially illegal union activity, the primary employer can file the charge alleging unlawful secondary activity with the NLRB and thereby cause the General Counsel to seek injunctive relief. The irreparable harm to justify the injunctive relief may be the primary employer's. The supposed object of statutory concern, the neutral employer, may take no side in the dispute, may take no active part in, and be indifferent to, the NLRB proceeding.

Another claimed purpose of section 8(b)(4) was that of "localizing" the dispute to the direct participants out of some sense of maintaining an economic balance of power. Nonetheless, the parties are free to exert direct, primary pressure without regard to relative economic parity. The resort by a weak union to secondary methods may actually serve to correct an imbalance of economic power.

A major justification advanced when Congress was considering the legislation was to bar minority unions from using secondary pressure to force recognition from an employer whose employees had chosen another union or no union. Yet Congress left a minority union free to picket directly for recognition in the same circumstance.[93]

In the absence of any particularized purpose, it is generally accepted that the crucial determination to be made as to the lawfulness of the activity is whether it is essentially primary or secondary in purpose, a distinction nowhere spelled out by the statute.

B. Primary vs. Secondary Activity

1. In General

The Board and courts have had to develop the reach of section 8(b)(4) of the Act based upon the logic of the primary-secondary distinction that conceptually anchors it. As important as the distinction is, however, Justice Frankfurter recognized that "it does not present a glaringly bright line." [94] In an early application of the provision in *International Rice Milling*,[95] steel workers were picketing the employer's plant for recognition. They succeeded in turning away trucks of suppliers. The Court held that the picketing was not unlawful, despite the fact that the pickets urged the truck drivers of the suppliers not to cross the line. Though the language of the Act literally applied to the pickets' action, the Supreme Court found that the amendments were not intended to outlaw unions' traditional *primary* activity, which by its very nature seeks to influence people doing business with the primary employer to honor its picket lines and enlist support for their cause. The Court described the effects on the supplier, the neutral secondary employer, as the "incidental" effects of traditional primary activity. What made the picketing in *Rice Milling* primary was that it took place on the premises of the employer with whom the union had a dispute. It is still the case that activity on the premises of a single primary employer is presumptively primary.

2. Common Situs Activity

It might be relatively easy to find picketing at the primary employer's premises as legitimate primary activity and picketing at the secondary employer's premises as illegal secondary activity. The lines become more difficult to draw, however, where either the primary or the secondary employer is located on the other's premises, or where the primary and other employers are on premises not their own, as is often the case with construction sites. The Supreme Court refused to treat construction site picketing as presumptively primary in *Denver Building & Const. Trades*.[96] In that case, the Court held that the picketing of a construction site by the Denver Building Trades Council over the employment of a nonunion electrical subcontractor violated the secondary boycott provisions of the Act. The Council argued that their primary dispute was with the general contractor and their objective was to have the general contractor hire only union subcontractors on the job. Applying the literal language of the statute, the Court rejected the argument, finding that because the general contractor had a contract with the subcontractor, who in turn employed the non-union employees, the only way the job could become union was to force the subcontractor off the job. The Court concluded that an object of the picketing was to force the general contractor to cease doing business with the subcontractor. The fact that the general contractor had subcontracted the work did not change the status of each as independent contractors. The Court indicated that had the general contractor employed the non-union employees directly, the strike would have been primary. The *Denver Building Trades* decision was much criticized as a too-literal application of the statute to the unique practices of the construction industry—where the special trades are employed by different contractors.[97]

Despite the *Denver Building Trades* decision, considerable activity by unions at construction sites is held to be primary under the *Moore Drydock* Standards, which both predated and postdated the *Denver Building Trades* decision. *Moore Drydock*[98] represented a compromise between the interest of employers and unions in common situs situations and established guidelines to separate primary from secondary activity in such circumstances. The case itself involved a union that had a dispute with the owner of a ship and had picketed the drydock where the ship had put in for repair. The Board set out criteria that permitted the union to picket the drydock. The Board reasoned that if the primary employer alone occupied the site, it would be clear that the union could picket the premises. The effects of such picketing could well persuade employees of others not to cross the line and perform services. Under the reasoning in *International Rice Milling*, it would be lawful primary activity. Further, when the situs of the primary employer is ambulatory—as in a truck or ship, the union may follow the situs and still maintain the primary nature of the dispute. When, however, the situs of the primary employer comes to rest at the premises of another employer, the problem becomes one of balancing the right of the union to engage in traditional primary activity and that of the secondary employer to be free of union activity in a dispute in which it is not directly involved. The Board holds that neither interest is absolute. The picketing will be lawful, provided that:

(1) Picketing is limited to times when the primary employer's employees are at the situs of the dispute, located on the picketed premises. Implicit in this rule is the conclusion that primary activity in such situations is activity aimed at enlisting the support of the primary employer's employees.[99] This rule is grounded in the presumption that if the picketing is carried on after the primary employees have gone, then the object of the union must be to appeal to secondary employees.

If the picketing otherwise meets *Moore Drydock*'s Standards, it is not made secondary by the refusal of secondary employees to work. The situation is viewed the same as if secondary employees refused to make pickups or deliveries at the site of a primary dispute. The rule has been given a common-sense application rather than a literal one. Thus, if the primary employees leave for short periods of time, a violation will not be found. If the primary employees come and go without notice, the picketing union cannot be held to have a secondary purpose by staying on the site. Conversely, notifying the picketing union of a schedule of the primary's work periods could obligate the union to picket at times the employer has indicated it will be present.[100]

(2) At the time of the picketing, the primary employer is engaged in its normal business at the situs. The balancing of interests underlying the rules require that the primary employer actually be engaged in the work that is in dispute. Otherwise the union would be merely using the presence of the primary employer as an excuse to picket the secondary employer. Questions then turn on the definition of "normal operations." The Board has held that a general contractor who subcontracted all the work was not engaged in normal business at the site. It was held that its normal business was in its office off site.[101]

(3) The picketing is limited to places reasonably close to the location of the primary employer or situs. This proviso has the obvious merit of limiting, to the maximum extent possible, the effects of the picketing on uninvolved neutrals. In *Crystal Palace Market*,[102] the Board found a violation where the primary employer, the owner of a market who leased some of the shops, had given the union permission to picket the owner's stands inside the market. The union refused and stayed outside and thereby picketed the entire market.

Cases involving picketing location raise the issue as to whether the union has to seek permission to enter the premises of the common site or merely picket at the public entrance closest to the primary employer. It would seem that the balancing test would place the burden on the party controlling the premises to offer the union the ability to picket on its property rather than on the union to seek permission. Certainly, a union requesting such permission and refused would have a valid defense to charges of picketing of a remote entrance. There is much confusion between the Board and the courts over the extent to which the union has to affirmatively seek to minimize the secondary effects of nominally primary picketing.[103]

(4) The picketing discloses clearly that the dispute is with the primary employer. The Board has held that the picket signs must clearly denote the object of the dispute. Signs must make clear to anyone seeing the pickets that the entire site is not involved in the dispute. Anything that serves to blur the distinction between the primary and other employers is an indication that the union's aim is secondary. Thus, a picket sign that stated that "This job is unfair" or "On strike" would be a violation because someone approaching the premises could conclude that everyone on the site is involved in the dispute and is being picketed.

The language of the *Moore Drydock* decision seems to imply that if the standards are met, the activity will be deemed primary. The later cases make clear, however, that the union will be judged by a "totality of conduct" approach. Thus, if the union by other acts reveals a secondary purpose, then the activity may be found unlawful, notwithstanding compliance with the standards.

The Board's changing attitudes in the application of these standards stems again from the lack of specific legislative objectives. Thus, when originally confronted with the primary employer on the secondary employer's premises, the Board enunciated rules that attempted to balance the interests of the union to conduct primary activity and the secondary employer to be free from picketing. The rules were therefore regarded as prescriptive rather than merely evidentiary. Following its balancing of interest approach, the Board subsequently found that despite conformity with the *Moore Drydock* standards, where the primary had another fixed location that could be "effectively" picketed, the picketing at the common site was a violation. Presumably, the existence of an alternative to the common situs to picket struck the balance against any picketing on the common site.[104] This application of *per se* rules gave way, after Supreme Court disapproval,[105] to an evidentiary approach whereby the *Moore Drydock* standards, as well as the presence of alternative sites for picketing, are weighed by the Board to determine whether the true purpose of the union was secondary or merely the incidental effects of primary activity.[106] The *Moore Drydock* rules, which were enunciated in a situation where the primary employer had located on the secondary employer's property, were also extended to construction sites where several contractors work on property owned by still another, as well as to areas where the secondary employer is present on premises owned by the primary employer.[107]

3. Reserved Gate

The rule that picketing at the premises of a primary employer is primary picketing is subject to one major exception. The primary employer may establish a special gate or entrance for the exclusive use of the neutral employers, and the union may not picket that entrance so long as the entrance is (a) clearly marked as exclusively reserved for use by neutral employers and their suppliers, (b) the work done by employees using the gate is unrelated to the normal operations of the primary employer, and (c) the work is of such a nature that if the primary employer were in full operations, it would necessitate curtailing these operations. The *General Electric* [108] decision, which enunciated these standards, was an extension of the *Moore Drydock* approach of balancing the interests of the parties at a common situs to a situation where the secondary employer was on the primary employer's premises.

The *General Electric* case involved General Electric's erection of a separate entrance for construction contractors making capital improvements to an industrial plant during an economic strike by the union representing General Electric's plant employees. The union continued to picket at the construction contractor's entrance. The Supreme Court rejected the union's argument that by allowing separate gates, the primary employer could insulate deliveries, customers, and employees from legitimate primary picketing. The Court stated that it was the *purpose* of those using the separate gate that would be determinative. If those using the gate were performing work unrelated to the primary's normal operations, they would be protected. On the other hand, customers and deliveries could not be so isolated because to do so would invade the union's recognized right to appeal to neutral employees whose tasks aid the employer's everyday operations.

a.   THE EXCLUSIVITY OF THE GATE

There are no hard and fast rules as to the adequacy of the reserved gate. The test involves the clarity of the notice to the union that the gate is to be used by neutrals only. Thus, if the names of neutral contractors are omitted, if the signs are posted sporadically, if the gate is "violated" by primary employees or suppliers or customers—these are factors to be weighed in determining the union's knowledge of the neutrality of the gate and weighing the purpose of its conduct.

A reserved gate "violated" by primary employees and suppliers may be picketed, although the violation must be more than sporadic. Once a gate has been violated, however, it may be rehabilitated and picketing restricted by sending the union notice of the reestablishment of the gate and seeing that its reserved nature was not again violated.[109]

If the gate is to be exclusively used by neutral employers, suppliers of the primary employer cannot use the gate. Nor can the suppliers deliver to a neutral employer for ultimate use by the primary employer. Thus, where supplies were delivered through the neutral gate and delivered to the neutral general contractor, but were to be used by the primary subcontractor, the Board found that the union could picket the gate because the issue was not title to the supplies but for whose use they were intended.[110]

b.   WORK UNRELATED TO NORMAL OPERATIONS

The second requirement of *General Electric*, that the work be unrelated to the normal or day-to-day operations of the primary employer, is easy to rationalize but harder to define. The alternative formulation is that the work must be of "a kind that would not, if done when the plant were engaged in its regular operations, necessitate curtailing those operations." [111]   A contractor building an addition to an existing factory or a new factory is generally held not to be performing related work notwithstanding the fact that the new addition or new plant is to be occupied by the primary employer.   The same is true of the installation of new systems.   Repairs and maintenance of existing equipment and structures are usually held to be related to regular work.   In *General Electric*, upon remand the Board found that because the contractor's employees also performed some maintenance functions, the work was related.[112]

The line between construction and repair is difficult to draw because obviously all the construction is in someway related eventually to the primary employer's normal operations.   To help inform the application of the standard, the Board needs to articulate why the related work requirement determines neutrality.   Without such an articulated reason, the application of the standard is inevitably inconsistent.

In subsequent cases, the Board and courts have not made clear what standards they were applying to construction site situations. Thus, the Board has simply stated in recent cases that the *Moore Drydock* standard requiring the picketing to be "reasonably close," rather than the *General Electric* standard, applies to picketing separate gates at construction sites.

The relationship among the *Denver Building Trades* decision, the *General Electric* decision, and the *Moore Drydock* standards as applied to construction sites was raised in *Markwell & Hartz, Inc. v. NLRB*.[113]   In that case, the Building Trades Council picketed union subcontractors' reserved gates in furtherance of a dispute over the non-building-trades-union status of the general contractor.   The Building Trades Council argued that because the work of the subcontractors was related, the picketing was lawful under *General Electric*, which it claimed had tacitly overruled *Denver Building Trades*.   The Board majority rejected the argument, finding that the picketing was not covered by *General Electric*, but by *Moore Drydock*.   The Board read *General Electric* narrowly, as applicable only to the picketing of manufacturers at their premises.   On construction sites, the Board held that where the contractors worked on premises not their own, a "true" common situs situation arose and *Moore Drydock's* requirement of picketing reasonably close to the situs of the dispute was violated by the union's picketing at the separate gate of a neutral employer. Moreover, the Board reasoned that to allow such picketing would implicitly overrule *Denver Building Trades*.   The Fifth Circuit affirmed 2–1.   One judge found that *General Electric* applied, but that *Denver Building Trades* had determined that the work of various contractors on a construction site was not related work and picketing the separate gate was illegal.   The second judge ruled that *Moore Drydock* applied to construction site disputes and limited *General Electric* to struck manufacturer cases. There has been criticism of the Board's decision in *Markwell & Hartz* on the grounds that it seems "to apply more rigid standards to the construction industry than to manufacturing industry." [114]

The Board has not explained the distinction between various construction contractors working on someone else's property and a manufacturing situation where the primary employer is using a subcontractor on its own premises. The distinction seems to fly in the face of both the Board's and the Supreme Court's previous statements that ownership of the property that is the site of the dispute is of little consequence.[115]

In a later decision, the Board indicated once again that ownership of the property was of little significance and extended the *Moore Drydock* standards to a construction site where the general contractor owned the premises.[116] Despite its tenuous underpinnings, the rule that the related work argument is unavailable in construction site picketing is now well settled and is regularly applied.[117]

4. The Ally Doctrine

The secondary boycott provisions are clear in their intent to insulate innocent third parties from becoming enmeshed in labor disputes in which they have no interest. The concept of neutrality is, however, difficult to define or apply. As Senator Taft stated in a post-legislative reflection: the protection of neutrals was "not intended to apply to a case where the third party is, in effect, acting in cahoots with or acting as a part of the primary employer." [118] In cases of expanded union activity, there is always some relationship between the primary and allegedly neutral employers, and the Board and courts must decide what relationships deprive the secondary employer of protection.

a. STRUCK WORK

If a company undertakes work for a struck company that, except for the strike, would be done by the employees then on strike, the Board and courts hold that the company undertaking the work thereby loses its status as a neutral employer and becomes an "ally" of the primary employer. The employees of the secondary employer are treated no differently conceptually than had the primary employer hired replacements for the strikers. The strikers would be permitted to picket and try to persuade them to join the strike. The arrangement between the struck employer and the ally need not be direct. In *Royal Typewriter*,[119] the struck company suggested to its customers that they have their Royal machines served during the strike by independent contractors the customers selected from the phone book and that Royal would reimburse the customers. The court held that the union's picketing of the independent repair companies was primary in that these companies were performing struck work and were indirectly paid by Royal.

The seeming simplicity of the logic of the "struck work" test—to hold as an ally a third party performing work that would be performed, but for the strike, by the strikers—is deceptive. It is not difficult to hold that a company agreeing to do struck work should be subject to the striker's activity. It is hardly an "unconcerned" party. However, the logic applies equally to an employer who takes advantage of a struck competitor and captures its business for itself. It is clear that such a competitor, acting contrary to the interest of the struck employer, is not an "ally," though one might question its neutrality or whether it can complain if it becomes enmeshed in the dispute. The competitor has clearly benefited from the strike by gaining new customers at the expense of the struck employer. In one sense, however, the threat of permanent loss of business posed by the competitor enhances the striking union's position. On the other hand, it could be argued that the union should be able to follow its work on the rationale that the "neutral" employer has become a third party to the dispute.

At present, however, the Board seems reluctant to hold that the performance of struck work *per se* makes one an ally, and the Board requires some relationship or arrangement to do struck work between the struck employer and the ally. It is clear that two firms doing business before a strike are not allies when they continue to do business during the strike and are not doing extra work caused by the strike.[120] If the struck employer arranges for a trucker to pick up its product and deliver it to the customer, the trucker becomes an ally. However, if the trucker is engaged by the customer, the Board will hold that it is not an ally.[121] The Board's requirement of some sort of arrangement excludes those firms that benefit from the strike by performing struck work, but at the behest of someone other than the struck employer. Plainly, the case where struck work is permanently obtained by a competitor could not be held within the rule. Temporary arrangements, however, created to avoid the impact of the strike, might be viewed as allied actions because the arrangements will ease the pressure on the struck employer even if the arrangement is made by the customer, by the supplier, or by an outside firm seeking a short-term opportunity.

The present Board view focuses on the relationship between the struck employer and the firm performing the struck work rather than on the underlying rationale of protecting neutral employers. The touchstone of the Board's ally doctrine is that the ally, by its efforts, is knowingly helping the primary employer to break the strike by undertaking work that the primary would be doing when the strike is over. Involvement of the third party is therefore an affirmative alliance rather than one of effect.   This being the case, it is necessary that the secondary employer have knowledge of the existing dispute and the fact that the work it is performing was formerly performed by the struck employer.   In most cases, the union will notify them of their role if they have been unaware to that point.   The secondary employers then have the option of refusing to perform the work and extricating themselves from the dispute.

If a secondary employer is an ally, it is subject to picketing for all its work, not just the struck work.[122]   This is because it has become a primary employer and has no separate protected status.

b.   Common Enterprises

The ally doctrine has also been applied to separate business entities that are closely tied together by common ownership, integration of operations, and management policies.   In this sense, the term "ally" is a misnomer because the relationship in this situation is not based on the fact that some third party is taking on struck work, but rather that the struck employer is so closely related with the other enterprise as to merge identities;   therefore, both constitute the primary employer.

In order for the doctrine to be applied in this respect, all three of the aforementioned ingredients must be present.   The Board has found that the separate divisions of the same corporation did not, without more, constitute a single person for purposes of section 8(b) (4).   Thus, the common ownership of a newspaper and television station in the same community did not make allies where day-to-day operations and labor relations policies were under the control of separate divisions.[123]   Similarly, common ownership of a newspaper in Michigan and one in Florida did not make them allies,[124] nor did the fact that two separately owned companies had integrated operations.[125] It is only where, in addition to common ownership, there is common control of day-to-day operations and labor policies and some integration of operations that two operations will be characterized as a single enterprise and an ally relationship will be found.[126]   There are, however, situations where the ingredients are not all present but the relationship between the two employers is so strong in the remaining areas that the employers can be treated as one.[127]

C.   Consumer Picketing and Handbilling

1.   The Statutory Scheme

The 1959 Landrum–Griffin amendments to the National Labor Relations Act included provisions that were aimed at closing so-called loopholes in the secondary boycott provisions of the law.   One of these was aimed at consumer boycotts—union pressure on retailers through picketing and handbilling to get them to cease doing business with struck manufacturers or suppliers.   There was also concern, however, that restrictions on unions peacefully publicizing their disputes to the buying public violated first amendment rights and unfairly restricted union efforts to seek public support.   The legislation that evolved expressly exempted from the reach of the secondary boycott language:

> "publicity other than picketing for the purpose of truthfully advising the public, including consumers and members of a labor organization, that a product or products are produced by an employer with whom the labor organization has a primary dispute and are distributed by another employer, as long as such publicity does not have the effect of inducing any individual . . . to refuse to pick up, deliver, or transport any goods or not to perform any services, at the establishment of the employer engaged in such distribution."

2. Consumer Picketing

In *NLRB v. Fruit & Vegetable Packers Local 760, Tree Fruits*,[128] the Supreme Court held that all consumer picketing was not implicitly outlawed because the statutory proviso protected only publicity *other* than picketing.   The Court read the legislative history as expressing concern only with picketing that urged the public to refrain from doing *any* business with the retailer selling the goods of the primary employer.   The Court held, therefore, that section 8(b)(4) did not apply to product picketing that was closely confined to the primary dispute.   In its decision, the Court held valid picketing by striking employees of firms supplying apples to Safeway stores in the Seattle area.   The employees had picketed with signs urging the public not to purchase Washington State apples.   The pickets were instructed to stay away from delivery entrances and did not picket when the store was closed to customers.   Store employees continued to work and deliveries were unimpeded.   The Court reasoned that "[W]hen consumer picketing is employed only to persuade customers not to buy the strike product, the union's appeal is closely confined to the primary dispute." [129]   The Court thus found that picketing confined to the product did not "coerce" Safeway to cease doing business with the Washington apple growers.

Several years after the *Tree Fruits* decision, the Court limited the protection afforded to product picketing.   In *NLRB v. Retail Store Employees Union, Local 1001 (Safeco)*,[130] the employees of an insurance company picketed the five offices of a title insurance company that received 90 percent of its income from the sale of insurance policies from the struck firm.   The Supreme Court held that "product picketing that reasonably can be expected to threaten neutral parties with ruin or substantial loss" was outside the *Tree Fruits* exception and a violation of section 8(b)(4).[131]   The Court concluded that because the picketing would, as a natural effect, urge consumers to not patronize the retailer at all, it was prohibited by the statute.

The approach taken in the *Safeco* decision is directly at odds with that taken in *Tree Fruits*. The *Tree Fruits* opinion virtually ignored the statutory language in order to permit peaceful picketing that was, in form, related only to the primary employer. In *Safeco*, the Court stressed the statutory language. The resulting test—whether the picketing "is reasonably likely to threaten the neutral party with ruin or substantial loss"—is obviously a vague one. How much loss is substantial is bound to be the subject of considerable litigation. The claim in this circumstance is that the product struck or boycotted is no longer distinguishable from the neutral employer's other products. The ironic result, of course, is that the closer the so-called neutral employer is tied economically to the primary employer, the greater its insulation from picketing publicizing the dispute with the source of its sole or major product.[132]

3. The Publicity Proviso

a. THE PRODUCER–DISTRIBUTOR RELATIONSHIP

The publicity proviso applies to products that are "produced" by a struck employer and are being "distributed" by another. In *NLRB v. Servette, Inc.*,[133] the Court made clear that the terms "produced" and "distributed" were not to be read literally nor limited to manufacturers and retailers, but to be applied to such relationships as supermarkets selling food from a wholesaler. The proviso has been held to reach as far as picketing a store whose products are advertised by a struck radio or television station. In these cases, it is hard to conceptualize the store that is advertising the products as the distributor of the product of the radio stations—the station being considered a "producer" of the products it advertises. The Court found that the First Amendment concerns that gave rise to the publicity proviso supported a view of "producer" as broad as the rule from which it was an exception.

This confusion between policy and language has led to disagreement among the circuits over the extent to which they should extend the statutory language to justify consumer boycotts other than picketing. Taking a reluctant lead from the Supreme Court's decision in *Servette*, the Ninth Circuit reversed itself and held that a television station was a producer of the products it advertised.[134] On the other hand, the Eight Circuit, in *Pet, Inc.*,[135] refused to enforce a Board finding that a struck employer was a producer for its parent corporation and the parent's other subsidiaries and divisions. The Eighth Circuit noted that in the cases where a producer-distributor relationship was found, the primary employer "worked on" the goods or services that it furnished the secondary. In this case, the court found that the primary struck-subsidiary did not work on any specific products of the parent.

The proviso has generated much confusion in construction cases where the union seeks to publicize the fact that the "product" has been built by non-union labor. The union attempts to publicize the dispute after the installation of the particular segment or the construction of the building by handbilling customers of the built facility. The Board has been inconsistent, finding legal the leafletting of mall customers advising that the mall was built by non-union employees, while finding illegal the picketing of a mall with the same message. As already noted, the Supreme Court limited the breadth of producer-distributor relationships in *DeBartolo*, finding that a producer-distributor relationship did not exist where the dispute was between the union and the nonunion contractor employed by one of the tenants to build a department store in the shopping center.[136]

The overriding problem is less judicial inconsistency than statutory inadequacy. The statutory requirement of producer-distributor does not articulate a sensible standard for determining when publicity aimed at the public should be permitted. Concern for legislative intent led to the expansive reading of "producer" in the *Servette* case, but concern with the statutory language led to a narrower reading of "distributor" in *DeBartolo* and *Safeco*.

Finally, however, first amendment considerations led the Court to find peaceful handbilling urging consumers not to patronize stores in a mall, outside of section 8(b)(4) even though it was not within the "producer-distributor" definition of the publicity proviso. In its second consideration of *DeBartolo*, the Court, expressly adopting a construction that avoided the constitutional issue, found the publicity was not "coercive". In *DeBartolo v. Florida Gulf Coast Building and Construction Trades Council*, (*DeBartolo II*) the Court rationalized that the proviso was not meant as an exception to an overarching ban on consumer publicity but intended merely to clarify the reach of section 8(b)(4) to certain types of publicity. Other types of peaceful publicity were outside of section 8(b)(4) and, therefore, not subject to the proviso's "producer-distributor" limits.

The Court seems to have ended the elaborate jurisprudence created by the Board and the courts construing the "producer-distributor" limitation by effectively reading it out of section 8(b)(4). The Court seems to be saying that peaceful consumer publicity other than picketing, is not to be construed as unlawful under the Act in order to stay clear of a first amendment violation. The reasoning in the second *DeBartolo* decision raises serious questions concerning past approaches with respect to all forms of peaceful union efforts at communication.

b. The Truthfulness of the Publicity

The proviso makes the truthfulness of the union's assertion relevant to its legality. The Board has held, however, that matters, even though truthful, that go beyond the scope of the proviso may make the union's action illegal. Thus the Board has held that where a union handbilled an airline at its terminal over the replacement of the union's employer by a non-union cleaning contractor, the activity was outside the proviso because the leaflets contained information about the airline's safety record in addition to the information concerning its dispute with the non-union cleaner.[137] The Board majority stated that although this information was truthful, it was unrelated to the dispute and, therefore, constituted "coercive" information that was not within the purpose of the proviso. The notion that truthful messages of a noncoercive type can turn otherwise lawful, peaceful handbilling into a violation of the law seems vulnerable to the same reasoning as in *DeBartolo II* supra.

D. Conclusion

The very technicality of the secondary boycott provisions and the difficulty in developing standards to apply their basic concepts has meant that neither Board, nor courts, nor commentators have attempted to summarize their operation in any but the most perfunctory manner. Nevertheless, even a perfunctory overview of the secondary boycott provisions reveals that they function in ways that are economically deceptive and ideologically confusing. The economic deception is that under section 8(b)(4), the announced purpose of which is to prevent the spread of economic disputes, there is an enormous amount of legal effort and attention devoted to preventing construction unions from shutting down relatively minor job sites. This seems like an odd focus under an Act that permits large industrial unions such as Teamsters and Autoworkers to strike, having enormous impact on thousands of neutral employers. The reason is that the provisions become triggered by the mere existence of two employers in a single economic dispute. The construction job site becomes the focus of secondary boycott attention because of the tradition of several small employers working together in a single location. If a single employer were *deemed* responsible for all the jobs, a strike by any of the crafts could be supported by refusals to work by all of them and the employer could not insulate any of them by use of a separate gate.

The ideological confusion stems from the fact that a union may appeal to managers of secondary enterprises to join with them and may appeal to customers at the secondary premises to a limited extent, but may not direct any appeal to secondary employees at a secondary location. Thus, a union has the least ability to appeal to those who have the most reason for making common cause with them.

Part V. Hot Cargo Agreements

A. Background

Union contracts sometimes provide that the covered employees are not required to handle, transport, or work on goods from an "unfair" company or from a company on strike. These so-called "hot cargo clauses" were partly developed in order to provide unions with a defense against secondary boycott claims: If the ABC Company was engaged in receiving and selling the products of XYZ Company and the latter had a dispute with its union, the ABC union, if it threatened to picket ABC unless it ceased doing business with XYZ, would be in violation of section 8(b)(4). However, if in advance of any dispute, the ABC union negotiated a hot cargo clause with ABC providing that ABC would cease doing business with any firm with which the union had a dispute, and then the union struck XYZ, the union would argue that demanding that ABC cease doing business with XYZ was its contractual right. If ABC balked, the union could argue that its dispute was with ABC over the enforcement of its contractual agreement and, therefore, primary activity. Similarly, if the clause provided that employees would not be required to handle goods from a non-union or struck employer, the union could argue that the boycott was merely individual members exercising their contractual rights. The hot cargo agreement thus seemed to allow by contract what the union couldn't achieve on an ad hoc, case-by-case basis. In 1958, the Supreme Court decided *Local 1976, United Brotherhood of Carpenters & Joiners v. NLRB (Sand Door)*,[138] a series of cases involving hot cargo contract provisions. One of the cases involved a contract that stated that members of the Carpenters union would not have to handle non-union material. Utilizing this provision, the Carpenters refused to install doors that had been manufactured off site by non-union labor. Two other cases involved Teamster drivers refusing to carry the goods of a manufacturer who was being struck by the machinists. The Teamsters relied on their contract, permitting them to refuse freight from an unfair company. Conceptually, the primary employers in these cases were, respectively, the non-union door manufacturer and the struck manufacturer, because it was these employers to whose policies the union objected. The Court held that while an employer was free to voluntarily agree to a boycott of another employer, it should be a decision made at the time the issue arises. Pressure to require the employer to live up to such a promise was not outside the reach of section 8(b)(4). The Court thus found that the union's use of economic pressure violated the secondary boycott provisions. The decision, however, did not make the execution of a hot cargo agreement a violation. The clauses were enforceable in arbitration or court action.

The Landrum–Griffin amendments enacted a year later sought to eliminate this so called "loophole" in the secondary boycott provisions. Section 8(e) made it an unfair labor practice for "any labor organization and any employer to enter into any contract . . ." in which the employer agrees "to cease . . . from handling . . . any of the products of any other employer . . . or to cease doing business with any other person . . ." and further declares that such agreements shall be unenforceable and void. Section 8(b)(4)(A) made it an unfair labor practice to coerce "any employer or self-employed person to . . . enter into any agreement which is prohibited by subsection 8(e) . . . ." Thus, the act of entering into the agreement, even if voluntary, is outlawed. Moreover, the attempt to enforce such an agreement by arbitration or court suit is held to be a fresh violation that is not time-barred by the six-month statute of limitations in the Act.[139]

There is much confusion engendered in the application of section 8(e) to various fact situations, especially those outside of the trucking context. The language of section 8(e) extends to contract clauses the primary-secondary dichotomy of section 8(b)(4) and, as such, incorporates the same conceptual difficulties of the secondary boycott provisions—complicated even further because it is in the form of language regulating future action.

B. Primary–Secondary Distinction

The basic issue to be resolved in determining the legality of "hot cargo" provisions is much the same as in section 8(b)(4) cases: Whether the employer that is party to the contract is to be regarded as a neutral or primary employer in view of the effect of the clause. The determination is conceptually difficult because of the tendency to regard the immediate employer as the primary employer and the fact that the "real" primary employer (the employer to whose labor policy the union objects) is often an abstract concept absent from the dispute.

1. Work Preservation or Union Interest Elsewhere

The central case dealing with the primary-secondary distinction is *National Woodwork Manufacturers Association v. NLRB.*[140] That case involved the Carpenters union, which had a contract with Frouge, a general contractor on a housing project, providing that no doors were to be handled that were fitted prior to being furnished on the job. The carpenters on the job site refused to install 3,600 doors that had been finished off-site by the manufacturer. The carpenters in the Philadelphia area customarily did the finishing work on the job site. The contractor had to return the doors and purchase blank doors. The National Woodwork Manufacturers Association filed charges claiming that the contract clause between the contractor and union was a violation of 8(e) because it was an agreement whereby the employer

(Frouge) had agreed to cease or refrain from handling the products of any other employer (the door manufacturer). The Association further claimed that in enforcing the provision by refusing to handle the doors, the union had also violated section 8(b)(4)(B), which prohibits forcing an employer to cease using the products of any other employer. The Supreme Court found that the provision was not a violation of section 8(e) because it had the objective of preserving work for the Frouge bargaining-unit employees that had traditionally been performed by them. As such, it was directed to the contractor and was lawful primary activity. The test of such clauses "is whether the agreement or its maintenance is addressed to the labor relations of the contracting employer vis-a-vis his own employees" or "calculated to satisfy union objectives elsewhere." [141] Applying the test to the facts in the case, the Court found that the clause and boycott were legal. The opinion pointed out that under the clause, the doors could not have been handled off-site even if cut by a union manufacturer. The basic test is simply stated and serves to extend the section 8(b)(4) primary-secondary distinction to contractual language. There are, however, some qualifications that the Court adverted to that make for difficulties.

In *National Woodwork*, the dispute involved work that had traditionally been done by the employees covered by the agreement. The Court indicated that a different result would apply where the provision was to be used to acquire work not traditionally performed by the bargaining unit. The Court reasoned that "the boycott in the present case was not used as a sword; it was a shield carried solely to preserve the members' jobs. We therefore have no occasion today to decide questions which might arise where the workers came on a boycott to reach out to monopolize jobs or acquire new job tasks when their own jobs are not threatened by the boycotted product. . . ." [142] The Court's distinction between work preservation and work acquisition does not correspond to a primary-secondary distinction. A union seeking to acquire work heretofore contracted out would still be seeking to affect the labor relations of the employer with whom it had contracted by creating more job opportunities for unit employees. As the dissent pointed out in *National Woodwork*, the distinction between work preservation and work acquisition seems to have been "created out of thin air." [143] In order to read the distinction into section 8(e), it is necessary to apply different modes of analysis to the two situations—first, analysis based on the primary-secondary distinction to work preservation, and next, analysis based on the statutory language to work acquisition situations.

The distinction also raised questions about the ability of unions to claim work arising from technological change. Because such work, by definition, has not been done previously by the union's members, would the union be able to claim it contractually? The issue arose in the context of an attempt by the International Longshoremen's Association to claim jurisdiction over the unloading of large containers, the use of which threatened to reduce drastically the traditional work of longshoremen. The union negotiated a provision with the shipping companies whereby they would perform the "stuffing" (loading) and the "stripping" (unloading) of any containers within a fifty-mile radius of the dock where they had traditionally loaded cargo. A Board majority held that the provision was an illegal attempt to acquire work that was previously performed by employees of the trucking companies.[144] The Board thus qualified its concept of work preservation by refusing to follow the work into a new technological form. The Supreme Court eventually reversed, holding that the Board was viewing the issue of preservation-acquisition from the trucking employee's view rather than that of the longshoremen.[145] According to the Court, the work in dispute was to be judged in light of its historical and functional relationship to the work previously performed by the longshoremen. Implicit in the Court's opinion was the conclusion that work acquisition as an objective was secondary and illegal and that work preservation was primary and legal, issues that were not resolved in *National Woodwork*.

The further history of the containerization litigation is instructive. The Board, on remand, reversed its ruling in all respects except for some small segment of work that had, historically, never been performed by longshoremen. It was reversed by the Third Circuit, who allowed all the work to be covered by the clause. Eventually, the Supreme Court upheld the Board. The decisions became muddled in an attempt to sort out a technical process and trace its functional origins. In the end, it seemed to have very little to do with concepts of neutral or primary employers.

The distinction insulating legitimate work preservation provisions from 8(e) runs only to the particular unit-employer's own employees. An 8(e) clause that preserved work in an industry that was traditionally performed by the union's members for most employers cannot serve as the basis for the claim of work preservation for an employer whose own employees have not traditionally performed this work. Thus, where a building contractor had traditionally subcontracted out the driving of building materials, the fact that the great majority of contractors in the area had employed the union's members for this work did not legitimize the clause as applied to the contractor. The union's effort to enforce the clause was held to be a violation.[146]

The work preservation standard has been applied with varying literalness. It has been held that work preservation clauses do not come within the exception to section 8(e) where they seek to recapture work once performed, but lost in previous years. However, if the work is "fairly claimable," that is, where the work has been reduced, but not to totally lost, it may be recaptured.[147]

2. Right of Control

Despite the Supreme Court's *National Woodwork* decision, even clauses that have the effect of preserving work may not be a defense to sections 8(e) and 8(b)(4) where the contracting employer has no control over the assignment of work. In *NLRB v. Enterprise Association of Pipefitters*,[148] the Court held that a subcontractor's clause providing that pipe threading and cutting be performed on the job site by the employer's union employees was no defense for the union's refusal to handle prefabricated climate control units where the general contractor had specified that certain prefabricated units were to be installed. The Court reasoned that because the struck subcontractor did not have the work, the subcontractor was neutral. The refusal to install was really directed at the general contractor, who was, therefore, the primary. The result is that the union can have a work restriction clause that does not violate section 8(e), but it may not be enforced by means that violate section 8(b)(4).

The right-of-control test represents another situation in which the Court shifts away from the primary-secondary distinction to a more literal application of the statute. A different result could have been justified easily under existing precedent. The subcontractor, having committed itself to a legal work preservation promise not to perform work on prefabricated units, could be held to be the primary employer where it freely undertook a job containing specifications that required the violation of its valid work-preservation union contract. The Court of Appeals, following this line, held that "an employer who is struck by his own employees for the purpose of requiring him to do what he has lawfully contracted to do to benefit those employees can never be considered a neutral bystander in a dispute not his own." [149] Finally, it would seem to be an easy evasion of the work preservation issue in construction to have the architect specify the type of material to be installed on the job. Because contractors would not have the right of control, union activity to enforce its agreement would be in violation of the Act. Theoretically, the union could enforce its contractual rights by pursuing the matter by lawful means: arbitration or court suits. These dispute-resolution alternatives would not justify a resort to a strike, but could provide damages for the "lost" work. The provisions would be enforceable by judicial means because the clauses are valid under section 8(e). Unions, however, seldom make use of this potentially potent avenue of enforcement.

C. Subcontracting Clauses

Clauses that ban all subcontracting are valid work preservation clauses and do not violate section 8(e). They seek to regulate the labor relations of the contracting employer and benefit the employees in the unit. The same is true of clauses that limit subcontracting on the basis of conditions unrelated to the union status of the employer to whom the work is subcontracted, e.g., full employment in the unit or not having equipment to perform the work. On the other hand, clauses that limit the employer's right to subcontract to employers who are signatories to the union's contract are in violation of section 8(e) because the objective of these provisions is to encourage subcontractors to unionize. Clauses that limit subcontracting to employers that meet the same standards of wage and fringes fall somewhere between the two types of provisions cited. The clause may be regarded as looking toward the labor relations of the potential subcontractor, because the clause seeks to regulate the type of employer rather than preserve work for the unit. However, the conditions placed on subcontracting serve to remove the incentive of subcontracting to undercut the standards of pay and benefits achieved by the bargaining unit. In this regard, the objective of the provision is aimed at the labor relations of the contracting employer. This latter rationale has been adopted by the Board, and these so-called "union standards" clauses are regarded as valid work preservation clauses. These clauses, however, are not valid if they require specific benefits rather than equivalent costs. In the former case, the clause may be deemed to go beyond providing a disincentive to subcontracting out and look to forcing a subcontractor to sign the union agreement.[150]

D. Picket Line Clauses

Many agreements contain provisions that protect employees who refuse to cross union picket lines.[151] To the extent that these provisions allow employees to honor a secondary line, the clause violates section 8(e). Conversely, a provision that is limited to honoring lawful primary picketing at the employer's premises will not be a violation. The same would be true where the clause allowed employees to refuse to cross a primary line at the premises of a primary employer not their own. Such refusal would be allowed as an incidental effect of primary picketing and would not violate section 8(e). The question to be determined in these cases is whether the picket line clause allows, in the furthest literal application of its terms, the honoring of picket lines that would be violative of section 8(b)(4).[152] Thus a clause that simply provides that employees cannot be disciplined for refusing to cross a picket line would be a section 8(e) violation, because it could apply to picket lines at a neutral employer's premises.

Section 8(b) of the Act contains a proviso. It states:

"Provided that nothing in this subsection shall be construed to make unlawful a refusal by any person to enter upon the premises of any employer (other than his own employer), if the employees of such employer are engaged in a strike ratified or approved by a representative of such employees whom such employer is required to recognize under this [Act] . . .."

The proviso expressly excepts from section 8(b)(4), and therefore from section 8(e), employees honoring the picket lines at the premises of another employer by incumbent unions. The Board initially held that honoring lines at the premises of another employer that did not meet the terms of the proviso would be violative of section 8(b)(4) and that contractual protection of such activity violated section 8(e). The courts have refused to support this restrictive interpretation, based upon the reasoning in *International Rice Milling*. That case determined that recognition picketing at the employer's premises, not by a union "whom the employer is required to recognize", was primary activity notwithstanding the fact that it served to turn away truck drivers employed by neutral employers. A clause that protected the truck drivers in such circumstances has therefore been held to be legal.[153]

A final issue involving these picket line clauses is whether clauses protecting decisions by individual employees not to cross picket lines of any nature amounts to prohibited *union* activity. Union arguments that individual decisions are outside of section 8(b)(4), and only union induced refusals are prohibited, have been rejected without much reasoning.[154]

E. Sympathy Clauses and Struck Goods Clauses

Some contracts provide that employees shall be protected if they refuse to perform work on any goods of a person, which work, but for a labor dispute, would be performed by the employees of that person. This type of clause has been held legal as a contractual adoption of the ally doctrine. However, it omits elements of that doctrine as it is currently applied, i.e., the struck work must be performed pursuant to some arrangement with the struck employer. Thus, the current Board might hold such a clause to be a violation of 8(e).

The more general struck goods clauses—the hot cargo clauses that gave the name to the type of illegality—are violations because they provide for the cessation of business with any employer in a dispute with its employees and a labor union. The fact that these clauses are worded in terms of protecting individual employee's decisions, not union inducements barred by section 8(b)(4), is of no effect. As stated above, the presumption is made, without much discussion, that individuals will act as their union tells them in such circumstances. Section 8(e) is construed as prohibiting contracts that theoretically permit conduct that is unlawful under section 8(b)(4). The contract language is judged by the theoretical reach of its terms rather than by its object or effect.

In all these situations, the employee's refusal may indeed be an individual judgment based on motivations ranging from fear of violence to feelings of solidarity with workers' causes. In either case, under section 8(e) the legality of their protection in the contract will turn on the nature of the picket line rather than individual motivation. Likewise, in the absence of any clause, sections 7 and 13 of the Act will protect them as economic strikers if the line is primary. Thus, they cannot be fired or discharged, but may be replaced.[155] Similarly, they will not be protected and may be discharged if their refusal to cross is in support of a secondary line.

F. The Construction Industry Proviso

In making hot cargo contracts illegal under section 8(e), Congress exempted contracts in the construction industry relating to the contracting or subcontracting of work to be done at the work site.[156] The proviso appears to have been a concession to the construction unions for Congress' failure to enact a common situs picketing bill that would allow various contractors on a work site to be treated as one employer and thus outside the reach of the secondary boycott restrictions imposed under *Denver Building Trades*. The result is that certain clauses that would otherwise violate section 8(e) are not illegal, and unions may strike to achieve them if limited to construction site work. Strikes to enforce such clauses are illegal, however, because the proviso applies only to section 8(e) and not to section 8(b)(4). Moreover, a union may not strike to obtain such a clause where there is an identifiable non-union contractor on the site. In such case, the immediate effect of striking for the clause is the same as striking neutral employers with the object of removing the non-union contractor.[157] Hot cargo provisions that come within the proviso may, however, be enforced by arbitration or court suits.[158]

The proviso does not exempt the construction industry as a whole, but relates only to work to be done at the site of construction. Materials delivered from off site to the site are not within the exemption for work to be done at the site of construction.[159] Nor is work performed off site that arguably could be performed on the site.[160]

As in so many instances in the area of secondary activity, the literal reach of the construction industry proviso to 8(e) has been qualified by other considerations. In *Connell Construction Co., Inc. v. Plumbers Local 100*,[161] a Plumbers local struck general contractors to obtain a contract guaranteeing that the contractors would only contract for on-site plumbing work with plumbing contractors under contract with the union. A contractor brought suit alleging the activity violated federal and state antitrust laws. The union defended the suit on the basis that such activity was expressly protected under the construction proviso to section 8(e). The Supreme Court decided that union subcontracting clauses where the general contractor had no employees affected by the proposal fell outside of the legislative intent to allow for hot cargo agreements on construction sites. Because a basis for the proviso was to avoid friction between union and non-union employees, the proviso did not apply to the general contractor in this case, who had no employees working with non-union employees. Moreover, the Court found that to allow unions to strike employers with whom the union had no collective bargaining relationship, for a contract restricting its subcontractors, was to create an organizational weapon for the unions never intended by Congress. It was allowing "top down" organizing, without regard to the wishes of the employees. Thus, the Court held that the construction industry proviso only sheltered agreements sought in the context of a collective-bargaining relationship.[162]

The *Connell* interpretation of the construction industry proviso was further refined in *Woelke & Romero Framing, Inc. v. NLRB.*[163] In that case, the Court resolved the issues of whether such clauses were within the proviso even though they were of application to all construction sites and not limited to those situations where non-union and union employees would be working on a job site. The Court held that so long as the subcontracting agreement was negotiated in the context of a collective-bargaining agreement, the proviso protected the clause.

The requirement of a collective-bargaining context may be satisfied by an agreement signed in advance of the hiring of any employees. Section 8(f) permits employers in the construction industry to enter into collective-bargaining agreements with construction unions in advance of any hiring or without the establishment of the union's majority status. Two circuits have held that because such bargaining relationships are legal and typical in the construction industry, a pre-hire type agreement satisfies the bargaining relationship required by *Connell.*[164]

G.   The Garment Industry Proviso

The second proviso to section 8(e) exempts the manufacturers, jobbers, and contractors in the garment industry from the protection of both section 8(b)(4) and section 8(e).[165] The provision was a reflection of the unique nature of the industry, where manufacturers are in effect brokers, contracting out the work to contractors who are thinly capitalized, unstable, and of short duration. The union's traditional approach had been to organize the manufacturers and limit their contracting to union contractors. The organizing of the contractor's employees was thus based on the manufacturer's agreement. In providing the garment industry unions leeway that was denied to others, the Congress was clearly mindful of the contrast between the International Ladies Garment Workers Union and the standards it had achieved by these types of agreements, and that of the Teamsters, whose activities had inspired the hot cargo legislation.[166]

The garment industry proviso also has been construed as exempting contractual organizing from the reach of section 8(b)(7). In

Hazantown, the Board held that picketing a jobber for a union subcontracting agreement was outside section 8(b)(7) because the union was not seeking to represent the jobber's employees nor the employees of the non-union contractors to whom it sent its work. The Board found the union's goal was to have Hazantown send its work to union contractors it already represented. As such, it was not covered by section 8(b)(4).[167]

Part VI.　Jurisdictional Disputes

A.　The Statutory Scheme: Section 8(b)(4)(D) and Section 10(k)

Ever since the development of early trade unions along craft lines, there have been disputes over work assignments that one union or another perceives as violating or threatening the traditional work of its members. These so-called "jurisdictional disputes" continue principally in industries in which the work is organized according to craft lines or particular skills (e.g., construction, printing, shipping), and the workers are organized by unions representing distinct crafts. In such industries, disputes may be prompted whenever new technology or new products blur traditional lines or merge job functions, or when an employer decides to alter the area practice in assigning the work usually given one trade to another.

Jurisdictional disputes can occur in a number of settings. They may arise where different unions represent groups of employees of the same employer or, as in construction, where different crafts work for specialty contractors performing that type of work on the same project. They also may occur where a group of employees working for one employer disputes work given to employees of a subcontractor. These claims to the work involved are almost always based on past custom and practice, and are, at the bottom, an aspect of work preservation. Yet while work preservation objectives have been recognized for purposes of section 8(e) as primary activity and are, therefore, exempted from the hot cargo provisions, the same impulse where two competing unions are concerned is viewed as "wasteful" and "indefensible."[168]

Among the activities made unfair labor practices by the 1947 Taft–Hartley amendments was the use of economic pressure by a union to force an employer to assign work to its members rather than to another group of employees. Section 8(b)(4)(D) proscribes:

> "Forcing or requiring any employer to assign particular work to employees in a particular labor organization or in a particular trade, craft, or class rather than to employees in another labor organization or in another trade, craft or class, unless such employer is failing to conform to an order or certification of the Board determining the bargaining representatives for employees performing such work. . . ."

The system for enforcing this provision is, however, unlike other unfair labor practices. Section 10(k) provides that when a charge under section 8(b)(4)(D) is filed, the Board shall "hear and determine the dispute" unless within ten days the parties submit evidence that they have "adjusted or agreed upon methods for the voluntary adjustment of the dispute." If, after the hearing, the Board's determination is complied with, or if there is a voluntary adjustment of the dispute, the charge is dismissed. Thus, if there is activity that constitutes a violation of section 8(b)(4)(D) and the union charged with the violation adjusts the dispute or agrees to comply with the Board's section 10(k) determination that the work goes to the other group, the charge will be dismissed. Likewise, if the charged union is awarded the work, the charge will be dismissed. If there is no adjustment, or the union refuses to comply with the Board determination, the Board will issue a complaint and will process the section 8(b)(4)(D) case as it would any other unfair labor practice.

The legislative purpose behind sections 8(b)(4)(D) and 10(k) was to encourage the permanent resolution of the underlying jurisdictional clash between the competing unions rather than to interpose the Board's sanctions on prohibited activity on an ad hoc basis. Congress also sought to encourage the private contractual resolution of these matters by the involved parties by allowing private dispute settlement machinery to oust the Board of jurisdiction to determine the dispute. If the parties to the dispute have their own settlement machinery, the Board will not hear the matter, deferring to their voluntary machinery. It was the intent of the legislation that the threat of government intervention would stimulate unions to set up machinery to settle these disputes privately.[169]

The Board will seek an injunction, however, where there is a strike or stoppage in support of a jurisdictional claim prior to the determination by the voluntary private machinery or the 10(k) hearing. The language of section 10(*l*) of the Act provides that the same procedures for injunctive relief applicable to other sections of 8(b)(4) should be applied "where such relief is appropriate." [170]

B. The Violation

1. Economic Pressure

In order to violate section 8(b)(4)(D), the union must threaten or resort to economic pressure in order to force the employer to assign it the work in dispute. A union seeking to enforce its claims by resort to arbitration or judicial process is not in violation.[171] The resort to so-called peaceful means of dispute resolution, however, may not ensure the resolution of the dispute. Frequently, different unions manage to achieve similar general contractual language that may be used to support conflicting claims to the same work. Resort to bilateral arbitration under one of the competing union's contracts omits the other competing union from the process and could result in conflicting arbitration awards. A subsequent award by the Board determining the dispute after a 10(k) hearing supercedes any arbitration award and ultimately decides which union is entitled to the work. So long as the unions do not resort to economic pressure, however, the issue will never reach the Board.

The necessity for economic force to trigger the Board's 10(k) machinery results in the anomaly that the dispute may never be finally resolved when both unions use only peaceful means to enforce their competing claims. It may unfortunately make practical sense for the union receiving the work assignment to threaten to strike if the work is removed in order to achieve a Board 10(k) award reinforcing the primacy of its claim.

2. Competing Claims

The Board has construed section 8(b)(4)(D) as requiring active, competing claims by two groups of employees for the work in order to find the existence of a jurisdictional dispute. Thus, a union may disavow its claim to the work and its disclaimer will result in a dismissal of the case by the Board, provided the evidence shows that its disavowal is clear and unqualified and not contradicted by union activities.[172]

The Board's requirement of active competing claims allows a union to legally strike or threaten to strike unless certain work is transferred to its members from another's, as long as the second union does not object or agrees to the transfer. Thus, an employer who is threatened with a stoppage by union A unless it gets the work now assigned to union B's members is without recourse if union B declares its agreement to the reassignment. This situation frequently obtains in the construction trades where the international unions that are members of the Construction Trades Department of the AFL–CIO have agreed to be bound by the decisions of its dispute resolution mechanism.[173] If the private machinery decision awarded some phase of construction to the Carpenters Union, for example, rather than the Sheetmetal Workers Union, a contractor's continued assignment of that work to Sheetmetal Workers could be met with a threatened or actual stoppage by Carpenters and the employer would be without recourse because of the Sheetmetal Workers agreement with the Carpenters' demand. The Board has required conflicting union claims ever since the Supreme Court's decision in *NLRB v. Radio and Television Broadcast Engineers Local 1212* (the *CBS* case).[174]

While the Court in *CBS* did not address the issue of the need for competing union claims, the Board in *Safeway*[175] found that requirement to be implied in the Court's decision. In *CBS*, the Court had directed the Board to decide which of two or more employee groups is right in claiming the work. The Court held that "implicit in the directive is the proposition that Sections 8(b)(4)(D) and 10(k) were designed to resolve competing claims between rival groups of employees, and not to arbitrate disputes between a union and an employer where no such claims are involved." [176]

The *Safeway* case illustrates the pre–*CBS* and post–*CBS* stance of the Board. In its 10(k) hearing, prompted by charges against a Teamster local's picketing over the employer's transfer of their work to other terminals where the employees were represented by two other Teamster locals, the Board determined that the picketing Teamsters were not entitled to the work. Following the *CBS* decision, the Board reconsidered the case and decided that because the locals to whom the work was transferred had not claimed the work, there was no jurisdictional dispute within the congressional intent. The Board determined that the picketing was no more than an attempt to retrieve jobs and to preserve the union's historical bargaining status. The Board noted that this was plainly not the "normal" jurisdictional dispute contemplated in *CBS*, where the unions are competing and the employer is willing to assign the work to either if only he could be let alone. Here, the Board pointed out, the employer had *created* the dispute by transferring the work away from the only group claiming the work.

A troubling aspect of the Board's *Safeway* decision is that the employer always creates the dispute in the sense that the employer makes the assignment triggering the conflicting claims. The language of the Board in *Safeway* and its characterization of the dispute is not helpful in drawing the line between a "traditional dispute" and the preservation of work. The jurisdictional dispute language is extremely broad, as are the other provisions of section 8(b)(4). The language literally covers union activities attempting to retrieve work for its members. These situations have simply been distinguished as not the "traditional" jurisdictional disputes Congress had in mind.[177]

In recent cases, the Board has required little evidence of an active claim from the beneficiaries of the employer's assignment. It has implicitly taken the position that the group's performance of the work in question is proof enough of its interest. Although the Board has not articulated this directly, it manifests this attitude in judging the sincerity of a union's disclaimer of the work. Where the union assigned the work disclaims it, there is no competing claim and, therefore, no dispute. Where, however, the union disclaiming the work suffers no hardship or sacrifices but actually continues working without any loss of pay or jobs, the Board has held that the disclaimer is ineffective and a dispute exists.[178]

The claim to the work will be a violation even if it is a claim made by the union whose members have been assigned the work, as long as the union announces that it will strike in the event the work is removed.   It can be a claim by the organized employees of a subcontractor for work assigned to the employer's unorganized employees.   It can also be the claim of the employees of one subcontractor for the work of another.   Questions arise when the jurisdictional claims are made in a context where the union threatens to strike if the employer contracts out work that the union claims should be performed by its members.   Protests of subcontracting, whether work preservation or work acquisition, are not traditionally thought of as jurisdictional disputes and have not been dealt with under section 8(b)(4)(D) despite the literal application of the language.[179]

3. The Section 10(k) Hearing

If the regional director finds reasonable cause to believe section 8(b)(4)(D) is being violated, he or she issues a notice of a section 10(k) hearing unless there is evidence of an agreed-upon method for resolving the dispute.   The hearing is held before a hearing officer of the regional office and is conducted like a representation proceeding, only the determination is made by the Board.   The Board must make an affirmative award of the work in dispute.   Prior to the *CBS* decision,[180] the Board took the position that if there was no Board order or certification, nor a clear contractual right running to the charged union, the employer's assignment was upheld.   The section 10(k) hearing was largely concerned with whether a jurisdictional dispute had, in fact, occurred within the literal language of section 8(b)(4)(D) and whether the striking union had a contract or Board order to support its claim.   If the union could not support its claim in that manner, the Board would determine that the union was "not entitled" to the work in dispute.   In *CBS*, the Supreme Court rejected the Board's view and held that the legislation clearly intended the section 10(k) hearing to *resolve* the underlying dispute, not merely to reject the union's claim if it was not based upon a Board order, certification, or contract right.

The Board's original interpretation of its function in the section 10(k) proceeding was based on the fact that it had no standards or expertise by which to judge which of two groups of employees should actually be assigned the work.   It resisted placing itself in the shoes of the employer.   It felt it could safely reverse only the employer's decision as to which employees should do the work where the employer had previously contracted the work to a given group or where the Board had ordered the employer to bargain with the union in circumstances where the work at issue was covered.   Otherwise, however, it had no experience or expertise in deciding work assignments on the "merits."

The Supreme Court's answer to this unusual claim of agency inexpertise was that the Board had "long experience . . . in similar labor problems."[181]   Moreover, the Board could use the standards used by arbitrators, unions, employers, and joint boards in dealing with such disputes. Finally, it could use "experience and common sense." The Court's determination that the Board should make an affirmative award stemmed from the generally held view of a jurisdictional dispute as one where two unions fought over a work assignment with the employer in the middle, just looking for the work to proceed and the matter to be settled. As the Court stated:

> "To determine or settle the dispute as between them (the competing unions) would normally require a decision that one or the other is entitled to do the work in dispute. Any decision short of that would obviously not be conducive to quieting a quarrel between two groups which here, as in most instances, is of so little interest to the employer that he seems perfectly willing to assign work to either if the other will just let him alone." [182]

In many situations, of course, it is of great concern to the employer which trade is awarded the work. In many cases, their skills are vastly different or their collective-bargaining agreements may call for different terms and conditions and, therefore, depending on the work involved, the choice of craft may affect costs and working conditions. The Board was now told, in effect, to substitute its judgment for that of the employer in choosing the trade or craft to perform the work. Not surprisingly, the Board selected standards for making the selection that would generally track the criteria that an employer would use.

Since *CBS,* the Board has made affirmative awards of the work basing its decisions on the following criteria:

1.   certification or collective bargaining agreements,

2.   efficiency and economy of operations,

3.   relative skills and safety,

4.   area industry and practice,

5.   employer's practice and preference.[183]

Despite the mandated change in approach, the Board usually awards the work to employees that have been originally assigned the work by the employer. Unions have criticized the Board's decisions as paying only lip service to the new criteria, but in reality continuing to uphold the employer's right to assign work.[184] The Board's criteria announced in *Jones,* however, usually supports the employer's assignment because, assuming no contractual obligation, the employer will normally choose the employees using the same criteria used by the Board, i.e., those who have the skills to most competently, efficiently, and economically perform the work. Indeed, in one case where the Board overruled the employer's decision, the Ninth Circuit remanded a section 8(b)(4)(D) case to the Board to explain why it had ruled contrary to the employer's preference.[185] The court found that the

Board, in its section 10(k) decisions, had decided in consonance with the employer's preference in almost every case and held that the Board could not, without explanation, depart from this long standing determination. The Board, on remand, initially rationalized its earlier refusal to go along with the employer's preference because it found it was not the most economic or efficient. The Board, however, reconsidered its view and agreed with the court that its decisions had consistently placed great weight on employer preference in making awards.[186] The few instances where the employer's preference does not prevail tend to arise where there is evidence of a clear and long-standing area practice.[187]

There has been occasional criticism of the Board for the conclusionary type of reasoning in its section 10(k) determinations. Frequently, the awards do not indicate the factors that the Board relies on in reaching its conclusion and, therefore, are of little help in predicting future decisions. However, the Board's ultimate support of the employer's choice in all but the most unusual circumstances gives adequate notice of its approach.

4. The Impact of the Hearing

Following the section 10(k) decision, if the charged union agrees to comply with the award, the charge will be dismissed. In the unusual case, where the charged union is awarded the work and the employer refuses to award the work, the union may strike because it is now "entitled" to the work. Thus the section 10(k) award legitimates activity that would otherwise be a violation of section 8(b)(4)(D). The section 10(k) decision is not a "final order" within the meaning of the Administrative Procedure Act and is not subject to appeal or review. If the union refuses to comply with the section 10(k) determination, a complaint issues and the section 8(b)(4)(D) is processed, usually finding the union in violation. The union can challenge the section 10(k) determination in the court proceeding on the enforcement of the section 8(b)(4)(D) violation.

5. The Voluntary Means of Adjustment

The jurisdictional dispute section of the Act is unique in that it has a legislatively built-in deferral mechanism where the parties to the dispute have established a private means of resolving their disputes. This was conceived with the intent of stimulating the establishment of private machinery as a preferred alternative to government intervention in those industries plagued by such disputes. In 1948, the building trades established The National Joint Board for the Resolution of Jurisdictional Disputes, (NJB) later called the Impartial Jurisdictional Dispute Board (IJDB). The Board has jurisdiction over all the construction trade unions. These unions are bound by its determinations through explicit agreement and by virtue of the international unions' membership in the Construction Trades Department of the AFL–CIO. Employers in the industry are bound to its decisions by provision in their collective-bargaining agreement with one or more of the unions. The Joint Board is made up of the representatives of the various trades and employer representatives from the large construction employer organizations. It has enjoyed different degrees of success at different times and, occasionally, some of the building trades unions have withdrawn or boycotted its proceedings. The NLRB during these periods has held that the unions were still bound because of their membership in the AFL–CIO's construction trade department, which in turn, committed its union members to the NJB.[188] Where an employer has not agreed to be bound by these procedures, however, a section 10(k) hearing will be held because not all the parties to the dispute have committed themselves to the private board resolution of the dispute.

The logic of requiring the employer to be bound to the private machinery as a party to the dispute where the unions were bound was explained in the *Plasterers Local 79* case.[189] In that case, the Plasterers claimed work that had been assigned to Tile Setters. The Plasterers, who unlike the Tile Setters, had no contract with the employers involved, submitted their claim to the Joint Board. The employers had not agreed to be bound by the Joint Board's decision. The Joint Board awarded the work to the Plasterers. The employers refused to change their assignment and the Plasters began picketing. The Board held a section 10(k) hearing and awarded the work to the Tile Setters. When the Plasterers refused to abide by the decision, the Board found a section 8(b)(4)(D) violation. The Plasterers argued that the situation should be treated as though the Tile Setters had disclaimed, in which case the section 10(k) hearing would be aborted. According to their argument, the Union's agreement to be bound by the Joint Board was tantamount to a disclaimer of jurisdiction and the employer should not be regarded as a party to the dispute.

The Supreme Court rejected the argument and affirmed the Board's long standing policy of viewing the employer as a "party to the dispute" by requiring the employer as well as the unions involved to be bound to any voluntary dispute settlement machinery. The Court pointed out that these disputes were "triangular" and that while, in many cases, the employer was not interested in the outcome, only in the prompt settlement of the dispute, there were other cases were the employer had a substantial economic interest in the outcome. The Court noted that a change in assignment could mean new terms and conditions of employment, a different union to bargain with, higher costs, and lower efficiency. It reasoned that in construction, where jobs are awarded by competitive bidding, a small change in costs can be extremely important.

The Court acknowledged the control the unions involved had in the Board's involvement in the dispute. If one union disclaims, the Board case evaporates because there are no competing claims to adjudicate. Where the employer continues to face real claims, however, the section 10(k) hearing is appropriate and the employer continues as a real party. The logic of the Court's decision is less than compelling. As the Court concedes, had the unions that were bound by the Joint Board decision agreed to its implementation, there would be no section 10(k) hearing and the employer's role would be academic, despite its interest in the outcome. The rule in *Plasterers* continues, however, so that where no real settlement occurs, as where the local union or employees continue to claim the work even after the parent union disclaims, the case will go forward.

If there is a voluntary means of adjustment, the Board will not issue a section 10(k) notice of hearing, but will hold the section 8(b)(4)(D) charge awaiting the voluntary resolution of the dispute. If a party rejects the voluntary determination or refuses to participate in the process, the Board will process the section 8(b)(4)(D) charge. Further, in cases where there is a strike or stoppage in support of a jurisdictional claim, the General Counsel is empowered to seek a section 10(*l*) injunction where such is "appropriate." This language is different from the other 8(b) sections where the General Counsel is mandated to seek an injunction. In practice, there is little difference in the treatment of such situations. Moreover, the General Counsel will seek an injunction even where there is a voluntary means of settling the dispute. The work stoppage itself is deemed to be evidence that the voluntary means are not working.

6. The Relationship Between Jurisdictional Disputes and Secondary Boycotts

The facts surrounding jurisdictional disputes often raise issues concerning other sections of the Act. Jurisdictional disputes that take place in construction settings frequently also involve secondary boycott violations because of the different employing specialty contractors. For example, if the carpenters claim work that has been awarded to sheetmetal members, and they strike in support of their claim, they will be striking their employer, the carpenter subcontractor, who would be a neutral employer, over the assignment by the general contractor to the sheetmetal contractor. Thus, the strike violates both provisions. That situations exist where a union violates both sections 8(b)(4)(B) and (D) was recognized in *NLRB v. Local 825, Operating Engineers (Burns & Roe).*[190] The Court found that the purposes of each section were different and that there was no indication that Congress intended either to have exclusive application.

CONCLUSION

Although section 7 defines concerted activity broadly and section 13 announces a general endorsement of the right to strike, the right has been significantly narrowed by virtue of section 8(b)(4) and section 8(b)(7). Anything other than a traditional strike over mandatory conditions of employment is suspect and may constitute an unfair labor practice. Unions are prohibited from striking to support each other, from striking for recognition or jobs, or in support of unusual bargaining demands. The restrictions are both broad and technical requiring both unions and employers to develop technical and legal expertise and making it difficult to predict the legal outcome of a given action. Thus, to the extent the law is significant, it seems to discourage militancy in favor of technical competence.

Part VII. Antitrust Laws and Labor Activity

A. Introduction

There has always been an historic tension between the national ideal of a free market economy driven by open and full competition and the ultimate aim of labor unions to organize otherwise competing businesses, to standardize workers' compensation and working conditions, and thereby to remove employee labor costs from competition.

A union's ability to establish relatively high standards of compensation, benefits, and working conditions depends ultimately on the organized employers' ability to compete profitably in the marketplace. Obviously, a union that organizes all the employers in an industry is able to bargain for improved conditions secure in the knowledge that no employer will be competitively disadvantaged by the package. Non-union employers paying less in wages or benefits, or free of restrictive work rules on manning or overtime, enjoy a competitive advantage and threaten to undermine the union's standards. Non-union employers limit the union's ability to negotiate improvements for fear of exacerbating the difference in unit labor costs between organized employers and their non-union competitors. A union negotiating for increased wages inevitably is concerned over the impact on competing employers of the wages negotiated with one group of employers. It may promise the employer, as the price of a wage increase, to secure no less from other employers.[191] In order to protect its standards, a union may seek to bar non-union competitors from the market by restricting subcontracting to union firms [192] or by limiting the goods it will work on to those made by union firms.[193]

All these actions tend, in one way or another, to restrict competition in the marketplace.

The national policy regarding union-generated restrictions on commercial competition has historically wavered from the original common law view of all union activity as a conspiracy in restraint of trade to the view that labor activity should be dealt with exclusively under the labor laws and remain absolutely exempt from the antitrust laws. The current policy is mixed. Union activity is held to be violative of antitrust laws depending on the plan or activity, on its goal, and on the parties in addition to the union agreeing to the plan. This is further complicated by the potential application to these same activities of the federal labor laws as well as the federal antitrust laws and the necessary accommodation of the conflicting policies they manifest.

B. The Antitrust Legislation—The Early Applications

The antipathy of the courts applying common law doctrines of tort and criminal conspiracy to labor activities—particularly to secondary boycotts—carried over to application of the federal antitrust laws to labor activities. While originally it was not at all clear that the Sherman Antitrust Act was intended to apply to labor disputes, the Supreme Court, in *Loewe v. Lawlor*,[194] found that the Sherman Act made no distinction between classes of disputes. It declared that "every contract, combination, or conspiracy, in restraint of trade . . . [was] illegal."[195] Thus, virtually all labor activity was made subject to the antitrust laws as an illegal combination in restraint of trade. This was far more restrictive than the common law means-ends test of civil tort law being applied to labor activities at the time.

The subsequent use of the Sherman Act to secure injunctions in labor disputes led to the enactment of the Clayton Act in 1914, which expressed a national policy exempting unions from antitrust law. Section 6 declared that:

> "[l]abor was neither a commodity nor an article of commerce, and that the Sherman Act should not be construed to forbid the existence and operation of labor, agricultural, or horticultural organizations, instituted for the purposes of mutual help. . . ."[196]

Thus, labor unions themselves and concerted refusals to work could not be deemed unlawful combinations in restraint of trade. Further, Section 20 of the Clayton Act barred injunctions in virtually all labor disputes.[197]

The effect of these provisions were severely limited by the Supreme Court's rulings in *Duplex Printing*.[198] In *Duplex*, which involved a secondary boycott, the Court construed section 20 as applying only to primary activities and held that the Clayton Act did not exempt the activities of employees who were not directly employed by the employer they were acting against. In a statement revealing the Courts' concern over broad-based labor activity, it declared that the Clayton Act was not meant to exempt employees as a class. Further, the activities that were exempt were only "legal" activities. The legality of these activities was presumably left for the courts to determine.

The Court's ruling served to establish a distinction between labor activities that were "local," directed to the primary employer (legal) and those directed at the marketplace (illegal). Thus in the *Coronado Coal* cases,[199] the violent strike of a mine operator was deemed lawful because it was found to be directed at the employer at the premises. The same activity, when later characterized as directed at restricting non-union products from competing in the market place, was found to be in violation of the antitrust laws.

The distinction has been criticized as irrelevant to the objectives of antitrust law and artificial in terms of labor policy.[200] In terms of the impact on the marketplace, it is of no consequence whether the union activity is aimed at impeding the flow of goods at the origin or at the destination. From the union's standpoint, organizing non-union employers and protecting union goods in the marketplace are integrated parts of the ultimate goal of maintaining high standards of wages and conditions by eliminating competition based on wage differences. The union therefore seeks to protect the union employers from non-union competition by either organizing the non-union employers or preventing them from competing with union employers.

The continued use of the labor injunction in labor disputes led to the enactment in 1932 of the Norris–LaGuardia Act.[201] Norris–LaGuardia, while not referring to the antitrust laws, legislatively overruled *Duplex* and the cases that reduced the reach of the Clayton Act. The Act declared that the federal courts were without jurisdiction to enjoin peaceful labor activity growing out of a "labor dispute." It broadly defined the term "labor dispute" as any controversy concerning terms or conditions of employment and specifically declared it to be of no consequence "whether or not the disputants stand in the proximate relation of employer and employee."[202]

Following the Norris–LaGuardia Act, in 1935 Congress enacted the National Labor Relations Act, which established affirmatively the right of employees to organize and join labor organizations, to bargain collectively, and to engage in concerted activities including strikes.[203] Moreover, employer practices obstructive of these employee rights were declared "unfair labor practices" and were made subject to the regulatory power of the National Labor Relations Board.

Although many believed that these statutes wholly exempted labor from any possible further application of the antitrust law, the Court later found that labor unions were still subject to the Sherman Act.[204]

In *Apex Hosiery v. Leader,*[205] the Hosiery Workers Union engaged in a sitdown strike to enforce its demand for a closed shop, thereby obstructing the manufacture and shipment of finished goods in interstate commerce. The Court held that the violent sitdown strike in *Apex* was not subject to the Sherman Antitrust Act. Justice Stone, writing for the majority, explained that the Sherman Act was not intended to cover conduct by a union unless it had a direct, substantial effect on commercial competition. The Courts' decision specifically recognized the inherent objective of labor organizations to restrain competition among employers over wages and working conditions. As the Court stated:

> "A combination of employees necessarily restrains competition among themselves in the sale of their services to the employer. . . . Since the enactment of . . . the Clayton Act . . . it would seem plain that restraints on the sale of the employee's services to the employer, however much they curtail competition among employees, are not themselves combinations or conspiracies in restraint of trade or commerce under the Sherman Act." [206]

The Court recognized that this objective required the restriction of competition from non-union employers, stating:

> "Since in order to render a labor combination effective it must eliminate the competition from non-union made goods, [citation omitted] an elimination of price competition based on differences in labor standards is the objective of any national labor organization." [207]

The Court's recognition of the union's inherent need to achieve market control of labor in order to protect labor standards also recognized the fundamental need to organize on an industry-wide basis. Implicit in *Apex* was the recognition that union monopoly was not only legitimate, but also a necessity if union standards were to be maintained and improved, and that antitrust laws had no application to this objective. Moreover, by declaring that the union's activity would not be subject to antitrust laws unless it had a direct effect on *commercial* competition, the Court distinguished the inevitable effects on competition by the union's elimination of differences in labor costs from price fixing or other market-restrictive agreements usually made by non-labor groups.

One year later, in *United States v. Hutcheson,*[208] the Supreme Court dismissed criminal antitrust indictments for strikes, picketing, and consumer leafletting by the Carpenters Union in a jurisdictional dispute with the Machinists Union. In *Hutcheson,* the defendant Carpenters' Union sought to force Anheuser–Busch to assign certain work to it in preference to the rival Machinists' Union. The union struck Anheuser–Busch and companies doing construction work for Anheuser–Busch. Justice Frankfurter, writing for the majority, declared that the Sherman Act, the Clayton Act, and the Norris–LaGuardia Act must be read together as "harmonizing texts" in deciding whether a labor union had violated the antitrust laws. Justice Frankfurter found that these activities were protected under section 20 of the Clayton Act as defined by Norris–LaGuardia's definition of "labor dispute." He reasoned that one could not hold the same conduct Congress intended to be free from injunctions to be criminal under another law. As he stated:

> "The Norris–LaGuardia Act reasserted the original purpose of the Clayton Act by infusing into it the immunized trade union activities as redefined in the later Act. In this light paragraph 20 removes all such allowable conduct from the taint of being a violation of any law of the United States' including the Sherman Law." [209]

Frankfurter's sweeping language seemed to free all traditional labor activity both primary and secondary from the antitrust laws. Moreover, the decision stated a clear standard for all future applications:

> "So long as a union acts in its self-interest and does not combine with non labor groups, the licit and the illicit under section 20 are not to be distinguished by any judgment regarding the wisdom or unwisdom, the rightness or wrongness, the selfishness or unselfishness of the end of which the particular activities are the means." [210]

Frankfurter's harmonizing of the texts of the three statutes in this way became known as the "statutory exemption."

The question as to how the Frankfurter test would be applied when a union combined with a non-labor group in collective-bargaining agreements to restrict competition from non-union contractors and manufacturers was answered a few years later in the *Allen Bradley* case.[211]

In *Allen Bradley,* Local 3, the electrical workers local in New York City, obtained closed-shop agreements with all local electrical equipment manufacturers and contractors. Under these agreements, contractors were obligated to buy equipment only from Local 3 manufacturers who, in turn, confined their New York City sales to Local 3 contractors. This industry-wide control included, in addition to agreements as to the terms and conditions of employment, price and market control arrangements. In order to achieve these ends, agencies were set up composed of representatives from the union, the contractors, and the manufacturers who policed these agreements. The Court found it to be a violation of the Sherman Antitrust Act for labor unions and their members, though furthering their own interests, to combine with employers and manufacturers of goods to restrain competition in goods and to monopolize the marketing of goods.

The combination the Court referred to was more than the collective-bargaining agreement. The illegality was in the total scheme, which allowed the contractors and manufacturers to monopolize all the business in New York City and to bar all others, enabling them to raise prices above competitive levels.

The Court noted that the means adopted by the union fell within the "specified acts" that section 20 of the Clayton Act had declared to be not violations of the Sherman Act and that, therefore, had there been no union-contractor-manufacturer combination, the union's acts would not have been violations of the Sherman Act. Thus, the same labor activities may or may not be violations depending on whether the union acts alone or in combination with business groups. The ruling applied the *Hutcheson* test, finding that in *Allen Bradley* the union had combined with non-labor groups and had not acted strictly in its own interest.

Implicit in the reasoning of *Apex, Hutcheson,* and *Allen Bradley* is the notion that collectively bargained agreements over mandatory subjects of bargaining are immune from the Sherman Act. Because, however, the union in a collective-bargaining agreement combines with a non-labor group, this rationale has become known as the "nonstatutory exemption." Some would call the term a misnomer because, if a union's activities to organize employers are within the so-called statutory exemption, the collective-bargaining agreement that flows from successful organizing is equally favored by national labor policy and should also be included in the statutory exemption.[212]

The Court's approach to reconciling the conflicting policies of the labor law and antitrust law seemed clearly charted by *Apex, Hutcheson,* and *Allen Bradley.* However, the conceptual approach was splintered by the *Pennington*[213] and *Jewel Tea*[214] cases decided together in 1965. Both decisions were by divided courts where no opinion commanded a majority.

In *Pennington,* the United Mine Workers and its welfare fund were sued by a small coal-operator, alleging that the union and the large coal-operators had entered into collective-bargaining agreements calling for substantial increases in wages and welfare payments. The Court found that the union had agreed to impose those terms on all the coal operators without regard to their ability to pay, with the aim of driving the small operators out of business. Justice White, writing for the majority, found the union not exempt under the *Hutcheson* approach, because the activity complained of was the product of an agreement with the employers, a non-labor group. He seemed to adopt a balancing approach, viewing the union's activity under the labor law and then balancing its labor law protection against the resulting market restriction. White found that the union's agreement to impose a uniform wage settlement on other coal operators would be a violation of the union's duty to bargain under the National Labor Relations Act. Further he held that an employer could not condition acceptance of a contract on the union's organizing a majority of the industry. He therefore concluded that there was little interest in national labor policy for this type of agreement. Weighed against that were the anti-competitive effects of an agreement to impose conditions on third parties at a level they could not pay and that would, therefore, drive them out of business. Justice White gratuitously offered his view that while unions are interested in establishing uniform wages, they need to be free to adjust that policy to the individual circumstances of each employer.

Douglas, Black, and Clark concurred in a separate opinion, finding the *Allen Bradley* reasoning applicable, presumably to find a combination with non-labor groups for non-labor purposes,—i.e., restricting the marketplace by driving out the marginal operators.

Jewel Tea involved the legality of a provision negotiated by the Meat Cutters union with a multiemployer group of food stores, restricting the sale of meat in Chicago stores to the hours between 9:00 A.M. to 6:00 P.M., Monday through Saturday. Jewel Tea, an independent employer, signed the agreement under threat of a strike. (Some 1000 independents and an association of 300 others agreed to the contract.) Jewel then sued, claiming that the restriction was a product of a conspiracy among the meat dealers to limit the hours to prevent the operation of self-service markets after 6:00 P.M. and that the unions were the enforcing agent of the conspiracy. Jewel, which had become basically a pre-packaged, self-service store, could operate after 6:00 p.m. without a butcher on duty.

The Court, with Justice White writing once again for himself and two others, applied the balancing approach. He rejected the union's argument that because the provision represented a mandatory subject of bargaining the case was within the NLRB's primary and exclusive jurisdiction. This characterization, he held, doesn't control the Sherman Act. He distinguished the case from *Pennington,* however, noting that the trial court had found no evidence of a union-employer conspiracy. Moreover, the union was seeking to impose a uniform condition, not pursuant to an agreement with some employers directed against others, but by unilaterally following its own interests. Therefore, the question became accommodating the coverage of the Sherman Act to the policy of the labor laws.

The crucial issue was how closely the marketing hours restriction related to wages, hours, and working conditions, so "that the union's successful attempt to obtain that provision through bona fide arm's length bargaining in pursuit of their own labor policies, and not at the behest of or in combination with non-labor groups, falls within the protection of the national labor policy and is therefore exempt from

the Sherman Act."[215]   The Court went on to find that though the
restriction's effect on competition was apparent and real, the concern
of the union members was direct and immediate.   Presumably this
direct interest was in seeing that work wasn't performed by others or
that they would be forced to work evening hours.   The Court
suggested that if the evidence showed that butcher workload and work
would not be affected by evening sales, the restriction would be an
unjustified restriction on self-service markets and not exempt from the
Sherman Act.

Justice Goldberg, joined by Justices Harlan and Stewart, concurred in both cases in a single opinion that would find both agreements outside of the antitrust law.   Justice Goldberg felt that the two
cases represented contrasting, but legitimate union policy judgments.
He noted in *Pennington* the union's longstanding philosophy that the
existence of marginal operators who couldn't pay the wages and
working conditions the union had negotiated with other operators
only served to depress working conditions.   Conversely, the Meat
Cutters in *Jewel* sought to protect the small, independent service
operators who couldn't operate at night without employing butchers,
from being disadvantaged by the large, automated, self-service markets.

Justice Goldberg pointed out that Justice White's balancing approach to the issues inevitably involved the Court in determining the
motives of the parties to collective-bargaining agreements but that the
motives of the parties to collective bargaining over wages often
coincide.   The union is seeking high wages and protection for its
members from low-wage, non-union competition.   The employers
who agree to pay high wages seek protection from competitors paying
lower wages.   The common motive, however, should not give rise to
a conspiracy in restraint of trade regardless of whether the bargaining
takes the form of a multiemployer arrangement or agreements with
the market leaders setting a pattern for the rest of the industry.
Justice Goldberg pointed to the latitude the balancing approach gives
judges to interpose their own views as to the appropriate goals of
collective bargaining, noting that Justices Douglas, Black, and Clark
would have found that the multiemployer agreement in *Jewel* was
evidence of a conspiracy.   Justice Goldberg would hold that the
collective-bargaining agreements on mandatory subjects of bargaining
under the labor law are *per se* not subject to the antitrust laws.

Implicit in this view was his rejection of the Court's view in
Pennington that the harmonizing of the Clayton Act and Norris–
LaGuardia was limited to a union's secondary activity and excluded
collective bargaining over mandatory subjects.   The statutory exemption, based on the logic that Congress would not specifically protect
certain activity under Norris–LaGuardia and the NLRA that would be

criminal under antitrust law, applies with at least equal force to collective bargaining, one of the highest objectives of the NLRA.

C. Post–*Pennington–Jewel* Applications

The application of antitrust laws to labor activities after *Pennington–Jewel* seemed to be based on the following principles:

1. If the union acts unilaterally, exerting economic pressure, and its activities could be described as acting alone in its own interest, its activities would be exempt under the so-called statutory exemption.

2. If the restriction at issue was the product of collective bargaining, the statutory exemption would not apply and the Court will balance the competing interests of the national labor policy and the policy represented by the antitrust laws.

If the union bargained in its own interest, at arms length, for a mandatory subject of bargaining or one that is closely related to wages and terms and conditions of employment, and did not agree to impose those terms on other employers, such would be deemed to be protected by national labor policy and outweigh any restrictive effects on the marketplace. Obviously, the absence of any of these factors and the perceived "directness" of the agreement's effect on market competition could result in the balance being struck in favor of antitrust coverage.

The Court's decisions were leading away from the clear principle outlined by *Apex* and *Hutcheson:* that union activity, whether unilateral economic pressure or collective-bargaining agreements seeking traditional union goals for its members' direct benefit, should be exempt from antitrust laws regardless of its effects on the marketplace. Following the "harmonizing" of Clayton and Norris–LaGuardia and adding to the mix the policy represented by the NLRA and its amendments, it would seem that the regulation of these activities should be left to the exclusive jurisdiction of the labor law as articulated by the NLRB. On the other hand, combinations of employers engaging in price fixing or other restrictions on commercial competition should not be insulated from the antitrust laws because of a union's participation in the combination by a collective-bargaining agreement or other arrangement. The touchstone of the legality of these combinations should be whether the agreement serves traditional union goals—immediately benefiting its employees. If it does, the resultant market restriction will then inevitably be the result of the elimination of competition over labor costs.

The balancing approach adopted in the two decisions leads to inconsistent results and involved the Court in a case-by-case judgment of the "validity" of the union's bargaining weighed against its impact on the marketplace. Whether the Court looks to the NLRA for guidance, as it did in *Pennington,* or follows its own notions of the justification of the union's restriction, as it did in *Jewel,* the Court is once again, as Justice Goldberg complained, involving itself in judging the legitimacy of the collective-bargaining agreement at issue. Moreover, a balancing analysis based on accommodating competing interests requires the Court's judgment as to whether the union, in its agreement, has chosen the means with the least restrictive impact on market competition in achieving its goals. This requires the Court to decide which of several alternatives was available and which the union should have negotiated.

The next judicial step away from *Apex–Hutcheson* was *Connell Construction Co.,*[216] where a union, clearly acting alone and not in combination with others, for its own self interest was found to be in violation of both the antitrust law and the hot cargo provisions of the labor law.

In *Connell* the Plumbers Local 100 picketed Connell, a general building contractor, for an agreement in which Connell would agree to subcontract all plumbing and mechanical work to firms under contract with Local 100. Connell, which employed no plumbers itself, signed under protest and later sued the union claiming that the agreement violated Sections 1 and 2 of the Sherman Act. (Connell had not filed charges with the NLRB because the NLRB had dismissed hot cargo charges filed earlier by another contractor faced with the same picketing.)

The district court, using a harmonizing approach, found that the subcontracting agreement was within the construction industry proviso of section 8(e) of the LMRA and that, therefore, the activity was exempt from the antitrust laws.[217]

The Fifth Circuit affirmed, finding the union's goal of organizing non-union subcontractors to be a legitimate union interest and, therefore, exempt. The Supreme Court reversed. The Court characterized *Hutcheson*'s synthesis of the Clayton Act and Norris–LaGuardia as creating a statutory labor exemption limited to specific unilateral union activities. The exemption, it went on to hold, did not apply to agreements between unions and employers. These agreements, the Court held, must be viewed by accommodating the national policy favoring collective bargaining and the policy favoring free competition. This accommodation could result in what it termed a limited nonstatutory exemption. The so-called nonstatutory exemption was rooted in the "strong" labor policy favoring elimination of competition over wages and working conditions, and therefore tolerates the consequent indirect effects on price competition.

However, the Court found that the nonstatutory exemption did not apply to what it termed was a "direct restraint" on competition. In *Connell,* the restraint agreement was deemed direct since the subcontracting clause eliminated non-union firms from the market despite the fact that they may have paid equivalent wages and benefits. Thus, the tolerance for restraints that resulted from the elimination of wage competition did not apply to exclusions based on unionization.

In terms that echoed the Courts' dark view in *Pennington* of the union's commitment to extend the same terms to other firms, the Court condemned the "most favored nations" clause, the provision promising that no signatory contractor would get more advantageous provisions. The Court found this clause revealed that the union's aim was to eliminate competition even on subjects unrelated to wages and working conditions. The Court went on to condemn the union's ultimate goal of controlling access to the market for subcontracting work. Here the Court speculated that such control could be used for illegal purposes such as excluding marginal firms, as in *Pennington*,[218] or outside contractors, as in *Allen Bradley*.[219] The Court conceded that there was no evidence of this nor any evidence of any conspiracy with the union employers, yet it found that because the direct exclusion of non-union contractors reduced competition that *might* not result from the elimination of competition concerning wages and hours, the balance was therefore to be struck in favor of competition.

The Court in *Connell* ignored the fact that the union's goal would have been of immediate benefit to the union and not the employers under contract. There was no evidence that the union had refused non-union contractors a union contract so as to exclude them from the market or that the union sought to impose a higher labor cost package than it had with the rest of its other employers. If it had done so, then its agreement would seem to suggest an alleged combination and could be examined. In *Connell,* however, the union was acting for its own immediate interest and that of its members.

A major factor in the balance was the fact that the contract sought by the union would not cover any of the general contractor's employees, so therefore, with echoes of *Duplex* and its requirement of proximate employee-employer relationship, the Court ruled that the union wasn't entitled to the support of the federal policy favoring collective bargaining. The Court held that the agreement was not protected by the construction proviso of section 8(e) of the labor law, because the proviso could not have been intended to apply to situations where the employer employed no employees and there was no collective-bargaining relationship. To apply the proviso to situations where there were no employees would allow the unions an unlimited tool to organize subcontractors from the top down through the general contractors.

Perhaps the most significant aspect of the Court's holding was that agreements that violated section 8(e) were not to be exclusively remedied by the NLRB. The Court managed this by some questionable reading of legislative history, distinguishing secondary boycotts outlawed under Taft–Hartley in 1947 (which clearly were intended to be exclusively remedied by the labor laws) from section 8(e), enacted in the Landrum–Griffin amendments in 1959. The 1959 amendments, the Court held, were not to be exclusively remedied by the Board. The anomaly of distinguishing section 8(e), enacted to outlaw hot cargo agreements and thus to close the "loophole" in the secondary boycott legislation, was not mentioned. Thus a union striking a neutral employer to achieve the cessation of business with a primary employer was to be exclusively remedied by the labor law while an agreement requiring the same result was also subject to antitrust law.[220]

The result of *Connell* was to move under judicial scrutiny the entire area of subcontracting clauses with its work preservation-work acquisition distinction and its concept of right of control. These are areas of continuing complexity still being developed by the NLRB, presumably the exclusive articulator of the labor laws. Yet under *Connell,* the Court in an antitrust context is the judge in the first instance as to whether the union's activity is an unfair labor practice and, then, whether its conduct constitutes a violation of the antitrust law.[221]

D. Current Applications

Two recent circuit court decisions, *Sun–Land Nurseries*[222] and *Altemose Construction Co.,*[223] indicate the difficulty and inconsistent results created by the *Jewel–Pennington–Connell* balancing approach. In *Sun–Land Nurseries,* the Ninth Circuit dealt with the issue that *Connell* had not answered: the application of antitrust law to a union subcontracting provision with a multiemployer group of contractors in the construction industry in the context of a collective-bargaining relationship.[224] The case involved a large landscape contractor whose employees were represented by an independent union and who complained of being excluded from work by general contractors because of their agreement with the Laborers Union to contract only with firms under Laborers contracts.

The district court granted summary judgment on the grounds that the agreement was valid under section 8(e) and therefore automatically exempt from antitrust liability. A panel of the Ninth Circuit disagreed with the holding that an automatic exemption followed protected activity and remanded to the district court for it to strike the appropriate balance between competing policies. Presumably, the legacy of *Connell* is for individual judges to weigh the relative values represented by the collective-bargaining agreement as against its anticompetitive effects. The Ninth Circuit, rehearing the matter *en banc,* read *Connell* in a more limited way, stating that while a collective-bargaining agreement valid under the labor law was not automatically exempt from antitrust liability, it cannot, by itself, without additional evidence of an illegal conspiracy, be the basis of an antitrust violation. Without denying the balancing approach, the court seemed to be creating a rebuttable presumption of exemption for activities that are legal under the labor law. It noted that the automatic exemption espoused by Justice Goldberg in *Jewel* had not been endorsed by a majority of the court. Yet the Ninth Circuit seemed impressed by its logic. As it stated: "Congress would not have exempted the construction industry from the prohibition against hot cargo clauses only to have such provisions create liability under the antitrust laws." [225]

In *Altemose,* the Third Circuit's opinion might be cited as a worst-case example of the consequences of the *Pennington–Connell* approach (or lack of same) to a typical unionized construction industry situation. In Philadelphia, the great bulk of commercial construction was carried on by the organized building trades. The trades belonged to the Building Trades Council, an umbrella association of unions that resolved interunion disputes and cleared and coordinated union efforts policing the industry to maintain all union construction projects. This was achieved by subcontracting clauses limiting contracting to employers under contract with the particular building trade union for the trade they employed. Altemose, a large non-union general contractor began work on the Valley Forge Plaza, a large commercial center consisting of a hotel, an office building, theaters and several stores. The Building Trades Council threatened Altemose that unless it signed an agreement, presumably committing it to employ union labor and subcontract work only to subcontractors employing union labor, it would picket. Thereafter, over 1,000 pickets appeared and considerable damage was done. Picketing took place at other Altemose job sites, and union subcontractors and suppliers were forced to cease doing business with Altemose. Altemose, in turn, secured an injunction restraining secondary activity pending the NLRB's determination of its charges, and also charged, and the Board eventually found, that the unions were guilty of section 8(b)(7)(C) violations by picketing for organizational purposes for more than thirty days.

In addition to pursuing its remedies at the NLRB, Altemose and an association of so-called open shop contractors sued the Building Trades Council alleging violations of the Sherman Act.

Altemose contended that the union had violated the law by (a) conspiring with non-labor groups and (b) by the unions and the Council conspiring together to exclude non-union contractors from the market.

The district court granted summary judgment for lack of evidence of any concert of action with non-labor groups. It found that the unions' pressure to have Altemose sign a subcontractors agreement, if illegal under section 8(e), would constitute, at most, secondary boycott activity under the labor law and as such would be exempt from antitrust law under the so-called statutory exemption. The same was true of the pressure on Altemose's suppliers and subcontractors. The district court distinguished *Connell*, where the contractor had actually signed an illegal hot cargo agreement, from the situation where the secondary activity had not resulted in an agreement.[226] The union's activity was also immune, it held, because of the nonstatutory exemption. The court found that the subcontracting clause was legal under section 8(e) because unlike *Connell* it was sought in the context of a bargaining relationship. The court cited the NLRB's finding that the union's picketing of Altemose was for organizational and recognitional objectives. The district court then rejected the claim of an illegal *Allen Bradley* type combination with employers to restrain trade on the product market. It held that the unions' attempt to organize the construction industry was a legal objective and that there was no evidence that the unions and employers tried to protect a select group of employers from competition. If anything, the court found, the evidence was to the contrary, that the union's purpose was to organize as many contractors as possible and non-union firms had the option when pressured to become union. Nor was the acquiescence of suppliers, contractors, and financial institutions evidence of a conspiracy. It would be contrary to the intent of the labor exemption if there was to be an inference of conspiracy from the favorable results of a union's secondary tactics.

The Third Circuit reversed. While conceding that the evidence of concert of action was "not overwhelming," it noted that the unions' secondary activities benefited union employers. It cited the lists of union contractors maintained by the unions' contractors (presumably to comply with their contract obligations to use only union contractors), the exclusion from the market of non-union firms, and the general contractors' hiring of only union firms rather than the lowest bidders, which the court felt was acting against their economic interest. In short, the court found evidence of a combination with non-labor groups based only on the traditional activities of the construction unions seeking to organize the industry. It went on to find that the unions and Council were not entitled to the statutory exemption because the unions' activity against Altemose could not be characterized as unilateral. The fact that Altemose, the object of the activity, hadn't signed an agreement did not distinguish the case from *Connell*. The court would look to the unions' agreement with other contractors to find that the activity should be judged by the nonstatutory exemption standards.

Under these standards, the court found that the unions' insistence on section 8(e) provisions might be illegal because Altemose had no bargaining relationship with the unions. It rejected, erroneously, the NLRB's earlier finding that the same picketing sought to organize

Altemose's employees. The court would not grant the Board's finding determinative status because it felt that Altemose, as the charging party, had no control over the factual or legal issues tried before the Board. The court thus ignored the fact that Altemose, having filed the section 8(b)(7)(C) charges, had alleged that the picketing was for organizational and recognitional purposes and that the Board had found merit to those charges. The court's decision here represents the final twist in the *Connell* antitrust intrusion into the NLRB's exclusivity. Not only are the courts to be free to determine in the first instance whether union activities constitute unfair labor practices under the labor law for purposes of ruling on the antitrust exemption, but now are to be free to ignore a specific Board decision on the same activity and decide the unfair labor practice issue *de novo* at a District Court trial.

E. Conclusion

Recent decisions illustrate the confusion in approach engendered by allowing the courts to apply antitrust law to labor activity free from the statutory moorings of the labor laws. Had the harmonizing rationale of *Hutcheson* been extended to collective-bargaining agreements, as Justice Goldberg argued in *Pennington* and *Jewel,* then the so-called statutory exemption would apply not only to union unilateral activity but also to restrictions in agreements that were mandatory subjects of bargaining or closely related to wages and terms and conditions of employment. Union activity for traditional union objectives would be dealt with exclusively under the labor law as administered by the NLRB.

Those instances where unions combined with non-labor groups in agreements that restricted competition would be tested under antitrust by the questions:

1. Is this a legitimate or traditional labor objective of immediate benefit to the union and its members?

2. Is the employers' interest in the agreement to gain an advantage over non-signers, or is it to assure that its signing doesn't work to its competitive disadvantage?

It would seem that the criteria should be clear, both to the courts applying the law and more important, to unions and employers who need to be able to understand and guide their actions accordingly.

The present statutory-nonstatutory approach has more or less immunized unions engaging in unilateral secondary activity but has tied the labor law to antitrust law in a way that leaves unions open to suits for antitrust liability whenever they have negotiated agreements including restrictions on subcontracting or the use of labor saving devices in order to preserve or acquire work or apply terms to other parties. In cases where the NLRB decides the activity is legal under the LMRA, some courts have determined that the exemption from antitrust is automatic, on the reasoning that what is legal and mandated by the labor law should not be subject to a lawsuit for treble damages and enjoinable under the antitrust law. However, as in *Sun-Land*, some courts will not find the exemption automatic when the NLRA finds the restriction within the labor law, but will, in such circumstances, insist on direct evidence of some unlawful combination for an unlawful end. Still other courts, as seen in *Altemose*, will look to decide the issue of whether the restriction is an unfair labor practice either de novo or in the first instance. An employer injured by union concerted activity has an option in such cases to either file a charge with the NLRB and hope to persuade the General Counsel of the merit of its charges and the need for an injunction; or it can file in antitrust and champion its own cause and, perhaps, convince a more sympathetic judge of the union's misconduct; or it can do both.

Where the NLRA has ruled that such agreements are illegal hot cargo clauses, the courts then purport to consider the agreement under a balancing approach. The balance seems to be weighed in favor of finding no exemption since the agreements are held to have lost the support of the national labor policy, and the restriction on competition can be said to outweigh the policy interest in collective bargaining.

Most recently, however, in *Richards v. Neilsen Freight Lines*,[227] the Ninth Circuit found that action that may be violative of the labor laws was not necessarily unlawful under the antitrust laws. In *Richards*, the trustee in bankruptcy for Foothills Express claimed *inter alia* that in an effort to gain recognition, the Teamsters had coerced other trucking companies not to do business with the small, non-union trucking company. Specifically, it was alleged that the union and other trucking companies had entered into discrete agreements not to use Foothills' trucking services until it became organized.

The trustee commenced an action claiming that the union's and other trucking companies' actions violated the antitrust laws. The district court, however, dismissed the action and the Ninth Circuit affirmed, finding that the defendants' actions were shielded by the nonstatutory exemption even though the alleged unlawful activity occurred outside the context of any collective-bargaining agreement and probably violated the labor law. The Court explicitly recognized the different policies advanced by the labor and antitrust laws:

> "It is not paradoxical that a labor law violation may still be within the antitrust exemption, for the violation will carry its own remedies under the labor laws, although we recognize that in some cases a violation of the labor laws may involve conduct whose consequences are so far-reaching that it falls outside the

exemption. Where, as here, there is no showing the alleged agreements pose actual or potential anticompetitive risks other than those related to a reduction in competitive advantages based on differential wages or working conditions, the nonstatutory labor exemption prevents antitrust scrutiny of the union activity.'' [228]

Judge Kennedy's decision finding that reducing competitive advantages in the areas of wages and working conditions is protected by the nonstatutory exemption comes very close to Justice Goldberg's analysis in *Jewel* and *Pennington,* i.e., that mandatory subjects of bargaining are exempt from the antitrust laws.

Tying antitrust application to findings of unfair labor practices results in a perverse concentration on the labor law to decide liability under another law with completely different concerns and objections. Whether a hot cargo clause is within the construction industry proviso or a violation of section 8(e), its effect on the market will be the same. The rulings on the labor law should not decide antitrust policy. Yet they do under the present approach, with unhappy and inconsistent results. The long and complex litigation over the containerization of cargo is a case in point. The ILA, the longshoremans union, correctly anticipated that the introduction of containers would eliminate the work of loading and unloading cargo ships. They negotiated rules with the New York Shipping Association restricting the stuffing and stripping of containers by freight consolidation within fifty miles of the pier for themselves at the pier. Some consolidators affected adversely by the rules filed hot cargo charges with the NLRB and sued in antitrust. The NLRB found the rules to be a violation in that they served to acquire the work of the consolidators. In a civil case, the Third Circuit, based on an NLRB ruling, found the agreement to be outside the nonstatutory exemption of antitrust and remanded to the District Court for a finding of damages.[229] The Supreme Court, however, found the NLRB's decision to be based on an erroneous characterization of the work in dispute as that of the consolidators when, in fact, it was the function formerly performed at the pier that was to be judged as the work at issue.[230] The Supreme Court then remanded the Third Circuit's antitrust decision back to the court to consider in light of its findings of the NLRB decision.[231] The Board then reviewed its decision and found the rules valid work preservation in all but a few instances.[232] Presumably, the antitrust ruling will follow the new findings under the labor law. Clearly, the union in this case acted out of traditional work preservation impulses and its conduct should be judged by such rather than tying antitrust liability to the legitimacy of the union's activity under the labor law.

FOOTNOTES

1. *Commonwealth v. Pullis,* Philadelphia Mayor's Court (1806).

2. This development is sketched out and relevant citations provided in Cox, Bok & Gorman, Labor Law 13 et seq., (10th ed. 1986).

3. 4 Met. 111 (1842).

4. Id.

5. 167 Mass. 92, 44 N.E. 1077 (1896).

6. Id.

7. Id. at 1078.

8. Id. at 1079–82.

9. See Caldwell, Trial by Judge and Jury, 33 Am.U.L.Rev. 33 (1899).

10. *Plant v. Woods,* 176 Mass. 492, 57 N.E. 1011 (1900).

11. 245 U.S. 229 (1917).

12. 26 Stat. 209 (1890), 15 U.S.C. §§ 1–7 (1982).

13. 208 U.S. 274 (1908).

14. 38 Stat. 730 (1914); 15 U.S.C. §§ 12–27 (1982).

15. 254 U.S. 443 (1921).

16. Id. at 471.

17. Frankfurter & Greene, The Labor Injunction (1930).

18. 47 Stat. 70 (1932), 29 U.S.C. §§ 101–15 (1982).

19. 312 U.S. 219 (1941).

20. 9 Stat. 449 (1935), 29 U.S.C. §§ 151 et seq. (1982).

21. Pub.L. No. 101, 80th Cong., 1st Sess., 61 (1947).

22. Pub.L. No. 257, 86th Cong., 1st Sess. (1959).

23. 310 U.S. 88 (1940).

24. Id. at 92.

25. Id. at 102.

26. *International Brotherhood of Teamsters, Local 695 v. Vogt, Inc.,* 354 U.S. 284 (1957).

27. 315 U.S. 769, 776 (1942) (Douglas, J., concurring).

28. 377 U.S. 58 (1964).

29. Id. at 63.

30. 447 U.S. 607 (1980).

31. Id. at 614.

32. Id. at 616.

33. Id. at 617–18 (Blackmun, J., concurring).

34. 458 U.S. 886 (1982).

35. Id. at 913.

36. See, e.g., Getman, Labor Law and Free Speech, The Curious Policy of Limited Expression, 43 Md.L.Rev. 4 (1984); Note, Labor Picketing and Commercial Speech, 91 Yale L.J. 938 (1982).

37. 28 LRRM 2001 (1988).

38. Partly because of constitutional concerns, Congress carved a major exception to the secondary boycott provisions:

"for publicity other than picketing, for the purpose of truthfully advising the public, including consumers and members of a labor organization that a product or products are produced by an employer with whom the union has a primary dispute and are distributed by another employer, as long as such publicity does not have an effect of

inducing any individual employed by any person other than the primary employee—
to refuse to pick up, deliver, or transport any goods or not to perform any service
. . ." *

The obvious goal of this proviso is to permit secondary handbilling aimed at getting
consumers, but not secondary employees, to make common cause with the union. While
the proviso is broad, it is limited to cases in which the primary employer is a producer
and the secondary employer is a distributor.

In order to avoid the constitutional issue, the Board and the courts of appeals read
the proviso broadly, expanding the categories of producer and distributor to include such
things as the relationship between a newspaper and an advertiser. The Supreme Court
endorsed an expansive reading of the proviso in *NLRB v. Servette, Inc.,*[39] in which it held
that a wholesale distributor of candy was a producer for these purposes. In *Edward J.
DeBartolo Corp. v. NLRB,*[40] however, the Supreme Court held that the proviso did not
protect handbilling in which consumers were asked to boycott a mall in which one of the
tenants used a nonunion general contractor to construct a department store. The Court
concluded that the contractor could be considered a producer and the store owner a
distributor for purposes of the proviso. Because the union's activity was directed towards
a general boycott of the mall, however, the Court found it to be outside the scope of the
proviso. The Court specifically reserved addressing the constitutional question. On
remand, the Board found that the union's activity violated the Act.[41]

    * 29 U.S.C. § 158(b)(4) (1982).

39. 377 U.S. 46 (1964).

40. 463 U.S. 147 (1983).

41. 273 N.L.R.B. 1431 (1985).

42. *ILA v. Allied Intern.,* 456 U.S. 212 (1982).

43. Id. at 226.

44. Id. at 225.

45. *NAACP v. Claiborne Hardware Co.,* 458 U.S. 886 (1982).

46. *United States v. O'Brien,* 391 U.S. 367, 377 (1968).

47. Section 8(b)(4)(C) states, in pertinent part,:

(b) It shall be an unfair labor practice for a labor organization or its agents—

* * *

    (4)(i) to engage in, or to induce or encourage any individual employed by any
person engaged in commerce or in an industry affecting commerce to engage in, a
strike or a refusal in the course of his employment to use, manufacture, process,
transport, or otherwise handle or work on any goods, articles, materials, or commodi-
ties or to perform any services; or (ii) to threaten, coerce, or restrain any person
engaged in commerce or in an industry affecting commerce, where in either case an
object thereof is:

* * *

    (C) forcing or requiring any employer to recognize or bargain with a particular
labor organization as the representative of his employees if another labor organization has been certified as the representative of such employees under the provisions
of section 9.

48. *NLRB v. Drivers Union Local 639,* 362 U.S. 274 (1960). The Board, in *Curtis Brothers,*
119 N.L.R.B. 232 (1957), *reversed,* 274 F.2d 551 (D.C.Cir.1958) *aff'd,* 362 U.S. 274 (1960), had tried
to apply section 8(b)(1)(A) to the recognition picketing of a non-union employer by a minority
union. The Board's reasoning was that the picketing forced the employees to suffer economic
hardship for exercising their Section 7 right to refrain from joining a union, and, therefore,
constituted illegal interference with those rights. The Supreme Court reversed the Board,
holding that Congress had specifically addressed peaceful picketing for recognition in Section
8(b)(4)(C) and therefore, the Board could not construe 8(b)(1)(A) to cover the same type of
picketing in non-union or non-certification situations.

49. See 105 Cong.Rec. 17898 (1959).

50. In cases where there is recognition or organizational picketing and no bar to an
election exists, the statute encourages resort to an NLRB election as a preferred
alternative to picketing in the resolution of the question of representation. An employer,

faced with picketing in such circumstances, can secure an election on an expedited basis by filing an 8(b)(7)(C) charge *and* a petition for an election. The Board will dispense with its usual hearing procedure on questions of appropriate unit and make a finding of appropriate unit based on its own investigation, and hold the election. If the picketing union then loses the election, it is prohibited from any further picketing by section 8(b)(7)(B) because a valid election has been held within twelve months. See, e.g., *International Hod Carriers Local 840 (C.A. Blinne)*, 135 N.L.R.B. 1153, 1158 (1962).

51. See Hellerstein, Picketing Legislation and the Courts, 10 N.C.L.Rev. 158, 186 (1931). According to Hellerstein:

A picketer may: (1) Merely observe workers or customers. (2) Communicate information, e.g., that a strike is in progress, making either true, untrue or libelous statements. (3) Persuade employees or customers not to engage in relations with the employer: (a) through the use of banners, without speaking, carrying true, untrue or libelous legends; (b) by speaking, (i) in a calm, dispassionate manner, (ii) in a heated, hostile manner, (iii) using abusive epithets and profanity, (iv) yelling loudly, (v) by persisting in making arguments when employees or customers refuse to listen; (c) by offering money or similar inducements to strike breakers. (4) Threaten employees or customers: (a) by the mere presence of the picketer; the presence may be a threat of, (i) physical violence, (ii) social ostracism, being branded in the community as a "scab," (iii) a trade or employee's boycott, i.e., preventing workers from securing employment and refusing to trade with customers, (iv) threatening injury to property; (b) by verbal threats. (5) Assaults and use of violence. (6) Destruction of property. (7) Blocking of entrances and interference with traffic. "The picketer may engage in a combination of any of the types of conduct enumerated above. The picketing may be carried on singly or in groups; it may be directed to employees alone or to customers alone or to both. It may involve persons who have contracts with the employer or those who have not or both.

52. See *Lumber and Sawmill Workers Local 2797 (Stoltze Land and Lumber Co.)*, 156 N.L.R.B. 388 (1965); see also *Blankenship Builders*, 204 N.L.R.B. 138 (1973) (weekend handbilling treated as part of a continuous course of conduct with weekday picketing).

53. 156 N.L.R.B. at 394. The language is very broad. The handbilling itself, however, recounted the history of the union's relationship to the employer, its strike and subsequent decertification. In addition, one employee was disciplined by the union for "crossing" the "handbilling line." The Board subsequently made clear that handbilling alone would not be equated with picketing. See *Lawrence Typographical Union No. 570 (Kansas Color Press)* 158 N.L.R.B. 1332 (1966), *order vacated and remanded on other grounds.* 376 F.2d 643 (10th Cir.1967) *on remand,* 169 N.L.R.B. 279 (1968) *enforced,* 402 F.2d 452 (10th Cir.1968).

54. *Teamsters Local 182,* 135 N.L.R.B. 851 (1962) *enforced,* 314 F.2d 53 (2d Cir.1963).

55. *NLRB v. Teamster Local 182,* 314 F.2d 53 (2d Cir.1963). The court cited Websters Dictionary for its definition of picketing. The Board, referred to Bouvier's and Black's Law dictionaries. Apparently, a picket sign on a wall or pole accompanied by a person who watches for deliveries and confronts those attempting the delivery is close to the situation where the picket patrols wearing a sign. However, where one of the elements is missing, as where the pickets posted signs and leave or do not come out to confront customers to either communicate with them or physically present themselves so that customers have to pass them, such would not be "picketing" because there were no identifiable pickets to physically challenge customers, employees or suppliers. See *NLRB v. United Furniture Workers (Jamestown Sterling Corp.),* 337 F.2d 936 (2d Cir.1964). The same is generally the case where there are people outside the premises of the dispute but they carry no signs. In one case, where the signs were absent, but 200 union representatives and strikers assembled in the vicinity of the employer, the Board held there was picketing because the action of the group was ambiguous. NLRB v. District 12 Mine Workers, 76 L.R.R.M. 2828 (7th Cir.1971).

The Board continues to apply a broad definition of picketing and has distinguished the situation where pickets are never seen from one where signs were posted near the entrance and former pickets gave out handbills to entering visitors. See *Lawrence Typographical Union No. 570,* 158 N.L.R.B. 1332 (1966) *vacated,* 376 F.2d 643 (10th Cir.1967).

56. *Laborers Local 840 (C.A. Blinne Const. Co.),* 135 N.L.R.B. 1153, 1158 n. 29 (1962). The congressional intent seems clear. It should be obvious, however, that the threat to picket is often more ambiguous than the picketing itself.

57. Id.

58. See *Calumet Contractors Ass'n*, 130 N.L.R.B. 78 (1961) *overruled*, 133 NLRB 512 (1961). This view was enunciated in an 8(b)(4)(C) case involving the picketing of an employer that had negotiated an allegedly substandard agreement with a certified union.

59. *Calumet Contractors Ass'n*, 133 N.L.R.B. 512 (1961).

60. See *NLRB v. Knitgoods Workers Union Local 155*, 403 F.2d 388, 391 (2d Cir. 1968).

61. Where the union has been previously engaged in "area standards" picketing without seeking recognition, it is supporting evidence of the union's claimed objective. Conversely, where the union claims an area standard purpose, but has never picketed other substandard employers, *Penny Constr. Co.*, 144 N.L.R.B. 1298 (1963), or its history is one of trying to organize all non-union employers *Teamsters Local 5 [Barber Bros.]*, 171 N.L.R.B. 30 (1968), *enforced*, 405 F.2d 864 (5th Cir.1968), its purpose will be seen as recognitional.

62. Compare *IBEW Local 953*, 154 N.L.R.B. 1301, 1306 (1965) (Board cites longstanding history of union efforts to organize employer to establish lack of abandonment of recognition objective) with *John's Valley Foods*, 237 N.L.R.B. 425 (1978) (no recognitional objective despite past finding that in earlier period of picketing, union's claim to have changed objective to area standards was a cover for continued recognition picketing).

63. See *Ogden Enterprises Ltd.*, 248 N.L.R.B. 290 (1980).

64. See *Altemose Constr. Co.*, 222 N.L.R.B. 1276 (1976), *enforced*, 547 F.2d 1158 (3d Cir.1976).

65. See *Fanelli Ford Sales, Inc.*, 133 N.L.R.B. 1468 (1961).

66. See *Waterway Terminals Co.*, 193 N.L.R.B. 477 (1971) *aff'd*, 473 F.2d 15 (9th Cir. 1973). In a case where the union sought the employment of one member employed by a former subcontractor, the Board distinguished *Waterway*, because, as in *Fanelli*, supra, the employer could have resolved the issue without recognizing the union. See *Teamsters Local 676 (Shell Chemical Co.)*, 199 N.L.R.B. 445 (1972) *enf'd* 495 F.2d 1116 (5th Cir.1974) *cert. denied*, 421 U.S. 963 (1975).

67. See *Laborer's Local 1298, (Roman Stone Constr. Co.)*, 153 N.L.R.B. 659 (1965).

68. In *Wood Surgeons*, 175 N.L.R.B. 390 (1969), the employer signed a pre-hire contract with the union and, in mid-term, cancelled it. The union filed charges of refusal to bargain and began picketing. The Board held that the charges were not valid because the employer was not in the construction industry, the pre-hire contract was unlawful and, therefore, the recognition was unlawful. The Board determined that because there was no lawful recognition, the picketing was subject to section 8(b)(7)(C) standards.

69. *Irvins, Inc.*, 134 N.L.R.B. 686 (1961).

70. For the prerequisites and procedures for holding an expedited election see *NLRB Rules and Regulations* (sub-part D) and *Statements of Procedure* (sub-part D).

71. See, e.g., *Carpet Cadillac, Inc.*, 209 N.L.R.B. 891 (1974).

72. See *Oakland G.R. Kinney Co.*, 136 N.L.R.B. 335 (1962).

73. 321 F.2d 771, 774 (10th Cir.1963).

74. 289 F.2d 41, 45 (2d Cir.1961).

75. See *Aztec Constr. Inc.*, 97 L.R.R.M. 1251, 1252 (1977).

76. See *Cuneo v. United Shoe Workers*, 181 F.Supp. 324 (D.N.J.1960) (10 days of picketing marked by violence); see also *Eastern Camera*, 141 N.L.R.B. 991 (1963) (26 days unreasonable and union petition thereafter is untimely).

77. See *NLRB v. Local 239, Teamsters*, 289 F.2d 41 (2d Cir.1961).

78. *Laborers Local 84 [C.A. Blinne I]*, 130 N.L.R.B. 587 (1961).

79. *Laborers Local 84 [C.A. Blinne II]*, 135 N.L.R.B. 153 (1962).

80. The Congress was concerned with preserving unions constitutional right to peacefully communicate. See 11 Legis. History of the Labor Management Reporting & Disclosure Act (1959), 1427, 1722.

81. *Crown Cafeteria I*, 130 N.L.R.B. 570 (1961) *reversed*, 135 N.L.R.B. 1183 (1962).

82. *Crown Cafeteria II*, 135 N.L.R.B. 1183 (1962); see also *Lebus v. Building & Construction Trades Council*, 199 F.Supp. 628 (E.D.La.1961).

83. *NLRB v. Local 3, IBEW (Jack Picault)*, 317 F.2d 193 (2d Cir.1963).

84. See *Local 3, IBEW (Jack Picault)*, 144 N.L.R.B. 5 (1963) *aff'd*, 339 F.2d 600 (2d Cir.1964).

85. See *Hotel, Motel & Club Employees Local 568 (Restaurant Mgt. Inc.)*, 147 N.L.R.B. 1060 (1964).

86. See *Carpenters Local 2133 (Cascade Employers Association)*, 151 N.L.R.B. 1378 (1965).

87. See *Hotel & Restaurant Employees Local 217 (Picadilly Square, Ltd.)*, 223 N.L.R.B. 1058 (1976).

88. See, e.g., *Barker Bros.*, 138 N.L.R.B. 478 (1962), *enf'd*, 328 F.2d 431 (9th Cir.1964).

89. Id.

90. At the same time Congress provided for a private right of action for damages by anyone injured as a result of a violation of section 8(b)(4) with the passage of Section 301.

91. See Legislative History of the Labor Management Relations Act (1947) at 1511 (1948).

92. 93 Cong.Rec. 4198 (1947).

93. In section 8(b)(4)(C), Congress barred picketing an employer for recognition where another union was certified. It did not get around to regulating recognition picketing in other situations until 1959 when the Landrum–Griffin amendments added section 8(b)(7) to the list of union unfair labor practices.

94. *Local 761, International Union, Electrical Workers v. NLRB*, 366 U.S. 667, 673 (1961).

95. *NLRB v. International Rice Milling*, 341 U.S. 665 (1951).

96. 341 U.S. 675 (1951).

97. There have been repeated attempts in Congress to amend the law to allow for contractors on construction sites to be treated as a single employer for purposes of the secondary boycott provisions. To date, these have been unsuccessful.

98. *Sailors Union of the Pacific (Moore Drydock Co.)*, 92 N.L.R.B. 547 (1950). Though *Denver Building Trades* involved a common site, the union picketed the entire site and openly directed its activity at the general contractor. The case turned on whether the general contractor was a primary or neutral secondary employer. Whether the union could have picketed the non-union subcontractor by changing its signs was not an issue involved in the case.

99. This is often fictional because in common situs cases the primary employer is often unorganized and the union's goal is to get the primary removed from the job through the refusal of unionized employees to cross the picket line.

100. *Teamsters Local 294 (Montgomery Ward & Co.)*, 192 N.L.R.B. 155 (1971).

101. *Los Angeles Bldg. Trades & Const. Council (Silver Crew Assoc.)*, 216 N.L.R.B. 307 (1975), *enforced*, 532 F.2d 1239 (9th Cir.1976).

102. *Crystal Palace Market (Retail Clerks Local 1017)*, 116 N.L.R.B. 856 (1956) *enf'd*, 249 F.2d 591 (9th Cir.1957).

103. See *Allied Concrete, Inc. v. NLRB Teamsters Local 83*, 607 F.2d 827 (9th Cir. 1979); *Texas Distributors, Inc. v. Plumbers, Local 100*, 598 F.2d 393 (5th Cir.1979).

104. See *Washington Coca Cola*, 107 N.L.R.B. 209 (1953).

105. *Local 861 Electrical Workers (Plauche Electric)*, 135 N.L.R.B. 250 (1962).

106. See *IBEW Local 400 (Texas City)*, 269 N.L.R.B. 119 (1984). The evidentiary use of the Moore Drydock test to ascertain the union's "true purpose," involves the tacit fiction that the union that seeks to picket a primary employer wants to minimize the effects of the picketing on neutrals as much as possible. It imputes to the union as a motive, the balance the Board has struck between allowing the union to picket the primary with as little effect on unoffending neutrals located at the same site. Treating Board policy as a union motive allows the Board to treat the *Moore Drydock* standards as evidentiary. If the union fails to abide by them, its true "motive" is seen as secondary. Treating adherence to the standards only as evidence of motive allows the finding that common situs picketing can be secondary, even where the standards are complied with if other evidence of the union's secondary motive can be shown. The change in approach from *per se* rules to an evidentiary search for the true purpose, made it much more difficult for unions to comply with an already complex set of proscriptions.

107. See *Local 55 (PBM)*, 108 N.L.R.B. 363 (1954), *enforced*, 218 F.2d 226 (10th Cir. 1954).

108. *Local 761, Electrical Workers v. NLRB*, 366 U.S. 667 (1961).

109. *Carpenters Local 470*, 224 N.L.R.B. 315 (1976).

110. *Electrical Workers Local 211 (Atlantic County Auth.)*, 277 N.L.R.B. 1041 (1985).

111. 366 U.S. at 681.

112. 138 N.L.R.B. 342 (1962).

113. 387 F.2d 79 (5th Cir.1967).

114. Id. (Wisdom J., dissenting).

115. *United Steelworkers of America v. NLRB*, 376 U.S. 492 (1964). Union picketing neutral's railroad right of way held to be legitimate primary activity where it was effectively the railroad entrance to struck employer. The fact that the "gate" was located on neutral's property was of no significance.

116. See *Carpenters Local 470 (Mueller–Anderson Co.)*, 224 N.L.R.B. 315 (1976), *enforced*, 564 F.2d 1360 (9th Cir.1977).

117. See, e.g., *Electrical Workers, Local 501 v. NLRB*, 756 F.2d 888 (D.C.Cir.1985).

118. 95 Cong.Rec. 8709 (1949).

119. *NLRB v. Business Mach. Local 450, IUE (Royal Typewriter Co.)*, 228 F.2d 553 (2d Cir.1955), *cert. denied*, 351 U.S. 962 (1956).

120. The extra work must be work formerly performed by the struck employer. Where a railroad company that was transporting some products for a struck company added more products because the struck employer's other shipper refused to continue because of the strike, the railroad company was held not to be an ally. *General Teamsters Local 959*, 266 N.L.R.B. 834 (1983), *aff'd*, 743 F.2d 734 (9th Cir.1984).

121. See *Laborers', Local 859 v. NLRB (Thos. Byrne & Co.)*, 446 F.2d 1319 (D.C.Cir.1971), where the court reversed a Board finding that a trucker hired by a customer to deliver struck products was not an ally. The D.C. Circuit held that the trucker was an ally because it was performing struck work and it was not important how the work was obtained.

122. See *Shopmen's Local 501, Iron Workers (Oliver Whyte Co.)*, 120 N.L.R.B. 856 (1958).

123. See *AFTRA v. NLRB*, 462 F.2d 887 (D.C.Cir.1972).

124. See *Miami Newspaper Pressmen's Local No. 46 v. NLRB*, 322 F.2d 405 (D.C.Cir. 1963); see also *Los Angeles Newspaper Guild, Local 69*, 185 NLRB 303 (1970), *aff'd*, 443 F.2d 1173 (9th Cir.1971) *cert. denied* 404 U.S. 1018 (1972).

125. See *Newspaper and Mail Deliveries Union of N.Y. (Gannett, Inc.)*, 271 N.L.R.B. 6011 (1984) (no straight line integration between publishers and distributor).

126. *Irwin–Lyons Lumber Co.*, 87 N.L.R.B. 54 (1949) (trucking firm that transported logs for commonly owned lumber company an ally because of integrated "straight-line operation").

127. *Acme Concrete and Supply Corp.*, 137 N.L.R.B. 1324 (1962): (companies shared premises, owners were related, interchange of supplies, did substantial business together). *Teamsters Local 560 (Curtin Matheson Scientific, Inc.)*, 248 N.L.R.B. 1212 (1980) (warehouses in distant states treated as one since serviced customers of parent corporation cross-shipped and would undoubtedly ship for other if it was struck).

128. 377 U.S. 58 (1964).

129. Id. at 72.

130. 447 U.S. 607 (1980).

131. Id. at 614–15.

132. Obviously, the effect on the neutral would be equally ruinous if the union's picketing of the primary was successful. Some commentators have suggested that there is little justification for insulating a secondary from direct pressures that would result indirectly from successful primary activity. See Meltzer and Henderson, Labor Law, Cases and Materials, 540, (3d Ed.1985).

133. 377 U.S. 46 (1964).

134. *Great Western Broadcasting Corp. v. NLRB,* 310 F.2d 591 (9th Cir.1962).

135. *Pet, Inc. v. NLRB,* 641 F.2d 545 (8th Cir.1981).

136. *Edward S. DeBartolo Corp. v. NLRB,* 463 U.S. 147 (1983). In the case, the Court found that the non-union contractor was a "producer" and the tenant for which the store was built, a "distributor." In an apparent flush of literalness, however, the Court found that the other tenants and the mall owner could not be considered distributors. To do so would extend the publicity proviso to virtually any secondary the union might want to boycott. Such a conclusion seemed inconsistent in view of the Court's expansive reading of "producer" in *Servette.* The Court's reading of the "producer-distributor" exception led the Board, on remand, to find the handbilling in violation of section 8(b)(4). In its second consideration of the case, the Court, faced with the Board's inevitable finding that peaceful handbilling outside the proviso was a violation of section 8(b)(4), avoided the first amendment issue by finding that such handbilling was not coercive and therefore, outside section 8(b)(4) altogether. *DeBartolo v. Florida Gulf Coast Building and Construction Trades Council,* ___ U.S. ___, 128 L.R.R.M. 2001 (1988). Its literal reading of the "producer-distributor" exception forced the Court, in effect, to eliminate it altogether as a limitation on legal peaceful non-picketing publicity.

137. See *Hospital and Service Employees Union, Local 399 (Delta Airlines),* 263 N.L.R.B. 996 (1982). The Ninth Circuit agreed with the Board's decision on the proviso but remanded on the issue of whether the activity was "coercive." *Hospital Service Employees Union Local 399 v. NLRB,* 743 F.2d 1417 (9th Cir. 1984).

138. 357 U.S. 93 (1958).

139. See, e.g., *Electrical Workers Local 684 (Walsh and Maddox),* 246 N.L.R.B. 549 (1979). (Board has consistently held that "enter into" encompasses the concepts of enforcement, maintenance and reaffirmation. Union citing clause in letter to employer was reaffirming the clause within the section 10(b) period.)

140. 386 U.S. 612 (1967).

141. Id. at 645.

142. Id. at 630.

143. Id. at 657 (Stewart, J., dissenting).

144. See *International Longshoremen's Ass'n (Dolphin Forwarding, Inc.),* 236 N.L.R.B. 525 (1978), *enf. denied,* 613 F.2d 890 (D.C.Cir.1979) *aff'd* 447 U.S. 490 (1980).

145. *NLRB v. International Longshoremen's Ass'n,* 447 U.S. 490 (1980).

146. *Teamsters Local 282 (DiFortunato, Inc.),* 197 N.L.R.B. 673 (1970).

147. *American Boiler Mfrs. Ass'n v. NLRB,* 404 F.2d 547 (8th Cir.1968) *cert. denied* 398 U.S. 960 (1970).

148. 429 U.S. 507 (1977).

149. *Plumbers Local 638 v. NLRB,* 521 F.2d 885, 903 (D.C.Cir.1975).

150. See, e.g., *General Teamsters Local 386, (Construction Materials Trucking, Inc.),* 198 N.L.R.B. 1038 (1972) (distinctions must be drawn protecting the unions' legitimate interest in preventing the undermining of the work opportunities and standards of employees in a contractual bargaining unit by subcontractors who do not meet the prevailing wage and benefit standards); *Local 437, Electrical Workers (Dimeo Construction Co.),* 180 N.L.R.B. 420 (1969) (clause requiring subs to adhere to seniority and grievance procedure provisions beyond standards needed to protect bargaining unit).

151. A typical provision may read: "It shall not be a violation of this agreement and it shall not be grounds for discharge or disciplinary action in the event an employee refuses to enter upon any property involved in a labor dispute or refuses to go through or work behind any picket line. . . ."

152. See, e.g., *Truck Drivers Local 413 v. NLRB,* 334 F.2d 539 (D.C.Cir.1964), *cert. denied,* 379 U.S. 916 (1964).

153. Id. at 545.

154. Id. at 543. In *Dan McKinney Co.,* 137 N.L.R.B. 649 (1962), the Board stated: "We see no real distinction between a contract which prohibits an employer from requiring that his employees do certain work and one prohibiting an employer from discharging his employees for refusing to perform such work." Id. at 652.

155. See *Overnite Transport Co.*, 212 N.L.R.B. 515 (1974).

156. Section 8(e) states, in pertinent part:

Provided that nothing in this subsection shall apply to an agreement between a labor organization and an employer in the construction industry relating to the contracting or subcontracting of work to be done at the site of the construction, alteration, painting or repair of a building, structure, or other work.

157. See *Northeastern Indiana Building and Constr. Trades Council (Centlivre Village Apartments)*, 148 N.L.R.B. 854 (1964), *dismissed*, 352 F.2d 696 (D.C.Cir.1965).

158. See, e.g., *Sheet Metal Workers, Local 48 v. Hardy Corp.*, 332 F.2d 682 (5th Cir. 1964).

159. See *Teamsters Local 559 (Connecticut Sand and Stone Corp)*, 138 N.L.R.B. 532 (1962).

160. *Electrical Workers Local 1516*, 172 N.L.R.B. 617 (1968).

161. 421 U.S. 616 (1975).

162. The Court noted that to hold otherwise would permit "stranger picketing" of an employer with whom the union had no bargaining relationship and whose employees it did not seek to represent, with the objective of signing a union signatory subcontracting agreement. The picketing would be outside of section 8(b)(7) because it was not for recognition and outside of section 8(b)(4)(A) since the language was literally excluded from section 8(e) by the construction industry proviso.

163. 456 U.S. 645 (1982).

164. See *A.L. Adams Const. Co. v. Georgia Power Co.*, 733 F.2d 853 (11th Cir.1984); *Donald Schriver, Inc. v. NLRB*, 635 F.2d 859 (D.C.Cir.1980), *cert. denied* 451 U.S. 976 (1981). Thus, where the employer has voluntarily entered into a collective bargaining agreement prior to employing any employees pursuant to section 8(f), it may include a hot cargo clause. The difference, of course, from *Connell*, is that a union may not coerce a section 8(f) agreement by economic pressure.

165. The proviso states:

That for the purposes of this subsection (e) and section 8(b)(4)(B) the terms "any employer," "any person engaged in commerce or in industry affecting commerce," and "any person" when used in relation to the terms "any other producer, processor, or manufacturer," "any other employer," or "any other person" shall not include persons in the relation of a jobber, manufacturer, contractor, or subcontractor working on the goods or premises of the jobber or manufacturer or performing parts of an integrated process of production in the apparel and clothing industry.

166. See 2 *Legislative History of the Labor Management Reporting & Disclosure Act (1959)* at 1385 (1959).

167. *Garment Workers Joint Board (Hazantown, Inc.)*, 212 NLRB 735 (1974). It should be noted that this was precisely the type of organizing prohibited by section 8(e) in a construction setting in *Connell*.

168. See President Truman, State of the Union as quoted in *Legislative History of the Labor Management Relations Act (1947)* at 608. As demonstrated, *infra*, a union's activity may violate both the secondary boycott and jurisdictional disputes provisions of the Act, or violate one and not the other.

169. *Legislative History of the Taft-Hartley Act, (1947)* at 480.

170. *McLoed v. National Maritime Union of America, AFL–CIO*, 457 F.2d 490 (2d Cir. 1972).

171. See, e.g., *The Newspaper Guild [Brockton]*, 275 NLRB 135 (1985) (no reasonable cause to believe section 8(b)(4)(D) violated where union threatened to "pursue all available remedies in securing disputed work where no evidence of intent to engage in prohibited activity).

172. *See Electrical Workers, Local 202 (W.B. Skinner, Inc.)*, 271 NLRB 171 (1984).

173. The AFL–CIO established the National Joint Board for the settlement of jurisdictional disputes (NJB) in 1948. It was composed of members of the Building Trade unions and employer representatives of the large contracting organizations. The NJB went through various stages of effectiveness, was disbanded, reconstituted and has been succeeded by the Industrial Joint Dispute Board.

174. 364 U.S. 573 (1961).

175. *Drivers Local 157 (Safeway),* 134 N.L.R.B. 1320, 1322 (1961).

176. 134 N.L.R.B. at 1322.

177. See e.g., *Franklin Broadcasting Company,* 126 N.L.R.B. 1212 (1960); *Longshoreman's Local 8, (Waterway Terminals Co.),* 185 N.L.R.B. 186 (1970). The reverse determination has been made by the Board where a jurisdictional dispute involves activity that facially invokes other sections of the Act. Thus, where a union has succeeded in displacing the members of another union, the discharges can be viewed as based on union membership and therefore a violation of section 8(a)(3) by the employer and section 8(b)(2) by the displacing union. However, the Board has held that a "bonafide jurisdictional dispute" does not raise such issues. *Brady–Hamilton Stevedore Co.,* 198 N.L.R.B. 147 (1972) *petition for review denied,* 504 F.2d 1222 (9th Cir.1974). However, as noted, infra, the Supreme Court recognized that a jurisdictional dispute can also involve illegal secondary activity and neither is exclusive. *NLRB v. Engineers Local 825,* 400 U.S. 297 (1971).

178. There are situations where the union disclaiming gives up some minor insignificant detail of work that really does not affect their members' work hours. See, e.g., *Electrical Workers, Local 610, (Landau Outdoor Sign Co.,* 235 N.L.R.B. 320 (1978) (switching on light for billboard); *Local 1291, International Longshoremen's Association (Pocohantas Steamship Company),* 152 N.L.R.B. 676 (1965), *aff'd,* 368 F.2d 107 (3d Cir. 1966) (dispute over hatch covers). *But see Teamsters Local 839 (Shurtleff & Andrews),* 249 N.L.R.B. 176 (1980), *reversed,* 682 F.2d 770 (9th Cir.1982). In *Shurtleff & Andrews,* the Board found no jurisdictional dispute when Teamsters picketed for a composite crew to operate a rig already operated by an Operating Engineer member. The Teamster claim was for the work of driving the rig on the site, something the Engineers didn't claim. The ruling exempting claims for a "composite crew," i.e., where no one competes for the work, but rather the claiming union demands that it be added for the crew performing a minor function seems clearly at odds with the previous cases.

179. See supra note 177 and accompanying text.

180. *NLRB v. Radio and Television Broadcast Engineers Local 1212 (Columbia Broadcasting System),* 364 U.S. 573 (1961).

181. Id. at 583.

182. Id. at 579.

183. See *J.A. Jones Constr. Co.,* 135 N.L.R.B. 1402 (1962). The Board announced that it would decide each case on the basis of these factors but would not fix the weight to be accorded each. The Board subsequently seemed to add as a consideration, the group that would lose jobs or whose jobs disappeared in a "substitute of function." See *Typographical Union Local 2 (Philadelphia Inquirer),* 142 N.L.R.B. 36 (1963).

184. See, e.g., *Carpenters Local 1026 (Intercounty Construction Corp.),* 266 N.L.R.B. 1050 (1983). (Union claimed Board hearing was a "sham").

185. *NLRB v. International Longshoremen's, Local 50,* 504 F.2d 1209 (9th Cir.1974) *cert. denied* 420 U.S. 973 (1975).

186. See *Longshoremen Local 50 (Brady–Hamilton Stevedore Co.),* 244 N.L.R.B. 275 (1979).

187. See *Longshoremen Local 380 (Stobeck Masonry, Inc.),* 267 N.L.R.B. 284 (1983). In these cases, it should be noted that the union, by picketing for a job assignment, can wind up with a Board supported claim that it would not otherwise have achieved by peaceful means. The Board has also overruled the employers assignment where the assignment is contrary to the employer's past practice and where there is a Joint Board award to which the employer is not bound. None of these rulings, however, have been consistent.

188. See, e.g., *NLRB v. Plasterers' Local 79,* 404 U.S. 116 (1971).

189. Id.

190. 400 U.S. 297 (1971).

191. See e.g., *United Mine Workers v. Pennington,* 381 U.S. 657 (1965).

192. See e.g., *Connell Construction Co., Inc. v. Plumbers Local 100,* 421 U.S. 616 (1975).

193. See e.g., *Allen Bradley Co. v. Local No. 3, IBEW,* 325 U.S. 797 (1945).

194. *Loewe v. Lawlor,* 208 U.S. 274 (1908).

195. 15 U.S.C. § 1 (1982).

196. 15 U.S.C. § 17 (1982).

197. 15 U.S.C. § 20 (1982).

198. *Duplex Printing Press Co. v. Deering*, 254 U.S. 443 (1921).

199. *Mine Workers v. Coronado Coal Co.*, "Coronado Coal I", 259 U.S. 344 (1922); *Coronado Coal Co. v. Mineworkers*, "Coronado II", 268 U.S. 295 (1925).

200. See, Meltzer, Labor Unions, Collective Bargaining and the Antitrust Laws, 32 U.Chi.L.Rev. 659, 676 (1965).

201. 29 U.S.C. § 101 *et seq.* (1982).

202. 29 U.S.C. § 113(c) (1982).

203. 29 U.S.C. § 151 *et seq.* (1982).

204. *Apex Hosiery Co. v. Leader*, 310 U.S. 469 (1940).

205. Id.

206. Id. at 502–503.

207. Id. at 503.

208. *United States v. Hutcheson*, 312 U.S. 219 (1941). As stated elsewhere, *Hutcheson* freed virtually all peaceful union activity from federal regulation. With the passage of the Taft–Hartley amendments to the National Labor Relations Act, certain types of secondary activity became unfair labor practices. The legitimacy of such action was to be determined exclusively by the NLRB.

209. *Hutcheson* at 236.

210. Id. at 232.

211. *Allen Bradley Co. v. Local 3 IBEW*, 325 U.S. 797 (1945).

212. See Handler and Zifchak, Collective Bargaining and the Antitrust Laws: The Emasculation of the Labor Exemption, 81 Columbia L.Rev. 459 (1981).

213. *United Mine Workers v. Pennington Coal Co.*, 381 U.S. 657 (1965).

214. *Local 189, Amalgamated Meat Cutters v. Jewel Tea Co.*, 381 U.S. 676 (1965).

215. 381 U.S. at 690.

216. *Connell Construction Co., Inc. v. Plumbers Local 100*, 421 U.S. 616 (1975).

217. Connell had also filed a state antitrust law claim. The District Court held that such was preempted by the federal labor law.

218. *United Mine Workers v. Pennington*, supra.

219. *Allen Bradley Co. v. Local 3 IBEW*, supra.

220. A strong case was made by the dissent for the exclusivity of remedy to be applied to section 8(e). They argued that the legislative history of Taft–Hartley indicates Congress believed that *Hutcheson* had eliminated any antitrust application to union activities. Taft–Hartley established union unfair labor practices. At the same time Congress rejected proposed amendments adding antitrust sanctions and enacted Section 303 providing compensatory damages for secondary boycott violations. It is hardly logical to infer, that by enacting section 8(e) to close a secondary boycott loophole, Congress intended to allow antitrust sanctions as well. Yet that is what *Connell* holds.

221. In *Connell*, it is arguable whether the finding on the antitrust violation is dependent on a finding of a section 8(e) violation. This was resolved in *Kaiser Steel Corp. v. Mullins*, 455 U.S. 72 (1982), where the Court stated that it was necessary in *Connell* to decide the section 8(e) issue first in order to determine whether the agreement was exempt from the antitrust law.

222. *Sun–Land Nurseries, Inc. v. Southern California District Council of Laborers*, 793 F.2d 1110, (9th Cir.1986) *cert. denied*, 107 S.Ct. 1299 (1987).

223. *Altemose Construction Co. v. Building & Const. Trades Council*, 751 F.2d 653 (3d Cir.1985), *cert. denied*, 475 U.S. 1107 (1986).

224. The Supreme Court had already indicated that *Connell* reasoning would not apply where there was a collective bargaining relationship. *Woelke & Romero Framing, Inc. v. NLRB*, 456 U.S. 645 (1982).

225. *Sun–Land Nurseries* at 1117.

226. Of course the court ignored the anomaly of holding that illegal secondary pressure to achieve a section 8(e) agreement was exclusively remedied by the labor law and exempt from antitrust law while the union's success in achieving the signing of such an agreement subjected it to antitrust liability as well. The distinction was first made by the Supreme Court in *Connell* which should have held that the section 8(e) agreement that was the fruit of the secondary activity was also to be exclusively remedied by the labor law. See Handler and Zifchak, Collective Bargaining and the Antitrust Laws: The Emasculation of the Labor Exemption, 81 Columbia L.Rev. 459 (1981).

227. *Richards v. Neilsen Freight Lines,* 810 F.2d 898 (9th Cir.1987).

228. Id. at 906.

229. *Consolidated Express, Inc. v. New York Shipping Ass'n,* 602 F.2d 494 (3d Cir. 1979), *vacated,* 448 U.S. 902 (1980).

230. *NLRB v. International Longshoremen's Association,* 447 U.S. 490 (1980).

231. *Consolidated Express v. New York Shopping Ass'n,* 448 U.S. 902 (1980).

232. *International Longshoremen's Ass'n,* 266 N.L.R.B. 230 (1983), *modified,* 734 F.2d 966 (4th Cir.1984), *aff'd,* 473 U.S. 61 (1985).

Relevant Books, Articles, and Suggested Reading

BOOKS:

Gorman, Labor Law Basic Text, Ch. X–XIV, (1976).

Thiebolt & Haggard, Union Violence: The Record and Response by Courts, Legislature, and the NLRB (1984).

Miller, Anti–Trust Laws and Employee Relations: An Analysis of Their Impact on Management and Union Policies (1984).

ARTICLES:

St. Antoine, "Integrity and Circumspection: The Labor Law Vision of Bernard D. Meltzer, 58 Univ. of Chicago L.Rev. (1986).

Modjeska, "Recognition Picketing Under the NLRA," 35 Univ. of Florida L.Rev. 633 (1983).

Gorman & Finken, "The Individual and the Requirement of Concert Under the National Labor Relations Act," 130 Univ.Penn.L.Rev. 286 (1981).

Getman, "Labor Law and Free Speech: The Curious Policy of Limited Expression," 43 Maryland L.Rev. 4 (1980).

Jaffe, "In Defense of the Supreme Court's Picketing Doctrine," 41 Michigan L.Rev. 1037 (1943).

Meltzer, "Organizational Picketing and the NLRB: Five on a See Saw," 30 Univ.Chicago L.Rev. 78 (1962).

Lesnick, "The Gravamen of the Secondary Boycott," 62 Columbia L.Rev. 1363 (1962).

Levin, "Wholly Unconcerned: The Scope and Meaning of the Ally Doctrine Under Section 8(b)4 of the NLRA," 119 Univ.Penn.L. Rev. 383 (1970).

Note, "Labor Picketing and Commercial Speech: Free Enterprise Values in the Doctrine of Free Speech," 91 Yale L.J. 938 (1982).

Chapter V

REGULATING THE NATURE OF UNION MANAGEMENT RELATIONS

Part I. Company Unions and Illegal Assistance

A. The Basic Statutory Concept

Section 8(a)(2) of the Act, by making it an unfair labor practice for an employer "to dominate or interfere with the formation of any labor organization or contribute financial or other support to it," seems to require that unions be independent, and that the relationship of a labor organization to the employer be one of strict separation, essentially adversarial in nature. The language thus suggests a commitment to traditional collective bargaining as the only appropriate relationship between employer and employee. In large part, this language reflects the concern of organized labor at the time the Wagner Act was passed that management could, through the device of company unions or through the granting of special benefits to preferred organizations, provide employees with the appearance of representation, while preserving employer control. "Collective bargaining becomes a mockery when the spokesman of the employees is the marionette of the employer." [1]

The term "company union" grew out of the effort during the period between the two world wars by various management officials to develop an alternative to collective bargaining in an attempt to forestall unionization. This concept led to the installation of "representation plans," "shop committees," and "communications programs"; all initiated by management, which played a significant part in their operation. The jurisdiction and power of the organizations that implemented these programs was typically quite limited. They acted to "advise" management, which retained the power of ultimate decision making. Such schemes were bitterly derided by unions and their supporters. It was the diversity of such schemes that led to the broad language of section 8(a)(2), the drafters of which recognized that the concept of a company union is an amorphous one, difficult to define. There are many types of organization that come within the area of statutory concern. On the other hand, it is not true that all unions that are limited to employees of a single employer are "company unions." Similarly, the concept of improper assistance is vague and hard to separate from the gains a union hopes to achieve through collective bargaining within the generally accepted connotations of the term. A strong union will obtain benefits through collective bargain-

306

ing such as union security arrangements, use of company premises, or union referral systems, all of which come within the literal language of section 8(a)(2). It is also the case that independent unions have been known to enter into so-called "sweetheart contracts" whereby the interests of the employees are sacrificed to advance those of the union leadership. As a result of the breadth of the problem and the lack of common understanding of its boundaries, Congress chose to use broad general language designed to prevent both company unions and sweetheart contracts while specifically mentioning neither.

B. The Components of Illegal Assistance

1. The Concept of Labor Organization

Crucial to application of section 8(a)(2) is the presence of a "labor organization." The term is defined by section 2(15) as "[A]ny organization of any kind or any agency, scheme, committee or plan in which employees participate and which exists for the purpose in whole or in part of dealing with employers concerning grievances, labor disputes, wages, rates of pay, hours of employment or conditions of work." The language employed makes clear that the concept of a labor organization is intended to be far broader than that of a union. Schemes or plans that are not called unions, which do not involve collective bargaining, strikes, or the settlement of grievance, may still constitute labor organizations.

The Supreme Court dealt with the meaning of this language in *NLRB v. Cabot Carbon Co.*[2] The employer in that case had set up a system of employee committees that met regularly with management "to consider and discuss problems of mutual interest." The Board held the committees to be dominated labor organizations, and the Supreme Court affirmed, stressing that the term "dealing with" should not be read as "synonymous with the more limited term 'bargaining with.'"

The Board, until recently, followed the Supreme Court's approach in *Cabot Carbon.* Systems under which employees were grouped together in order to discuss or act upon matters within the language of section 8(a)(2) were found to be labor organizations. However, as is discussed below, the courts of appeals have for some time rejected this approach and more recently the Board has done so as well.

2. Domination

The Board distinguishes domination from other forms of proscribed employer involvement with a labor organization. A finding that a labor organization is dominated is equivalent to finding it a company union whose primary allegiance is to the employer rather than to the employees, and which functions to give the appearance of representation while maintaining control in the employer. When the Board determines that a labor organization is dominated, it will order it "disestablished," which means that the employer is forbidden from ever bargaining, recognizing, or dealing with the organization.[3] This remedy, which denies the possibility of reform, is obviously meant to totally eliminate the dominated entity.

The theory of disestablishment must be based on the idea that the element of coercion is so built into the structure of a dominated labor organization that no simple change in structure or behavior could cure it. While the remedy is obviously intended to be an extremely powerful one, its potency turns to a considerable extent on the way in which the Board's order is interpreted and enforced. This depends upon how likely it is that the Board will find a new program or newly established employee organization is in reality the dominated or tainted labor organization under a new name.

In *Duro Test Corp.,*[4] the Board recognized the possibility of a lawful independent entity being established following the disestablishment of a dominated organization. The test is whether there is a "line of fracture" between the two organizations, which involves a clear disavowal, a break in time, and changes in structure and leadership. The concept of a "line of fracture" like most legal metaphors is easier to visualize than employ, and the question of when it occurs has not been a major problem only because it has rarely been addressed.

The distinction between domination and lesser forms of violation is far from clear. The Board has defined a dominated labor organization as one whose "organization is directly instigated and encouraged or directly participated in by supervisors or other managerial employees and the employer provides financial or other direct support to the organization."[5] Despite this definition, however, the degree of employer involvement in the formation of a labor organization necessary for domination is unclear. The fact that the employer expresses approval is not enough, nor is an employer suggestion that is then acted upon independently. Indeed, such expressions would seem to be exercises of the employer's first amendment rights and within the scope of section 8(c). The hallmark of domination is significant supervisory involvement. However, not all supervisory involvement constitutes domination. The line between illegal and legal supervisory involvement is a hazy one, as is the distinction between involvement that constitutes illegal domination and that which constitutes illegal support. The opinions in cases in which domination is found frequently involve little more than the listing of factors followed by a characterization of domination.[6]

3. Illegal Support

Illegal assistance falling short of domination is generally characterized as unlawful "support." Where such illegal support is found, the

Board does not issue a disestablishment order; it will, however, invariably order the employer to cease recognizing the improperly assisted labor organization until such time as the coercive effects of the illegal behavior have been expunged.   Illegal support takes many forms, reflecting the various policies that section 8(a)(2) helps to police.   Common forms of illegal support include any direct financial contribution by the employer to an incumbent union, the bestowal of benefits such as the use of company resources or facilities upon one of two unions, the granting of recognition at a point at which a union is not legally entitled to it, and the inclusion in a collective agreement of an invalid union security arrangement.

In *ILGWU v. NLRB*,[7] the Supreme Court held that a grant of recognition by an employer to a minority union violated section 8(a)(2) even if undertaken in the good faith belief that the union had a majority support.   In such cases, a violation will be found and a *Resnick* (derecognition) remedy applied, despite the wishes of the employees at the time the charge is filed or the remedy imposed.   The purpose of imposing such a remedy is obviously to keep it from being worthwhile for a union to seek recognition before it achieves majority status.   The risk in such cases is that the employer will not adequately contest the violation since section 8(a)(2) is a company violation but the remedy is one that punishes the union.   In such cases, the union involved is usually named as a party in the NLRB complaint and can defend its own interest in the event the employer is less than fully committed to defending the charges.

C. The Legitimation of Company Involvement: Support v. Cooperation

The question that has provoked the greatest amount of scholarly comment and that has received the most careful judicial attention concerns the extent to which section 8(a)(2) freezes labor relations into an adversarial mold, outlawing everything other than the choice between total managerial discretion and formal collective bargaining. Does the Act recognize a distinction between company unions and job enrichment, between efforts to thwart employee choice and programs to improve communication?   If such distinctions exist, what are their statutory manifestations, and what are the standards that govern their application?   While none of those questions have yet been answered, the law in this area shows steady movement toward greater permissiveness.   Several of the courts of appeals have steadfastly refused to apply section 8(a)(2) literally despite the Supreme Court's decision in *Cabot Carbon*.   They have developed a series of analytic techniques for limiting its application.   These include a judicially created distinction between support and cooperation, a requirement that the coercive effect be proved, a requirement of unlawful intent, and a judicial narrowing of the definition of labor organization.[8]   Several courts of appeals have taken the position that the concept of free choice should apply to the forms of organization held permissible. The Board in the past has taken a more restrictive and literal approach. However, the courts' opinions, together with criticism by scholars of the harmful effects of rigidly applying section 8(a)(2), has recently affected the Board, which has begun to apply section 8(a)(2) more narrowly.

The first significant opinion restricting the application of section 8(a)(2) was *Chicago Rawhide Mfg. Co. v. NLRB*,[9] in which the employer provided extensive assistance to employee committees, which were permitted to hold meetings on company premises and company time, and to post election notices on company bulletin boards. Time spent in committee meetings was compensated for by the employer. The Board found the committees to be dominated labor organizations.

The Court refused to enforce the Board's order on the grounds that the company had engaged only in permissible "cooperation," which the Court distinguished from illegal "support." It described the distinction in the following passage:

> " 'Support' is proscribed because, as a practical matter, it cannot be separated from influence. A line must be drawn, however, between support and cooperation. Support, even though innocent, can be identified because it constitutes at least some degree of control or influence. Cooperation only assists the employees or their bargaining representative in carrying out their independent intention. If this line between cooperation and support is not recognized, the employer's fear of accusations of domination may defeat the principal purpose of the Act, which is cooperation between management and labor. In this case the Board seems to have confused cooperation by the Company with the employees through the Employees Committees with improper domination interference and support."

In deciding that the employer had engaged only in permissible cooperation, the Court focused on the Board's failure to prove two things: first, that the employer intended to coerce the employees' choice of bargaining representative; second, that the employer, in fact, dominated the employer assistance committees: "Actual domination must be shown before a violation is established." The addition of these motive and effects tests, which have been frequently adopted by other courts, invites a complex factual determination in each case and substantially reduces the likelihood of finding a violation. If the structure once completed generally functions independently, actual domination is hard to show and any system that looks cooperative may be explained in terms of legitimate employer motive.

Chicago Rawhide was followed by a series of similar decisions in a variety of circuits including the First, Sixth, Seventh, and Ninth. The Sixth and Seventh being particularly adamant in rejecting the Board's approach. The requirement that the Board show actual rather than potential domination has been utilized in a variety of cases. Thus, in *Hotpoint Co. v. NLRB,*[10] the Court found that supervisory involvement in calling meetings and in shaping bylaws, together with the company providing office facilities, amounted only to "potential means of control."

In *Coppus Engineering Corp. v. NLRB,*[11] in finding illegal support and domination by the employer, the Board relied on the fact that the Employees' Shop Committee lacked provisions for membership of employees generally and was provided the use of company property and time for meetings. The Court refused enforcement, holding that the employer assistance provided "shows no more than cooperation by petitioner and a possibility of control," rather than illegal support itself. Judge Magruder's concurrence made clear the necessity of a finding of interference with the employees' free choice, as evidenced, for example, by employee dissatisfaction with the Shop Committee. He argued that although the Shop Committee seemed to have been feeble, "the choice was the employees', and the Act guarantees to them freedom to exercise that choice, unimpeded by employer interference or coercion."

In *Modern Plastics Corp. v. NLRB,*[12] the NLRB found a section 8(a)(2) violation in the company's support and domination of employee committees. The basis of its finding included the facts that the committee received no dues from its members, had no source of income, owned no property, and didn't operate under a constitution or bylaws. Members' meetings were held only infrequently; the committee held monthly meetings with the plant manager. Many grievances were settled with no committee participation, and the plant manager's secretary was involved in the mechanics of the election of committee members. The court cited a number of considerations in refusing to enforce the Board's finding. Among these considerations was that there was no showing of actual coercion and that the employees hadn't shown dissatisfaction with the committee itself or with the particular type of representation it provided. The court also indicated its reluctance to abort, through a finding of illegal support, the harmonious relation that it claimed existed between the employer and the employee committee.

The case that best illustrated the basic difference in approach between the Board and the courts was *Hertzka and Knowles v. NLRB.*[13] The case arose in the aftermath of a decertification election lost by a union that had been unable to negotiate an agreement with the employer. After the election, a meeting was held in which "five in-house committees were established to deal with 'professional stature—remuneration—minimum standards, efficiency and physical environment. Each committee was comprised of five employees and one management representative." The Board found domination and ordered the committee disestablished. The Court denied enforcement of this part of the Board's order. After pointing out that "[c]ourts have emphasized that there is a line between cooperation which the Act encourages and actual interference or domination," the court concluded that substantial evidence was not presented to show "that the employees' free choice either in type, organization or in the assertion of demands is stifled by the degree of employer involvement at issue."

Although the finding was cast in terms of evidence, the difference seems to be one of law, with the court rejecting the Board's assumption that substantial employer involvement in a labor organization constitutes domination within the meaning of the Act. The court's reliance on employee choice is implicitly based on the notion that if the employees are dissatisfied with the arrangement, they can petition for a "real" labor organization. These informal groups would not be a bar to any elections. The focus choice seems misplaced. Because the theory of 8(a)(2) is that such an organization prevents the expression of choice through the Board's regular processes.

The Board has not openly changed its approach, adopted the distinction between cooperation and support, or adopted the requirement that there be a showing of illegal motive or actual domination. Nevertheless, recent Board opinions in a variety of areas have responded to the judicial coolness toward section 8(a)(2) by requiring a greater degree of demonstrated hostility to unions before a violation is found. Without overruling any of its earlier precedent, the Board has begun to construe the statute to permit greater flexibility and to encourage experimentation with forms of employer-employee relations other than collective bargaining.[14]

D. Worker Participation and Section 8(a)(2)

1. Historical Background

The tendency to narrowly construe section 8(a)(2) was given impetus by the favorable publicity given to the concept of "worker participation" during the 1960s and 1970s. The concept was advertised as a technique for "democratizing the work place" and "restructuring the employment relationship." The term "worker participation" does not have a well-defined meaning. It has been applied to everything from informal grievance programs to semi-autonomous work teams. In general, however, there are four basic participation models: (a) the Italian–French model of participation through works councils; (b) the Swedish model of participation through reorganizing the production process to utilize teams of employees exercising considerable autonomy; (c) the German model of participation through election of worker representatives to corporate boards of directors; and (d) the Japanese model of participation through quality circles, meetings in which employees and management together discuss questions of quality, productivity, and personnel policy.[15]

All of these approaches have been experimented with to some extent in the United States, although the appointment of worker representatives on boards of directors has been used only rarely. In part this is because corporate structures vary between the United States and Europe and partly because the labor movement that spearheaded this idea in Europe has been ambivalent or negative about it in the United States. Generally the major difference between U.S. and European approaches is that in Europe participation programs tend to be operated in coordination with trade unions whereas in the United States they have primarily been utilized in non-unionized enterprises. The major exception is quality circles, which have been utilized as a joint union-management technique particularly in the automobile industry, where their role is limited to avoid interfering with contractually established standards and the grievance system.

2. Legal Issues

Almost all worker participation programs are suspect in theory and analytically vulnerable to a finding that they are labor organizations. Their approach is to give workers a collective voice in running an enterprise under conditions set and subject to change or elimination by management. The theory of section 8(a)(2) has historically been that only a system of worker participation independently established and not subject to unilateral elimination or alteration by management thereafter is meaningful. Many unions are concerned that work teams and participation programs will lull workers into believing that traditional collective bargaining would be superfluous. Thus to many in the union movement, worker participation programs pose a new variation of the threat historically posed by company unions. Moreover, the breadth of the language used in section 8(a)(2) reflects the fact that historically, company unions and participation plans had a common theory, similar goals, and were indistinguishable in practice. The term "labor organization" applies to an "organization of any kind, or any agency or employee representation committee or plan in which employees participate." It would be difficult to argue that worker participation programs do not constitute a "plan in which employees participate." Therefore, section 8(a)(2) would seem to apply whenever worker participation programs exist for the purpose in whole or in part of dealing with employers.

For most forms of worker participation, interaction with the employer is a crucial part of the process. The extent to which work teams in practice deal with management varies. Some have involved frequent meetings in which worker ideas are approved or rejected, but in other programs, particularly those modeled on the "Volvo" system, the work teams function almost autonomously within the sphere assigned to them. It is arguable that the inevitable managerial veto over employee decisions, particularly if exercised regularly, together with the fact that management establishes the team and sets its limits and usually engages in constant discussion with the team or its leader constitutes "dealing".[16] Certainly such a definition would be consistent with *Cabot Carbon.*

The possibility that application of section 8(a)(2) would limit experiments with worker participation has been the subject of considerable scholarly concern since the 1960s. Until recently, most of the writing has decried the possibility that section 8(a)(2) would impose rigid boundaries on U.S. labor relations, imposing a 30's type model on attempts at cooperative systems. However, as already noted, the trend of the case law gives little reason for worry on this score. Decisions by the courts of appeals, narrowing the definition of labor organizations, have exemplified the courts' concern that section 8(a)(2) might unduly limit the nature of labor management relations. The decision that most strongly points in this direction is *NLRB v. Steamway Div. of Scott & Fetzer Co.,*[17] in which the employees established an "in-plant representation committee" that involved regular meetings between management officials and elected employee representatives for the purpose of making suggestions concerning grievances and working conditions. The Sixth Circuit, virtually limiting *Cabot Carbon* to its particular facts, concluded that the committee was not a labor organization. The court distinguished *Cabot Carbon* on the grounds that it "involved a more active ongoing association between management and employees which the term dealing connotes than is present here." The opinion by Judge Engle also relied upon the short terms of the elected representatives, which created an "individual" rather than a "representative" basis in their discussions with management, and the absence of anti-union animus, a factor which had not previously been required and that was also absent in *Cabot Carbon.* In a passage with considerable implication for future construction of section 8(a)(2), the court stressed the fact that the committee did not "resemble a 'labor organization' in the ordinary sense of the term."

The opinion is laden with questionable analytic and historic statements. Characterizing meetings of a formally structured representation committee as "individual" dealing is a feat of linquistic interpretation available only to those for whom an outcome rather than language is the standard. Moreover, the legislative history, broad language, and traditional interpretation of section 8(a)(2) have all heretofore made clear that resemblance to a traditional union is irrelevant, as is employer motive. It is clear that the court was straining the language in order to avoid the conclusion implicit in *Cabot Carbon* that section 8(a)(2) limits employer ability to communicate directly with its employees in innovative and non-adversarial ways. As Judge Engle put it, "the adversarial model of labor relations is an anachronism." The clearest statement of the industrial relations policy that undergirds opinions such as *Scott & Fetzer* is contained in the dissent by Judge Wisdom in *NLRB v. Walton Mfg. Co.*,[18] which is quoted at length by the majority in *Scott & Fetzer:* "To my mind an inflexible attitude of hostility toward employee committees defeats the Act. It erects an iron curtain between employers and employees . . . preventing the development of a decent, honest constructive relationship between management and labor."

That the Board, too, has been moved by the combination of critical praise for worker participation programs and criticisms of the Act's inflexibility is suggested by the handling of the one case in which the Board dealt with the status of semi-autonomous work teams under section 8(a)(2).[19] The case involved the highly publicized "Pet Foods" plan under which employee work teams were established that made job assignments, prepared work schedules, and met with management to discuss grievances and working conditions. The administrative law judge found that the teams were not labor organizations. He justified this conclusion in part on the astounding grounds that the system had been initiated "for reasons quite apart from labor relations." Presumably this is an attempt to separate the goal of increased productivity from labor relations, a futile effort as shown by his further conclusion that team meetings served as "occasions for management to communicate directly with its employees and vice versa." He also made much of the fact that the teams were not established in response or in order to thwart an organizational drive, and that the team organization was unlike that of a union in part because all members participated in the program and therefore there was no element of representation by the team. The Board affirmed both the conclusion and its reasoning. Once again, the earnestness of the effort to legitimate is more impressive than the reasoning.

Similarly, the Board has restricted the definition of labor organization in order to permit flexibility in the area of academic representation. It has held that a faculty senate is not a labor organization because it makes only "recommendations," not bargaining demands.

It is perhaps worth noting that scholarly enthusiasm with worker participation outside the union sector may be waning. Recent articles have pointed out that such programs tend to be short-lived, that they rarely lead to significant change, and that they are often instituted primarily to prevent unionization. Commentators have begun to question the wisdom of the courts lessening commitment to collective bargaining.[20] Perhaps such criticism will lead to greater willingness to apply section 8(a)(2) in the future.

In any case, neither the device of the company union nor the development of employee participation programs is likely to play a major role in preventing union organization. Such programs are generally costly to management and, as a result, are not frequently adopted. Their value as a union avoidance technique is questionable. They provide a target for some unions, an opportunity for take over in other circumstances—they are not always easy to control—and by their very weakness may put employees in mind that they need a more powerful and independent representation.

Part II. The Duty of Neutrality

A. The *Midwest Piping* Doctrine

1. The Basic Doctrine

The courts have been willing to apply section 8(a)(2) to situations in which an employer has given help to one union that it has refused to give to its rival. Where two unions compete for employee support, the employer is required to treat both unions neutrally. He may express a preference, but he may not grant benefits to one union or its supporters that he denies to the other. The courts have been less willing to apply section 8(a)(2) in situations in which the improper aid has taken the form of granting recognition to one of the competing unions. In a situation involving two competing unions, the Board, under its *Midwest Piping* doctrine,[21] has historically required the employer to withhold recognition even where the union recognized had majority support that it was able to demonstrate. Essentially the doctrine required an employer to withhold or withdraw recognition when "faced with conflicting claims of two or more rival unions which give rise to a real question concerning representation. . . ." In this formulation of the doctrine, a "question concerning representation" is a term of art derived from section 9(c)(1) of the act which provides that the Board may direct an election after a hearing "if the Board finds upon the record of such hearing that . . . a question of representation exists." In representation proceedings, the Board uses the terms "question of representation" and "question concerning representation" interchangeably. Therefore, in every election there has been a prior determination that a question concerning representation exists.

The Board did not explain its decision to make the doctrine coextensive with the existence of a question concerning representation. Such an approach did, however, simplify the Board's task in deciding whether or not to apply the doctrine. Moreover, the approach was consistent with the Board's underlying view that the purpose of the doctrine is to protect the integrity of the Board's election processes.

The courts that had accepted the Board's verbal formulation of the doctrine in terms of the existence of a question concerning representation used the term to signify a situation in which the employer is ignorant of the wishes of his employees. As a result, many Board decisions applying the doctrine were reversed when brought to the courts for enforcement. The courts have accepted the *Midwest Piping* doctrine solely as a technique for preventing the employer from imposing his own choice of a bargaining representative upon his employees.[22]

2. Application of the *Midwest Piping* Doctrine to Negotiation of an Agreement With an Incumbent Union

In 1954, in *William D. Gibson Co.*,[23] the Board created an exception to the *Midwest Piping* doctrine to meet the case where an employer contracted with an incumbent union in the face of a rival claim. This exception was overruled without discussion in *Shea Chemical Corp.*[24] The *Shea Chemical* doctrine lasted from 1958 until 1981. The closest the Board has ever come to an explanation was when it adopted the language of the trial examiner in the *St. Louis Independent Packing Co.* case:[25] "The situation is no different where one of the competing unions has been the incumbent bargaining representative of the employees involved. The right of employees to change their bargaining representative carries no less dignity in the statutory scheme than their right to choose in the first instance between unions competing for representative status."

The Board has recently, over strong dissent, substantially amended the *Midwest Piping* doctrine. In *RCA del Caribe*,[26] the Board returned to the *Gibson* doctrine holding that an employer need not withdraw recognition from an incumbent union. The Board majority simply reversed one of the justifying assumptions of *Shea Chemical* and concluded that withdrawal of recognition might signal to the employees that the employer favors a change, a signal the Board had traditionally concluded would somehow corrupt the process. The significance of employer signaling is far from obvious given that the employer has the right to state his preference unequivocally. Presumably, signaling behavior is somehow more coercive than direct expression, but the Board has never explained why. The Board in *RCA* also justified its return to *Gibson* by virtue of the strong presumption of continuing majority status that under Board doctrine is accorded to an incumbent union.

In *Grossman*,[27] the Board further narrowed the reach of the *Midwest Piping* doctrine in the context of initial organizing by holding that absent other factors the duty to refrain from recognition did not attach until a petition was filed, rather than at the point at which rival claims were known. Those decisions have brought the Board closer to the approach generally taken by the courts.

The one part of the *Midwest Piping* doctrine about which the Board and the courts apparently still disagree concerns the situation in which the employer recognizes a union after a petition is filed, based upon convincing proof of its majority status. If, as it has suggested, the Board continues to find a violation in such situations, the courts presumably will continue to reject that conclusion.

Part III. The Legal Significance of Supervisory Participation in the Organization and Functioning of a Legitimate Labor Organization

A. The Basic Concepts

One of the classic features of a company union was the key role of low-level supervisory personnel acting on behalf of management. Such employees played a dual role, serving both as the primary vehicle for managerial control and as a symbol of the nonadversarial nature of the organization. Supervisory prominence is thus a common feature of blatantly manipulative company-dominated systems. But supervisory involvement may have other, less sinister, significance. In some industries, particularly construction, supervisors typically maintain a strong sense of identification with the rank and file. Their continuing involvement with a union gives it status and power. Sometimes supervisors who become active in the union do not consider themselves a part of management in any meaningful way. Moreover, the frequently noted ambiguous status of low-level supervisors makes them ideally suited to play a key role in a labor organization committed to the concept of cooperative relations, serving as a means by which management can be informed of the needs of employees, and employees can be made to understand the legitimate claims of management. That a hazy line, at best, may be drawn between such a cooperative role and the manipulative role associated with the traditional company union should be apparent. The appropriate characterization may turn more on delicate questions of motive and self-perception than on the supervisor's status job or role in the union. Does the supervisor see herself primarily as a spokeswoman for the employees or as an agent of management? Does management intend to utilize the supervisor to prevent the union from taking positions furthering the interests of the employees at the expense of the employers? The issue posed of distinguishing legitimate from illegitimate use of supervision is obviously quite similar to and often is an aspect of the effort to distinguish cooperation from improper support.

Thus in general, the division between the Board and the courts and the difference among the circuits in dealing with that issue are paralleled in their treatment of the role of the supervisors.

B.   Evaluating Supervisory Participation in Union Affairs

Both the Board and the courts hold that low-level supervisors may participate in some union affairs without violating section 8(a)(2). However, the standards by which such behavior is judged are unclear. In general, the Board looks to a series of variables in making a determination. These include: the level of supervision, the nature of the industry, the nature of the employer's operation, whether such supervisors have historically been represented by the union, and the nature of the union activity in which the supervisors engage. The seminal case concerning supervisory involvement in the administration of a labor union is *Nassau and Suffolk Contractor's Association.*[28] There master mechanics (low-level supervisors) attended union meetings, voted on matters of union business, and served on the union's collective bargaining committee. Several officers and high-level supervisors of the employer who had retained their union memberships also attended the meetings and voted on issues of union administration.

Acknowledging that supervisory involvement in union affairs often creates employer liability, the Board nevertheless stated that in certain instances a supervisor may be "acting in his individual rather than in his representative capacity," and that the employer cannot be held responsible for such actions. Because of the longstanding tradition of including master mechanics in the bargaining unit, as well as the perception of the mechanics as loyal union supporters, the Board found no section 8(a)(2) violation. The Board indicated that there would be a violation only if the employer instigated or ratified the mechanics' activities, or if the employer somehow led the rank and file to believe that the supervisors were acting on behalf of the management.

The employer's officers and high-level supervisors, however, were found to have interfered with the administration of the union by voting in the union elections. The Board said that while it "may not be unlawful for company executives and high-ranking supervisors to retain the union membership they acquired as rank-and-file employees, that does not make it lawful for them to participate in elections to determine who is to administer the affairs of the union."

The Board also found a violation based on the master mechanics' role on the union negotiating committee, the Board held such activity unlawful assistance under section 8(a)(2):

> "[E]mployees have the right to be represented in collective-bargaining negotiations by individuals who have a singleminded loyalty to their interests. Conversely, an employer is under a duty to refrain from any action which will interfere with that employee's rights and place him even in a slight degree on both sides of the bargaining table."

Though the Board in other parts of the decision stressed the master mechanics' loyalty to the union, it here stated that even those low-level supervisors "remain in part agents of their employers with a resulting divided loyalty and interests."

The right of supervisors to engage in various types of union activity has been frequently questioned. Such issues as (a) membership in the union, (b) attendance at union meetings, (c) voting on union issues, and (d) holding union office have all been dealt with by the Board and the courts.

Although the court's *Nassau and Suffolk* opinion stated that a high-level supervisor may retain membership, this permission has not always been granted when the circumstance otherwise suggested improper management support. Thus, in *The Brescome Distributors Corp.,*[29] the trial examiner, whose findings were upheld by the Board, found that "[t]he continued membership in the Association of two supervisors, one of whom . . . was an officer in the organization, would necessarily serve to emphasize the status of the Association as an agency favored by the Respondent." The trial examiner stated that "where such supervisory activity has been held permissible, the involvement has not only been on a limited basis, but has had a normal relation to a union which represented the supervisor in respect to his own working conditions." Since the supervisors at issue in *Brescome* made their own individual contracts concerning working conditions, the trial examiner felt justified in finding interference based on their membership alone. *The Brescome Distributors Corp.* case also found unlawful interference in the presence of supervisors at an important straw vote. In general, such activity has not been enough to sustain a charge of interference with the administration of a labor union. In *Stahl–Meyer, Inc.,*[30] a chief engineer who was a member of the union "took no part whatsoever in any union activity during the period of his employment except to attend occasional meetings and speak from the floor on general matters." He never voted, held union office, or became involved in contract negotiation. Without even deciding whether the engineer was a supervisor, the trial examiner dismissed the charge because no possible violation could be predicated upon the engineer's actions. To hold to the contrary, he determined, "would be to read the first clause of section 14(a) out of the statute."

1. Voting

No generally accepted rule regarding supervisors voting on union affairs has emerged. *Nassau and Suffolk* has been subject to various interpretations on this issue, and the only part of the issue that has been resolved is that very high-ranking supervisors and executives may not vote on union affairs and that voting by low-level supervisors may be one factor considered in determining whether a violation was committed.

In *Banner Yarn Dyeing Corp.,*[31] however, it was held that a supervisor who was within the bargaining unit could vote in all union elections unless the voting was instigated by his employer or the voting led employees to believe that the supervisor was acting on behalf of management. The Board determined the general rule to be that supervisors who were members of the unit could vote, while those outside the unit, even if members of the union, could not.

The *National Gypsum*[32] case added an additional test based upon the level of authority held by the supervisor at issue. Voting by those who exercised "managerial functions" was held improper. The reason given by the Board for distinguishing high-level supervisors from low-level ones is the same one given in *Nassau and Suffolk*—that in a close vote, high-level supervisory involvement in effect allows the supervisors to choose those union representatives that they will deal with in their roles as agents of the employer.

2. Being Active in Union Affairs

The determination of whether unlawful interference results from low-level supervisors holding union office is made on a case-by-case basis. High-level supervisors may not hold union offices.

Supervisors also will be found guilty of interference with the administration of the union's affairs any time their union office results in an actual conflict of interest. Thus in *Narragansett Restaurant Corp.,*[33] where a supervisor served as a union steward and also aided the employer in the maintenance of a quota system for union and non-union personnel, a violation was found.

As the discussion above suggests, the Board has responded to the competing considerations by proceeding on a case-by-case, situation-by-situation basis in judging the legitimacy of supervisory involvement. The courts of appeals have generally gone along. However, a recent opinion by Judge Winter of the Second Circuit suggested that the Board has not adequately appreciated the potential for coercion in situations in which supervisors play a role in the day-to-day running of a labor organization:

> "Supervisors as a class have interests of their own and an organization which is itself governed in part by supervisors will tend to reflect at least in part those interests. For example, the authority of supervisors vis a vis rank and file employees is usually a major issue in collective bargaining. An organization in which supervisors play a significant governing role will have difficulty in isolating and reflecting only the views of the rank and file on that issue. Staff of the professional organization who are employed at the pleasure of a board of directors containing supervisors cannot

easily cast aside the knowledge that supervisory employees have a say in their own employment when they advise employees on bargaining positions and negotiate on their behalf. Moreover, it is tunnel vision to assume that this influence will be of importance only when a supervisor of employees in a particular unit is a member of the board of directors of the certified bargaining representative." [34]

The court also rejected the Board's claim that it could determine whether actual interference occurred on a case-by-case basis: "evidence of explicit interference in collective bargaining of the kind demanded by the Board may not be available even in cases in which the structure of a professional organization leads to a pervasive supervisory influence." This opinion puts into question the legal status under the act of professional associations in many fields which have historically included supervisors and rank and file with little or no distinction.

3. The Nature of the Industry

Nassau and Suffolk and several other leading cases involved the building trades, but the rules set forth in them have been applied to various other industries. The Board and the courts occasionally refer to construction cases as "special." Nevertheless, the application of section 8(a)(2) does not depend upon the industry but upon the factors discussed in the previous section, which vary from industry to industry. In *Nassau and Suffolk,* the Board stated that "in quite a number of industries foremen are members of the same union and are included in the same bargaining contract as rank-and-file production workers. This is particularly true in building trades." Later, in discussing why a case-by-case analysis of supervisory involvement was necessary, the Board said, "Certainly in the printing, publishing, and construction industries, where the inclusion of foremen in rank-and-file units and unions is a practice of long-standing, employers would ridicule the idea that they dominate or interfere with the administration of such union because some of their foremen may be active within the union's administration.[35]

Part IV. Assistance Through Collective Bargaining

A. Union Security and Dues Checkoff

A proviso to section 8(a)(3) specifically legalizes:

"making any agreement with a labor organization . . . to require as a condition of employment membership therein on or after the thirtieth day following the beginning of such employment or the effective date of such agreement whichever is the latter. . . . Provided further that no employer shall justify any discrimination against an employee for non-membership in a labor organization if . . . he has reasonable grounds for believing that membership was terminated for reasons other than failure of the employee to tender the periodic dues and initiation fees uniformly required as a condition of acquiring or retaining membership."

The stated purpose of the proviso, which contravenes both the policy of section 8(a)(2) and the policy against discrimination on the basis of union activity, was to permit unions to deal with the problem of "free riding," i.e., employees who obtain the benefits of union representation without paying for it. The decision to permit such an exception was sufficiently controversial that Congress in section 14(b), included by the Taft–Hartley Amendments, permitted states to prohibit such agreements, and Congress also initially provided that such agreements had to be authorized by a majority vote of the affected employees. This latter provision was quickly dropped at the instance of employers, who were its initial supporters. It turned out that the authorization votes, which were disruptive in terms of time spent and sentiment stirred, were overwhelmingly favorable to the inclusion of such clauses. These results reflected the strength of employee sentiment in unionized enterprises concerning free riding, and they gave great impetus to the unions' claim.

Section 14(b) giving jurisdiction to the states has been far more significant and lasting. Twenty states now have laws prohibiting the type of union security arrangements permitted by the proviso. (In some of these "right to work" states the union is permitted to charge an "agency fee" whereby non-members are required to pay to cover the costs of collective bargaining.) It is not clear how important such laws have been. Early studies suggested that they have little or no impact on union membership or power, but these studies have recently been subject to sophisticated methodological criticism and the validity of their findings is subject to doubt.

Wherever union security agreements are legal, unions will invariably seek to obtain them, together with a "checkoff" provision whereby dues are automatically deducted from the employees' pay. Most employers are willing to grant a checkoff provision. It is an easy way to demonstrate willingness to deal fairly with the union, and its institution prevents the disruption that might result from union efforts to collect dues during working time. Employers who are strongly opposed to unions may resist the checkoff on the grounds that they do not intend to be a "collection agency" for the union, but it is rare for this attitude to prevail over the course of bargaining. More resistance is encountered with respect to union security. Some employers have a strong ideological resistance to forcing anti-union employees to join up. Many think of this as selling out the company's "loyal supporters" during the organizational campaign. Also, denying such clauses to the union may weaken the union financially and perhaps cause dissension. Thus an employer who strongly opposes unions may resist and perhaps even take a strike over this issue. For most employers, however, it is a proposal that because of the strength of the union's desire, can be used to obtain provisions that management feels strongly about, such as a broad no-strike or management-rights clause. Acceptance of a union security clause is a good way to acquire the good will of union officials, and this is not a minor benefit for an employer.

B. The Use of Funds Obtained Under Union Security Clauses

In a series of cases culminating in *C.W.A. v. Beck* [35a] the Supreme Court has limited the use to which unions might put funds obtained from non-members by virtue of union security clauses. The effect of these decisions is to require unions to rebate to those who elect not to become members, that proportion of their dues used for purposes other than collective bargaining. The series began with *Abood v. Detroit Board of Education* [36] in which the Supreme Court held that a state could not constitutionally permit a public sector union to collect from objecting agency-fee payers that portion of union dues that was not allocable to collective bargaining. The Court in its opinion accepted the conclusion that any forced payment for causes and purposes to which the employee objected to some extent interfered with first amendment rights. The Court held that such interference was acceptable only so long as it was undertaken for purposes of collective bargaining.

In *Ellis v. Brotherhood of Railways, Airline and Steamship Clerks,* [37] the Supreme Court dealt similarly with the question of which activities could be charged to dissenting employees under the Railway Labor Act. Although it found an acceptable scheme provided for in the Act, the Court based on constitutional principles its conclusion that dissenting employees could be charged only for those activities "necessarily or reasonably incurred for the purposes of performing the duties of exclusive representation." The Court also found inadequate the system whereby the union deducted the full amount of the dues and then refunded to the agency-fee payer an amount based on the percentage of dues money spent on matters other than collective bargaining, because "the union obtains an involuntary loan for purposes to which the employee objects."

The general standard of relationship to collective bargaining was made more specific in the *Ellis* opinion through application to five specific areas of union activity: organizing, litigation, conventions, social activities, and publications.

The Court concluded that general organizing expenses were not properly chargeable to dissenters. Justice White's opinion stated that where a union security agreement was in force, "by definition organizing expenses are spent on employees outside the collective bargaining unit already represented. Using dues exacted from an objecting employee to recruit members among workers outside the bargaining unit can afford only the most attenuated benefits to collective bargaining on behalf of the dues payer." In a footnote, the Court dealt with efforts to organize the agency-fee payers themselves, and it concluded that "it would be perverse [to allow] the union to charge objecting nonmembers part of the costs of attempting to convince them to become members." Justice White's opinion does not deal with the cost of activity directed to maintaining the allegiance of current members.

The Court stated that the expenses of litigation "incident to negotiating and administering the contract or to settling grievance and disputes arising in the bargaining unit are clearly chargeable." Litigation not so tied to the interests of the bargaining unit, such as the union's challenge to the airline industry's mutual aid pact, was held to be non-chargeable.

The Court held that the expenses of the union's national convention were totally chargeable. It noted that at conventions "unions establish bargaining goals and priorities and formulate overall union policy." It quoted with approval the court of appeals conclusion that such activities "guide the union's approach to collective bargaining." Similarly, the cost of union social activities were held chargeable in their entirety on the grounds that while "not central to the collective bargaining they are sufficiently related because they bring about harmonious working relationships, promote closer ties among employees and create a more pleasant environment for union meetings." The Court's treatment of these categories is noteworthy because it was willing to classify them as totally chargeable without requiring that they be analyzed more minutely to determine whether they included non-chargeable components. It is almost inevitable, for example, that conventions include discussion of organizing and highly likely that they will involve some partisan political activity. This approach is in marked contrast with that taken with regard to union publications. The Court accepted the legitimacy of charging agency-fee payers with the cost of "communicating with the employees, including the objecting ones"; but it insisted that objectors could not be charged for writing about activities such as political caucuses and organizing for which it could not charge directly.

Thus, in the course of a brief opinion, the Court took a variety of different approaches construing the concept of collective bargaining: narrowly in some areas and broadly in others; requiring that a system of specific allocation be employed for some activities but not for others; apparently tying the chargeability of some expenditures but not others to their connection with the employee's bargaining unit. The opinion did not purport to lay down precise guidelines for determining the chargeability of all union activities. Such major areas as lobbying, administration, general advertising, and education programs are not even discussed.

While there is no explanation given for requiring greater precision with regard to litigation and publication expenses than for such items as convention expenditures, such activities may be differentiated on the grounds of their connection to first amendment concerns. Publication is the union activity most directly connected to the expression of ideas and litigation to the advocacy of causes.

The task facing unions after *Ellis,* to develop a workable scheme for determining the percentage of dues for which agency-fee payers were responsible that would pass Constitutional scrutiny, was a formidable one. First, they were required to analyze expenditures in such a way as to permit them to determine which categories were chargeable. Second, they had to develop a technique for resolving disputes with agency-fee payers without undergoing a process of continual federal court litigation over this issue. Unions with many agency-fee payers were aware that such groups as the "Right to Work Foundation," which opposes the concept of involuntary unionism or anything related to it, are ready to underwrite judicial challenges to their processes and determinations. Many unions attempted to develop schemes by which neutral arbitrators would have the final say in the process. Some hired established arbitrators to analyze their expenditures and make the necessary allocations; others established hearing panels of well-recognized neutrals to rule on objections to their determinations. In *Chicago Teachers Union Local No. 1 v. Hudson,*[38] the Supreme Court passed upon the constitutionality of one such effort. The union in that case made its own determination of the amount chargeable. Thereafter, the agency-fee payers could challenge the assessment through a series of steps, the final one of which was a hearing before an arbitrator selected by the union president from a list maintained by the Illinois Board of Education. The Court found this process inadequate. Its concern for the importance of the interests implicated in union security arrangements was repeatedly stressed. "First, although the government interest in labor peace is strong enough to support an 'agency shop,' notwithstanding its limited infringement on nonunion employees' constitutional rights, the fact that those rights are protected by the first amendment requires that the procedure be carefully tailored to minimize the infringement." The Court opinion emphasized this point by quoting Madison and Jefferson. Justice Stevens concluded: "The amount at stake for each individual dissenter does not diminish this concern. For whatever the amount the quality of respondents' interest in not being compelled to subsidize the propagation of political or ideological views that they oppose is clear."

The strength of the first amendment interests involved led the Court to insist that any process meet three requirements. First, that the amount initially deducted be calculated to correspond to the amount actually chargeable. Second, that dissenting members had to be given enough "information about the basis for the proportionate share . . . to gauge the propriety of the union's fee." Third, the union must "provide for a reasonably prompt decision by an impartial decisionmaker." The Court found the process developed by the union inadequate in all three areas. In particular, it announced that "review by a Union-selected arbitrator is also inadequate because the selection represents the Union's unrestricted choice. . . ."

The problem of developing adequate procedures that are monetarily feasible has occupied considerable effort by public sector unions since the *Hudson* decision. The easiest of the tasks is likely to be obtaining an impartial hearing officer. Some state laws have been amended to provide such a service, and the American Arbitration Association working with the affected unions has developed a special, expedited procedure for choosing arbitrators selected by the association as qualified in such cases. Such problems such as whether the union should pay for the arbitrator remain, but the basic scheme seems likely to pass muster. More difficult to determine is how much information the union must provide when it first establishes a proportionate share. Both the process of calculation and the process of allocation are complex. Their explication to be understandable would require a lengthy document, and even then the adequacy of the union's investigation and the integrity of its determinations could not easily be established. Thus it is likely that a long process of litigation to refine the standards set forth in *Hudson* will be necessary.

The opinions dealing with public sector and Railway Labor unions did not apply directly to the National Labor Relations Act, but in *C.W.A. v. Beck* the Court held that the principles of *Street* and *Ellis* controlled the interpretation of the proviso to section 8(a)(3). The Court concluded that the reach of the proviso permitting union security was limited by its purpose, which was to permit unions to charge those employees who obtain the benefits of collective bargaining with their share of its cost. Thus employees who chose not to be members could not be required to help finance other union activity. The Court did not base its conclusion on Constitutional grounds although it indicated that a contrary result would raise "serious doubts as to [its] constitutionality,". It focused instead on the ground that no basis existed for treating the N.L.R.A. differently from the other statutes which it had already interpreted to require rebates. Comparing section 8(a)(3) with section 2 Eleventh of the R.L.A. the Court concluded that "Given the parallel purpose structure and language of

8(a)(3) we must interpret that provision in the same manner." While the Court did not discuss the applicability of *Hudson* under the N.L. R.A. its reasoning indicated that all rights pertaining to union security, applicable to non members, under other statutes apply under the N.L. R.A. as well. Thus the difficult and time consuming processes of special book keeping, detailed explanations and impartial hearings to separate out collective bargaining from other union activities are now universally required whenever union security agreements are in force.

C. Union Hiring Halls

In industries such as construction and longshore where jobs are generally of short duration and the union is frequently the employee's permanent tie to the industry, it is common for unions to operate hiring halls through which employees sign up and obtain jobs with employers who contact the union for this purpose. The use of the union's referral service is often the best way for an employer to obtain skilled help quickly without running the risk of labor troubles. Collective agreements in such industries often specify that the union hiring hall shall be the exclusive source of labor for the jobs covered by it. It is well-settled law that referrals may not legally take into account union membership or activity. This is also generally specified by the agreement. As a practical matter, however, where union hiring halls exist and where unions thereby control much of the supply of competent labor, it is inevitable that union considerations affect the hiring process. The idea that a non-member should be referred out when members are looking for work has never been accepted by most union business agents.

At one time the Board made a determined effort to regulate the operation of union hiring halls in this regard. In *Mountain Pacific Chapter*,[39] the Board held that the very existence of an exclusive hiring hall encouraged union membership unless certain detailed safeguards were in place to regulate how the hiring system operated. The Supreme Court specifically rejected the *Mountain Pacific* doctrine in *Local 357 Teamsters v. NLRB*.[40] In rejecting the Board's claim that the very existence of a hiring hall is discriminatory, the Court stated: "Nothing is inferable from the . . . hiring hall provision . . . there is no evidence that it was in fact used unlawfully. We cannot assume that a union conducts its operations in violation of law. . . ."

For some time after this decision the Board gave up its efforts to regulate hiring halls. However, a 1984 decision, *Bechtel Power Corp.*[41] announced a new standard that appears much like the Board's old *Mountain Pacific* approach. It held that a referral system to be valid had to be based on an "objective nondiscriminatory standard" that was made known to the employees. This approach has been well-received by the courts. Thus in *NLRB v. Ironworkers Local Union No. 505*,[42] the Ninth Circuit upheld a finding of violation based upon the union's application of an unwritten exception to its posted rules. Rejecting the union's claim that evidence of improper intent was necessary the court stated: "A union violates [section 8(b)(1)(a)] . . . if it wields its power invidiously or arbitrarily for such conduct gives notice that its favor must be curried, thereby encouraging membership. . . . This court has indicated that when the hiring hall deviates from written rules without adequate justification, even pursuant to longstanding exceptions routinely applied, the Board may rationally conclude that the union is wielding its power arbitrarily." This opinion, like the Board's decision in *Bechtel Power Corp.,* reflects the conclusion that the passage of time has made the Supreme Court's decision in the *Teamster Local 357* case no longer controlling. The likelihood is that this assumption is correct given the Court's increased concern with arbitrary union power. As a result, a union seeking to maintain the legality of a hiring hall provision would be well advised to consider adopting standards in conformity with the *Mountain Pacific* standards of long ago.

FOOTNOTES

1. Brooks, Unions of Their Own Choosing (1939). For a good analysis of the theory and development of section 8(a)(2), see Kohler, Models of Worker Participation: The Uncertain Significance of Section 8(a)(2), 27 Boston Col.L.Rev. 499.

2. 360 U.S. 203 (1959).

3. *Carpenter Steel Co.,* 76 N.L.R.B. 670 (1948).

4. 81 N.L.R.B. 976 (1949).

5. See New Standards For Domination and Support under § 8(a)(2), 82 Yale L.J. 510 (1973).

6. Compare *University of Chicago Library,* 205 N.L.R.B. 220, with *Texas Bolt Co.,* 135 N.L.R.B. 1182 (1982).

7. 366 U.S. 731 (1961).

8. See, e.g., Jackson, An Alternative to Unionization and the Wholly Unorganized Shop: A Legal Basis for Sanctioning Joint Employer Employee Committees and Increasing Employee Free Choice, 28 Syr.L.Rev. 18099 (1977); Note, New Standards for Domination and Support Under Section 8(a)(2), 82 Yale L.J. 510 (1973), *Federal–Mogul Corp. v. NLRB,* 394 F.2d 915 (6th Cir.1968).

9. 221 F.2d 165 (7th Cir.1955).

10. 289 F.2d 683 (7th Cir.1961).

11. 240 F.2d 564 (1st Cir.1957).

12. 379 F.2d 201 (6th Cir.1967).

13. 503 F.2d 625 (9th Cir.1974).

14. *General Foods Corp.,* 231 N.L.R.B. 1232 (1977).

15. Kohler, Models of Worker Participation: The Uncertain Significance of Section 8(a)(2), 27 B.C.L.Rev. 499 (1986).

16. Note, Does Employer Implementation of Employee Production Teams Violate Section 8(a)(2) of the National Labor Relations Act? 49 Ind.L.J. 516 (1974).

17. 691 F.2d 288 (6th Cir.1982).

18. 289 F.2d 177 (5th Cir.1961).

19. *General Foods Corp.,* 231 N.L.R.B. 1231 (1977).

20. See Note, Collective Bargaining as an Industrial System: An Argument Against Judicial Revision of Section 8(a)(2) of the National Labor Relations Act, 96 Harv.L.Rev. 1661 (1983); Kohler (supra).

21. 63 N.L.R.B. 1060 (1945). See Estreicher & Telsey, The Recast *Midwest Piping* Doctrine: The Case for Acceptance, Jan. 85 Labor L.J. 14 (1985); Margulies, Employees Pipe Dream (The *Midwest Piping* Doctrine Revised), 33 Depaul L.R. 75 (1983); Getman, The *Midwest Piping* Doctrine: An Example of the Need for Reappraisal of Labor Board Dogma, 3 U.Chi.L.Rev. 292 (1964).

22. See Getman, The *Midwest Piping* Doctrine: An Example of the Need for Reappraisal of Labor Board Dogma, 3 U.Chi.L.Rev. 292 (1964).

23. 110 N.L.R.B. 660 (1954).

24. 121 N.L.R.B. 1027 (1957).

25. 129 N.L.R.B. 662 (1960).

26. 266 N.L.R.B. 1088 (1982).

27. 262 N.L.R.B. 955 (1982).

28. 118 N.L.R.B. 174 (1957).

29. 179 N.L.R.B. 787 (1967).

30. 138 N.L.R.B. 265 (1962).

31. 139 N.L.R.B. 1018 (1962).

32. 139 N.L.R.B. 916 (1962).

33. 243 N.L.R.B. 125 (1975).

34. *NLRB v. North Shore University Hospital,* 724 F.2d 269 (2d Cir.1983).

35. Although it is sometimes said that the construction industry is treated specially for purposes of Section 8(a)(2) with respect to the issue of supervisory involvement, only one case may be cited for this conclusion, *Beach Electric Co.,* 174 N.L.R.B. 210 (1969), in which minor supervisors held a number of top level union positions and the Board found no violation due to "the nature of the industry involved."

35a. ___ U.S. ___ (1988).

36. 431 U.S. 209 (1977).

37. 466 U.S. 435 (1984).

38. 475 U.S. 292 (1986).

39. Mountain Pacific Chapter of Assoc. Gen. Contractors, 119 N.L.R.B. 883 (1957).

40. *Local 357, Teamsters v. NLRB,* 365 U.S. 667 (1961).

41. 268 N.L.R.B. 766 (1984).

42. 794 F.2d 1474 (9th Cir.1986).

Relevant Books, Articles, and Suggested Reading

BOOKS:

Bradley & Gelb, Worker Capitalism: The New Industrial Relations (1983).

Siegel & Weinber, Labor Management Cooperation: The American Experience (1982).

Martin & Kassalow (ed.), Labor Relations in Advanced Industrial Societies: Issues and Problems (1980).

Dept. of Labor Report U.S. Labor Law and the Future of Labor Management Cooperation 1987–1988.

ARTICLES:

Canter, "Uses and Abuses of the Agency Shop," 59 N.D.L.Rev. 61 (1983).

Mayer, "Union Security and the Taft–Hartley Act," Duke L.J. 505 (1961).

Moberly, "New Directions in Worker Participation and Collective Bargaining," 87 West L.Rev. 765 (1985).

Kohler, "Models of Worker Participation: The Uncertain Significance of Section 8(a)(2)," 27 Boston Col.L.Rev. (1986).

Olson, "Union Experience with Worker Ownership," Wis.L.Rev. 729 (1982).

Getman, "The Midwest Piping Doctrine: An Example of the Need for Reappraisal of Labor Board Dogma," Univ.Chicago L.Rev. 292 (1964).

Estreicher & Telsey, "The Recast Midwest Piping Doctrine: The Case for Judicial Acceptance," Labor L.J. 14 (Jan 1985).

*

Chapter VI

FEDERAL PREEMPTION OF STATE LABOR LAWS

Part I. The Preemption Issue: Historical Note

Prior to the enactment of the National Labor Relations Act in 1935, the law regulating labor relations was a crazy quilt of state conspiracy doctrines, common law torts, and state statutes of general application applied to union activities. The federal influence in the area was limited to the Sherman and Clayton antitrust statutes and, by 1932, the Norris–LaGuardia Act and several state "baby" Norris–LaGuardia acts limiting the use of injunctions in labor disputes.

The NLRA was a comprehensive statute, creating and declaring the rights of employees to organize and join labor organizations and to engage in other concerted activities and setting forth a code of conduct for employers to prevent interference with these rights. The Act established the mechanism for determining the employees' will on the issue of union representation and provided an agency—the National Labor Relations Board—to administer the Act and its processes. After twelve years of regulating employer conduct in labor relations, the law was amended in 1947 and again in 1959 to extend the Act's reach to regulate and limit certain union activity as well.

This sweeping legislation, involving both substantive rights and procedural mechanisms, immediately raised questions concerning the relationship of existing state laws as enforced in the courts and the new federal law and the administrative agency created to administer it. More specifically, how much of the previous patchwork of state laws and new federal legislation was to coexist, and how much had been preempted? What conduct was to be concurrently regulated, and what was to be the exclusive jurisdiction of the NLRB?

The issue of preemption with regard to the NLRA and its subsequent amendments is in some ways no different from the issue raised whenever Congress legislates in an area previously unregulated or left to the states. The ultimate supremacy of the federal law is clear. The question is how much of the field did Congress intend to preempt.

The preemption issues with regard to the NLRA are particularly troublesome, however, because, unlike the other issues of federal-state relationships, labor relations were mostly a matter of state concern up until the New Deal legislation. An early attempt by Congress to legislate organizing rights for railroad employees was struck down in 1908 when the Supreme Court held that Congress could not, by exercise of its authority under the commerce power, regulate in this area.[1]   The state legal systems had created a labor jurisprudence complete with laws, regulations, and precedents that in most cases directly conflicted with the new federal legislation, in some cases complemented the legislation, and in some cases seemed to cover situations where the NLRA was silent.   This last was especially true in the continued state regulation of union activity before the 1947 Taft–Hartley amendments added union unfair labor practices to the federal labor law.[2]

In the area of labor relations, the Congressional approach was a broad and sudden break with the past.   There were no preceding smaller legislative steps from which to draw guidance as to congressional intent.[3]   Prior to the NLRA, the federal law applied to labor relations raised no significant preemption issues.   The Sherman [4] and Clayton Acts [5] affected labor jurisprudence concurrently with state legislation and case law and so raised no issues of preemption. Indeed, the relationship between the federal antitrust laws and the federal labor law raises issues continuing to date.[6]   The Norris–LaGuardia Act was limited to the jurisdiction of federal courts so it did not speak to state regulation, and, therefore, did not raise issues of preemption.

The question of preemption posed in 1935 by the enactment of a comprehensive federal labor law, national in scope and endowed with an agency to make its rulings uniform in effect and application, created issues that were without precedent in the area of federal-state relations and that are still being debated and developed today.

Part II. Basic Principles in Preemption Cases

The conceptual approach to labor preemption issues developed by the courts is governed by principles that are easier to articulate than apply.[7]   First, the supremacy clause of the Constitution mandates that where Congress has intended to legislate in the field, state law is preempted.[8]   The ultimate issue then is to determine what aspects of the conduct being regulated by the states Congress intended to preempt.   Outside of a few explicit exceptions, Congress has not set down any clear guidelines.[9]   The silence of Congress as to the extent of its intent to occupy the field has led to the conclusion that it did not intend to occupy the field fully.[10]   The question of how much is left to state regulation becomes one of divining congressional intent from the expression of the policies in the NLRA and weighing their significance against asserted state interests.   The courts have developed a two-pronged analytical approach to the question based upon the so-called *Garmon* and *Machinists* rules,[11] although an alternative "balancing of interests" approach seems to be emerging as articulated in the lower courts and by some commentators.[12] The remainder of this chapter explores the development of these rules and their application in current situations.[13]

Part III. Early Development of Preemption Policy

A. State Regulation of Rights Protected by the Act

The federal labor law as originally enacted declared a national policy favoring employee-union organization and collective bargaining. In the early days of the NLRA, courts were sensitive to any state regulation, regardless of the local interest asserted, that seemed to modify or qualify the newly granted employee rights to pursue those goals.

Early preemption issues were raised by state attempts to modify or condition rights guaranteed employees by section 7 of the Act. The Supreme Court struck down a Florida statute that required the licensing of union representatives and that limited issuance of the license to persons free of criminal convictions and of good moral character.[14] The Court reasoned that the state law interfered with the employees' section 7 right to freely choose their representative for collective bargaining and therefore was preempted under the supremacy clause. State laws requiring a union membership vote prior to a strike [15] or limiting the rights of employees of public utilities to strike [16] similarly were held preempted by section 7's seemingly unlimited grant to employees to engage in concerted activities.

B. Taft–Hartley Amendments: Union Conduct Regulated

The NLRA as enacted in 1935 restricted only employer conduct and provided for the resolution of questions of union representation. Union strikes, picketing, and boycotts were left unregulated by the Act, but presumably were defined as protected concerted activities under section 7 of the Act.[17] In *Allen Bradley v. IBEW, Local 3*,[18] a case involving union threats and violence, the Supreme Court found that because such conduct was not regulated by the Act, the states were free to continue to regulate such misconduct. Outside of this instance, issues of conflicting substantive law regarding union activity did not arise until the Taft–Hartley amendments specified certain union activity as unfair labor practices under the Act.

Taft–Hartley raised basic issues of substantive conflict and primary jurisdiction. First, did the fact that the NLRA now outlawed certain union conduct heretofore regulated by the states serve to limit all such regulation exclusively to the NLRA, or could the states continue to regulate activity not prohibited by the Act? Second, where state and federal law prohibited the same conduct, did the federal interest in the primary jurisdiction of the NLRB preempt the activity of state agencies and courts in remedying the same activity?

The Supreme Court soon made it clear that preserving the primary jurisdiction of the NLRB was the basis for preemption in cases where both state and federal law regarded the union's conduct as prohibited. In Pennsylvania, which had enacted a "Baby–Wagner Act," the state board's finding that picketing for recognition by a minority union was a violation of both the state law and section 8(b)(2) of the NLRA was held preempted.[19] State agencies, the Court held, could not apply state law because the NLRA had preempted the field and the states could not enforce federal law or provide state remedies unless and until the NLRB had acted. Where the NLRB had acted and secured an injunction of certain limited forms of picketing, a state court injunction of all the picketing could not stand.[20]

In these cases, the Supreme Court recognized the danger to the establishment of a uniform national labor policy of applying different sanctions or remedies even where both state law and the NLRA prohibited the conduct. Some justices in these cases, however, would allow state court action to parallel NLRB action precisely because the state allows monetary damages, a remedy that the NLRB cannot provide.[21] This view reasons that the availability of an enhanced remedy available in a state tort action is of deeply rooted local interest and the interference with the federal policy is of little significance because no substantive conflict is involved.

C. State Regulation of Union Violence

The states' traditional exercise of their police power to regulate violence was not limited by the NLRA. As stated earlier, the issue raised by a parallel body of federal law prohibiting the same conduct did not arise until the 1947 Taft–Hartley amendments added union unfair labor practices. The first case concerning union violence to reach the Supreme Court after the amendments involved the ability of a state court to award damages to a construction contractor whose business had been damaged by the United Mineworkers in a violent campaign to prevent the employment of AFL employees.[22] The Court upheld the award of damages despite its recognition that the union's activity was governed by the NLRA. The Court characterized the NLRB's cease-and-desist remedy as preventive and of prospective effect and the state's as dealing with the consequences of already-committed tortious conduct. Because the remedies did not conflict, the state should be able to award damages for wrongs. The Court did not rely on the state's traditional police power over violent activity as the basis for the decision. A state award to employees for compensatory and punitive damages caused by union violence was subsequently upheld on the same basis.[23]   The Court soon made clear that aside from the fact that differing remedies were available, the state's basic, traditional interest in regulating violent conduct was not preempted and state court injunctions for violent activity would lie despite the NLRB's authority to grant similar relief.[24]

D. Discretionary Jurisdiction of the NLRB

One of the early preemption issues arose over the question of state regulation in areas where the Board chose not to assert jurisdiction.   The NLRA extended the reach of the labor laws coextensively with the commerce power from major industries to small enterprises. In an early case, the Supreme Court upheld the Board's finding that even employers not directly engaged in interstate commerce, but having a "substantial impact" on the flow of goods across state lines, were within its reach.[25]   The Board eventually decided, for reasons of economy, to limit its jurisdiction to firms meeting certain minimum standards of size.   The courts, in these early cases, were sensitive to the primacy of the new agency and made clear that the Board's decision not to exercise its jurisdiction in certain areas did not open those areas to state regulation.   Thus, in 1946, the Supreme Court held that the Board's refusal to certify a union of foremen did not allow New York State's Labor Board to certify the union under its "Little Wagner Act." [26]   The Court found that the NLRB's exercise of discretion, even deciding not to assert jurisdiction, did not allow another body to assert jurisdiction over the same subject matter.   State regulation was preempted to the extent of the NLRB's *potential* jurisdiction, rather than to that of the NLRB's self-imposed limitations. In the 1947 amendments, the NLRB was specifically authorized to cede jurisdiction to the states.[27]   However, the failure of the Board to assert jurisdiction was not construed as a cession of jurisdiction.[28]   The Supreme Court subsequently made clear that unless the Board made an explicit agreement to cede jurisdiction, a state labor board could not act even though the Board had expressly declined to take jurisdiction.[29]   The ruling precluded the various states from asserting a variety of labor laws, from "baby-Wagner Acts" that tracked the NLRA to restrictive labor legislation.   The ruling created a no-man's land over labor disputes where the NLRA had declined to assert jurisdiction and the states were precluded from acting.   The situation was resolved by the enactment of section 14(c) in 1959, which permitted state regulation in areas where the Board had declined jurisdiction.[30]   The practical effect of section 14(c) is that the issue of the jurisdictional standard of the NLRB becomes, in some cases, a litigated issue depending on the parties' view as to which labor law, federal or state, it regards as more favorable.

The early preemption cases were more or less decided on a case-by-case basis.   The Supreme Court, in fashioning a preemption doctrine, was clearly impressed with the bold sweep of the new legislation and was sensitive to any state laws that might impinge upon or modify the grand federal scheme. Yet the issues were varied and complex and the lower state courts, who were dealing with these new defenses of preemption in their heretofore traditional suits for injunctions of strikes, boycotts, and picketing, or suits for damages for tortious conduct, needed definitive standards to apply. This remained to be supplied by Justice Frankfurter's opinion in *San Diego Building Trades Council v. Garmon.*[31]

Part IV. *Garmon*: The Basic Principles Established

The Supreme Court's approach to labor law preemption issues was given its clearest expression in *Garmon,* in which Justice Frankfurter took the opportunity to synthesize the previous case law and enunciate the guiding principles in the area.

Garmon involved picketing by a minority union to pressure the employer to sign a collective-bargaining agreement. The NLRB declined to take jurisdiction because the employer did not meet the Board's jurisdictional standards. The employer then sued in California state court, which granted an injunction against the picketing and awarded damages. The California Supreme Court upheld the decision of its lower court on the ground that the NLRB's refusal to take jurisdiction left the matter for state action. It then determined that the union conduct constituted a violation of section 8(b)(2) of the NLRA.

The case came to the Supreme Court on the issue of whether the states could regulate activities otherwise preempted when the NLRB declined to assert jurisdiction. The Court ruled that the NLRB's action did not leave the states free to regulate in the area. The Court remanded the case to the California courts on the issue of the impact of state law on the issue. On remand, the California court set aside the injunction but found authority under California law to award damages.

Before the Supreme Court a second time, on the issue of whether the state court could award damages for peaceful union activity, Frankfurter found the state could not enjoin union activity or award damages because the union's activity was arguably protected under section 7 and arguably prohibited as an unfair labor practice under section 8. He then set forth the principles to apply to this and, presumably, to future preemption cases.

He noted that the law raised difficult problems of federal and state relations and involved "a more complicated and perceptive process than is conveyed by the delusive phrase, ascertaining the intent of the legislature," and that the court had to implement the federal scheme in accordance with its broadly outlined aims and social policy.

The determination of what was to be left to state regulation and what was preempted had to be determined on the basis of potential areas of conflict—inconsistent standards of substantive law and differing remedial schemes. Remedies that differed were no less disruptive of a uniform labor policy than were substantive conflicts. Frankfurter saw the NLRB as the "unifying consideration"—the agency entrusted by Congress to administer the national labor policy.

Frankfurter set out the following principles:

First, if an activity is clearly protected by section 7 or prohibited by section 8, the state's jurisdiction is displaced. This is only giving "due regard for the federal enactment." Not only activities clearly within the ambit of either section 7 or 8 are preempted. Even those activities over which the Act's coverage is not clear cannot be left to the states or federal courts to decide. These issues are to be decided exclusively by the NLRB in the first instance so that it can exercise its "primary competence." Thus, even activities "arguably" protected by section 7 or prohibited by section 8 have to be left to the Board. This applies whether the state laws at issue are of broad general application or specifically directed at labor relations. The potential for frustration of the national scheme would be the same. In *Garmon* itself, because the NLRB had not determined the status of the picketing, the state's jurisdiction was displaced.

Second, if the Board decides the activities are neither protected nor prohibited, the question then becomes whether the activity may be regulated by the states. However, where the Board has not taken a clear position—either by declining jurisdiction, refusing to issue a complaint, or taking some other ambiguous action—the state's action is still precluded. "The governing consideration is that to allow states to control activities that are potentially subject to federal regulation involves too great a danger of conflict with national labor policy."

Finally, Frankfurter attempted to reconcile the Court's past preemption decisions by carving out two exceptions to the preemption rule. He found that:

"When the exercise of state power over a particular area of activity threatened interference with the clearly indicated policy of industrial relations, it has been judicially necessary to preclude the States from acting. However, due regard for the presuppositions of our embracing federal system, including the principle of diffusion of power not as a matter of doctrinaire localism but as a promoter of democracy, has required us not to find withdrawal from the states of power to regulate where the activity regulated a merely peripheral concern of the Labor Management Relations

Act . . . or where the regulated conduct touches interests so deeply rooted in local feeling and responsibility that, in absence of compelling congressional direction, we could not infer that Congress had deprived the States of the power to act." [32]

Thus, state courts are able to award damages and injunctions in instances of labor violence as an exception to the general preemption rule, based on the states' compelling interest in maintaining domestic peace. This interest is "so deeply rooted in local feeling and responsibility" that it should not be overridden in the absence of clear congressional direction.

Frankfurter expressly rejected the Court's earlier rationale in *Laburnum,* that state action was appropriate because the state remedy had no federal counterpart. The awarding of damages could be as effective a form of state regulation as injunctive relief. "In fact, since remedies form an ingredient of any integrated scheme of regulation, to allow the State to grant a remedy here which has been withheld from the National Labor Relations Board only accentuates the danger of the conflict." [33] The real basis for *Laburnum* and the other cases allowing state courts to grant injunctions or award damages for conduct marked by violence and threats to public order was, according to Frankfurter, because the "compelling state interest . . . in the maintenance of domestic peace is not overridden in the absence of clearly expressed congressional direction." [34]

The other basic exception recognized in *Garmon* covers cases such as *Machinists v. Gonzales,* [35] which involved an expelled union member's suit against his union for breach of contract under California law. Here again, Frankfurter ignored the Supreme Court's rationale in that case of no federal counterpart to the state remedy and recharacterized the case as appropriate for state jurisdiction because the activity, involving the union's internal affairs, was merely a "peripheral concern" of the Act.

The guiding principal behind *Garmon* is that the NLRA expresses a congressional purpose to establish a national labor policy to be uniformly administered by a central agency, the NLRB. This purpose would be defeated if federal and state courts were free, without limitation, to exercise jurisdiction over activities that are subject to regulation by the NLRB. Thus, two impulses drive *Garmon*. The first is the avoidance of conflicting rulings on substantive rights—i.e., either the states' enjoining or restricting conduct that the NLRB would find was legal and protected, or conversely, the states' enforcing or permitting conduct the NLRB would hold was prohibited. [36] The second impulse concerns the congressional interest that the national labor law be uniformly administered by investing primary jurisdiction in the NLRB. This is based upon the view that the "judicial attitudes, court procedures and traditional judicial remedies, state and federal, were as likely to produce adjudications incompatible with national labor policy as were different rules of substantive law." [37]

In following a *Garmon* analysis, the courts suggest a difference in result depending on whether the interest at issue is protection of the conduct or protection of the primary jurisdiction of the Board, although these interests are not always easy to separate. In situations where preemption is concerned with state regulation of conduct actually protected by the Act, the Court has recently asserted that there can be no exceptions for local state interests no matter how "deeply rooted." The issue is one of the supremacy of federal law. Where, however, the interest is in the primary jurisdiction of the Board in areas of *arguably* protected or prohibited conduct, the exceptions to preemption for matters of peripheral concern and for deeply rooted state interests may be considered and the interests of the state may outweigh the resulting interference with the federal regulatory scheme.[38]

The principles enunciated by Frankfurter were intended to provide a clear guide for subsequent decisions in this area. This may have reflected the court's early enthusiasm for a new and developing area of federal law. Yet the clarity and reach of the principles were perhaps overstated. Frankfurter's determination that *Gonzales* was "peripheral" was conclusory and has been distinguished to the point of elimination in subsequent cases.[39] His rejection of the "alternative remedy" theory of *Laburnum* was disputed by the concurring judges in *Garmon,* and the theory has proved a viable, if pernicious, rationale in state tort actions in this area once again.[40] The "local interest" exception has led to a balancing test where the balance has frequently been struck in favor of the state's interest.[41]

The Supreme Court seems to have strayed from Frankfurter's primary focus on the type of activity regulated and its implications for national labor policy and has focused instead on whether the state results conflict with those of the NLRB. This may signify a waning of the justices' regard for the primacy of the law of labor-management relations *per se* over the competing interests in private property and individual rights and freedom.

Garmon still provides the basic principles from which to approach questions of preemption. Its viability was underscored in several recent Supreme Court cases, all starting their analysis by determining whether the conduct was arguably protected or prohibited by the Act.[42] This appears to be only the beginning of the process, however, rather than the conclusion, in determining what is to be allowed to the states and what is preempted.

Part V. Applications of *Garmon*

In applying *Garmon,* the Court discovered that it had not succeeded in formulating a "bright line" rule that could always be used to determine which state laws are preempted and which are not. Congressional intent proved to be complex, and the Justices soon found themselves creating new tests to achieve desired results in particular cases.

A. State Regulation of Unions

A state law providing for licensing union business agents was struck down as interfering with the employees' section 7 right to choose a bargaining representative. In *Hill v. Florida,*[43] a statute requiring the licensing of union agents and requiring good moral character, ten years of citizenship, and a record free of felony convictions was struck down as "repugnant" to the NLRA. The Court reasoned that the legislative history made clear that Congress was mindful of the issue of labor racketeering and the historic use of criminal law in labor situations. Its omission of any qualifications for a bargaining representative was regarded as deliberate.

The decision in *Hill v. Florida* was recently undercut by the Supreme Court in *Brown v. Hotel Workers Local 54*[44] when it upheld sections of the New Jersey Casino Control Act that required the registration of labor unions representing casino employees and provided for disqualification if their officers or agents were identified as "career offenders" (persons who used criminal methods) or as "members of a career offender cartel" (members of a group using criminal methods). Disqualification barred the union from collecting dues or handling pension funds. These provisions, enacted as part of the law legalizing gambling in New Jersey, were applied to disqualify the union certified by the NLRB to represent casino employes in Atlantic City. The Third Circuit held that establishing qualifications for union office interfered with section 7 and that *Hill v. Florida* controlled. In reversing the Third Circuit, Justice O'Connor's opinion reviewed the basic *Garmon* argument that this legislation, aimed at ensuring the integrity of legalized gambling, fell within the exception for "state interests deeply rooted in local feeling and responsibility." The *Garmon* exceptions, she pointed out, are not available where the activity regulated is "actually" protected. In such cases, there can be no balancing of interests, since federal rights are paramount. Where the conduct is only arguably protected, the interest served by preemption is in the NLRA's primary jurisdiction and as such may be subordinated, in the interest of federalism, to significant interests that outweigh the resulting interference with the federal scheme. The New Jersey Act, however, like that in *Hill v. Florida,* interfered with rights actually protected by section 7.

Nevertheless, the Court found that Congress had indicated, subsequent to *Hill v. Florida,* that it did not intend to preempt all state regulation that touched on employees' rights to choose a bargaining representative. The Court pointed to two sections of the Labor Management Reporting and Disclosure Act (LMRDA) of 1959 indicating that some state regulatior of union officials was contemplated. In section 504, convicted felons were barred from serving as union officials for five years from the date of conviction or the end of imprisonment. While this apparent modification of section 7 rights was made by Congress, it indicated some room for state action since criminal convictions would be based on each state's criminal law, and therefore contemplated a consequent lack of uniformity in standards. Section 602(a) of the LMRDA specifically provided that the Act was not meant to preempt state legislation relating to unions or their officials. To the Court, the most compelling evidence of a change in Congressional intent was its approval of the New York Waterfront Commission Act, which, in language almost identical to that used in the New Jersey Casino Act, prohibited unions from collecting dues if their officers had been convicted of a felony. The Act was in furtherance of an interstate compact between New York and New Jersey and therefore had to be approved by Congress. Such approval had been challenged on the basis of *Hill* and the Supreme Court had upheld the Act based upon clear evidence of Congressional intent.[45] These instances indicated a change of Congressional intent regarding limitations on the choice of union representatives and the Court found the New Jersey regulations were not preempted. However, it remanded the case to determine whether by not allowing the union to collect dues or administer the pension fund, the law was, in effect, destroying the union. If such was found, the Court indicated it might reconsider its determination because that would clearly interfere with the employees' right to select a union. The decision may be read as consistent with *Garmon* principles. Its only innovation is in its finding of an explicit indication of changed legislative intent based upon actions taken by Congress subsequent to the enactment of the basic federal labor statutes.

B.　State Regulation of Collective Bargaining

The Supreme Court has consistently followed a policy of preemption where states attempt to restrict a union's resort to peaceful economic weapons protected by section 7. State laws requiring a vote by the membership prior to a strike [46] or restricting strikes by employees of public utilities,[47] laws specifically aimed at limiting labor activities, are preempted because they are in direct conflict with the federal Act.

Equally preempted are state laws not specifically aimed at labor activity but which nonetheless result in outlawing or restricting activity the Act protects.   In this regard state antitrust laws applied to union conduct are preempted as to activity that is either arguably protected or prohibited.   *Teamsters, Local 24 v. Oliver* [48] involved the application of Ohio's antitrust law to a collective-bargaining agreement in which the employers had agreed to a minimum truck lease rate when hiring independent truckers.   The Court found that the purpose of the minimum lease rate was to protect the integrity of the negotiated wage rate.   As such, the minimum lease rate was related to wages, a mandatory subject of bargaining, and state laws could not interfere or limit the range of solutions the parties could negotiate in the exercise of their duty to bargain under federal labor law.   An attempt to apply local restraint-of-trade laws to a union jurisdictional strike was struck down in *Weber v. Anheuser-Busch, Inc.* [49] as impinging upon arguably protected activity.

In these cases the fact that the state laws were of general application and not specifically aimed at labor relations was of no significance.   It was the conduct that was regulated that was the focus of the analysis.

The fact that the parties are negotiating on a mandatory subject cannot, however, mean that any arrangement reached is insulated from the reach of state regulation.   Thus, the Supreme Court indicated in *Teamsters Local 24 v. Oliver* that it might regard contract terms that conflict with local health and safety regulation as not shielded by preemption.   These latter interests presumably would be in furtherance of maintaining state standards for the welfare of all its citizens regardless of whether they were subject to collective bargaining agreements.

How far the exception for general health and welfare standards will go in avoiding preemption might well depend on how close the regulation is to the states' basic interest.   Thus, state OSHA standards, anti-discrimination laws, minimum wages, and laws of garnishment would probably not be preempted despite the fact that the laws probably restrict collective bargaining on mandatory subjects.   On the other hand, we already have seen that antitrust laws and laws barring strikes of public utilities would be preempted.   The line becomes vague and unpredictable where traditional union conduct clashes with the states' basic interest in the general welfare.   Such a clash occurs when the state pays unemployment benefits to strikers.   In *New York Telephone v. New York State Department of Labor,* [50] the state sought to justify the payments as pursuant to its interest in the welfare of its citizens.   The employer argued that the state was underwriting protected activity—activity meant by Congress to be free of outside influences and left to the free play of economic forces.   Six justices decided that paying benefits to strikers was clearly an interference with the congressional design of the free play of economic forces in bargaining disputes.   Three of these justices felt it was an interference that Congress had intended. Three dissented. The three remaining justices, in the plurality opinion, advanced the distinction, discredited in *Garmon,* between state laws of general application as opposed to specific state labor regulation. They held that the states' unemployment laws should be exempt from normal preemption analysis because they represented a general state concern with the security of the unemployed, only incidentally involved participants in a labor dispute, and were not directed at labor-management relations. They went on to find that the benefits were a state interest deeply rooted in local feeling and responsibility. A majority of the court, then, for divided reasons, concluded that unemployment benefits, and, by inference, welfare payments, may be paid strikers as either a congressionally-recognized exception to the free play doctrine or by inference of congressional intent.

C. State Regulation of Property Rights: Trespass and *Sears, Roebuck*

The area of trespass represents the first sign of judicial retreat from an absolutist approach to preemption issues where protected activity is concerned. Trespass cases in labor disputes arise in two ways. A union that is picketing or leafletting on private property in a parking lot or shopping mall or industrial park is ordered off the property by the owner. In the first scenario, the union can file section 8(a)(1) charges with the Board alleging interference with section 7 rights. In the second scenario, the employer can sue for an injunction based on trespass in state court if the union refuses to leave. The unfair labor practice case will result in a Board determination as to whether the union activity is protected and whether the employees' section 7 rights are superior to the property rights of the owner.[51] The injunction suit in state court raises the issue of preemption because the finding of an unpermitted entry on private property would be without reference to the possibility that it was in conflict with an overriding federal interest. The difference in the way the issue arises was to prove a great source of confusion. The issue raised in the context of unfair labor practice charges was treated by the Supreme Court in *NLRB v. Babcock & Wilcox,*[52] which held that it was for the NLRB to strike a balance to allow the fullest exercise of section 7 rights with the least interference to property rights. The Court made clear, however, that property rights would have to be subordinated in instances where the employees had no reasonable alternative means for communication concerning section 7 matters. The Board has been elaborating this standard for over a decade. The line of decisions was sidetracked for almost eight years by the Supreme Court holding in 1968 in *Amalgamated Food Employees v. Logan Valley Plaza,*[53] which alleged trespassory picketing in a shopping center was protected by the "business-district" concept of the first amendment.[54] In *Sears Roebuck & Co. v. San Diego Council of Carpenters,* the Court finally faced the preemption issue it avoided in *Logan.*[55]

This case concerned a state court injunction secured by Sears against picketing by the Carpenters Union on the property of a single store, requesting the store to sign a union agreement and to use carpenters sent from the union hiring hall. The Court found that the state court was not preempted unless and until the case was brought before the NLRB, despite the fact that the picketing was both arguably protected (area standards) and arguably prohibited (recognitional—Section 8(b)(7)(C) or work assignment—section 8(b)(4)(D)).

The Court dealt with the "arguably prohibited" branch of *Garmon* by noting that the issue before the state court was not the same issue that would be considered by the NLRB. The trespass case would be concerned with the location of the picketing; the NLRA was concerned with the object of the picketing. The Court established two criteria for exempting state action from preemption in cases where the conduct is arguably prohibited: "(1) there is a significant state interest in protecting the citizen from the challenged conduct and (2) although the challenged conduct occurred in the course of a labor dispute and an unfair labor practice charge could have been filed, the exercise of state jurisdiction . . . entails little risk of interference with the regulatory jurisdiction of the Labor Board." The Court went on to find that since the controversy to be presented to the court was not identical to that which would be presented to the Board, there was no realistic risk of interference with the NLRB's primary jurisdiction to determine unfair labor practices and therefore a state finding of trespass was not to be preempted. The Court thus added the "identical controversy" standard to *Garmon's* "arguably prohibited" branch of preemption doctrine.

The Court then turned to the "arguably protected" branch of *Garmon.* It regarded the possibility of conflict caused by state interference with federally protected activity as a more serious issue than with "arguably prohibited" conflicts. State regulation of conduct prohibited by the federal Act violates only the primary jurisdiction of the NLRB, whereas state limits on protected activity violates the supremacy of the federal law as well.

While the state court determination of an injunction in this case could directly conflict with a decision that might be made by the NLRB as to whether the trespassing activity was protected by federal law, the Court found there was no practical chance of conflict because the case was not before the Board. The employer could not raise the issue by filing an unfair labor practice charge. By ordering the union off its property, it had given the union an opportunity to bring the issue to the Board, but the union had not done so. Under the circumstances the Court saw the employer being faced with three alternatives. It could allow the union to remain on its property and thereby forego its property rights; it could resort to self-help and evict the pickets by force, which could result in violence; or it could proceed in state court. The last was the only avenue that promised an orderly resolution to the question of the legality of the union's activity. If the union had filed a charge, the primary jurisdiction of the NLRB would have ousted the state's jurisdiction. But where, as here, the employer had no way to invoke the Board's jurisdiction and the union had not done so, the possibility of a conflicting ruling was not sufficient to preempt the state. In this type of case, in which the employer cannot obtain a Board determination, "only labor activity that is actually, rather than arguably, protected under federal law should be immune from state judicial control." Insofar as the rationale for preemption was based on primary jurisdiction, it would not be sufficient in this type of case.

The Court then examined whether the danger of state conflict with federal rights made a jurisdictional hiatus preferable to state rulings that may frustrate national labor policy. The Court noted that the Board had found that in some cases under its *Babcock & Wilcox* balancing analysis, a union's trespass was protected. The judgment as to where the Board might have struck the balance in this case was speculative and therefore the activity was certainly only "arguably" protected. The Court went on to find that the risk of interference with Board policy was slight because, reviewing the Board cases, the Court decided the Board probably would find the activity unprotected. While there was some risk of state courts enjoining activity the Board would find protected, those instances were probably cases where the union would file charges with the Board and thereby avoid the state action. Moreover, the Court indicated the union could always invoke the Board's jurisdiction even after the state court action had commenced. Justice Blackmun, concurring, sought to clarify the majority opinion to declare that any time the union invoked the Board's processes the state action would be stayed until the General Counsel had dismissed the charge or the Board had finally ruled. Justice Powell, also concurring, disagreed, feeling that the Board's processes were too time consuming to accommodate Blackmun's view that state jurisdiction was ousted upon the filing of a charge. He would find state jurisdiction ousted only after a Board decision.

The decision in *Sears* thereby created an exception to *Garmon* in the area of "arguably protected" rights whenever the state interest is great or interference with the federal law is slight, and the employer has no opportunity to test the protected nature of the union's activity. As the dissent pointed out, the exception allows a state court to decide both the state interest in allowing the conduct to be restrained and the chances that the Board would find the activity protected. The dissent would have continued a "flat rule" or absolute approach to arguably protected activity on the grounds that the balance between competing federal and state interests had been struck by Congress when it enacted section 7. All activity coming under its protection was to be free of state regulation. The dissent went on to illustrate its disagreement by finding that the Board in making its *Babcock & Wilcox* analysis would have probably found the locus of accommodation on the side of permitting the trespass.

The differing views of the Court seem to represent, at bottom, differing views on the relative importance of the Act to other interests. The majority was ultimately moved by the situation where preemption would leave an employer unable to secure a definitive judgment on trespassory picketing. The dissent felt that the requirements of the uniform application of section 7 rights warranted the social cost. The *Sears* approach could apply to any number of "arguably protected" activities where other interests are at issue and section 7 rights are not raised unless the employer commits unfair labor practices and the union chooses to file a charge. The practical result of *Sears* should be a union's immediate resort to the NLRB to avoid state jurisdiction in these situations.

D. Intentional Torts and the *Farmer* Balancing Test

When activity that is arguably prohibited by the Act is regulated by the state, the preemption doctrine is based, as discussed above in *Sears,* on the primary jurisdiction of the NLRB. The state's alternate processes and remedies for conduct prohibited by the NLRA are not complementary, but disruptive of uniform policy, because they create the possibility of conflicting substantive rules. The administration of the Act by the Board is crucial because differing judicial attitudes, procedures, and remedies are seen "as likely to produce adjudications incompatible with national labor policy as were different rules of substantive law." [56]

It was recognized early, however, that the states' traditional interest in preserving the peace and protecting the health and safety of their citizens was not intended to be diminished by the NLRA. State courts continue to have jurisdiction to enjoin violent union conduct and to award damages for violent union activity even though the conduct is also arguably an unfair labor practice. A more difficult question is posed when other types of tortious conduct are alleged that are arguably prohibited, and the states' basic interest is less clear. The Supreme Court has been loathe to eliminate the individual's traditional ability to seek a remedy for a "wrong" and yet is aware of the potential conflict with the primary jurisdiction of the NLRB. The result has been a series of compromises separating out so-called egregious torts from the basic labor dispute, allowing private suits for the former and preempting suits involving the latter. The Supreme Court in *Linn v. United Plant Guards* [57] allowed a suit for malicious libel where the alleged acts were committed in a union election campaign by union adherents characterizing an employer official. In an area heavily regulated by Board law, the Court recognized that libel *per se* situations were preempted by NLRB rulings allowing propaganda in election campaigns even when it is marked by extreme charges and vituperation. Libel suits would represent "an unwarranted intrusion" into the robust exchange of views. The Court, however, carved out malicious libel for state jurisdiction. It saw little likelihood of conflict with the federal scheme since the NLRB would focus on the coercive nature of the speech and the state court on its falsity and the intent to harm. *Linn* marks the Court's change of focus from the conduct regulated to the different issues raised by different bodies of law.

This approach was followed in *Farmer*,[58] in which a member sued his union for the intentional infliction of emotional distress and discrimination in operating the union hiring hall. The Court allowed the suit for damages for the malicious tort, but held that the discrimination part of the complaint was preempted as arguably prohibited by section 8. The plaintiff had previously filed charges with the NLRB alleging discrimination in an earlier job referral and collected back pay. The state court of appeals found the action preempted. The Supreme Court, however, followed the line of cases from the union violence cases to *Linn,* finding that these extreme types of intentionally tortious conduct were of overriding state interest. Stating that *Garmon* was not to be applied mechanically, the Court elaborated on the local interest exception, setting forth a balancing test to be applied on a case-by-case basis.

First, the Court looked to whether the underlying conduct was protected. If not, there would be little risk of state regulation of conduct intended by Congress to be protected. Second, the Court looked to whether there was an overriding state interest. The third factor was the risk of state interference with effective administration of national labor policy. The Court then went on to find that the intentional tort was actionable because the federal interest was peripheral inasmuch as the conduct was not protected by the Act. The state interest in protecting its citizens from outrageous conduct was deep and could provide a remedy that the NLRB could not. Since the decision before the Court would not involve the determination of the underlying labor dispute, the potential for interference with the federal labor scheme was minimal. Thus, the balance was struck in favor of allowing the tort action. The Court cautioned that the tortious conduct considered in the state action had to be separate from the emotional distress that normally would result from the discriminatory acts.

Farmer, in advocating a case-by-case balancing approach, directly challenged the *Garmon–Lockridge* recognition of the need for broad principles to provide guidance and easy application by lower courts. Moreover, by relying on the difference between the controversy presented to the court and that which would be presented to the NLRB, the Court moved away from the *Garmon* focus on the conduct to be regulated to a focus on the regulatory scheme applied by the state court. This focus on whether the issue presented to the court was identical to the issue presented to the Board was further articulated in *Sears* and has become a well-used distinction in preemption cases involving allegations of intentional torts.

The "identical controversy" standard has proved to be a source of confusion for lower courts.[59] That is because state tort claims usually will require different findings to establish a claim than an NLRA violation. That would also be the case with clearly protected activity—as, say area standards picketing—that could be an intentional interference with contractual relations. The controversy before the state court would be different, but the conflict with the federal scheme is obvious and recognized. Yet the doctrine continues to be applied where conduct is arguably prohibited, probably because the results are seen as not conflicting but complementary, providing differing remedies for the same wrong.

The limits of the Court's "identical controversy" analysis were indicated in *Engineers Local 926 v. Jones*,[60] in which the Court refused to extend its *Farmer–Sears* holdings to a damage suit by a supervisor who alleged that the defendant union had brought about his discharge. The union's conduct was arguably a violation of section 8(b)(1)(B)— "coerc[ing] . . . an employer in the selection of his representatives for the purpose of collective bargaining or the adjustment of grievances." The supervisor argued that the issue before the state court would be different because he didn't need to prove coercion, merely that the union caused his termination. He urged the Court to separate out the allegations that did not involve coercion and allow them to be litigated in state court. The Court refused, pointing out that this would permit the state court to determine whether the union's acts were coercive in order to decide its jurisdiction, and that that issue was for the NLRB. Further, it held that unlike *Sears,* where the issues were "completely unrelated," the issue of causation of the discharge was fundamentally the same in both forums. As the dissent noted, this is a somewhat more restrictive definition of the "identical controversy" standard.

Finally, the Court, simply citing Frankfurter's decision, signaled some continuing respect for the *Garmon* view on differing remedies by flatly rejecting the argument for state action because the plaintiff could have been awarded punitive damages and attorneys fees by the state court. The threat to a national labor policy by differing remedies was later recognized in a decision in which the Supreme Court struck down a Wisconsin statute that prohibited firms that had been found guilty of violating the National Labor Relations Act three separate times in a five-year period from doing business with the state.[61]   The Court unanimously found that the Wisconsin law sought to provide supplemental sanctions that conflicted with the Act's comprehensive remedial scheme.   The state's argument, that it was not regulating labor activity but merely exercising its spending power, was dismissed as a "distinction without a difference."

The Court has had difficulty in treating the preemption issue in union-union member disputes.   As noted earlier, in *Gonzales* the Supreme Court held that a union member could sue his union under state law for wrongful expulsion from membership.   It noted that the protection of union members and their rights had not been undertaken by federal law and the "remote possibility of some entanglement with the Board's enforcement of national policy" was not sufficient to deny the union member a state court remedy.[62]   In *Garmon,* the case was characterized as one of "only peripheral interest" to the regulatory scheme.

The exception from preemption rules for union member suits was extended in *Vaca v. Sipes* [63] to suits by members alleging a union's violation of its duty of fair representation, although by the time of *Vaca,* in 1967, the NLRB had found that a union's violation of its duty of fair representation was an unfair labor practice and, therefore, a union member's suit against his or her union could no longer be characterized as outside the labor law.   The Court emphasized that the doctrine of the duty of fair representation had been judicially developed and only belatedly adopted by the NLRB and, therefore, did not raise the issue of primary jurisdiction.   Moreover, the Court cited the close relationship of these suits to state court section 301 suits alleging a discharge in breach of the collective bargaining agreement.   (Section 301 suits would involve the union's conduct as a basic issue in satisfying a member's exhaustion of remedies requirement where there was a grievance procedure to be followed.)   On balancing the interests asserted against the "effect on the administration of national labor policies of concurrent judicial and administrative remedies" the court in *Vaca* held that duty of fair representation suits were not preempted. A few years later in *Lockridge,*[64] the Court found the balance in favor of preemption where a union member sued his union over his suspension from membership, resulting in his discharge by his employer under a negotiated union security clause.   Except for this latter aspect, the case was on all fours with *Gonzales,* but the Court found that *Gonzales* involved purely internal union matters whereas it characterized *Lockridge* as involving an area of pervasive federal concern.   The result in *Lockridge* seemed to reflect the Court's obvious desire to reaffirm the preeminence of the *Garmon* rule over its exceptions.   The "peripheral concern" exemption for union-member disputes was probably eliminated by *Lockridge*.   The term was originally applied by Frankfurter to characterize *Gonzales*. It was conclusory on his part and has never been cited since as a separate exception but always as part of the "deeply rooted" exception. Moreover, because the 1959 Labor–Management Reporting and Disclosure Act amendments to the labor law gave protection and rights to union members, the original "peripheral concern" rationale for the exception—that such issues were unregulated by federal law—no longer obtained. Frankfurter's attempt to reconcile cases in *Garmon* seems least successful in these so-called "peripheral" cases. In each there is a possible NLRB violation that might be invoked. The "peripheral interest" seems more of an arbitrary characterization than a meaningful distinction.

Frankfurter's view in *Garmon* that the "counterpart remedy" rationale contributes to a lack of uniform policy seems correct. The NLRB provides make-whole remedies for violations of the Act. These include remedial money damages as well as cease-and-desist orders. Private state suits for punitive damages or exemplary damages for intentional torts in labor-management activity seem to have been deliberately rejected by the enactment of the NLRA. The specific statutory provisions in section 303 of the Act for private damage actions in cases involving violations of sections 8(b)(4) and 8(b)(7) would seem to indicate clearly a congressional intent to preclude all other types of private damage suits for union activity that is arguably prohibited. The Court's decisions to allow such suits for malicious libel in *Linn* and for outrageous conduct in *Farmer* seem to reflect a lower regard for the protection of labor activity in the national jurisprudence. The judicial concern that preemption might leave a victim without recourse and the *Sears* test of the identical issue reflect a retreat to the pre-*Garmon* focus on the type of remedy available or on whether the issue presented would be identical to that presented to the Board. This shifts the focus from the conduct being regulated and from the confusion engendered when the same conduct is subject to differing laws administered by differing forums.

Part VI. The Free Play of Economic Forces: The *Machinists* Approach

There is a preemption issue raised by state regulation of conduct that is neither arguably protected by section 7 nor prohibited by section 8. The question to be resolved where the Act is silent is whether Congress meant this activity to be free of any regulation, state or federal, and therefore left to the free play of economic forces, or whether Congress was indifferent to state regulation in the area.

The concept of the free play of economic forces is based on the view of the federal labor law as an attempt by Congress to establish a balance of power between labor and management that would provide a context for truly free collective bargaining. The parties are free to support their positions by engaging in economic pressure. The union may picket, strike, or boycott. The employer may lock out, replace, or relocate. The use of these economic weapons has been limited by Congress with an eye towards some national equilibrium. To allow the states to further regulate such activity upsets the balance struck by Congress, which intended that labor-management relations not regulated by the Act be left to the free play of economic forces.[65]

A. Development of the *Machinists* Rule

Because the NLRA as originally enacted in 1935 contained no union unfair labor practices, the question was raised as to whether all union activity was to be free of state regulation. In *Allen–Bradley Local 1111 United Electrical Workers v. Wisconsin Employment Relations Board,*[66] the Supreme Court answered the issue with regard to union violence. States could regulate in this area because Congress had not addressed violent activity in the NLRA and the Court felt that the state could still exercise its "historic powers" over such traditionally local matters as public safety and order. After the Taft–Hartley amendments added union unfair labor practices, the Supreme Court in the *Briggs–Stratton* case allowed state regulation to bar intermittent job stoppages.[67] The Court recognized that traditional strikes in support of a collective bargaining position were protected, but, the Court held, the union's quickie stoppages were not in the nature of protected activity and the state police power was therefore not superseded.

The determination in *Briggs–Stratton* was reversed in several steps. First, the union conduct that the Court decided was unprotected and, therefore, subject to state regulation, was subsequently found to be a permissible union pressure tactic in *NLRB v. Insurance Agents' International Union.*[68] In that case, the Court noted that economic pressure was integral to the bargaining process and for the government to intervene and regulate the choice of economic weapons would be to interfere with the substance of the negotiations. As it had stated in *Garner:* "For a state to impinge on an area of labor combat designed to be free is quite as much an obstruction of federal policy as if the state were to declare picketing free for purposes or by methods which the federal Act prohibits." [69] The concept that certain economic activity was to be left unregulated by any level of government also applied to preempt state sanctions of secondary activity that did not constitute a section 8(b)(4) violation.[70] In that case, the fact that Ohio law outlawed secondary activity that was not prohibited by section 8(b)(4) presented a clear conflict: a state remedy for activity the Act did not regulate. To the Court, a state suit would upset the balance of power expressed in national labor policy. The decision in *Briggs–Stratton* was finally directly overruled by the *Machinists* case,[71] where the Court articulated its view that there was, in addition to the *Garmon*-type approach, a second line of preemption analysis involving conduct that was neither arguably protected nor prohibited. This analysis centers on the issue of whether Congress intended the activity to be unregulated because it had been left "to be controlled by the free play of economic forces." The Court expressly rejected the *Briggs–Stratton* view that activity neither protected nor prohibited by the Act left the states free to regulate. Some activity, the court held, would be protected by federal law not because it fell within section 7 but because Congress intended that it was an activity that should be unrestricted by any governmental authority.

The Court found that the congressional scheme envisioned a system of free collective bargaining in which economic warfare was a basic ingredient. As one commentator noted, when the states outlaw an area unregulated by the federal law, it is not merely filling a gap "but denying to one party an economic weapon that Congress meant him to have available".[72] The Court in the *Machinists* case then went on to find that the union's activity—refusing to work overtime—was within the arsenal of self-help allowed to the parties in the bargaining process. The Court's decision in this regard reaffirms the view that the use of economic pressure in labor disputes was "part and parcel" of the collective-bargaining process. The fact that in the view of the Board or a state court one party has an economic advantage over the other is irrelevant to the issue. Tactics that were to be outlawed were to be done so specifically by federal statute. The Court, in completing its description of the "free play" doctrine, pointed out that the employer in the case could have retaliated by locking out the employees or by hiring permanent replacements.

The ringing endorsement of the "free play" branch of preemption analysis in *Machinists* has been modulated in recent cases, revealing a lack of its uniform acceptance by the Court.

B. Applications of *Machinists*: Employer Conduct

In *Belknap, Inc. v. Hale,*[73] the *Machinists* branch of preemption was found "too remote" an interest to prevent a state suit by strike replacements for breach of contract and misrepresentation against an employer who had initially hired them with assurances of permanence and then terminated them pursuant to a settlement agreement with the striking union to reinstate the strikers. The employer argued preemption based on the *Machinists* view that the state suit severely burdened the employer's use of one of its main weapons in a strike: the hiring of permanent replacements. If replacements would be able to sue for their jobs it would inhibit the employer's hiring them in the first instance and, once hired, inhibit any settlement with the union since the return of the strikers is usually the basic union condition for any strike settlement. The Court felt otherwise: "It is one thing to hold that the federal law intended to leave the employer and the union free to use their economic weapons against one another, but quite another to hold that either the employer or the union is also free to injure innocent third parties without regard to the normal rules of law governing those relationships. We cannot agree with the dissent that Congress intended such a lawless regime." [74]

The analysis is flawed by characterizing the replacements as "innocent third parties" seemingly outside the dispute. They could more accurately be regarded as parties who took sides in the dispute by taking jobs held by strikers. Moreover, Congress has created substantive rights for innocent third parties in sections 8(a) and 8(b) of the Act. The Act applies to replacements' rights as well as to strikers'. Their termination, in some circumstances, might be an unfair labor practice and, in some circumstances, part of the resolution of the dispute. To allow a state-court contract obligation to attach to a permanent strike replacement seems to directly involve the state in the economic battle and adds additional pressures to the parties that inhibit the resolution of the dispute. If the hiring of a permanent replacement during a strike locks the employer into an unalterable employment obligation, the employer may be hesitant to use replacements and the union may, therefore, be freer to use the strike weapon. On the other hand, once having employed replacements, the employer may be unable to ever settle the dispute since a fundamental condition for settlement of any strike is the reinstatement of the strikers. Moreover, by holding the employer to an obligation of permanence, the replacements may run afoul of Board precedent outlawing grants of special privileges to strike replacements and discrimination against strikers.[75] The Court's decision in *Belknap* involves a conflict with the NLRB's administration of the Act given that the reinstatement of the strikers was a condition of the settlement of the union's unfair labor practice charges. Thus, the basic NLRB processes became obstructed by allowing the NLRB settlement to be attacked by state action.

The retreat, in this instance, from the free play doctrine seems to be consistent with the recent Court rulings reducing the reach of preemption and the centrality of federal labor policy and increasing the focus on the competing rights of individuals affected by labor activity.

C. State Regulation of Strike Situations: Unemployment Benefits to Strikers

The *New York Telephone* case involved a challenge by struck telephone companies to the New York State policy of paying unemployment benefits to strikers after an eight-week waiting period. The impact of the benefits paid to strikers was found by all nine justices to alter the balance in collective bargaining by increasing the striking employees' willingness to remain on strike and on the employer's costs of the strike since the employer contributions to the unemployment system would be increased. However, the plurality opinion by Justice

Stevens and supported by Justices White and Rehnquist chose to distinguish the state unemployment law from the state regulation involved in *Machinists* on the basis that it was not aimed at regulating private conduct in labor relations but rather was a law of general application aimed at providing public benefits to ensure employee security. Therefore, they held, the *Machinists* analysis would not be controlling, and the *Garmon* exception for state laws "deeply rooted in local feeling and responsibility" would be invoked. The Court found that the legislative history revealed that Congress, in enacting Social Security legislation within weeks of the NLRA, had intended to provide the states with wide leeway in establishing programs of unemployment insurance and that in the absence of compelling congressional direction, preemption should not be inferred.

The three concurring justices making up the rest of the majority expressed the traditional Frankfurter approach to preemption. They expressly disavowed the main opinion's distinction between laws of general and specific application. They felt that the *Machinists* free play approach was equally applicable to laws of general application and that the touchstone of preemption was the impact of the law on the conduct to be regulated. As they stated: "The crucial inquiry is whether the exercise of state authority frustrate[s] the effective implementation of the Act's processes, not whether the state's purpose was to confer a benefit on a class of citizens." [76] They felt that the "local interest" exception of *Garmon* should be limited to state interests that are at the "core of the State's duties and traditional concerns"— basically torts. The concurring justices, however, would uphold the state system on the basis of legislative history that revealed congressional intent to permit the states to implement an unemployment system regardless of its impact on the balance of bargaining power.

The three dissenting judges felt that the *Machinists* analysis was controlling. They traced the Court's rejection of the NLRB's attempts to restrict the economic weapons of the parties in negotiation disputes in *Insurance Agents* (union quickie strikes) and *American Ship Bldg. Co.* (employer lockouts) [77] and reasoned that the states had no more authority than the NLRB to upset the balance of power struck by Congress. The dissent disputed the legislative history, finding nothing that would support the view that Congress intended unemployment benefits for strikers.[78] The decision may be read as reaffirming the vitality of the *Machinists* analysis. A majority of the Court—the six judges that made up the concurring and the dissenting opinions—made clear their belief in its applicability. However, the plurality opinion continued to sound the distinction between laws of general application and those specifically directed at labor relations so emphatically rejected by Frankfurter in *Garmon,* but revised in *Sears.*

The distinction carved out by Congress for state discretion in its social security legislation was determinative in *Baker v. General Motors*

Corp.,[79] where the Court upheld a Michigan statute that denied unemployment benefits to strikers who finance strike benefits through means other than dues. The Court, in a 6–3 decision, followed the *New York Telephone* decision that allowed states freedom to decide whether or not to pay unemployment benefits to strikers.

In *Fort Halifax Packing Co. v. Coyne*,[80] the Supreme Court held that a state statute mandating severance pay for employees whose employers have relocated is not preempted by the NLRA. The Court held that since the statute applies equally to both union and non-union employees, it does not undercut collective bargaining and held that the establishment of minimum substantive labor standards is a traditional police power of the state that merely provides a neutral "backdrop" to negotiations. On this basis, the Court concluded that the *Machinists* doctrine did not apply. Free play is still free, regardless of the substantive backdrop against which the bargaining takes place.

Where, however, the state or local governments act with specific regard to labor relations, the *Machinists* analysis continues to apply with less difficulty. Thus, in *Golden State Transit Corp. v. City of Los Angeles*,[81] the Supreme Court held that the city's conditioning of a taxi franchise renewal upon the settlement of the employer's dispute with its drivers was preempted. The Court rejected the Ninth Circuit's finding that the city was basically regulating transportation and as such was engaged in an issue of peripheral concern to national labor policy. The city's action was specifically tied to a labor issue (a bargaining impasse) and, as such, served to limit the employer's right to hold out for an unlimited period and the city's action therefore upset the balance of power designed by Congress. Justice Rehnquist in a lone dissent marked more by eloquence than reason complained that from *Bethlehem Steel* and *Garner*, two "sensible acorns," the court had raised "the mighty oak of [the] Court's pre-emption doctrine, which sweeps ever outward though still totally uninformed by any express directive from Congress."[82]

Part VII. The "Balancing" Test

The confusion in the application of either the *Garmon* or *Machinists* approaches leads some lower courts to apply a straight "balancing" test, weighing the interests as outlined by the Court in *Farmer*. The reasoning is that in the absence of specific congressional expression, all private conduct is either arguably regulated by the Act under *Garmon* or unregulated by the Act and intended to be left to the free play of economic forces under *Machinists*.

The crucial issue then in either case is the second step—whether the activity is within the peripheral-deeply rooted local interest exception articulated in *Garmon* and also applied in *Machinists*. This involves the balancing of the states' legitimate non-labor interest in regulating the activity against the federal interest in uniform labor regulation and the degree to which the state regulation will interfere with those interests.[83]

The "balancing test" has received the support of some commentators and lower courts, and reflects still another step away from the high judicial regard for the Act reflected in *Garmon* and *Lockridge*. By regarding the *Farmer* balancing of the local interest exceptions as the "second step" of preemption analysis, these courts have elevated the exception to greater significance than the rule. In each case approached in this manner, preemption becomes subject to being outweighed by the balance struck by the particular court. In the end it leaves the individual lower courts without the clear guidelines that the Court attempted to set out in *Garmon*.

CONCLUSION

The preemption principles seem to be clear and easy to apply in cases of state interference with organizational activity and traditional union economic pressures, strikes, picketing, and boycotts. However, there is a growing concern expressed by some members of the Court over whether individual victims of intentional torts should be prevented from having their day in court because of concern for a uniform policy of labor law that limits relief to the NLRB and its remedial powers. The interests in individual rights sparked by the Civil Rights Acts and the struggle of minorities and women to enter the workplace may have shifted the focus in labor-management law from collective rights to individual rights. The Court also may be influenced by a concern that union members not be disadvantaged in comparison with unorganized employees by having lesser recourse to the state court machinery. This shift has caused a corresponding shift from the basic *Garmon* and *Machinists* rules to a more complex, and thus more malleable, analysis.

The Supreme Court may reflect those interests in the balances it strikes between competing interests in the future.

FOOTNOTES

1. *Adair v. United States*, 208 U.S. 161 (1908). This ruling was the reason that the Norris–LaGuardia Act spoke in terms of limiting the jurisdiction of federal courts because Congress felt it had to be based upon the Congressional power to regulate the federal courts in order to pass constitutional muster.

2. As one commentator noted, the Taft–Hartley Act, initially branded by organized labor as "slave labor" legislation, by prohibiting some forms of union economic activity as unfair labor practices, provided an argument for the preemption of more restrictive state statutes and court decisions. Cox, Recent Developments in Federal Labor Law Preemption, 41 Ohio State L.J. 277 (1980).

3. The Railway Labor Act enacted in 1923 created substantive rights of organizing and collective bargaining and limited certain actions of the railroads. However, no agency was created to elaborate and interpret the Act and the Act's coverage was limited to railway (and later airline) employees.

4. 15 U.S.C. § 1 et seq.

5. 15 U.S.C. § 12 et seq.

6. See Chapter 4, supra, at p. 279.

7. See the various approaches of the Justices to preemption in *New York Telephone Co. v. New York State Dept of Labor*, 440 U.S. 519 (1979) and *Local 926, Intern. Union of Operating Engineers v. Jones*, 460 U.S. 669 (1983).

8. U.S. Const. Art. VI, Sec. 2. Preemption, accordingly, is not a waivable defense. *International Longshoremen's Ass'n v. Davis*, 476 U.S. 380 (1986).

9. Sec. 164(c) of the NLRA, as added by Title VII of the Labor–Management Reporting and Disclosure Act of 1959, 73 Stat. 541, 29 U.S.C. § 164(c)(2), allows state agencies and courts to assert jurisdiction over suits for breaches of collective bargaining agreements when the Board has declined jurisdiction.

10. See, e.g., *Weber v. Anheuser–Busch, Inc.*, 348 U.S. 468 at 480 (1955).

11. *San Diego Building Trades Council v. Garmon*, 359 U.S. 236 (1959); *Local 76, Intern. Ass'n of Machinists v. Wisconsin Employment Relations Commission*, 427 U.S. 132 (1976).

12. See, e.g., Cox, *Recent Developments*, supra; *Palm Beach Co. v. Journeymen's and Production Allied Services, Local 157*, 519 F.Supp. 705 (S.D.N.Y.1981).

13. The preemption of private rights of action by the dispute resolution procedures of collective bargaining agreements under LMRA § 301 presents different issues, and is not within the scope of this discussion.

14. *Hill v. Florida*, 325 U.S. 538 (1945). But see *Brown v. Hotel and Restaurant Employees Union Local 54*, 468 U.S. 491 (1984), where the Court upheld a similar licensing requirement for union officials representing employees in New Jersey gambling institutions.

15. *International Union, United Autoworkers v. O'Brien*, 339 U.S. 454 (1950).

16. *Amalgamated Ass'n of Street Employees, Division 998 v. Wisconsin Employment Relations Board*, 340 U.S. 383 (1951).

17. In addition, Sec. 13 of the Act provides: "Nothing in this Act, except as specifically provided for herein, shall be construed so as either to interfere with to impede or diminish in any way the right to strike, or to affect the limitation or qualifications on that right.

18. 325 U.S. 795 (1945).

19. *Garner v. Teamsters Union, Local 776*, 346 U.S. 485 (1953).

20. *Capital Service v. NLRB*, 347 U.S. 501 (1954).

21. *United Construction Workers v. Laburnum Constr. Corp.*, 347 U.S. 656 (1954).

22. Id.

23. *International Union, United Auto Workers v. Russell*, 356 U.S. 634 (1958).

24. *United Auto Workers v. Wisconsin Employment Relations Board*, 351 U.S. 266 (1956).

25. *NLRB v. Fainblatt*, 306 U.S. 601 (1939).

26. *Bethlehem Steel Co. v. New York State Labor Relations Board*, 330 U.S. 767 (1947).

27. *La Crosse Telephone Co. v. Wisconsin Employment Relations Board*, 336 U.S. 18 (1949).

28. Id.

29. *Guss v. Utah Labor Relations Board*, 353 U.S. 1 (1957).

30. Section 14(c) provides that "[t]he Board, in its discretion, may . . . decline to assert jurisdiction over any labor dispute involving any class or category of employers where . . . the effect of such labor dispute on commerce is not sufficiently substantial to warrant the exercise of its jurisdiction." The provision goes on to state that states could assert jurisdiction over those labor disputes that the Board had declined.

31. 359 U.S. 236 (1959).

32. Id. at 243–44.

33. Id. at 247.

34. Id. at 247.

35. 356 U.S. 617 (1958).

36. *New York Telephone v. New York State Department of Labor*, 440 U.S. 519, at n. 12 (1979).

37. *Garner*, supra note 19, at 490–91 (1953).

38. *Brown*, supra note 14. The claim that an activity is "arguably protected" may not be pleaded conclusorily; it must be shown that the Board has not authoritatively rejected such a view and that there is sufficient evidence to uphold such a view. *International Longshoremen's Ass'n v. Davis*, 476 U.S. 380 (1986).

39. *Amalgamated Ass'n of Street Employees v. Lockridge*, 403 U.S. 274 (1971).

40. *Farmer v. Carpenters*, 430 U.S. 290 (1977); *Linn v. United Plant Guard Workers, Local 114*, 383 U.S. 53 (1966); *Belknap, Inc. v. Hale*, 463 U.S. 491 (1983).

41. *Brown*, supra note 14.

42. Id.; *Sears, Roebuck & Co. v. San Diego Council of Carpenters*, 436 U.S. 180 (1978).

43. 325 U.S. 538 (1945).

44. Supra, note 14.

45. *De Veau v. Braisted*, 363 U.S. 144 (1960).

46. *International Union, United Autoworkers v. O'Brien*, supra, note 15.

47. *Amalgamated Ass'n of Street Employees Division 998 v. Wisconsin Employment Relations Board*, supra, note 16.

48. 358 U.S. 283 (1959).

49. 348 U.S. 468 (1955).

50. 440 U.S. 519 (1979).

51. *NLRB v. Babcock and Wilcox Co.*, 351 U.S. 105 (1956). The Board's current formulation of this analysis appears in *Fairmont Hotel*, 282 N.L.R.B. 27 (1986).

52. Id.

53. 391 U.S. 308 (1968).

54. Interestingly enough, the court refused to deal with the preemption issue (the property owner had sued for a state court trespass injunction), saying it was unnecessary in view of the finding on the constitutional issue. After first limiting *Logan Valley* to shopping centers in *Central Hardware Co. v. NLRB*, 407 U.S. 539 (1972) (business district concept does not apply to union activity in single store parking lot) and to labor activity in *Lloyd Corp. v. Tanner*, 407 U.S. 551 (1972) (First Amendment protection not applicable to general political activity in shopping center), the court finally overruled *Logan* in *Hudgens v. NLRB*, 424 U.S. 507 (1976) (First Amendment doesn't apply; Board should use *Babcock & Wilcox* balancing test in cases of union activity on private property).

55. 436 U.S. 180 (1978).

56. *Garner*, supra note 19 at 490–91.

57. 383 U.S. 53 (1966).

58. See note 40 supra.

59. See, e.g., *Sherman v. St. Barnabas Hosp.*, 535 F.Supp. 564 (S.D.N.Y.1982); *Adkins v. General Motors Corp.*, 556 F.Supp. 452 (S.D.Ohio 1983).

60. Supra, note 7.

61. *Wisconsin Department of Industry, Labor and Human Relations v. Gould Inc.*, 475 U.S. 282 (1986).

62. *Machinists v. Gonzales*, 356 U.S. 617 (1958).

63. *Vaca v. Sipes*, 386 U.S. 171 (1967).

64. See note 39, supra.

65. See *Machinists*, supra, note 11.

66. 315 U.S. 740 (1942).

67. *International Union United Auto Workers, Local 232 v. Wisconsin Employment Relations Board*, 336 U.S. 245 (1949).

68. 361 U.S. 477 (1960).

69. *Garner*, supra note 19 at 500.

70. *Teamsters Local 20 v. Morton*, 377 U.S. 252 (1964). This case involved the union's solicitation of customers of the employer to stop renting its trucks during the dispute. Since the solicitation did not involve threats or other coercive measures, the solicitation was held not to violate section 8(b)(4).

71. See note 11, supra.

72. Lesnick, Preemption Reconsidered: The Apparent Reaffirmation of Garmon, 72 Colum.L.Rev. 469 (1972).

73. *Belknap, Inc. v. Hale*, 463 U.S. 491 (1983).

74. Id. at 500.

75. *NLRB v. Erie Resistor Corp.*, 373 U.S. 221 (1963) (granting strike replacements "super seniority" over strikers illegally discriminates against the strikers).

76. *New York Telephone*, supra note 36, at 550 (Blackmun, J.).

77. *American Ship Building Co. v. NLRB*, 380 U.S. 300 (1965).

78. The three dissenting justices, Powell, Burger and Stewart, agreed with the concurring justices that the "deeply rooted" exception in *Garmon* should be limited to personal torts or violence to property.

79. 478 U.S. 621 (1986).

80. *Fort Halifax Packing Co., Inc. v. Coyne*, 107 S.Ct. 2211 (1987).

81. 475 U.S. 608 (1986).

82. Id. at 475 U.S. at 622, 106 S.Ct. 1403.

83. See Cox, *Recent Developments, supra, Palm Beach Co. v. Journeymen's and Prod. Allied Services Local 157*, 519 F.Supp. 705 (S.D.N.Y.1981).

Relevant Books, Articles, and Suggested Reading

BOOKS:
Gorman, Basic Text on Labor Law (1976).

ARTICLES:
Michelman, "State Power to Govern Concerted Employee Activities," 74 Harv.L.Rev. 641 (1961).

Meltzer, "the Supreme Court, Congress, and State Jurisdiction Over Labor Relations," 59 Columbia L.Rev. 6 (1959).

Cox, "Labor Law Preemption Revisited," 85 Harv.L.Rev. 1337 (1972).

Lesnick, "Preemption Reconsidered: The Apparent Reaffirmation of Garman," 72 Columbia L.Rev. 469 (1972).

Cox, "Recent Developments in Federal Labor Law Preemption," 41 Ohio State L.J. 277 (1980).

*

Appendix A

NATIONAL LABOR RELATIONS ACT

49 Stat. 449 (1935), as amended; 29 U.S.C. §§ 151–69 (1982).

FINDINGS AND POLICIES

Sec. 1. The denial by some employers of the right of employees to organize and the refusal by some employers to accept the procedure of collective bargaining lead to strikes and other forms of industrial strife or unrest, which have the intent or the necessary effect of burdening or obstructing commerce by (a) impairing the efficiency, safety, or operation of the instrumentalities of commerce; (b) occurring in the current of commerce; (c) materially affecting, restraining, or controlling the flow of raw materials or manufactured or processed goods from or into the channels of commerce, or the prices of such materials or goods in commerce; or (d) causing diminution of employment and wages in such volume as substantially to impair or disrupt the market for goods flowing from or into the channels of commerce.

The inequality of bargaining power between employees who do not possess full freedom of association or actual liberty of contract, and employers who are organized in the corporate or other forms of ownership association substantially burdens and affects the flow of commerce, and tends to aggravate recurrent business depressions, by depressing wage rates and the purchasing power of wage earners in industry and by preventing the stabilization of competitive wage rates and working conditions within and between industries.

Experience has proved that protection by law of the right of employees to organize and bargain collectively safeguards commerce from injury, impairment, or interruption, and promotes the flow of commerce by removing certain recognized sources of industrial strife and unrest, by encouraging practices fundamental to the friendly adjustment of industrial disputes arising out of differences as to wages, hours, or other working conditions, and by restoring equality of bargaining power between employers and employees.

Experience has further demonstrated that certain practices by some labor organizations, their officers, and members have the intent or the necessary effect of burdening or obstructing commerce by preventing the free flow of goods in such commerce through strikes and other forms of industrial unrest or through concerted activities which impair the interest of the public in the free flow of such commerce. The elimination of such practices is a necessary condition to the assurance of the rights herein guaranteed.

It is hereby declared to be the policy of the United States to eliminate the causes of certain substantial obstructions to the free flow of commerce and to mitigate and eliminate these obstructions when they have occurred by encouraging the practice and procedure of collective bargaining and by protecting the exercise by workers of full freedom of association, self-organization, and designation of representatives of their own choosing, for the purpose of negotiating the terms and conditions of their employment or other mutual aid or protection.

DEFINITIONS

Sec. 2. When used in this Act—

(1) The term "person" includes one or more individuals, labor organizations, partnerships, associations, corporations, legal representatives, trustees, trustees in bankruptcy, or receivers.

(2) The term "employer" includes any person acting [in the interest of] as an agent of an employer, directly or indirectly, but shall not include the United States or any wholly owned Government corporation, or any Federal Reserve Bank, or any State or political subdivision thereof, [or any corporation or association operating a hospital, if no part of the net earnings inures to the benefit of any private shareholder or individual,] or any person subject to the Railway Labor Act, as amended from time to time, or any labor organization (other than when acting as an employer), or anyone acting in the capacity of officer or agent of such labor organization.

(3) The term "employee" shall include any employee, and shall not be limited to the employees of a particular employer, unless the Act explicitly states otherwise, and shall include any individual whose work has ceased as a consequence of, or in connection with, any current labor dispute or because of any unfair labor practice, and who has not obtained any other regular and substantially equivalent employment, but shall not include any individual employed as an agricultural laborer, or in the domestic service of any family or person at his home, or any individual employed by his parent or spouse, or any individual having the status of an independent contractor, or any individual employed as a supervisor, or any individual employed by an employer subject to the Railway Labor Act, as amended from time to time, or by any other person who is not an employer as herein defined.

(4) The term "representatives" includes any individual or labor organization.

(5) The term "labor organization" means any organization of any kind, or any agency or employee representation committee or plan, in

which employees participate and which exists for the purpose, in whole or in part, of dealing with employers concerning grievances, labor disputes, wages, rates of pay, hours of employment, or conditions of work.

(6) The term "commerce" means trade, traffic, commerce, transportation, or communication among the several States, or between the District of Columbia or any Territory of the United States and any State or other Territory, or between any foreign country and any State, Territory, or the District of Columbia, or within the District of Columbia or any Territory, or between points in the same State but through any other State or any Territory or the District of Columbia or any foreign country.

(7) The term "affecting commerce" means in commerce, or burdening or obstructing commerce or the free flow of commerce, or having led or tending to lead to a labor dispute burdening or obstructing commerce or the free flow of commerce.

(8) The term "unfair labor practice" means any unfair labor practice listed in section 8.

(9) The term "labor dispute" includes any controversy concerning terms, tenure or conditions of employment, or concerning the association or representation of persons in negotiating, fixing, maintaining, changing, or seeking to arrange terms or conditions of employment, regardless of whether the disputants stand in the proximate relation of employer and employee.

(10) The term "National Labor Relations Board" means the National Labor Relations Board provided for in section 3 of this Act.

(11) The term "supervisor" means any individual having authority, in the interest of the employer, to hire, transfer, suspend, lay off, recall, promote, discharge, assign, reward, or discipline other employees, or responsibly to direct them, or to adjust their grievances, or effectively to recommend such action, if in connection with the foregoing the exercise of such authority is not of a merely routine or clerical nature, but requires the use of independent judgment.

(12) The term "professional employee" means—

(a) any employee engaged in work (i) predominantly intellectual and varied in character as opposed to routine mental, manual, mechanical, or physical work; (ii) involving the consistent exercise of discretion and judgment in its performance; (iii) of such a character that the output produced or the result accomplished cannot be standardized in relation to a given period of time; (iv) requiring knowledge of an advanced type in a field of science or learning customarily acquired by a prolonged course of specialized intellectual instruction and study in an institution of higher learning or a hospital, as distinguished from a general academic education or from an apprenticeship or from training in the performance of routine mental, manual, or physical processes; or

(b) any employee, who (i) has completed the courses of specialized intellectual instruction and study described in clause (iv) of paragraph (a), and (ii) is performing related work under the supervision of a professional person to qualify himself to become a professional employee as defined in paragraph (a).

(13) In determining whether any person is acting as an 'agent' of another person so as to make such other person responsible for his acts, the question of whether the specific acts performed were actually authorized or subsequently ratified shall not be controlling.

(14) The term "health care institution" shall include any hospital, convalescent hospital, health maintenance organization, health clinic, nursing home, extended care facility, or other institution devoted to the care of sick, infirm, or aged person.

NATIONAL LABOR RELATIONS BOARD

Sec. 3. (a) The National Labor Relations Board (hereinafter called the "Board") created by this Act prior to its amendment by the Labor Management Relations Act, 1947, is continued as an agency of the United States, except that the Board shall consist of five instead of three members, appointed by the President by and with the advice and consent of the Senate. Of the two additional members so provided for, one shall be appointed for a term of five years and the other for a term of two years. Their successors, and the successors of the other members, shall be appointed for terms of five years each, excepting that any individual chosen to fill a vacancy shall be appointed only for the unexpired term of the member whom he shall succeed. The President shall designate one member to serve as Chairman of the Board. Any member of the Board may be removed by the President, upon notice and hearing, for neglect of duty or malfeasance in office, but for no other cause.

(b) The Board is authorized to delegate to any group of three or more members any or all of the powers which it may itself exercise. The Board is also authorized to delegate to its regional directors its powers under section 9 to determine the unit appropriate for the purpose of collective bargaining, to investigate and provide for hearings, and determine whether a question of representation exists, and to direct an election or take a secret ballot under subsection (c) or (e) of section 9 and certify the results thereof, except that upon the filing of a request therefor with the Board by any interested person, the Board may review any action of a regional director delegated to him under this paragraph, but such a review shall not, unless specifically ordered by the Board, operate as a stay of any action taken by the regional director. A vacancy in the Board shall not impair the right of the remaining members to exercise all of the powers of the Board, and three members of the Board shall, at all times, constitute a quorum of the Board, except that two members shall constitute a quorum of any group designated pursuant to the first sentence hereof. The Board shall have an official seal which shall be judicially noticed.

(c) The Board shall at the close of each fiscal year make a report in writing to Congress and to the President [stating in detail the cases it has heard, the decisions it has rendered, the names, salaries, and duties of all employees and officers in the employ or under the supervision of the Board, and an account of all moneys it has disbursed.] summarizing significant case activities and operations for that fiscal year.

(d) There shall be a General Counsel of the Board who shall be appointed by the President, by and with the advice and consent of the Senate, for a term of four years. The General Counsel of the Board shall exercise general supervision over all attorneys employed by the Board (other than administrative law judges and legal assistants to Board members) and over the officers and employees in the regional offices. He shall have final authority, on behalf of the Board, in respect of the investigation of charges and issuance of complaints under section 10, and in respect of the prosecution of such complaints before the Board, and shall have such other duties as the Board may prescribe or as may be provided by law. In case of a vacancy in the office of the General Counsel the President is authorized to designate the officer or employee who shall act as General Counsel during such vacancy, but no person or persons so designated shall so act (1) for more than forty days when the Congress is in session unless a nomination to fill such vacancy shall have been submitted to the Senate, or (2) after the adjournment sine die of the session of the Senate in which such nomination was submitted.

Sec. 4. (a) Each member of the Board and the General Counsel of the Board [shall receive a salary of $12,000 per annum,] shall be eligible for reappointment, and shall not engage in any other business, vocation, or employment. The Board shall appoint an executive secretary, and such attorneys, examiners, and regional directors, and such other employees as it may from time to time find necessary for the proper performance of its duties. The Board may not employ any attorneys for the purpose of reviewing transcripts of hearings or preparing drafts of opinions except that any attorney employed for assignment as a legal assistant to any Board member may for such Board member review such transcripts and prepare such drafts. No administrative law judge's report shall be reviewed, either before or after its publication, by any person other than a member of the Board or his legal assistant, and no administrative law judge shall advise or consult with the Board with respect to exceptions taken to his findings, rulings, or recommendations. The Board may establish or utilize such regional, local, or other agencies, and utilize such voluntary and uncompensated services, as may from time to time be needed. Attorneys appointed under this section may, at the direction of the Board, appear for and represent the Board in any case in court. Nothing in this Act shall be construed to authorize the Board to appoint individuals for the purpose of conciliation or mediation, or for economic analysis.

(b) All of the expenses of the Board, including all necessary traveling and subsistence expenses outside the District of Columbia incurred by the members or employees of the Board under its orders, shall be allowed and paid on the presentation of itemized vouchers therefor approved by the Board or by any individual it designates for that purpose.

Sec. 5. The principal office of the Board shall be in the District of Columbia, but it may meet and exercise any or all of its powers at any other place. The Board may, by one or more of its members or by such agents or agencies as it may designate, prosecute any inquiry necessary to its functions in any part of the United States. A member who participates in such an inquiry shall not be disqualified from subsequently participating in a decision of the Board in the same case.

Sec. 6. The Board shall have authority from time to time to make, amend, and rescind, in the manner prescribed by the Administrative Procedure Act, such rules and regulations as may be necessary to carry out the provisions of this Act. [Such rules and regulations shall be effective upon publication in the manner which the Board shall prescribe.]

RIGHTS OF EMPLOYEES

Sec. 7. Employees shall have the right to self-organization, to form, join, or assist labor organizations, to bargain collectively through representatives of their own choosing, and to engage in other concerted activities for the purpose of collective bargaining or other mutual aid or protection, and shall also have the right to refrain from any or all of such activities except to the extent that such right may be affected by an agreement requiring membership in a labor organization as a condition of employment as authorized in section 8(a)(3).

UNFAIR LABOR PRACTICES

Sec. 8. (a) It shall be an unfair labor practice for an employer—

(1) to interfere with, restrain, or coerce employees in the exercise of the rights guaranteed in section 7;

(2) to dominate or interfere with the formation or administration of any labor organization or contribute financial or other

support to it: Provided, That subject to rules and regulations made and published by the Board pursuant to section 6, an employer shall not be prohibited from permitting employees to confer with him during working hours without loss of time or pay;

(3) by discrimination in regard to hire or tenure of employment or any term or condition of employment to encourage or discourage membership in any labor organization: Provided, That nothing in this Act, or in any other statute of the United States, shall preclude an employer from making an agreement with a labor organization (not established, maintained, or assisted by any action defined in section 8(a) of this Act as an unfair labor practice) to require as a condition of employment membership therein on or after the thirtieth day following the beginning of such employment or the effective date of such agreement, whichever is the later, (i) if such labor organization is the representative of the employees as provided in section 9(a), in the appropriate collective-bargaining unit covered by such agreement when made, [and has at the time the agreement was made or within the preceding twelve months received from the Board a notice of compliance with Section 9(f), (g), (h)], and (ii) unless following an election held as provided in section 9(e) within one year preceding the effective date of such agreement, the Board shall have certified that at least a majority of the employees eligible to vote in such election have voted to rescind the authority of such labor organization to make such an agreement: Provided further, That no employer shall justify any discrimination against an employee for nonmembership in a labor organization (A) if he has reasonable grounds for believing that such membership was not available to the employee on the same terms and conditions generally applicable to other members, or (B) if he has reasonable grounds for believing that membership was denied or terminated for reasons other than the failure of the employee to tender the periodic dues and the initiation fees uniformly required as a condition of acquiring or retaining membership;

(4) to discharge or otherwise discriminate against an employee because he has filed charges or given testimony under this Act;

(5) to refuse to bargain collectively with the representatives of his employees, subject to the provisions of section 9(a).

(b) It shall be an unfair labor practice for a labor organization or its agents—

(1) to restrain or coerce (A) employees in the exercise of the rights guaranteed in section 7: Provided, That this paragraph shall not impair the right of a labor organization to prescribe its

own rules with respect to the acquisition or retention of member-ship therein; or (B) an employer in the selection of his represent-atives for the purposes of collective bargaining or the adjustment of grievances;

(2) to cause or attempt to cause an employer to discriminate against an employee in violation of subsection (a)(3) or to discriminate against an employee with respect to whom member-ship in such organization has been denied or terminated on some ground other than his failure to tender the periodic dues and the initiation fees uniformly required as a condition of acquiring or retaining membership;

(3) to refuse to bargain collectively with an employer, pro-vided it is the representative of his employees subject to the provisions of section 9(a);

(4)(i) to engage in, or to induce or encourage [the employ-ees of any employer] any individual employed by any person engaged in commerce or in an industry affecting commerce to engage in, a strike or a [concerted] refusal in the course of [their] his employment to use, manufacture, process, transport, or other-wise handle or work on any goods, articles, materials, or com-modities or to perform any services[,]; or (ii) to threaten, coerce, or restrain any person engaged in commerce or in an industry affecting commerce, where in either case an object thereof is—

(A) forcing or requiring any employer or self-employed person to join any labor or employer organization [or any employer or other person to cease using, selling, handling, transporting, or otherwise dealing in the products of any other producer, processor, or manufacturer, or to cease doing business with any other person;] or to enter into any agreement which is prohibited by section 8(e);

(B) forcing or requiring any [any employer or other] person to cease using, selling, handling, transporting, or otherwise dealing in the products of any other producer, processor, or manufacturer, or to cease doing business with any other person, or forcing or requiring any other employer to recognize or bargain with a labor organization as the representative of his employees unless such labor organiza-tion has been certified as the representative of such employ-ees under the provisions of section 9[;]; Provided, That nothing contained in this clause (B) shall be construed to make unlawful, where not otherwise unlawful, any primary strike or primary picketing;

(C) forcing or requiring any employer to recognize or bargain with a particular labor organization as the representa-tive of his employees if another labor organization has been certified as the representative of such employees under the provisions of section 9;

(D) forcing or requiring any employer to assign particular work to employees in a particular labor organization or in a particular trade, craft, or class rather than to employees in another labor organization or in another trade, craft, or class, unless such employer is failing to conform to an order or certification of the Board determining the bargaining representative for employees performing such work:

Provided, That nothing contained in this subsection (b) shall be construed to make unlawful a refusal by any person to enter upon the premises of any employer (other than his own employer), if the employees of such employer are engaged in a strike ratified or approved by a representative of such employees whom such employer is required to recognize under this Act: Provided further, That for the purposes of this paragraph (4) only, nothing contained in such paragraph shall be construed to prohibit publicity, other than picketing, for the purpose of truthfully advising the public, including consumers and members of a labor organization, that a product or products are produced by an employer with whom the labor organization has a primary dispute and are distributed by another employer, as long as such publicity does not have an effect of inducing any individual employed by any person other than the primary employer in the course of his employment to refuse to pick up, deliver, or transport any goods, or not to perform any services, at the establishment of the employer engaged in such distribution:

(5) to require of employees covered by an agreement authorized under subsection (a)(3) the payment, as a condition precedent to becoming a member of such organization, of a fee in an amount which the Board finds excessive or discriminatory under all the circumstances. In making such a finding, the Board shall consider, among other relevant factors, the practices and customs of labor organizations in the particular industry, and the wages currently paid to the employees affected; [and]

(6) to cause or attempt to cause an employer to pay or deliver or agree to pay or deliver any money or other thing of value, in the nature of an exaction, for services which are not performed or not to be performed[.]; and

(7) to picket or cause to be picketed, or threaten to picket or cause to be picketed, any employer where an object thereof is forcing or requiring an employer to recognize or bargain with a labor organization as the representatives of his employees, or forcing or requiring the employees of an employer to accept or select such labor organization as their collective bargaining repre-

sentative, unless such labor organization is currently certified as the representative of such employees:

(A) where the employer has lawfully recognized in accordance with this Act any other labor organization and a question concerning representation may not appropriately be raised under section 9(c) of this Act.

(B) where within the preceding twelve months a valid election under section 9(c) of this Act has been conducted, or

(C) where such picketing has been conducted without a petition under section 9(c) being filed within a reasonable period of time not to exceed thirty days from the commencement of such picketing: Provided, That when such a petition has been filed the Board shall forthwith, without regard to the provisions of section 9(c)(1) or the absence of a showing of a substantial interest on the part of the labor organization, direct an election in such unit as the Board finds to be appropriate and shall certify the results thereof: Provided further, That nothing in this subparagraph (C) shall be construed to prohibit any picketing or other publicity for the purpose of truthfully advising the public (including consumers) that an employer does not employ members of, or have a contract with, a labor organization, unless an effect of such picketing is to induce any individual employed by any other person in the course of his employment, not to pick up, deliver or transport any goods or not to perform any services.

Nothing in this paragraph (7) shall be construed to permit any act which would otherwise be an unfair labor practice under this section 8(b).

(c) The expressing of any views, argument, or opinion, or the dissemination thereof, whether in written, printed, graphic, or visual form, shall not constitute or be evidence of an unfair labor practice under any of the provisions of this Act, if such expression contains no threat of reprisal or force or promise of benefit.

(d) For the purposes of this section, to bargain collectively is the performance of the mutual obligation of the employer and the representative of the employees to meet at reasonable times and confer in good faith with respect to wages, hours, and other terms and conditions of employment, or the negotiation of an agreement, or any question arising thereunder, and the execution of a written contract incorporating any agreement reached if requested by either party, but such obligation does not compel either party to agree to a proposal or require the making of a concession: Provided, That where there is in effect a collective-bargaining contract covering employees in an industry affecting commerce, the duty to bargain collectively shall also mean that no party to such contract shall terminate or modify such contract, unless the party desiring such termination or modification—

(1) serves a written notice upon the other party to the contract of the proposed termination or modification sixty days prior to the expiration date thereof, or in the event such contract contains no expiration date, sixty days prior to the time it is proposed to make such termination or modification;

(2) offers to meet and confer with the other party for the purpose of negotiating a new contract or a contract containing the proposed modifications;

(3) notifies the Federal Mediation and Conciliation Service within thirty days after such notice of the existence of a dispute, and simultaneously therewith notifies any State or Territorial agency established to mediate and conciliate disputes within the State or Territory where the dispute occurred, provided no agreement has been reached by that time; and

(4) continues in full force and effect, without resorting to strike or lock-out, all the terms and conditions of the existing contract for a period of sixty days after such notice is given or until the expiration date of such contract, whichever occurs later:

The duties imposed upon employers, employees, and labor organizations by paragraphs (2), (3), and (4) shall become inapplicable upon an intervening certification of the Board, under which the labor organization or individual, which is a party to the contract, has been superseded as or ceased to be the representative of the employees subject to the provisions of section 9(a), and the duties so imposed shall not be construed as requiring either party to discuss or agree to any modification of the terms and conditions contained in a contract for a fixed period, if such modification is to become effective before such terms and conditions can be reopened under the provisions of the contract. Any employee who engages in a strike within [the sixty-day] any notice period specified in this subsection, or who engages in any strike within the appropriate period specified in subsection (g) of this section, shall lose his status as an employee of the employer engaged in the particular labor dispute, for the purposes of sections 8, 9, and 10 of this Act, but such loss of status for such employee shall terminate if and when he is reemployed by such employer. Whenever the collective bargaining involves employees of a health care institution, the provisions of this section 8(d) shall be modified as follows:

(A) The notice of section 8(d)(1) shall be ninety days; the notice of section 8(d)(3) shall be sixty days; and the contract period of section 8(d)(4) shall be ninety days.

(B) Where the bargaining is for an initial agreement following certification or recognition, at least thirty days' notice of the existence of a dispute shall be given by the labor organization to the agencies set forth in section 8(d)(3).

(C) After notice is given to the Federal Mediation and Conciliation Service under either clause (A) or (B) of this sentence, the Service shall promptly communicate with the parties and use its best efforts, by mediation and conciliation, to bring them to agreement. The parties shall participate fully and promptly in such meetings as may be undertaken by the Service for the purpose of aiding in a settlement of the dispute.

(e) It shall be an unfair labor practice for any labor organization and any employer to enter into any contract or agreement, express or implied, whereby such employer ceases or refrains or agrees to cease or refrain from handling, using, selling, transporting or otherwise dealing in any of the products of any other employer, or to cease doing business with any other person, and any contract or agreement entered into heretofore or hereafter containing such an agreement shall be to such extent unenforcible and void: Provided, That nothing in this subsection (e) shall apply to an agreement between a labor organization and an employer in the construction industry relating to the contracting or subcontracting of work to be done at the site of the construction, alteration, painting, or repair of a building, structure, or other work: Provided further, That for the purposes of this subsection (e) and section 8(b)(4)(B) the terms "any employer", "any person engaged in commerce or an industry affecting commerce", and "any person" when used in relation to the terms "any other producer, processor, or manufacturer", "any other employer", or "any other person" shall not include persons in the relation of a jobber, manufacturer, contractor, or subcontractor working on the goods or premises of the jobber or manufacturer or performing parts of an integrated process of production in the apparel and clothing industry: Provided further, That nothing in this Act shall prohibit the enforcement of any agreement which is within the foregoing exception.

(f) It shall not be an unfair labor practice under subsections (a) and (b) of this section for an employer engaged primarily in the building and construction industry to make an agreement covering employees engaged (or who, upon their employment, will be engaged) in the building and construction industry with a labor organization of which building and construction employees are members (not established, maintained, or assisted by any action defined in section 8(a) of this Act as an unfair labor practice) because (1) the majority status of such labor organization has not been established under the provisions of section 9 of this Act prior to the making of such agreement, or (2) such agreement requires as a condition of employment, membership in such labor organization after the seventh day following the beginning of such employment or the effective date of the agreement, whichever is later, or (3) such agreement requires the employer to notify such labor organization of opportunities for employment with such employer, or gives such labor organization an opportunity to refer qualified applicants for such employment, or (4) such agreement specifies minimum training or experience qualifications for employment or provides for priority in opportunities for employment based upon length of service with such employer, in the industry or in the particular geographical area: Provided, That nothing in this subsection shall set aside the final proviso to section 8(a)(3) of this Act: Provided further, That any agreement which would be invalid, but for clause (1) of this subsection, shall not be a bar to a petition filed pursuant to section 9(c) or 9(e).

(g) A labor organization before engaging in any strike, picketing, or other concerted refusal to work at any health care institution shall, not less than ten days prior to such action, notify the institution in writing and the Federal Mediation and Conciliation Service of that intention, except that in the case of bargaining for an initial agreement following certification or recognition the notice required by this subsection shall not be given until the expiration of the period specified in clause (B) of the last sentence of section 8(d) of this Act. The notice shall state the date and time that such action will commence. The notice, once given, may be extended by the written agreement of both parties.

REPRESENTATIVES AND ELECTIONS

Sec. 9. (a) Representatives designated or selected for the purposes of collective bargaining by the majority of the employees in a unit appropriate for such purposes, shall be the exclusive representatives of all the employees in such unit for the purposes of collective bargaining in respect to rates of pay, wages, hours of employment, or other conditions of employment: Provided, That any individual employee or a group of employees shall have the right at any time to present grievances to their employer and to have such grievances adjusted, without the intervention of the bargaining representative, as long as the adjustment is not inconsistent with the terms of a collective-bargaining contract or agreement then in effect: Provided further, That the bargaining representative has been given opportunity to be present at such adjustment.

(b) The Board shall decide in each case whether, in order to assure to employees the fullest freedom in exercising the rights guaranteed by this Act, the unit appropriate for the purposes of collective bargaining shall be the employer unit, craft unit, plant unit, or subdivision thereof: Provided, That the Board shall not (1) decide that any unit is appropriate for such purposes if such unit includes both professional employees and employees who are not professional employees unless a majority of such professional employees vote for inclusion in such unit; or (2) decide that any craft unit is inappropriate for such purposes on the ground that a different unit has been established by a prior Board determination, unless a majority of the employees in the proposed craft unit vote against separate representation or (3) decide that any unit is appropriate for such purposes if it includes, together with other employees, any individual employed as a guard to enforce against employees and other persons rules to protect property of the employer or to protect the safety of persons on the employer's premises; but no labor organization shall be certified as the representative of employees in a bargaining unit of guards if such organization admits to membership, or is affiliated directly or indirectly with an organization which admits to membership, employees other than guards.

[(c) Whenever a question affecting commerce arises concerning the representation of employees, the Board may investigate such controversy and certify to the parties, in writing, the name or names of the representatives that have been designated or selected. In any such investigation, the Board shall provide for an appropriate hearing upon due notice, either in conjunction with a proceeding under section 10 or otherwise, and may take a secret ballot of employees, or utilize any other suitable method to ascertain such representatives.]

(c)(1) Whenever a petition shall have been filed, in accordance with such regulations as may be prescribed by the Board—

(A) by an employee or group of employees or any individual or labor organization acting in their behalf alleging that a substantial number of employees (i) wish to be represented for collective bargaining and that their employer declines to recognize their representative as the representative defined in section 9(a), or (ii) assert that the individual or labor organization, which has been certified or is being currently recognized by their employer as the bargaining representative, is no longer a representative as defined in section 9(a); or

(B) by an employer, alleging that one or more individuals or labor organizations have presented to him a claim to be recognized as the representative defined in section 9(a);

the Board shall investigate such petition and if it has reasonable cause to believe that a question of representation affecting commerce exists shall provide for an appropriate hearing upon due notice. Such hearing may be conducted by an officer or employee of the regional office, who shall not make any recommendations with respect thereto. If the Board finds upon the record of such hearing that such a question of representation exists, it shall direct an election by secret ballot and shall certify the results thereof.

(2) In determining whether or not a question of representation affecting commerce exists, the same regulations and rules of decision shall apply irrespective of the identity of the persons filing the petition or the kind of relief sought and in no case shall the Board deny a labor organization a place on the ballot by reason of an order with respect to such labor organization or its predecessor not issued in conformity with section 10(c).

(3) No election shall be directed in any bargaining unit or any subdivision within which, in the preceding twelve-month period, a valid election shall have been held. Employees [on strike] engaged in an economic strike who are not entitled to reinstatement shall [not] be eligible to vote under such regulations as the Board shall find are consistent with the purposes and provisions of this Act in any election conducted within twelve months after the commencement of the strike. In any election where none of the choices on the ballot receives a majority, a run-off shall be conducted, the ballot providing for a selection between the two choices receiving the largest and second largest number of valid votes cast in the election.

(4) Nothing in this section shall be construed to prohibit the waiving of hearings by stipulation for the purpose of a consent election in conformity with regulations and rules of decision of the Board.

(5) In determining whether a unit is appropriate for the purposes specified in subsection (b) the extent to which the employees have organized shall not be controlling.

(d) Whenever an order of the Board made pursuant to section 10(c) is based in whole or in part upon facts certified following an investigation pursuant to subsection (c) of this section and there is a petition for the enforcement or review of such order, such certification and the record of such investigation shall be included in the transcript of the entire record required to be filed under section 10(e) or 10(f), and thereupon the decree of the court enforcing, modifying, or setting aside in whole or in part the order of the Board shall be made and entered upon the pleadings, testimony, and proceedings set forth in such transcript.

(e)(1) Upon the filing with the Board, by 30 per centum or more of the employees in a bargaining unit covered by an agreement between their employer and a labor organization made pursuant to section 8(a)(3), of a petition alleging they desire that such authority be rescinded, the Board shall take a secret ballot of the employees in such unit, and shall certify the results thereof to such labor organization and to the employer.

(2) No election shall be conducted pursuant to this subsection in any bargaining unit or any subdivision within which, in the preceding twelve-month period, a valid election shall have been held.

[Subsections (f), (g) and (h) were deleted by the Labor–Management Reporting and Disclosure Act.]

PREVENTION OF UNFAIR LABOR PRACTICES

Sec. 10. (a) The Board is empowered, as hereinafter provided, to prevent any person from engaging in any unfair labor practice (listed in section 8) affecting commerce. This power shall not be affected by any other means of adjustment or prevention that has been or may be established by agreement, law, or otherwise: Provided, That the Board is empowered by agreement with any agency of any State or Territory to cede to such agency jurisdiction over any cases in any industry (other than mining, manufacturing, communications, and transportation except where predominantly local in character) even though such cases may involve labor disputes affecting commerce, unless the provision of the State or Territorial statute applicable to the determination of such cases by such agency is inconsistent with the corresponding provision of this Act or has received a construction inconsistent therewith.

(b) Whenever it is charged that any person has engaged in or is engaging in any such unfair labor practice, the Board, or any agent or agency designated by the Board for such purposes, shall have power to issue and cause to be served upon such person a complaint stating the charges in that respect, and containing a notice of hearing before the Board or a member thereof, or before a designated agent or agency, at a place therein fixed, not less than five days after the serving of said complaint: Provided, That no complaint shall issue based upon any unfair labor practice occurring more than six months prior to the filing of the charge with the Board and the service of a copy thereof upon the person against whom such charge is made, unless the person aggrieved thereby was prevented from filing such charge by reason of service in the armed forces, in which event the six-month period shall be computed from the day of his discharge. Any such complaint may be amended by the member, agent, or agency conducting the hearing or the Board in its discretion at any time prior to the issuance of an order based thereon. The person so complained of shall have the right to file an answer to the original or amended complaint and to appear in person or otherwise and give testimony at the place and time fixed in the complaint. In the discretion of the member, agent, or agency conducting the hearing or the Board, any other person may be allowed to intervene in the said proceeding and to present testimony. [In any such proceeding the rules of evidence prevailing in courts of law or equity shall not be controlling.] Any such proceeding shall, so far as practicable, be conducted in accordance with the rules of evidence applicable in the district courts of the United States under the rules of civil procedure for the district courts of the United States, adopted by the Supreme Court of the United States pursuant to section 2072 of Title 28.

(c) The testimony taken by such member, agent, or agency or the Board shall be reduced to writing and filed with the Board. Thereafter, in its discretion, the Board upon notice may take further testimony or hear argument. If upon [all] the preponderance of the testimony taken the Board shall be of the opinion that any person named in the complaint has engaged in or is engaging in any such unfair labor practice, then the Board shall state its findings of fact and shall issue and cause to be served on such person an order requiring such person to cease and desist from such unfair labor practice, and to take such affirmative action including reinstatement of employees with or without back pay, as will effectuate the policies of this Act: Provided, That where an order directs reinstatement of an employee, back pay may be required of the employer or labor organization, as the case may be, responsible for the discrimination suffered by him: And provided further, That in determining whether a complaint shall issue alleging a violation of section 8(a)(1) or section 8(a)(2), and in deciding such cases, the same regulations and rules of decision shall apply irrespective of whether or not the labor organization affected is affiliated with a labor organization national or international in scope. Such order may further require such person to make reports from time to time showing the extent to which it has complied with the order. If upon [all] the preponderance of the testimony taken the Board shall not be of the opinion that the person named in the complaint has engaged in or is engaging in any such unfair labor practice, then the Board shall state its findings of fact and shall issue an order dismissing the said complaint. No order of the Board shall require the reinstatement of any individual as an employee who has been suspended or discharged, or the payment to him of any back pay, if such individual was suspended or discharged for cause. In case the evidence is presented before a member of the Board, or before an administrative law judge or judges thereof, such member, or such judge or judges, as the case may be, shall issue and cause to be served on the parties to the proceeding a proposed report, together with a recommended order, which shall be filed with the Board, and if no exceptions are filed within twenty days after service thereof upon such parties, or within such further period as the Board may authorize, such recommended order shall become the order of the Board and become effective as therein prescribed.

(d) Until [a transcript of] the record in a case shall have been filed in a court, as hereinafter provided, the Board may at any time, upon reasonable notice and in such manner as it shall deem proper, modify or set aside, in whole or in part, any finding or order made or issued by it.

(e) The Board shall have power to petition any [United States] court of appeals of the United States [(including the United States court of appeals for the District of Columbia)] or if all the courts of appeals to which application may be made are in vacation, any [United States] district court of the United States, within any circuit or district, respectively, wherein the unfair labor practice in question occurred or wherein such person resides or transacts business, for the enforcement of such order and for appropriate temporary relief or restraining order, and shall [certify and] file in the court [a transcript of] the [entire] record in the proceedings, [including the pleadings and testimony upon which such order was entered and the findings and order of the Board.] as printed in section 2112 of Title 28. Upon [such filing] the filing of such petition, the court shall cause notice thereof to be served upon such person, and thereupon shall have jurisdiction of the proceeding and of the question determined therein, and shall have power to grant such temporary relief or restraining order as it deems just and proper, and to make and enter [upon the pleadings, testimony, and proceedings set forth in such transcript] a decree enforcing, modifying, and enforcing as so modified, or setting aside in whole or in part the order of the Board. No objection that has not been urged before the Board, its member, agent, or agency, shall be considered by the court, unless the failure or neglect to urge such objection shall be excused because of extraordinary circumstances. The findings of the Board with respect to questions of fact if supported by substantial evidence on the record considered as a whole shall be conclusive. If either party shall apply to the court for leave to adduce additional evidence and shall show to the satisfaction of the court that such additional evidence is material and that there were reasonable grounds for the failure to adduce such evidence in the hearing before the Board, its member, agent, or agency, the court may order such additional evidence to be taken before the Board, its member, agent, or agency, and to be made a part of [the transcript] record. The Board may modify its findings as to the facts, or make new findings, by reason of additional evidence so taken and filed, and it shall file such modified or new findings, which findings with respect to questions of fact if supported by substantial evidence on the record considered as a whole shall be conclusive, and shall file its recommendations, if any, for the modification or setting aside of its original order. Upon the filing of the record with it the jurisdiction of the court shall be exclusive and its judgment and decree shall be final, except that the same shall be subject to review by the appropriate circuit court of appeals if application was made to the district court as hereinabove provided, and by the Supreme Court of the United States upon writ of certiorari or certification as provided in section 1254 of Title 28.

(f) Any person aggrieved by a final order of the Board granting or denying in whole or in part the relief sought may obtain a review of such order in any United States court of appeals in the circuit wherein the unfair labor practice in question was alleged to have been engaged in or wherein such person resides or transacts business, or in the United States Court of Appeals for the District of Columbia, by filing in such court a written petition praying that the order of the Board be modified or set aside. A copy of such petition shall be forthwith [served upon the Board] transmitted by the clerk of the court to the Board and thereupon the aggrieved party shall file in the court [a transcript of] the [entire] record in the proceeding, certified by the Board, [including the pleading and testimony upon which the order complained of was entered, and the findings and order of the Board.] as provided in section 2112 of Title 28. Upon [such filing,] the filing of such petition, the court shall proceed in the same manner as in the case of an application by the Board under subsection (e) of this section, and shall have the same exclusive jurisdiction to grant to the Board such temporary relief or restraining order as it deems just and proper, and in like manner to make and enter a decree enforcing, modifying, and enforcing as so modified, or setting aside in whole or in part the order of the Board; the findings of the Board with respect to questions of fact if supported by substantial evidence on the record considered as a whole shall in like manner be conclusive.

(g) The commencement of proceedings under subsection (e) or (f) of this section shall not, unless specifically ordered by the court, operate as a stay of the Board's order.

(h) When granting appropriate temporary relief or a restraining order, or making and entering a decree enforcing, modifying, and enforcing as so modified, or setting aside in whole or in part an order of the Board, as provided in this section, the jurisdiction of courts sitting in equity shall not be limited by sections 101 to 115 of title 29, United States Code.

(i) [Repealed.]

(j) The Board shall have power, upon issuance of a complaint as provided in subsection (b) charging that any person has engaged in or is engaging in an unfair labor practice, to petition any United States district court within any district wherein the unfair labor practice in question is alleged to have occurred or wherein such person resides or transacts business, for appropriate temporary relief or restraining order. Upon the filing of any such petition the court shall cause notice thereof to be served upon such person, and thereupon shall have jurisdiction to grant to the Board such temporary relief or restraining order as it deems just and proper.

(k) Whenever it is charged that any person has engaged in an unfair labor practice within the meaning of paragraph (4)(D) of section 8(b), the Board is empowered and directed to hear and determine the dispute out of which such unfair labor practice shall have arisen, unless, within ten days after notice that such charge has been filed, the parties to such dispute submit to the Board satisfactory evidence that they have adjusted, or agreed upon methods for the voluntary adjustment of, the dispute. Upon compliance by the parties to the dispute with the decision of the Board or upon such voluntary adjustment of the dispute, such charge shall be dismissed.

(l) Whenever it is charged that any person has engaged in an unfair labor practice within the meaning of paragraph (4)(A), (B), or (C) of section 8(b), or section 8(e) or section 8(b)(7) the preliminary investigation of such charge shall be made forthwith and given priority over all other cases except cases of like character in the office where it is filed or to which it is referred. If, after such investigation, the officer or regional attorney to whom the matter may be referred has reasonable cause to believe such charge is true and that a complaint should issue, he shall, on behalf of the Board, petition any United States district court within any district where the unfair labor practice in question has occurred, is alleged to have occurred, or wherein such person resides or transacts business, for appropriate injunctive relief pending the final adjudication of the Board with respect to such matter. Upon the filing of any such petition the district court shall have jurisdiction to grant such injunctive relief or temporary re- straining order as it deems just and proper, notwithstanding any other provision of law: Provided further, That no temporary restraining order shall be issued without notice unless a petition alleges that substantial and irreparable injury to the charging party will be una- voidable and such temporary restraining order shall be effective for no longer than five days and will become void at the expiration of such period[.]: Provided further, That such officer or regional attorney shall not apply for any restraining order under section 8(b)(7) if a charge against the employer under section 8(a)(2) has been filed and after the preliminary investigation, he has reasonable cause to believe that such charge is true and that a complaint should issue. Upon filing of any such petition the courts shall cause notice thereof to be served upon any person involved in the charge and such person, including the charging party, shall be given an opportunity to appear by counsel and present any relevant testimony: Provided further, That for the purposes of this subsection district courts shall be deemed to have jurisdiction of a labor organization (1) in the district in which such organization maintains its principal office, or (2) in any district in which its duly authorized officers or agents are engaged in promoting or protecting the interests of employee members. The service of legal process upon such officer or agent shall constitute service upon the labor organization and make such organization a party to the suit. In situations where such relief is appropriate the procedure specified herein shall apply to charges with respect to sections 8(b)(4)(D).

(m) Whenever it is charged that any person has engaged in an unfair labor practice within the meaning of subsection (a)(3) or (b)(2) of section 8, such charge shall be given priority over all other cases except cases of like character in the office where it is filed or to which it is referred and cases given priority under subsection (*l*) of this section.

INVESTIGATORY POWERS

Sec. 11. For the purpose of all hearings and investigations, which, in the opinion of the Board, are necessary and proper for the exercise of the powers vested in it by section 9 and section 10—

(1) The Board, or its duly authorized agents or agencies, shall at all reasonable times have access to, for the purpose of examination, and the right to copy any evidence of any person being investigated or proceeded against that relates to any matter under investigation or in question. The Board, or any member thereof, shall upon application of any party to such proceedings, forthwith issue to such party subpenas requiring the attendance and testimony of witnesses or the production of any evidence in such proceeding or investigation requested in such application. Within five days after the service of a subpena on any person requiring the production of any evidence in his possession or under his control, such person may petition the Board to revoke, and the Board shall revoke, such subpena if in its opinion the evidence whose production is required does not relate to any matter under investigation, or any matter in question in such proceedings, or if in its opinion such subpena does not describe with sufficient particularity the evidence whose production is required. Any member of the Board, or any agent or agency designated by the Board for such purposes, may administer oaths and affirmations, examine witnesses, and receive evidence. Such attendance of witnesses and the production of such evidence may be required from any place in the United States or any Territory or possession thereof, at any designated place of hearing.

(2) In case of contumacy or refusal to obey a subpena issued to any person, any district court of the United States or the United States courts of any Territory or possession, or the District Court of the United States for the District of Columbia, within the jurisdiction of which the inquiry is carried on or within the jurisdiction of which said person guilty of contumacy or refusal to obey is found or resides or transacts business, upon application by the Board shall have jurisdiction to issue to such person an order requiring such person to appear before the Board, its member, agent, or agency, there to produce evidence if so ordered, or there to give testimony touching the matter under investigation or in question; and any failure to obey such order of the court may be punished by said court as a contempt thereof.

[(3) No person shall be excused from attending and testifying or from producing books, records, correspondence, documents, or other evidence in obedience to the subpena of the Board, on the ground that the testimony or evidence required of him may tend to incriminate him or subject him to a penalty or forfeiture; but no individual shall be prosecuted or subjected to any penalty or forfeiture for or on account of any transaction, matter, or thing concerning which he is compelled, after having claimed his privilege against self-incrimination, to testify or produce evidence, except that such individual so testifying shall not be exempt from prosecution and punishment for perjury committed in so testifying.]

(4) Complaints, orders, and other process and papers of the Board, its member, agent, or agency, may be served either personally or by registered mail or by telegraph or by leaving a copy thereof at the principal office or place of business of the person required to be served. The verified return by the individual so serving the same setting forth the manner of such service shall be proof of the same, and the return post office receipt or telegraph receipt therefor when registered and mailed or telegraphed as aforesaid shall be proof of service of the same. Witnesses summoned before the Board, its member, agent, or agency, shall be paid the same fees and mileage that are paid witnesses in the courts of the United States, and witnesses whose depositions are taken and the persons taking the same shall severally be entitled to the same fees as are paid for like services in the courts of the United States.

(5) All process of any court to which application may be made under this Act may be served in the judicial district wherein the defendant or other person required to be served resides or may be found.

(6) The several departments and agencies of the Government, when directed by the President, shall furnish the Board, upon its request, all records, papers, and information in their possession relating to any matter before the Board.

Sec. 12. Any person who shall willfully resist, prevent, impede, or interfere with any member of the Board or any of its agents or agencies in the performance of duties pursuant to this Act shall be punished by a fine of not more than $5,000 or by imprisonment for not more than one year, or both.

LIMITATIONS

Sec. 13. Nothing in this Act, except as specifically provided for herein, shall be construed so as either to interfere with or impede or diminish in any way the right to strike, or to affect the limitations or qualifications on that right.

Sec. 14. (a) Nothing herein shall prohibit any individual employed as a supervisor from becoming or remaining a member of a labor organization, but no employer subject to this Act shall be compelled to deem individuals defined herein as supervisors as employees for the purpose of any law, either national or local, relating to collective bargaining.

(b) Nothing in this Act shall be construed as authorizing the execution or application of agreements requiring membership in a labor organization as a condition of employment in any State or Territory in which such execution or application is prohibited by State or Territorial law.

(c)(1) The Board, in its discretion, may, by rule of decision or by published rules adopted pursuant to the Administrative Procedure Act, decline to assert jurisdiction over any labor dispute involving any class or category of employers, where, in the opinion of the Board, the effect of such labor dispute on commerce is not sufficiently substantial to warrant the exercise of its jurisdiction: Provided, That the Board shall not decline to assert jurisdiction over any labor dispute over which it would assert jurisdiction under the standards prevailing upon August 1, 1959.

(2) Nothing in this Act shall be deemed to prevent or bar any agency or the courts of any State or Territory (including the Commonwealth of Puerto Rico, Guam, and the Virgin Islands), from assuming and asserting jurisdiction over labor disputes over which the Board declines, pursuant to paragraph (1) of this subsection, to assert jurisdiction.

Sec. 15. [Reference to repealed provisions of the Bankruptcy Act.]

Sec. 16. If any provision of this Act, or the application of such provision to any person or circumstances, shall be held invalid, the remainder of this Act, or the application of such provision to persons or circumstances other than those as to which it is held invalid, shall not be affected thereby.

Sec. 17. This Act may be cited as the "National Labor Relations Act."

Sec. 18. [This section, which refers to the now-repealed Sections 9(f), (g), (h), is omitted.]

INDIVIDUALS WITH RELIGIOUS CONVICTIONS

Sec. 19. Any employee who is a member of and adheres to established and traditional tenets or teachings of a bona fide religion, body, or sect which has historically held conscientious objections to joining or financially supporting labor organizations shall not be required to join or financially support any labor organization as a condition of employment; except that such employee may be required in a contract between such employee's employer and a labor organization in lieu of periodic dues and initiation fees, to pay sums equal to such dues and initiation fees to a nonreligious, nonlabor organization charitable fund exempt from taxation under section 501(c)(3) of title 26 of the Internal Revenue Code [section 501(c)(3) of title 26], chosen by such employee from a list of at least three such funds, designated in such contract or if the contract fails to designate such funds, then to any such fund chosen by the employee. If such employee who holds conscientious objections pursuant to this section requests the labor organization to use the grievance-arbitration procedure on the employee's behalf, the labor organization is authorized to charge the employee for the reasonable cost of using such procedure.

Appendix B

NORRIS–LAGUARDIA ACT

47 Stat. 70 (1932), 29 U.S.C. §§ 101–15 (1982).

Sec. 1. No court of the United States, as herein defined, shall have jurisdiction to issue any restraining order or temporary or permanent injunction in a case involving or growing out of a labor dispute, except in a strict conformity with the provisions of this Act; nor shall any such restraining order or temporary or permanent injunction be issued contrary to the public policy declared in this Act.

Sec. 2. In the interpretation of this Act and in determining the jurisdiction and authority of the courts of the United States, as such jurisdiction and authority are herein defined and limited, the public policy of the United States is hereby declared as follows:

Whereas under prevailing economic conditions, developed with the aid of governmental authority for owners of property to organize in the corporate and other forms of ownership association, the individual unorganized worker is commonly helpless to exercise actual liberty of contract and to protect his freedom of labor, and thereby to obtain acceptable terms and conditions of employment, wherefore, though he should be free to decline to associate with his fellows, it is necessary that he have full freedom of association, self-organization, and designation of representatives of his own choosing, to negotiate the terms and conditions of his employment, and that he shall be free from the interference, restraint, or coercion of employers of labor, or their agents, in the designation of such representatives or in self-organization or in other concerted activities for the purpose of collective bargaining or other mutual aid or protection; therefore, the following definitions of, and limitations upon, the jurisdiction and authority of the courts of the United States are hereby enacted.

Sec. 3. Any undertaking or promise, such as is described in this section, or any other undertaking or promise in conflict with the public policy declared in section 2 of this Act, is hereby declared to be contrary to the public policy of the United States, shall not be enforceable in any court of the United States and shall not afford any basis for the granting of legal or equitable relief by any such court, including specifically the following:

Every undertaking or promise hereafter made, whether written or oral, express or implied, constituting or contained in any contract or agreement of hiring or employment between any individual, firm, company, association, or corporation, and any employee or prospective employee of the same whereby

(a) Either party to such contract or agreement undertakes or promises not to join, become, or remain a member of any labor organization or of any employer organization; or

(b) Either party to such contract or agreement undertakes or promises that he will withdraw from an employment relation in the event that he joins, becomes, or remains a member of any labor organization or of any employer organization.

Sec. 4. No court of the United States shall have jurisdiction to issue any restraining order or temporary or permanent injunction in any case involving or growing out of any labor dispute to prohibit any person or persons participating or interested in such dispute (as these terms are herein defined) from doing, whether singly or in concert, any of the following acts:

(a) Ceasing or refusing to perform any work or to remain in any relation of employment;

(b) Becoming or remaining a member of any labor organization or of any employer organization, regardless of any such undertaking or promise as is described in section 3 of this Act;

(c) Paying or giving to, or withholding from, any person participating or interested in such labor dispute, any strike or unemployment benefits or insurance, or other moneys or things of value;

(d) By all lawful means aiding any person participating or interested in any labor dispute who is being proceeded against in, or is prosecuting, any action or suit in any court of the United States or of any State;

(e) Giving publicity to the existence of, or the facts involved in, any labor dispute, whether by advertising, speaking, patrolling, or by any other method not involving fraud or violence;

(f) Assembling peaceably to act or to organize to act in promotion of their interests in a labor dispute;

(g) Advising or notifying any person of an intention to do any of the Acts heretofore specified;

(h) Agreeing with other persons to do or not to do any of the acts heretofore specified; and

(i) Advising, urging, or otherwise causing or inducing without fraud or violence the acts heretofore specified, regardless of any such undertaking or promise as is described in section 3 of this Act.

Sec. 5. No court of the United States shall have jurisdiction to issue a restraining order or temporary or permanent injunction upon the ground that any of the persons participating or interested in a labor dispute constitute or are engaged in an unlawful combination or conspiracy because of the doing in concert of the acts enumerated in section 4 of this Act.

Sec. 6. No officer or member of any association or organization, and no association or organization participating or interested in a labor dispute, shall be held responsible or liable in any court of the United States for the unlawful acts of individual officers, members, or agents, except upon clear proof of actual participation in, or actual authorization of, such acts, or of ratification of such acts after actual knowledge thereof.

Sec. 7. No court of the United States shall have jurisdiction to issue a temporary or permanent injunction in any case involving or growing out of a labor dispute, as herein defined, except after hearing the testimony of witnesses in open court (with opportunity for cross-examination) in support of the allegations of a complaint made under oath, and testimony in opposition thereto, if offered, and except after findings of fact by the court, to the effect—

(a) That unlawful acts have been threatened and will be committed unless restrained or have been committed and will be continued unless restrained, but no injunction or temporary restraining order shall be issued on account of any threat or unlawful act excepting against the person or persons, association, or organization making the threat or committing the unlawful act or actually authorizing or ratifying the same after actual knowledge thereof;

(b) That substantial and irreparable injury to complainant's property will follow:

(c) That as to each item of relief granted greater injury will be inflicted upon complainant by the denial of relief than will be inflicted upon defendants by the granting of relief;

(d) That complainant has no adequate remedy at law; and

(e) That the public officers charged with the duty to protect complainant's property are unable or unwilling to furnish adequate protection.

Such hearing shall be held after due and personal notice thereof has been given, in such manner as the court shall direct, to all known persons against whom relief is sought, and also to the chief of those public officials of the county and city within which the unlawful acts have been threatened or committed charged with the duty to protect complainant's property: Provided, however, That if a complainant shall also allege that, unless a temporary restraining order shall be issued without notice, a substantial and irreparable injury to complainant's property will be unavoidable, such a temporary restraining order may be issued upon testimony under oath, sufficient, if sustained, to justify the court in issuing a temporary injunction upon a hearing after notice. Such a temporary restraining order shall be effective for no longer than five days and shall become void at the expiration of said five days. No temporary restraining order or temporary injunction shall be issued except on condition that complainant shall first file an undertaking with adequate security in an amount to be fixed by the court sufficient to recompense those enjoined for any loss, expense, or damage caused by the improvident or erroneous issuance of such order or injunction, including all reasonable costs (together with a reasonable attorney's fee) and expense of defense against the order or against the granting of any injunctive relief sought in the same proceeding and subsequently denied by the court.

The undertaking herein mentioned shall be understood to signify an agreement entered into by the complainant and the surety upon which a decree may be rendered in the same suit or proceeding against said complainant and surety, upon a hearing to assess damages of which hearing complainant and surety shall have reasonable notice, the said complainant and surety submitting themselves to the jurisdiction of the court for that purpose. But nothing herein contained shall deprive any party having a claim or cause of action under or upon such undertaking from electing to pursue his ordinary remedy by suit at law or in equity.

Sec. 8. No restraining order or injunctive relief shall be granted to any complainant who has failed to comply with any obligation imposed by law which is involved in the labor dispute in question, or who has failed to make every reasonable effort to settle such dispute either by negotiation or with the aid of any available governmental machinery of mediation or voluntary arbitration.

Sec. 9. No restraining order or temporary or permanent injunction shall be granted in a case involving or growing out of a labor dispute, except on the basis of findings of fact made and filed by the court in the record of the case prior to the issuance of such restraining order or injunction; and every restraining order or injunction granted in a case involving or growing out of a labor dispute shall include only a prohibition of such specific act or acts as may be expressly complained of in the bill of complaint or petition filed in such case and as shall be expressly included in said findings of fact made and filed by the court as provided herein.

Sec. 10. Whenever any court of the United States shall issue or deny any temporary injunction in a case involving or growing out of a labor dispute, the court shall, upon the request of any party to the proceedings and on his filing the usual bond for costs, forthwith certify as in ordinary cases the record of the case to the circuit court of appeals for its review. Upon the filing of such record in the circuit court of appeals, the appeal shall be heard and the temporary injunctive order affirmed, modified, or set aside with the greatest possible expedition, giving the proceedings precedence over all other matters except older matters of the same character.

Sec. 11.   In all cases arising under this Act in which a person shall be charged with contempt in a court of the United States (as herein defined), the accused shall enjoy the right to a speedy and public trial by an impartial jury of the State and district wherein the contempt shall have been committed: Provided, That this right shall not apply to contempts committed in the presence of the court or so near thereto as to interfere directly with the administration of justice or to apply to the misbehavior, misconduct, or disobedience of any officer of the court in respect to the writs, orders, or process of the court.

Sec. 12.   The defendant in any proceeding for contempt of court may file with the court a demand for the retirement of the judge sitting in the proceeding, if the contempt arises from an attack upon the character or conduct of such judge and if the attack occurred elsewhere than in the presence of the court or so near thereto as to interfere directly with the administration of justice.   Upon the filing of any such demand the judge shall thereupon proceed no further, but another judge shall be designated in the same manner as is provided by law.   The demand shall be filed prior to the hearing in the contempt proceeding.

Sec. 13.   When used in this Act, and for the purposes of this Act—

(a) A case shall be held to involve or to grow out of a labor dispute when the case involves persons who are engaged in the same industry, trade, craft, or occupation; or have direct or indirect interests therein; or who are employees of the same employer; or who are members of the same or an affiliated organization of employers or employees; whether such dispute is (1) between one or more employers or associations of employers and one or more employees or associations of employees; (2) between one or more employers or associations of employers and one or more employers or associations of employers; or (3) between one or more employees or associations of employees and one or more employees or associations of employees; or when the case involves any conflicting or competing interests in a "labor dispute" (as hereinafter defined) of "persons participating or interested" therein (as hereinafter defined).

(b) A person or association shall be held to be a person participating or interested in a labor dispute if relief is sought against him or it, and if he or it is engaged in the same industry, trade, craft, or occupation in which such dispute occurs, or has a direct or indirect interest therein, or is a member, officer, or agent of any association composed in whole or in part of employers or employees engaged in such industry, trade, craft, or occupation.

(c) The term "labor dispute" includes any controversy concerning terms or conditions of employment, or concerning the association or representation of persons in negotiating, fixing, maintaining, changing, or seeking to arrange terms or conditions of employment, regardless of whether or not the disputants stand in the proximate relation of employer and employee.

(d) The term "court of the United States" means any court of the United States whose jurisdiction has been or may be conferred or defined or limited by Act of Congress, including the courts of the District of Columbia.

Sec. 14. If any provision of this Act or the application thereof to any person or circumstance is held unconstitutional or otherwise invalid, the remaining provisions of the Act and the application of such provisions to other persons or circumstances shall not be affected thereby.

Sec. 15. All Acts and parts of Acts in conflict with the provisions of this Act are hereby repealed.

INDEX

References are to Pages

†